Ubuntu® Linux® Desktop

Your visual blueprint™ to using the Linux® operating system

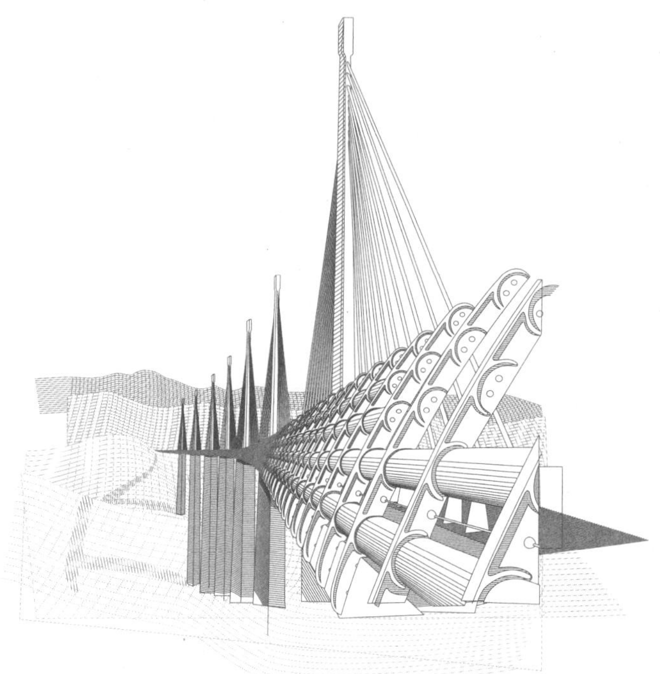

by Ric Shreves

WILEY

Wiley Publishing, Inc.

Ubuntu® Linux® Desktop: Your visual blueprint™ to using the Linux® operating system

Published by
Wiley Publishing, Inc.
10475 Crosspoint Boulevard
Indianapolis, IN 46256
www.wiley.com

Published simultaneously in Canada

Library of Congress Control Number: 2009922177

ISBN: 978-0-470-34520-7

Mannufactured in the United States of America

10 9 8 7 6 5 4 3 2 1

Trademark Acknowledgments

Contact Us

For general information on our other products and services, please contact our Customer Care Department within the U.S. at (800)762-2974 and outside the U.S. at (317)572-3993 or fax (317)572-4002.

For technical support, please visit www.wiley.com/techsupport.

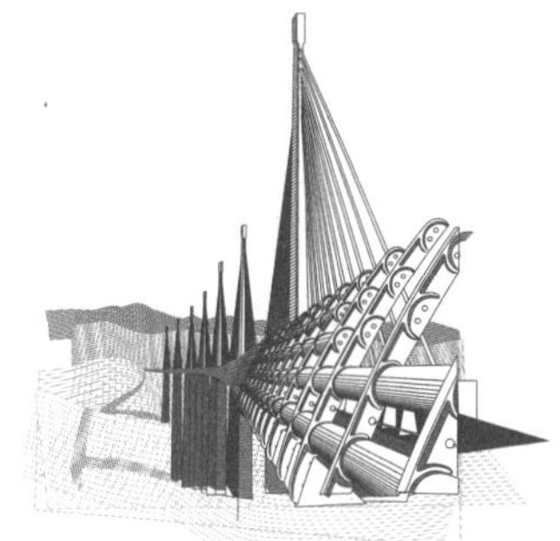

WILEY

Sales

Contact Wiley
at (800) 762-2974
or (317) 572-4002.

Praise For Visual Books...

"This is absolutely the best computer-related book I have ever bought. Thank you so much for this fantastic text. Simply the best computer book series I have ever seen. I will look for, recommend, and purchase more of the same."

—David E. Prince (NeoNome.com)

"I have several of your Visual books and they are the best I have ever used."

—Stanley Clark (Crawfordville, FL)

"I just want to let you know that I really enjoy all your books. I'm a strong visual learner. You really know how to get people addicted to learning! I'm a very satisfied Visual customer. Keep up the excellent work!"

—Helen Lee (Calgary, Alberta, Canada)

"I have several books from the Visual series and have always found them to be valuable resources."

—Stephen P. Miller (Ballston Spa, NY)

"This book is PERFECT for me — it's highly visual and gets right to the point. What I like most about it is that each page presents a new task that you can try verbatim or, alternatively, take the ideas and build your own examples. Also, this book isn't bogged down with trying to 'tell all' — it gets right to the point. This is an EXCELLENT, EXCELLENT, EXCELLENT book and I look forward to purchasing other books in the series."

—Tom Dierickx (Malta, IL)

"I have quite a few of your Visual books and have been very pleased with all of them. I love the way the lessons are presented!"

—Mary Jane Newman (Yorba Linda, CA)

"I am an avid fan of your Visual books. If I need to learn anything, I just buy one of your books and learn the topic in no time. Wonders! I have even trained my friends to give me Visual books as gifts."

—Illona Bergstrom (Aventura, FL)

"I just had to let you and your company know how great I think your books are. I just purchased my third Visual book (my first two are dog-eared now!) and, once again, your product has surpassed my expectations. The expertise, thought, and effort that go into each book are obvious, and I sincerely appreciate your efforts."

—Tracey Moore (Memphis, TN)

"Compliments to the chef!! Your books are extraordinary! Or, simply put, extra-ordinary, meaning way above the rest! THANK YOU THANK YOU THANK YOU! I buy them for friends, family, and colleagues."

—Christine J. Manfrin (Castle Rock, CO)

"I write to extend my thanks and appreciation for your books. They are clear, easy to follow, and straight to the point. Keep up the good work! I bought several of your books and they are just right! No regrets! I will always buy your books because they are the best."

—Seward Kollie (Dakar, Senegal)

"I am an avid purchaser and reader of the Visual series, and they are the greatest computer books I've seen. Thank you very much for the hard work, effort, and dedication that you put into this series."

—Alex Diaz (Las Vegas, NV)

Credits

Project Editor
Dana Rhodes Lesh

Senior Acquisitions Editor
Stephanie McComb

Copy Editor
Dana Rhodes Lesh

Technical Editor
Joseph Neal

Editorial Manager
Robyn Siesky

Business Manager
Amy Knies

Senior Marketing Manager
Sandy Smith

Manufacturing
Allan Conley
Linda Cook
Paul Gilchrist
Jennifer Guynn

Book Design
Kathryn Rickard

Project Coordinator
Kristie Rees
Erin Smith

Layout
Carrie A. Cesavice
Andrea Hornberger
Jennifer Mayberry

Screen Artist
Ana Carrillo

Cover Illustration
Cheryl Grubbs

Proofreader
Mildred Rosenzweig

Quality Control
Amanda Graham

Indexer
Valerie Haynes Perry

Special Help
Mark D. Lesh

Vice President and Executive
Group Publisher
Richard Swadley

Vice President and Executive Publisher
Barry Pruett

Composition Director
Debbie Stailey

About the Author

Ric Shreves is an author and Web applications consultant specializing in open source. Ric is a partner in the Web development firm water&stone (www.waterandstone.com), where he practices what he preaches and uses Ubuntu for both servers and desktop PCs. He lives in Bali with his wife, a dog, 2.5 cats, 4 turtles, and an uncountable number of fish.

Author's Acknowledgments

I would like to thank the team at Wiley & Sons for bringing me another interesting open-source project. Ubuntu 8.10 deserves more attention, and this is a worthy effort to help it gain more exposure. I would also like to extend a big thanks (and an even bigger hug) to my wife for putting up with the short delivery times associated with this project; she was very patient with my shifting part of my other workload to her for the interim!

TABLE OF CONTENTS

TABLE OF CONTENTS

TABLE OF CONTENTS

HOW TO USE THIS BOOK

Ubuntu Linux Desktop: Your visual blueprint to using the Linux operating system uses clear, descriptive examples to show you how to set up and get started with the Ubuntu Linux desktop. If you are already familiar with Ubuntu Linux, you can use this book as a quick reference for many tasks, including using the system utilities and the bundled office and home software. The clear steps in each chapter cover all of the most common tasks that you will encounter using the Ubuntu Linux desktop. The OpenOffice suite is also covered in some detail, allowing you to increase your work productivity and efficiency.

Who Needs This Book

This book is for the experienced computer user who wants to find out more about the Ubuntu Linux desktop system. It is also for more experienced Linux users who want to expand their knowledge of the different features that the Ubuntu desktop has to offer.

Book Organization

Ubuntu Linux Desktop: Your visual blueprint to using the Linux operating system has 14 chapters:

Chapter 1, "Getting Started with Ubuntu," provides the information needed to obtain a copy of the Ubuntu Linux system, together with instructions for installing it on your machine.

Chapter 2, "Configuring the Desktop," introduces you to the Ubuntu desktop and explains how to arrange and organize your desktop to suit your needs.

Chapter 3, "Managing Files and Folders," covers the Ubuntu file system and explains how to use it to locate, organize, and manage your files and folders.

Chapter 4, "Setting Preferences," helps you to tailor the Ubuntu desktop system to your particular needs and work habits.

Chapter 5, "Administering the System," provides you with all the information you need to manage and administer the Ubuntu system, including how to manage network services and install additional software and hardware.

Chapter 6, "Using the Included Accessories," covers how to use the numerous accessories that come bundled with the Ubuntu system.

Chapter 7, "Working with Photos and Graphics," focuses on using the image editing and management software included with the Ubuntu desktop.

Chapter 8, "Communicating over the Internet and Managing Your Schedule," helps you use your Ubuntu system to connect to the Internet, send email, make calls with VoIP, and browse the Web.

Chapter 9, "Creating and Editing Documents with OpenOffice.org Writer," provides basic information to help you get started with OpenOffice's word-processing software.

Chapter 10, "Creating and Editing Spreadsheets with OpenOffice.org Calc," covers using the Calc application to create and edit spreadsheets.

Chapter 11, "Creating and Editing Presentations with OpenOffice.org Impress," helps you create presentations with the OpenOffice Impress software.

Chapter 12, "Creating Illustrations with OpenOffice.org Draw," introduces you to the OpenOffice Draw illustration program.

Chapter 13, "Playing and Recording Music and Sound," focuses on using Ubuntu's tools to play and record music and sound on your computer.

Chapter 14, "Using the Command Line," shows you how to unlock the power of the Ubuntu Terminal window.

What You Need to Use This Book

To get the most out of this book, you will need a PC with sufficient memory and CPU capacity to install and run Ubuntu Linux. Ubuntu will run well with a 700MHz x86 processor or better, at least 384MB of RAM, and 8GB of disk space. If you want visual effects to run well, it is recommended that you have a 1.2GHz processor or better and a supported graphics card. Your PC should also have a sound card, a microphone and speakers, or a headset with a microphone, a CD-R drive, and a connection to the Internet.

The Conventions in This Book

A number of styles have been used throughout *Ubuntu Linux Desktop: Your visual blueprint to using the Linux operating system* to designate different types of information.

`Courier Font`

Indicates the use of Terminal commands.

Bold

Indicates information that you must type.

Italics

Indicates a new term.

Apply It

An Apply It section takes the example from the preceding task one step further. Apply It sections enable you to take full advantage of advanced techniques and special features of the system.

Extra

An Extra section provides additional information about the preceding task. Extra sections contain the inside information to make working with the Ubuntu Linux desktop easier and more efficient.

Download Ubuntu

Before you can begin using Ubuntu Linux, you will have to first obtain a copy. There are currently four different methods of obtaining Ubuntu. One option is to request a CD from Canonical. Although this CD is free of charge, it does tend to take some time; there is a backlog for the CDs because there is more demand than can be readily provided for free. If you really want to have the official release on CD, you may want to order an Ubuntu CD online directly from Canonical or Amazon. This incurs a charge, but it is faster. If you do not need a CD, there are two other options. By far the most popular way to get Ubuntu is to download it. Downloading the installer is cheap and easy, but be aware that the files are very large. The faster your connection, the better your experience because the image is roughly 700MB in size. As an alternative, if you know someone who is running Ubuntu, you can ask them to make you an installation disc.

The most current release of the Ubuntu operating system is 8.10. This version is also known as *Intrepid Ibex.* The version number comes from the year 2008 and the month October. The code name convention uses African animals for the informal version names. For more on the history of the naming convention, visit https://wiki.ubuntu.com/DevelopmentCodeNames.

There are also two primary variants of Ubuntu 8.10. The first is the Ubuntu Desktop, which is the focus of this book. The other is the Server edition, and it is primarily for handling tasks within a data center or a network. Server provides mail servers, file servers, and application servers. In general, it is all the back-office plumbing that your typical corporate desktop would connect to for services.

Download Ubuntu

1. Open Internet Explorer.
2. Navigate to www.ubuntu.com/getubuntu/download.
3. Click Please Select a Location.
4. Click the location nearest you.
5. Click Begin Download.

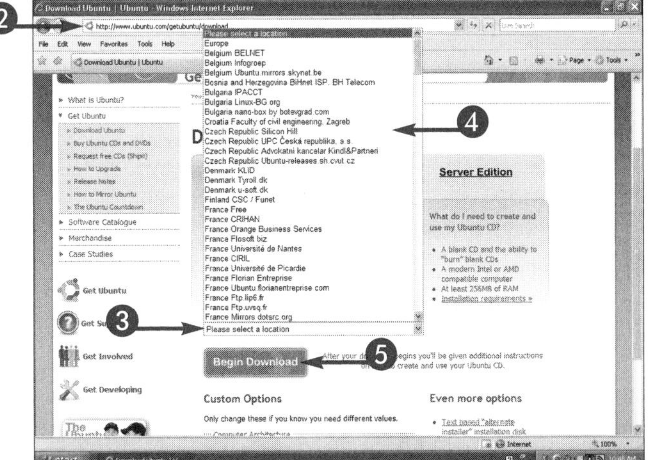

The download page appears, and the File Download dialog box opens.

Note: *Depending on your security settings, you may have to click in the top of the browser to allow the download to start.*

6. Click Save.

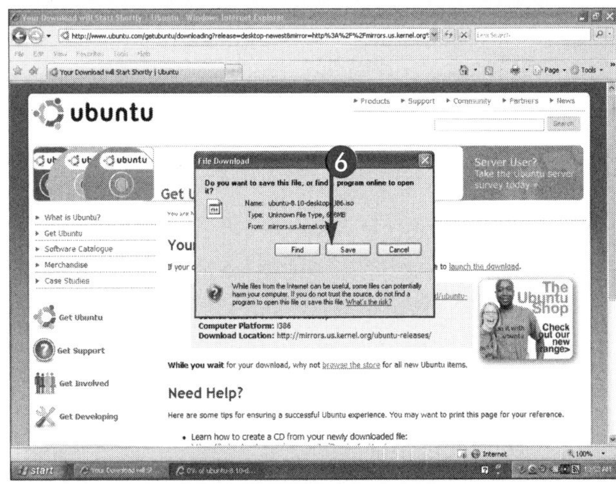

7 Navigate to a location to save the file.

8 Click Save.

The download begins.

Note: *Depending on the speed of your Internet connection and the load on the download servers, this operation could take up to several hours.*

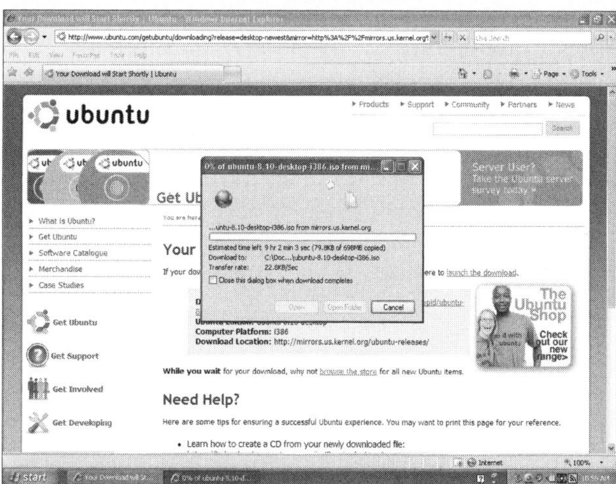

Extra

Ubuntu is built on the Debian Linux distribution. Debian was started over 10 years ago by Ian Murdock when he was a student at Purdue University. Over the years, the project has grown to over 1,000 volunteer developers and 20,000 different software packages. The base package format and package-management utilities behind Ubuntu come from Debian. Ubuntu works on improving the consumability of the underlying operating system. That effort has primarily focused on assembling a more targeted, consistent set of applications that can be bundled with the base Linux OS to make a complete desktop or server.

Although Ubuntu draws from Debian, it adds features as well. The Ubuntu release always includes the latest version of the GNOME desktop user interface. Other important differences include newer versions of the X Window Server and the compiler GCC. These differences are documented in the feature goals for the release on the Ubuntu Web site.

The essential thrust of the Ubuntu project is to be more consistently updated, patched, and recent than the base Debian distribution and to enhance the system and promote it to users. The Ubuntu project is largely supported by Canonical, which also provides commercial support services.

Burn Ubuntu to a CD

After you download the Ubuntu installation file from the Internet, you need to write the file to CD in order to generate a bootable CD. You will use the resulting CD to install Ubuntu on your destination computer. This is a fairly simple task, yet there are many different ways to accomplish it. The instructions in this section detail how to burn the CD on a machine running any Microsoft Windows version from 95 up through Vista. Note that you must have a CD drive capable of recording CDs and at least one writable CD that is compatible with that drive.

The Ubuntu installation file that you downloaded was actually an archive of the data. When this data is stored to a CD, the computer will use the data on the CD to install the new operating system on the computer's internal hard disk drive. The installation files create a CD that has all the right bootstrap data to support running the computer from the CD during the installation process. This process is called *creating an .iso file,* or burning a disc image.

Although burning a disc image sounds simple, many operating systems do not include this capability by default. To perform this task, you will use a third-party piece of software to burn the image file to the CD. Although you may already have such software on your machine, this software varies widely with manufacturer. The one used in this section is Nero Express. It ships with many systems built by PC vendors.

Burn Ubuntu to a CD

1. Launch the CD-burning application that you plan to use.
2. Choose to burn a CD image.

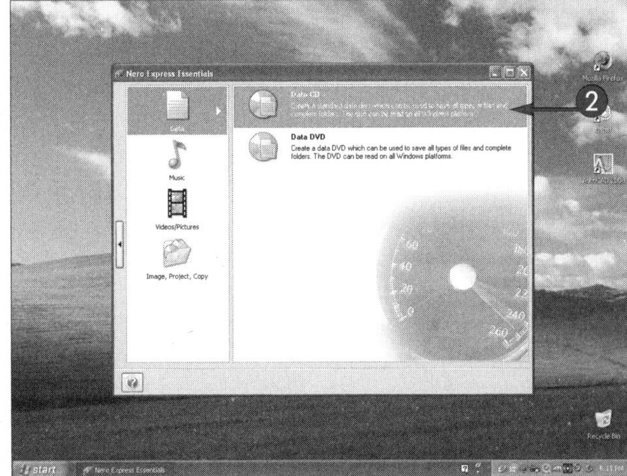

3. Navigate to the location of your Ubuntu .iso file.
4. Click the .iso file.
5. Click Add (or Open).

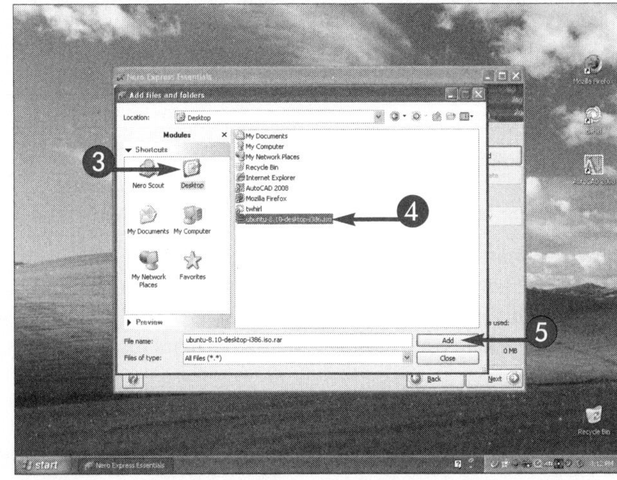

- Optionally, you can ensure data integrity by clicking Verify Data on Disc After Burning.

6 Click Burn.

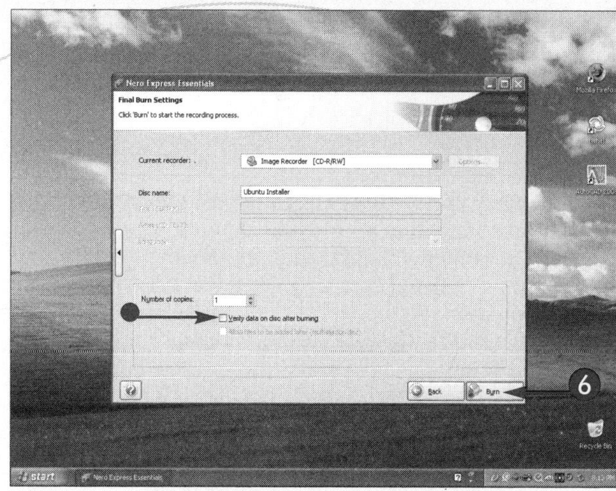

The burning begins.

When the burning is complete, the disc will eject.

Extra

If your hardware or operating system configuration is different from the one discussed, you can go to https://help.ubuntu.com/community/BurningIsoHowto for help. The main issues you may encounter are media and hardware related. One common problem is trying to burn faster than the media you have in the drive can support. This will frequently result in a bad CD. Sometimes the burning software will detect that a bad burn has occurred, but other times it will not, and you will not know until you try the CD in the destination machine. Another common problem that can be the source of great frustration is insufficient temporary disk space. This error means that you have to clear off files from your computer in order to open up enough room to hold the data for the burn. The most difficult problem to remedy is hardware misconfiguration. This is where the operating system on your source machine does not properly recognize the burning capabilities of the drive or possibly even the drive's existence at all. In such a case, you will need to consult any documentation that came with your drive or computer to get it configured properly before attempting to burn the Ubuntu CD.

Boot from the Ubuntu Live CD and Verify Hardware

You can easily check the compatibility of most of your hardware before you install Ubuntu. The image that you download in the section "Download Ubuntu" is what is known as a *live CD.* This means that it contains a fully working operating system and the CD is bootable. This enables you to simply insert the CD in the computer and boot from it instead of your hard drive. You can take Ubuntu for a test drive, or you can check your hardware for compatibility.

Historically, one of the consistent challenges with Linux was hardware support. This was due to the lack of support by the hardware vendors, who would not provide documentation of their drivers or would use driver software that only ran on a specific operating system. This is mainly a thing of the past, but if you are installing on any extremely old, exotic, or cutting-edge hardware, it is always best to check compatibility prior to performing an installation of Ubuntu; otherwise, you may lose some or all of the functionality of that hardware.

After you boot, you will want to verify your computer's basic hardware functionality. The video card is one of the first things you should check. The Screen Resolution program will enable you to verify that you have the appropriate resolutions available to you that you want to use. If the video card does not function at all, you will know pretty quickly. You will end up with a black console screen with a login prompt. There are several options available at the boot that you can try to use a more conservative graphics mode.

Boot from the Ubuntu Live CD and Verify Hardware

BOOT FROM THE LIVE CD

1. Start Ubuntu Linux from the live CD.

Note: *See the section "Burn Ubuntu to a CD."*

The Language screen appears.

2. Choose your language.

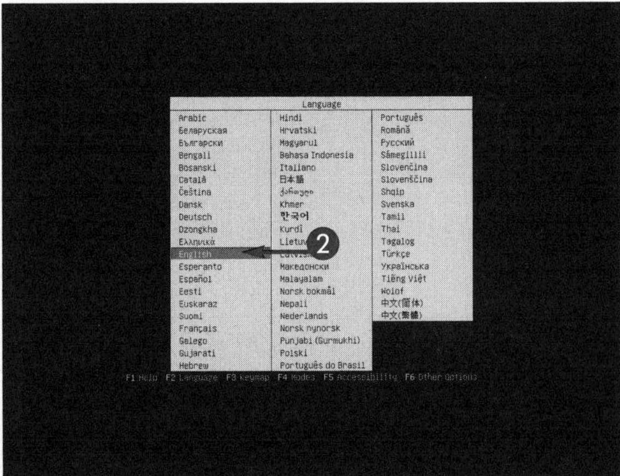

The Ubuntu screen appears.

3. Choose Try Ubuntu Without Any Change to Your Computer.

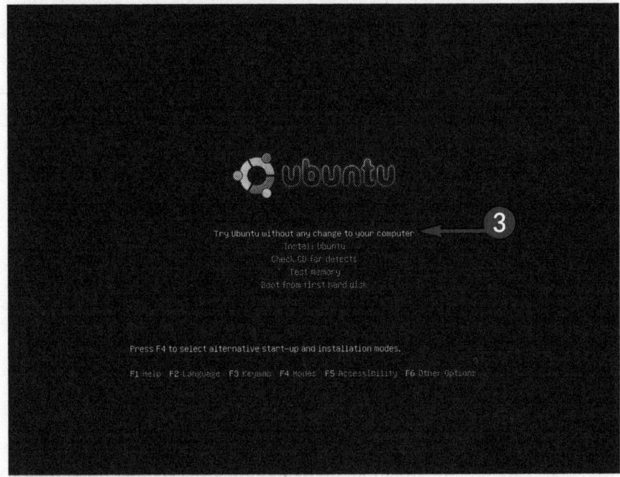

Ubuntu Linux loads.

VERIFY THE AVAILABLE RESOLUTIONS

1. Click System ➔ Preferences ➔ Screen Resolution.

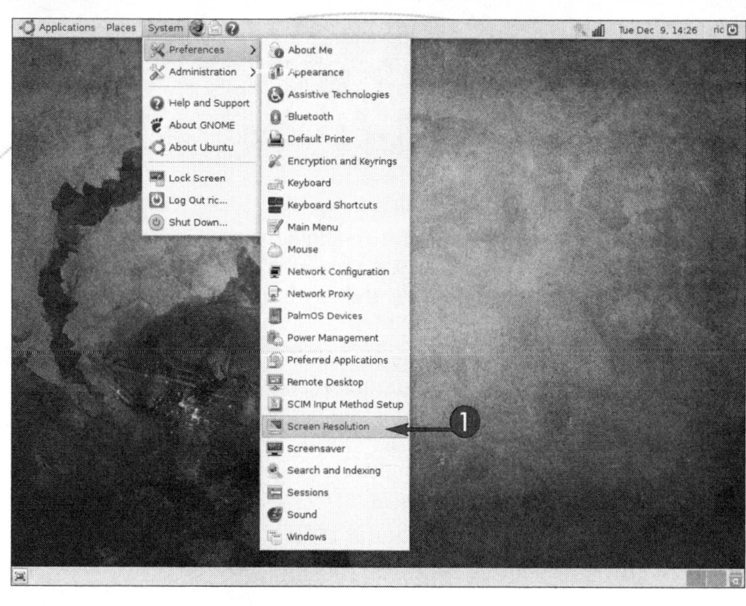

The Monitor Resolution Settings dialog box appears.

2. Click here and verify that the list of available resolutions includes the one that you want to use.

3. Click Close.

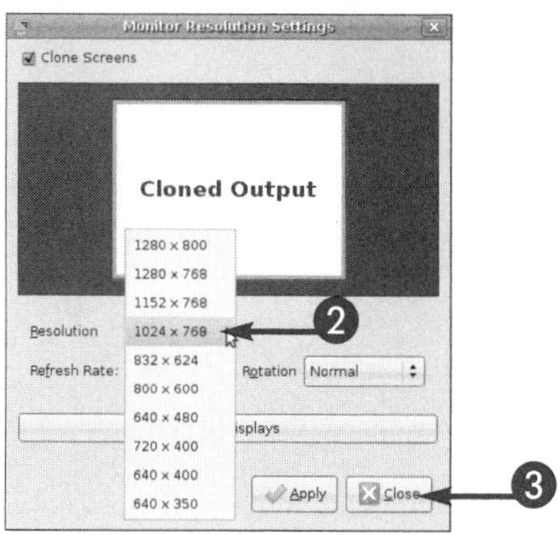

Extra

Ubuntu provides many language and accessibility options. Accessibility support is provided directly from the initial screen of the live CD, enabling selection of everything from a high-contrast screen theme to full Braille support and even screen reading.

The Modes selection on the first boot screen enables you to pick different major modes of operation for the boot process itself. The Normal mode is the default bootup for the CD. The Safe Graphics mode provides a low-resolution, yet safe, way to boot Ubuntu on older hardware or hardware with an unrecognizable graphics card. You can also use a driver update CD or a manufacturer installation.

The Other Options selection on the initial boot screen allows you to enable and disable certain features that are normally, but not always, supported by hardware. This can help if you have problems booting or experience strange behaviors due to hardware not conforming to the standard. Advanced Configuration and Power Interface (ACPI) is a feature that sometimes has hardware support issues. It replaced an older standard and may or may not be supported fully by your hardware. The Advanced Programmable Interrupt Controller (APIC) support is another common source of issues for similar reasons.

continued ➔

Boot from the Ubuntu Live CD and Verify Hardware (continued)

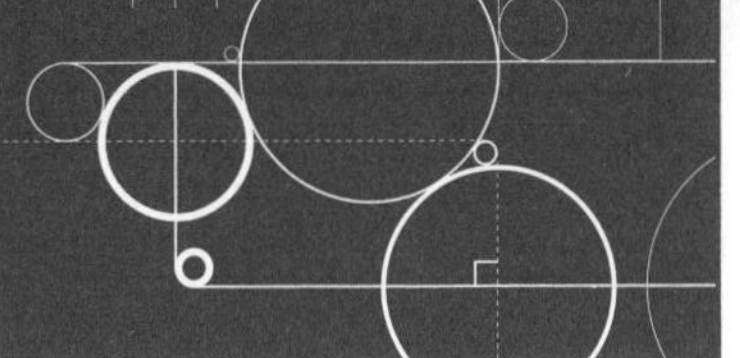

After you boot, you will want to check the compatibility of all your hardware. In addition to the video card, you should be concerned with your network connections, your sound devices, and anything else that is essential or unusual about your system.

A quick check of the network monitor applet will allow you to verify that you have a network address and that the connection is functioning normally. Before you perform this step, make sure that you are plugged in to your network cable or that your wireless device is functioning properly; otherwise, the results are likely to be meaningless.

Note that although an Internet connection is optional, a fast network connection with access to the Internet will enhance your Ubuntu experience greatly. Ubuntu gains much of its flexibility and security from frequent updates via the Internet. The full software library available to Ubuntu is quite large. In fact, many more packages are available than can fit on a CD or DVD. This being the case, you will find many more software options available to you if you have an Internet connection.

Finally, you should verify that your sound hardware is functioning properly. Make sure that you have speakers or a pair of headphones handy to perform this test. The Sound application under the Preferences menu will enable you to check the sound system. Although this is not a complete list of all possible hardware items to check, this should get you up and running.

If there are additional hardware or peripherals you use regularly, you should check them as well.

Boot from the Ubuntu Live CD and Verify Hardware *(continued)*

VERIFY THE NETWORK CONNECTION

1. Click System ➔ Preferences ➔ Network Configuration.

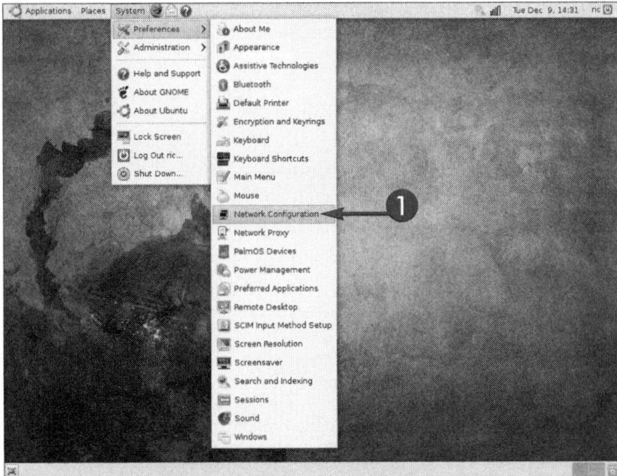

The Network Connections dialog box appears.

2. Verify your network connection information.
3. Click Close.

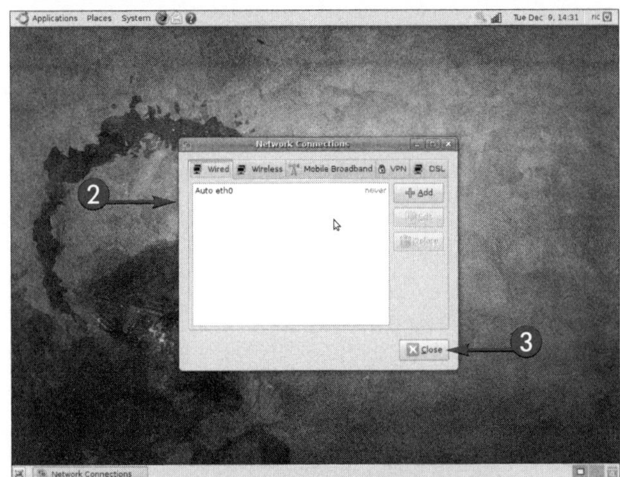

VERIFY THE SOUND HARDWARE

1. Click System ➔ Preferences ➔ Sound.

   The Sound Preferences dialog box appears.

2. Click Test.

   Ubuntu tests your sound events.

3. Click Test.

   Ubuntu tests the sound for music and movies.

4. Click Test.

   Ubuntu tests the receiving of sound for audio conferences.

5. Click Test.

   Ubuntu tests the sending of sound for audio conferences.

6. Click Close.

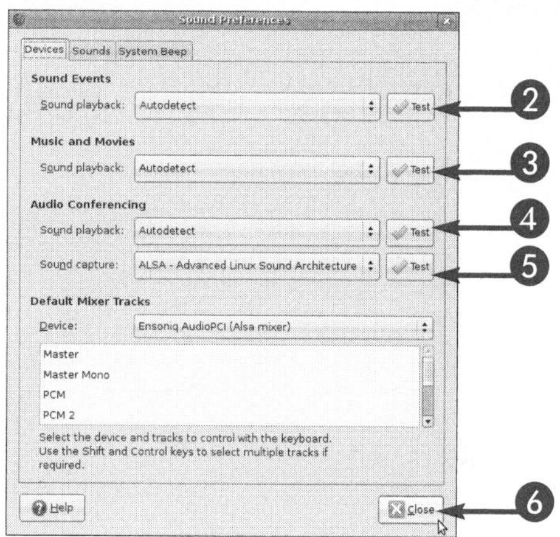

Extra

To check external drives such as memory card readers, external disk drives, and external CD/DVD drives, you will want to click the Computer option under the Places menu. This allows you to see all the file storage volumes connected to your machine, even if you are currently not connected to them by the operating system, or in other words, they are not currently mounted, such as a drive located on the network.

Linux can read a variety of formats, including FAT, FAT32, NTFS, Minix, Ext2, Ext3, and Apple HFS. The Ubuntu kernel has built-in support for all USB drives and for FireWire (IEEE1394) drives as well. Due to the vast array of file systems that Linux supports, you should be able to read just about anything that registers as a drive on the computer screen.

When you see a volume listed, you can double-click it to open the file system, causing a mount operation to occur in the background. Once successfully mounted, the File Browser will show you the contents of the drive. You can unmount the drive from the computer window of the File Browser by right-clicking it and selecting Unmount.

Install Ubuntu

You can install Ubuntu directly from the live CD. The process is quick and easy, and you can even surf the Internet while you install. Because the live CD already has a fully working environment, you actually do the installation from within the same environment you will experience after the system is fully installed.

Historically, installing Linux was fairly arcane, but recent Linux distributions actually rival or beat the ease of installation of other operating systems. With the live CD and the capability to ensure that the hardware is working prior to actually installing the software, you gain the confidence that the process will be a success before investing the time for a full install.

The first half of the Ubuntu installation process primarily asks questions about locale-driven items — specifically, your local time zone, your preferred language, and your keyboard layout. The most technical question posed during the installation relates to disk preparation, that is, whether you want to partition the drive.

Partitioning is a scheme in which a physical disk can contain multiple, logically separate areas that an operating system can view as separate volumes. These separate areas can also host other operating systems, and with the correct boot loader setup, you can boot various operating systems on the same machine.

If you want to keep the data that is presently on the machine, if any, you must create a new partition, rather than wipe out the machine with a completely fresh installation. Moreover, if you want to keep the present operating system on the machine and install Ubuntu as an additional system, you must partition the drive.

Install Ubuntu

1. Double-click the installer.

   The Install dialog box appears, showing the Welcome page.

2. Click your preferred language.
3. Click Forward.

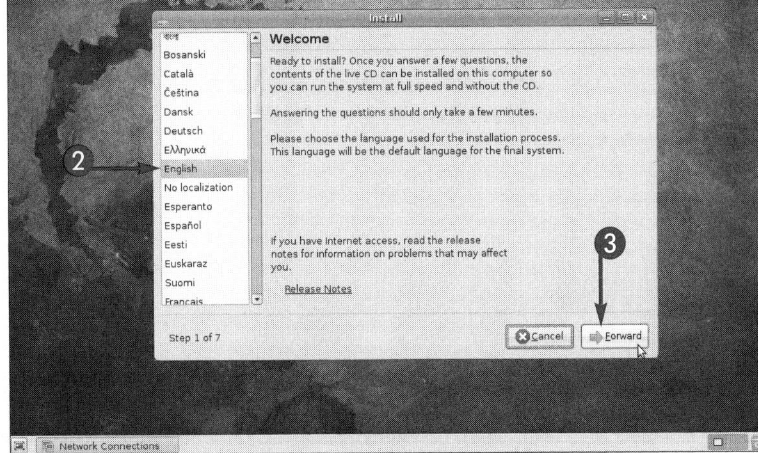

The Where Are You? page appears.

4. Click here and select a city in your time zone.
5. Click Forward.

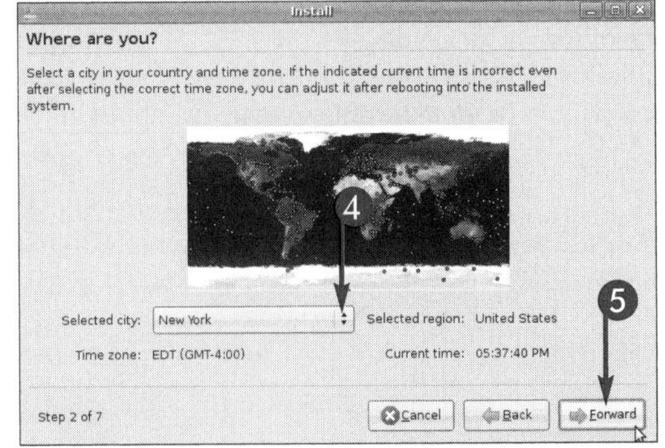

The Keyboard Layout page appears.

6 Click your keyboard layout.

7 Click Forward.

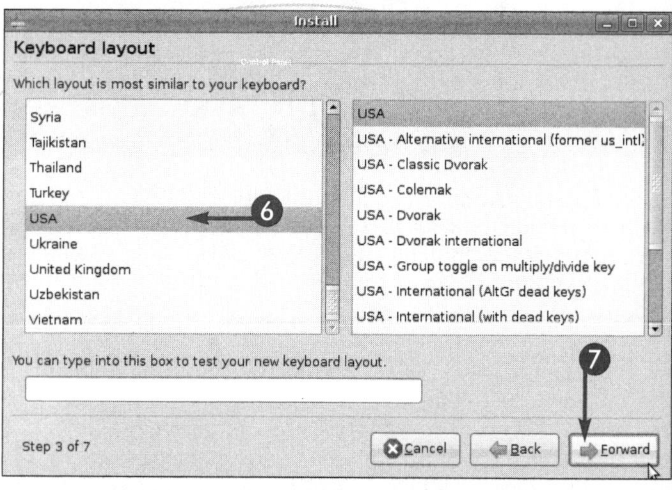

The Prepare Disk Space page appears.

8 Verify that you want to use the recommended partitioning for the drive.

Note: *Double-check that you have any important data from the drive backed up.*

9 Click Forward.

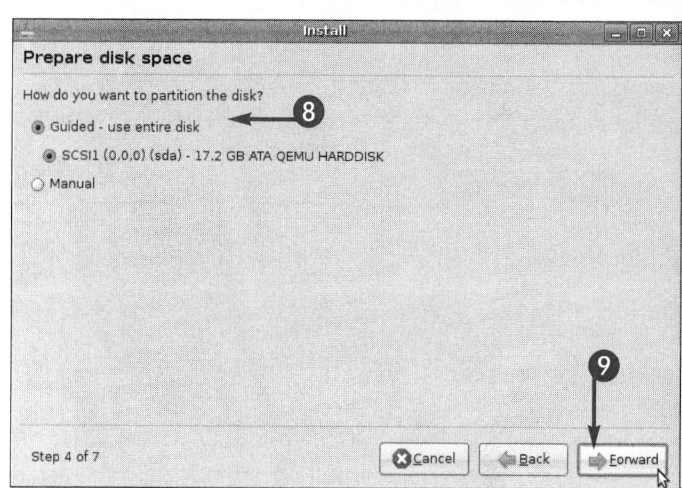

Extra

Partitioning schemes on Linux have a long tradition. The original UNIX operating systems ran on large multiuser machines. When upgrades were performed on the operating system of these large machines, it was paramount to not adversely affect the users. Consequently, rather than have all the users' files on the same set of disks as the operating system files, they were kept on separate disks. This allowed system administrators to completely rewrite programs or the principle system if needed. The segregation of the user files meant that when the system came back up, all the user files would be left untouched.

Partitions were also important for the operating system itself, as the swap file for the operating system was also maintained on a separate disk. This allowed a performance boost by having a dedicated set of disks for pushing memory pages into and out of magnetic storage.

Aside from swap, the /tmp folder was often kept on separate disk volumes. This usually had more to do with access speed, as UNIX and all UNIX-like operating systems create tremendous traffic in the form of temporary files.

continued

Install Ubuntu (continued)

Installing Ubuntu involves not only getting the software on to your computer, but also setting up your account to use the software. Controlling user access and privileges is one of the keys to keeping your Ubuntu system safe.

The proliferation of viruses and malware has been accelerated by the use of unsecured administrative privileges on machines connected to the Internet. A common scenario for malware is to trick users into running a malicious piece of software on their computers that, because they have administrative privileges, allows this program to set up backdoors into the system that can be used remotely by the person or persons who authored the program. This kind of attack is called a *Trojan.*

Similar, though more sophisticated, is the virus attack. This relies on a vulnerability in either software or access mechanisms to gain access to a system. If the account breached has sufficient privileges, the virus can propagate to other accounts on the system or even propagate out to other systems.

To avoid these problems, it is paramount to have strong and not easily guessed passwords for user accounts and to protect them vigorously. Never share your password with another user and never run any program if you are unsure of its authenticity. Ubuntu subscribes to a least-privilege approach, meaning that your user account has the minimum privileges necessary to accomplish your day-to-day tasks. Whenever you request to perform an operation that requires additional privileges, a dialog box will be presented to ask you for your password. This is a warning sign. Whenever you are asked for your password by the system, be certain of the actions that you are performing.

Install Ubuntu *(continued)*

The Who Are You? page appears.

10 Type in your full name.

11 Type in the login name that you want to use.

12 Choose a password.

13 Retype the password, making sure that it matches the first one.

14 Type in the name for your machine.

15 Click Forward.

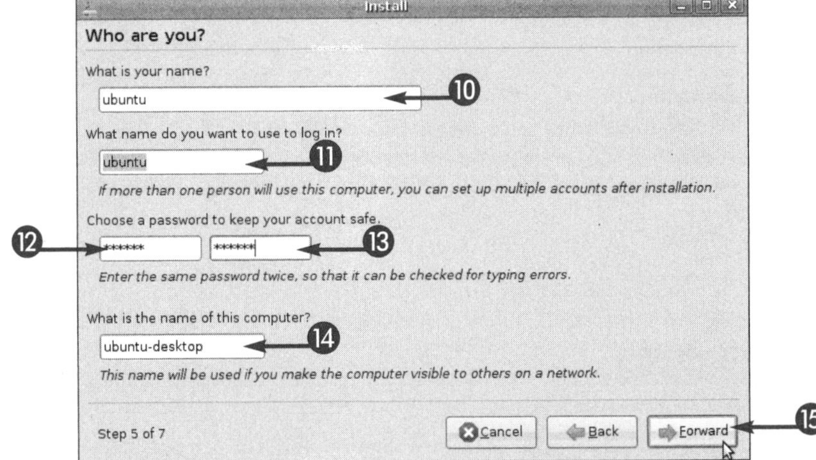

The Ready to Install page appears.

16 Click Install.

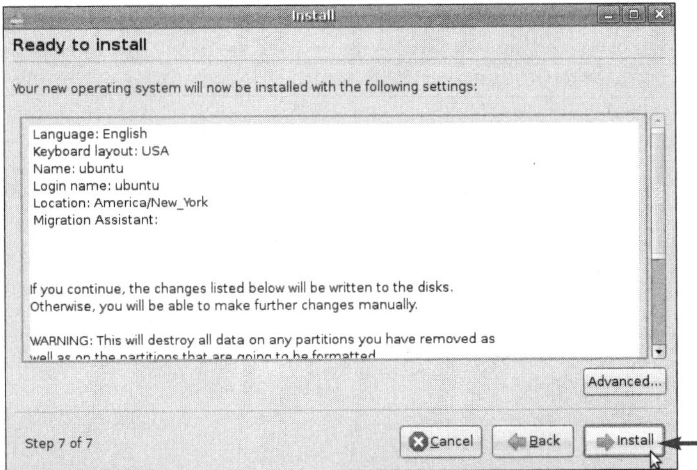

The installation begins.

Note: *This can take from 10 to 40 minutes, depending on your machine's CPU and disk capabilities.*

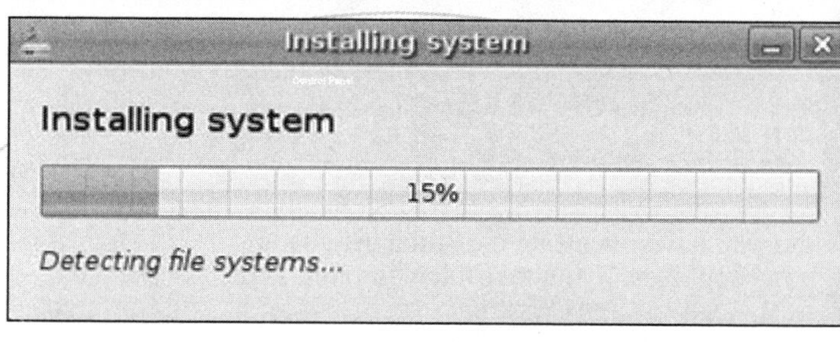

When the installation is finished, the Installation Complete dialog box appears.

17 Click Restart Now.

Note: *Remove the CD from the machine before the next boot.*

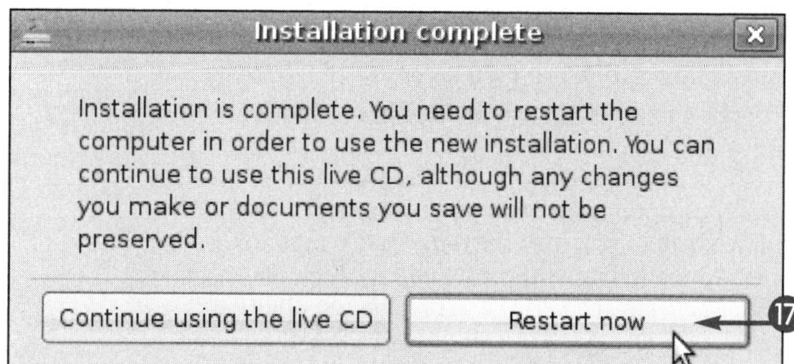

Extra

Choosing a strong password is essential to keeping your system safe. There are a couple general principles to help you avoid your password being compromised. The longer the password, the harder it will be to crack it with brute force. For example, if you have a three-digit password that is only made up of numbers, then it can be cracked in under 1,000 tries. If the number of digits is longer, obviously, it will take more tries to crack. The same principle applies to the characters you use. To make your password strong, use different types of characters. Use numbers, letters of both upper- and lowercase, and punctuation. This greatly increases the number of tries it takes to crack a password by brute force.

Hackers are aware of these strategies, however, and try to skew the odds in their favor by using dictionaries of common passwords and variations on them to reduce the number of tries needed. To thwart this type of attack, avoid proper nouns and words that can be found in the dictionary. A common technique is to use the first letter of each word of a phrase to allow for a combination of letters not common in any language.

Log Into/Out of the System for the First Time

After you have completed the initial installation, you should get in and take a look around your fresh Ubuntu Linux system.

When Ubuntu first boots up, it brings up the login screen. You will need to provide the login and password you used during installation in order to gain access to the system.

A couple options present themselves to you on this first screen. From the Options menu, you can select a different language to use during your session. You may also select from a variety of options for starting your session. Most of these explicitly say to only use them if you are unable for some reason to log in any other way, and a couple have some additional utility. One of the options is the ability to log into other machines with the secure shell (SSH) protocol. Although this sounds very useful, it is limited to only users who have an account on the local machine.

Another useful option is the ability to connect to remote machines that are running XDMCP. XDMCP is a protocol for establishing remote X11 connections. The host computer, not the one you are using, broadcasts its availability on the network, and typically, dedicated X terminals see these broadcasts and allow you to select from an available host and initiate a login. Then the X11 session is directed to this X terminal as if the session were running on the console of the host. Using this option on Ubuntu allows an Ubuntu desktop to be used just like a dedicated X terminal.

Other options are pretty much standard login screen types of operations. These include restarting or shutting down the machine, along with sending the machine into either hibernation or suspend (standby) modes.

Log Into/Out of the System for the First Time

LOG IN

1. Type in the login username you created during installation and press Enter.

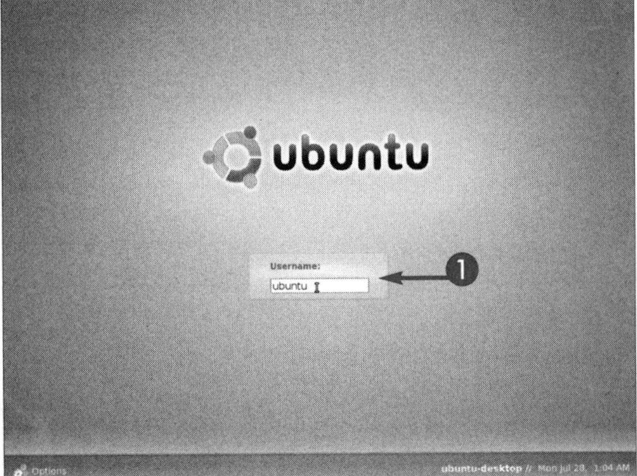

2. Type in the password you chose during installation and press Enter.

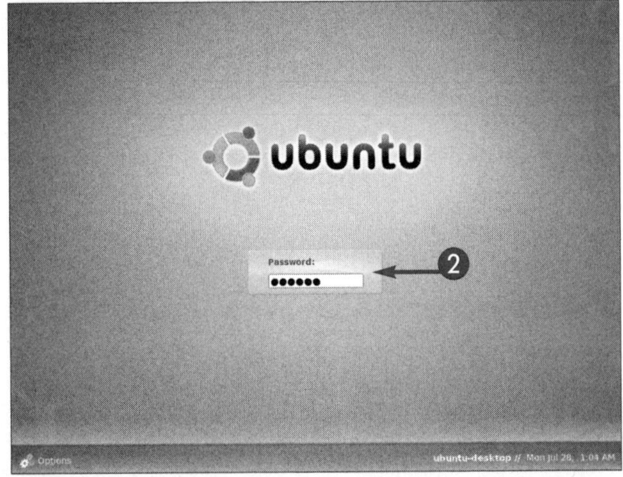

The Ubuntu desktop launches.

LOG OUT

1. Click the Quit applet.
2. Click Log Out.

You are logged out of the system.

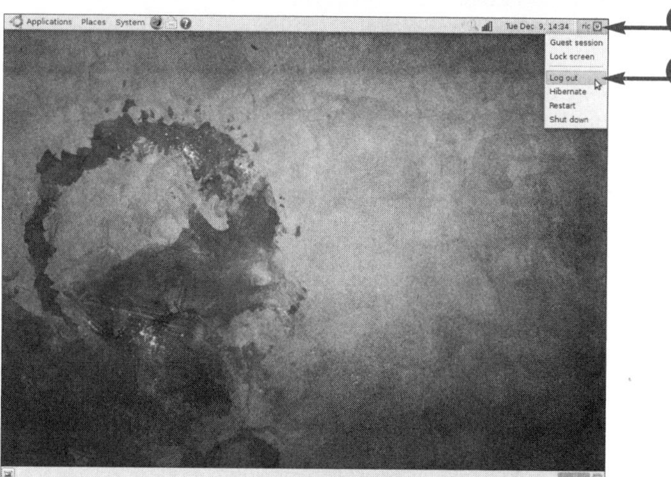

Extra

When logging out, notice the other options presented. Ubuntu allows for you to switch to another user without having to log out. This is especially handy when you are sharing a computer. The most important option on the logout display is the Lock Screen option. Locking the screen when you are away from your computer is a good line of defense against hacking. Most hacking in corporations happens within the confines of the company itself, rather than a person or persons on the Internet. Good computer security starts right at your desk. Whenever you are not at your computer, lock the screen. Then you will not have to worry about others looking at, editing, or — worse yet — accidentally deleting your files.

Another useful option is hibernation. This choice puts the computer to sleep without shutting it down completely. If you have never used hibernation before, consider it because it is a great way to be able to shut down your machine and conserve either AC line power or battery power without losing your place within your work. When a machine is hibernated, it is completely shut off, drawing no power.

Organize Desktop Icons and Panels

You can reorganize the GNOME desktop to suit your own tastes. If you configure your desktop more intuitively, you can increase your productivity by having files, folders, and icons located more conveniently for rapid access.

The GNOME desktop is organized in much the same manner as other computer systems, such as Windows or Apple's Macintosh OS. The desktop consists of icons across the surface of the screen and one or more panels about its edges. These desktop icons can be moved by dragging them around the desktop surface or even into a panel.

On any unoccupied space on the desktop surface, you can right-click and get a context menu of icon options. One of these options is Create Launcher. A *launcher* is a small text file that operates as a shortcut to launch a program or a file.

Another option is Create Folder. With this, you can create new directories directly within the Desktop folder.

If you have any document templates installed, you will also have the option to select them and create a document with that template. There are no default templates installed with Ubuntu, but you can use the Create Document option to create an empty file on the desktop surface.

There are several housekeeping items on this right-click menu as well. Clean Up by Name arranges all the icons on the desktop surface alphabetically against the top left of the screen. Keep Aligned spaces the icons evenly according to an invisible grid that each icon will gravitate toward when released from a drag operation.

You can also access a dialog box to change the background image and color of the desktop surface.

Organize Desktop Icons and Panels

ADD A LAUNCHER

1. Right-click any unoccupied desktop area.
2. Click Create Launcher.

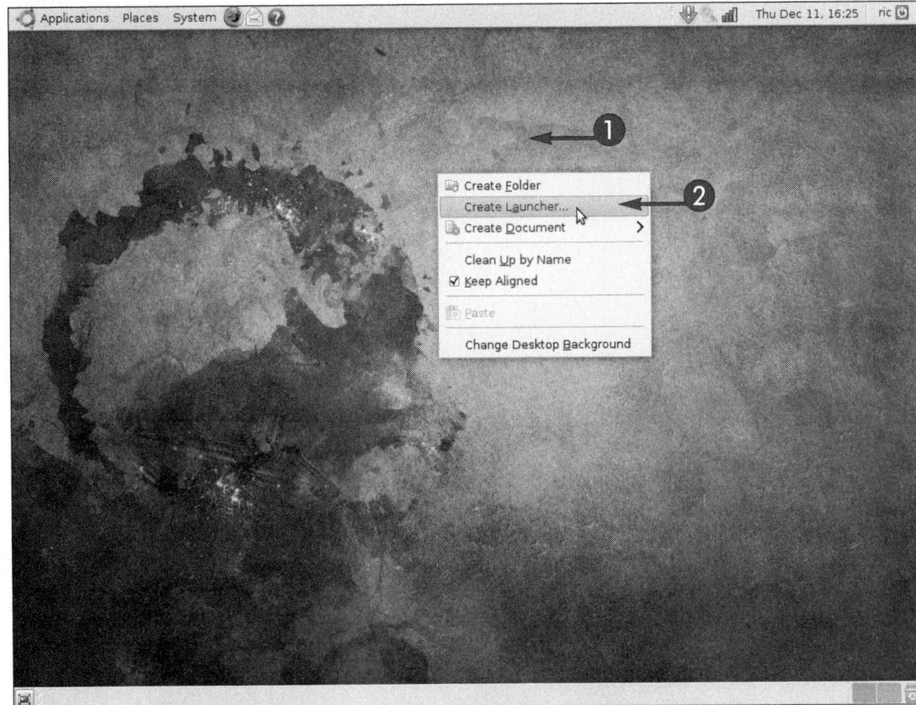

The Create Launcher dialog box appears.

3. Type the name of the application for which you would like to create a launcher, such as **XEyes** in this example.
4. Type the command to launch that application, such as **xeyes** in this example.

Note: *You can find a description of launcher commands online at https://help.ubuntu.com/7.04/user-guide/C/launchers.html.*

5. Click OK.

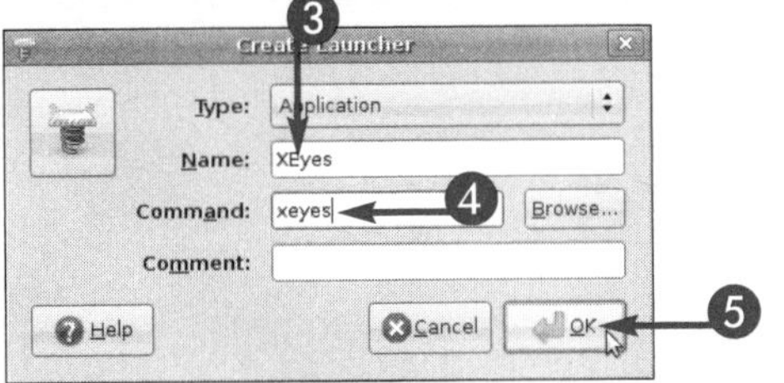

6 Double-click the new launcher.

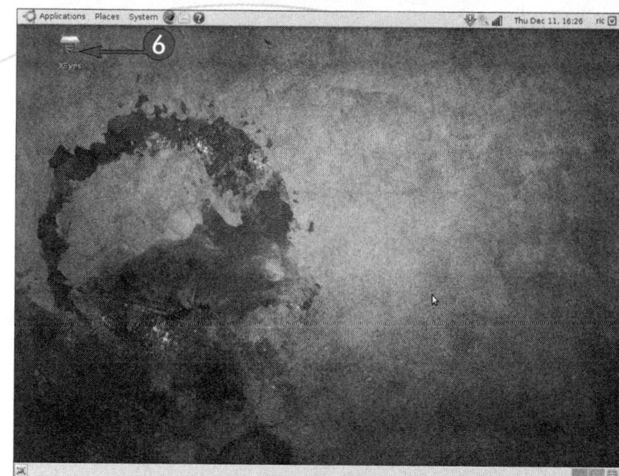

- The associated application launches.

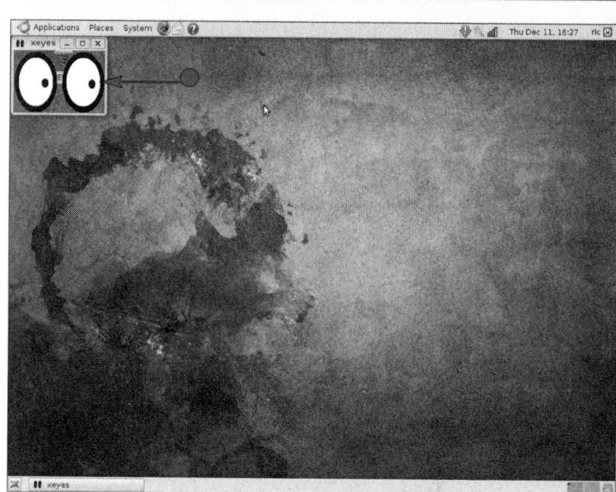

Extra

After you have created the launcher, you can move it around anywhere on the desktop. You can also move it into a folder to keep the desktop clean. Another way to keep the launchers handy for use even when you have an application maximized is to take it and drag it into one of the panels.

A launcher can also open a uniform resource locator (URL). In order to do this, you need to select Location in the Type box in the Create Launcher dialog box. These are very similar to the application launcher files in that they are stored with the .desktop files in the Desktop folder. But they have a different type specified in the metadata that tells the operating system (OS) to determine that they should be opened with the Firefox Web browser application instead of the Nautilus File Browser application. You can drag a link from the browser out to the GNOME desktop surface to create a URL launcher as well. Along with the standard http:// reference, it can also open locations of the file:// variety.

continued

Organize Desktop Icons and Panels (continued)

The default installation presents the user with two panels, one across the top of the screen and one across the bottom. These panels are used to host launchers, menus, and applets to offer rapid access to software or directories on the machine. A menu provides hierarchical access to a set of applications, grouped together by category or function. An applet is a program with a very tiny user interface (UI), allowing it to be embedded within the UI of another application. This allows the hosting application to aggregate componentized functionality that it does not have to provide itself.

The left half of the top panel has the main menu, a launch icon for the browser, another for email, and a third for help. The right half of this panel has the User Switcher, the System Updater Status applet, the Network Monitor applet, the Volume Control applet, the Time and Date applet, and the Quit applet.

The bottom panel contains the Show Desktop applet; the Window List applet, which shows icons and text for each open application; the Workspace Switcher applet; and the Trash applet.

If you right-click any panel, you are presented with several configuration options. One of these options opens the Panel Properties dialog box, which enables you to tweak the orientation, thickness, whether the panel will expand to fill the entire screen edge, whether it will automatically hide itself when not in use, and whether to show the hide buttons.

Another configuration option on the panel right-click menu enables you to create a new panel on any of the edges of the screen.

Organize Desktop Icons and Panels *(continued)*

CREATE A NEW PANEL

1. Right-click a panel.
2. Click New Panel.

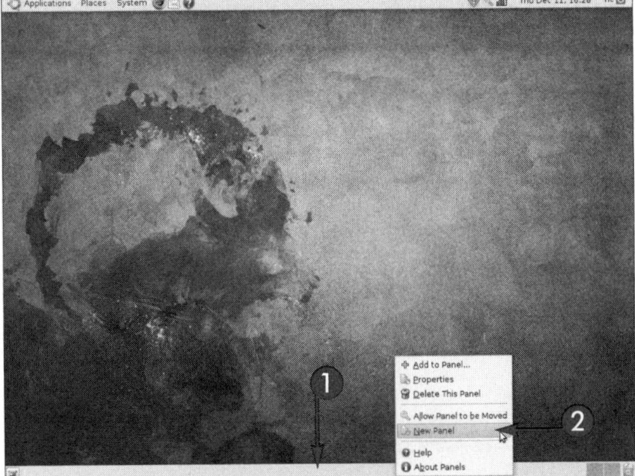

- A new panel appears.

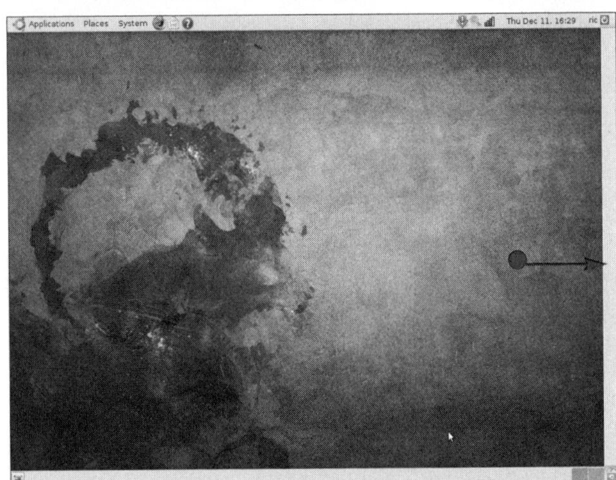

3. Right-click the new panel.
4. Click Properties.

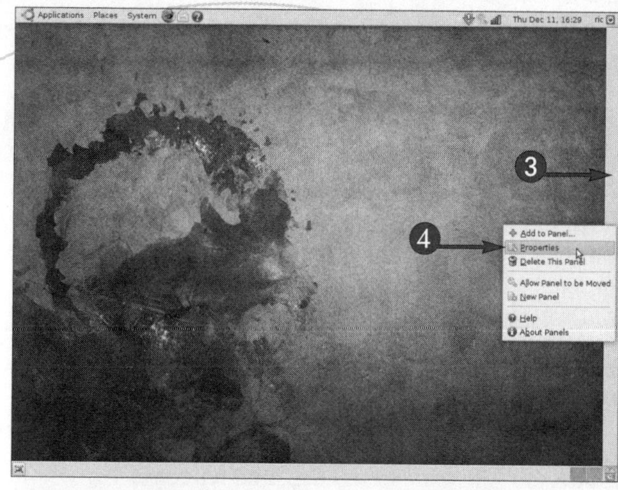

The Panel Properties dialog box appears.

5. Make any changes to the new panel that you want.

Note: *For example, if Expand is checked, you can click to deselect it.*

- If you uncheck Expand, the panel shrinks.

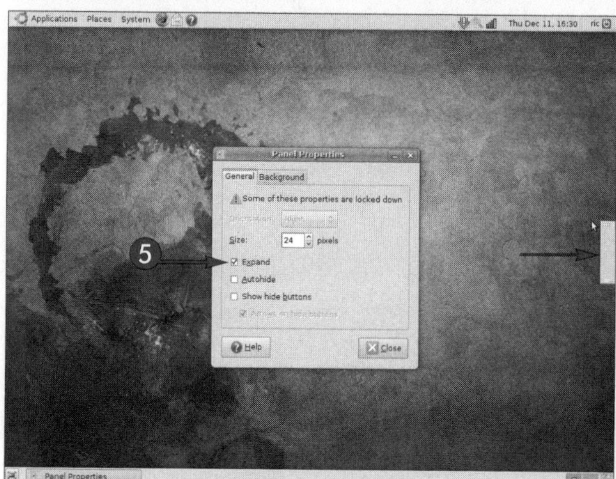

Extra

Panels can be made to have backgrounds of their own, or even become semitransparent. To do this, you right-click a non-applet-occupied area of a panel and click Properties. In the Panel Properties dialog box, click the Background tab. The default is to just use the system color/style theme. To change the color, you can select Solid Color, click the color sample, and select a different color in a color chooser dialog box. Then you can adjust the slider for a transparent look. To add an image as a panel background, click Background Image and navigate to the image that you want to use. This image will repeat if it is smaller than the surface of the panel.

Panels can be dragged around to virtually anywhere on the desktop. If the Expand option of the panel is active, however, the panel can only be placed along an edge of the desktop. When this option is out of play, the smaller panels displayed can be dragged out onto the open surface of the desktop or attached to any point along one of the desktop edges.

Change the Number of Workspaces

Although switching between applications allows you to multitask, sometimes the number of applications to toggle between becomes a hindrance to productivity. Workspaces, many times called *virtual desktops,* can alleviate some of that overhead by allowing you to group the applications that you switch between onto different spaces. Each workspace has its own list of applications to switch between. This enables you, for example, to place your email and administrative windows on one desktop, all your graphics editing and task-related tools on another desktop, and reference materials on still another desktop. This is nearly as if you had three computers next to each other, all with different sets of applications running.

Although these workspaces can be conceived of as separate computers, they are more closely related to having multiple monitors. That is due to the fact that applications can be moved from desktop to desktop easily via the right-click menu on the top of the window border. Options presented there include moving an application to a workspace right or left of the current workspace.

The ability to switch between workspaces is presented by the Workspace Switcher as the Pager applet. This applet shows a small representation of each of the workspaces and the applications on them. By clicking in a given workspace representation, you can switch to that workspace. Additionally, you can move applications from workspace to workspace by dragging the representation of an application on the task switcher to another of the workspaces on the switcher.

Change the Number of Workspaces

1. Right-click the desktop switcher.
2. Click Preferences.

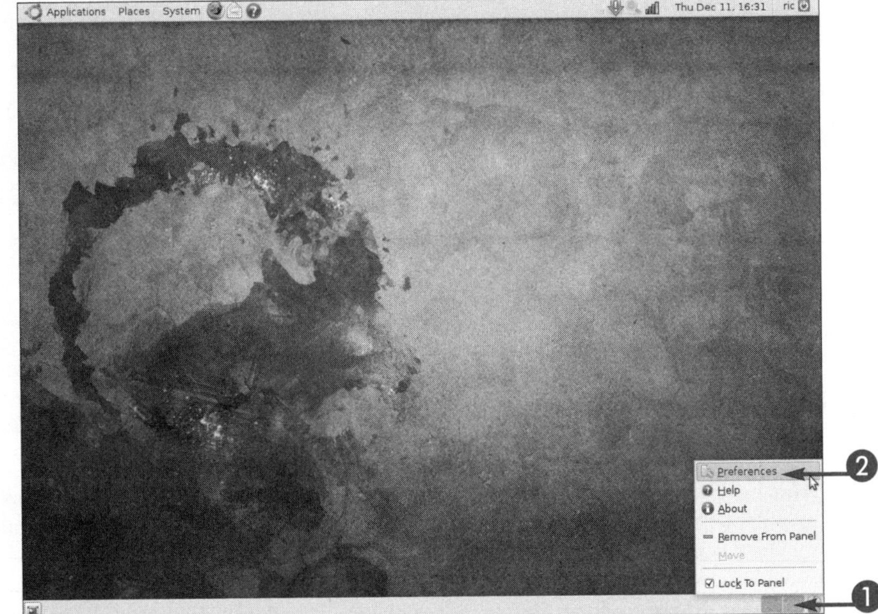

The Workspace Switcher Preferences dialog box appears.

3. Change the number of workspaces from 2 to the number that you want.
4. Press Tab.

- The lower pane of the dialog box now shows the number of desktops that you chose.

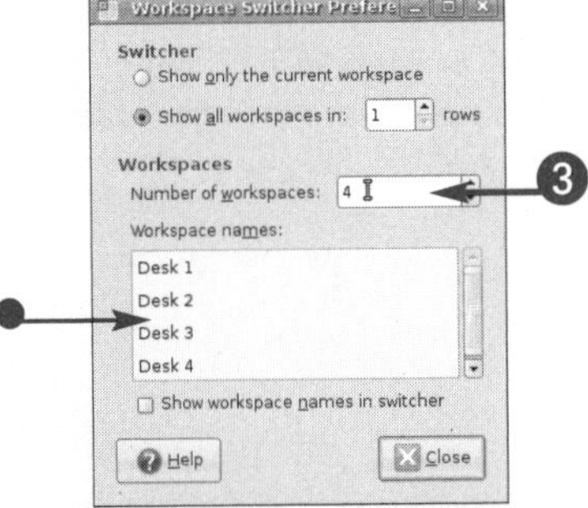

Add a Panel Applet

There are many small tasks that you access frequently, such as changing the system volume, checking the time or weather, or checking the state of the system battery. These tasks are usually provided via the omnipresent GNOME panel applets. Adding new applets to the panel enables you to customize the access to frequently used items.

The GNOME panel is the primary means of launching applications on an Ubuntu-based machine. The panel consists of applets. Even the main menu is a special form of applet. This allows for great flexibility and configurability in accessing your applications and tools.

There are so many available applets that the Add to Panel dialog box has its own search at the top to help you to quickly locate an applet for your need. The dialog box also lists all available applets and provides short descriptions of each.

Some of the more useful applets are for the standard types of things that many operating systems put in a system tray. The Clock and Calendar applet on Ubuntu enables you to see your appointments in the Evolution email application as well as the usual simple date and time. The User Switcher applet allows switching the currently logged-in user and provides various security options such as locking the screen when a user is switched. The Network Monitor applet gives you information about your LAN or Internet connection's activity. There are many other interesting applets such as the CPU Frequency Scaling Monitor applet, the Dictionary Lookup applet, the Sticky Note applet, and of course the Trash applet, which moves the file-recovery functionality to the system tray instead of being on the desktop surface itself as it is on other operating systems.

Add a Panel Applet

1. Right-click a panel.
2. Click Add to Panel.

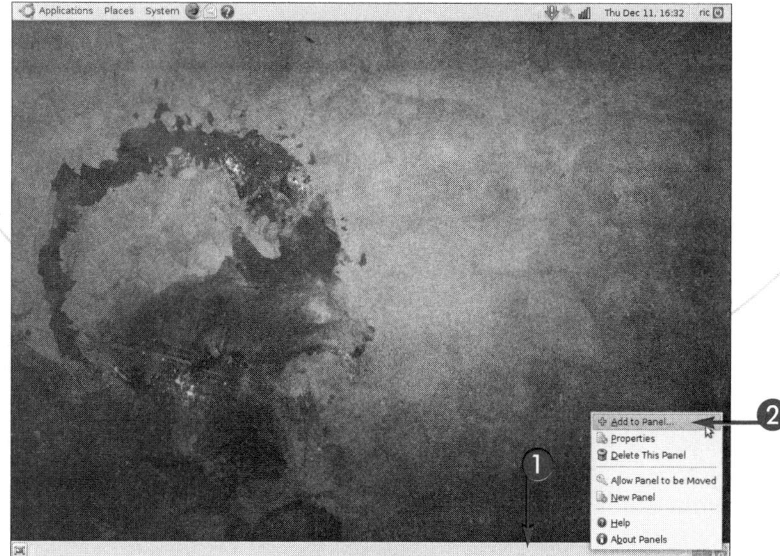

The Add to Panel dialog box appears.

3. Click an applet to add.
4. Click Add.

The new applet appears on the panel.

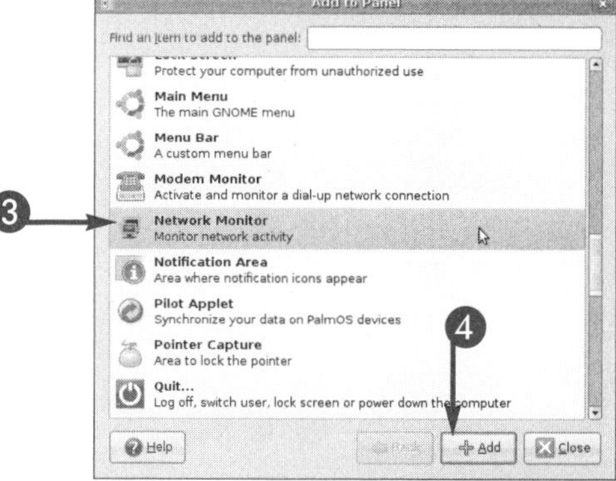

Add Frequently Used Applications to the Desktop or Main Panel

Sometimes there are applications that you use so frequently that the navigation of the menus becomes tiresome. Other times, you would like to access an application or folder usually found on the desktop without having to minimize other applications, or the number of icons become too much clutter on the desktop. To help solve these problems, you can place application shortcuts from the main menu onto the desktop or into the panel for quick, easy access.

The panel and desktop use launchers, which, as mentioned earlier, contain metadata regarding the action that should be taken when they are opened, the type of entity they refer to, and the icon for the launcher to present on the desktop or panel. Launchers are stored in small files ending in the extension .desktop and are plain text. To create a new launcher, see the section "Organize Desktop Icons and Panels."

Once added to either the desktop or the panel, these applications can be accessed by either a single click for the panel or a double-click for the desktop. Their removal is as easy as a right-click and selecting either Remove from Panel for panel launchers or Move to Trash for desktop launchers.

Add Frequently Used Applications to the Desktop or Main Panel

ADD AN ITEM TO THE MAIN PANEL

1. Click Places.
2. Click the folder location that you want to add to the main panel.
3. Drag the location icon from the menu to the panel.

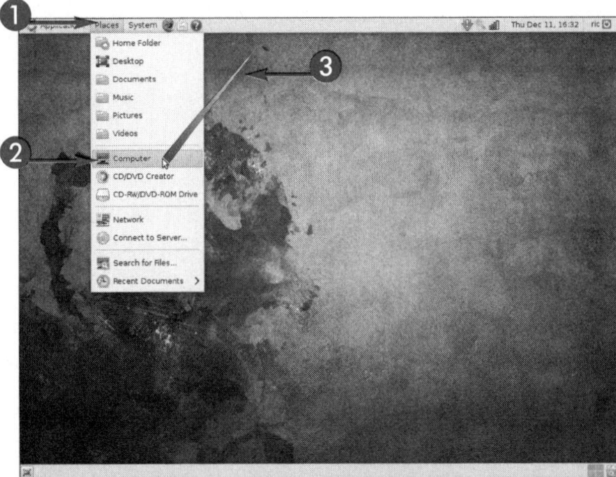

- Its icon appears on the panel.

ADD AN ITEM TO THE DESKTOP

1. Click Applications.
2. Click the submenu containing the application that you want to add to the desktop.
3. Click the application.
4. Drag it to the desktop.

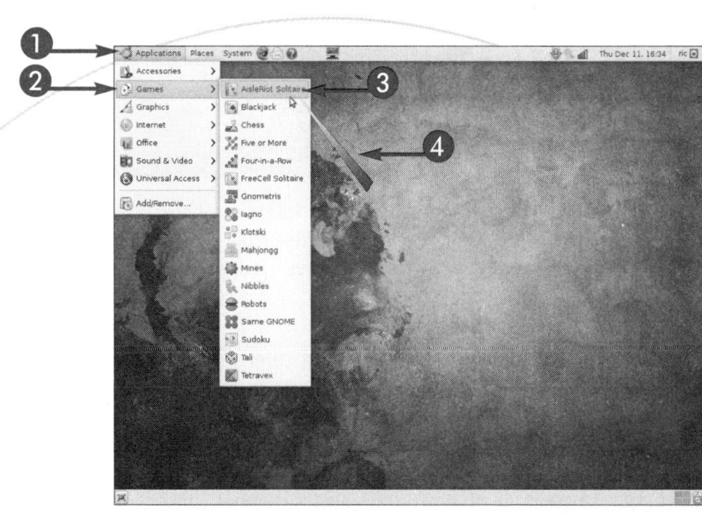

- A launcher icon appears on the desktop.

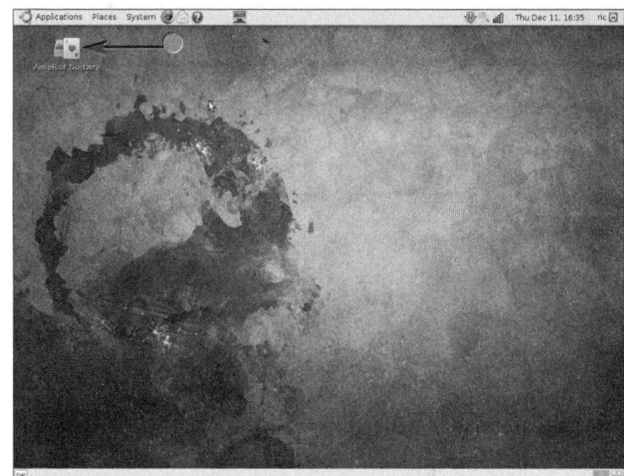

Extra

A panel can also hold a specialized applet called a *drawer* that can contain more launchers, applets, or menus. Drawers can also extend panels in a similar fashion to menus. These drawers act like little versions of the panels themselves, popping up like a menu when clicked on. They can hold all the same things that a panel can. And they can receive the same drag-and-drop operations that the main panels can. This means of course that you can drag any launcher or location into these drawers as well, further organizing the contents of your desktop. Even applets such as the Calendar or Trash can be placed within a drawer if you want to make the panel very minimalist.

Drawers are a great way to expose files or applications located inside the deeper layers of your file structure. You can also use a drawer to hold an entire set of URLs, giving you instant access to your favorite Web sites by clicking.

Adjust the Sound Volume

One of the frequently configured items on any system is the volume. You can adjust the master volume level of the computer and vary the relative volumes of each of the channels of input using the Volume Control applet.

The Volume Control applet has two modes of operation. With a single click, you can view and make a quick adjustment of the master volume of the sound card. The other mode of operation, accessed by a double-click, allows for modifying the volume of the input channels and recording channels. It also enables you to adjust the balance of the channels, mute, and access any special features supported by your sound card and its drivers.

The options on the Volume Control applet depend on the hardware on your machine. The most common options are Master, PCM (for pulse code modulation), Line-in, and CD. Channels that support stereo have a pair of chain links indicated below the sliders, which when clicked, will allow you to modify the left and right volumes for that channel independently.

You may also see Switches and Options tabs. The Switches tab contains special features such as audio expansion, microphone gain boost, and output adjustment for headphones. The Options tab sets which microphone input to capture audio from and other options.

Using the Volume Control Preferences dialog box, you can add any additional channels that your sound card and its drivers support.

Adjust the Sound Volume

ADJUST THE VOLUME

1. Double-click the Volume Control applet.

   The Volume Control applet launches.

2. Adjust the volume channel that you want to change.

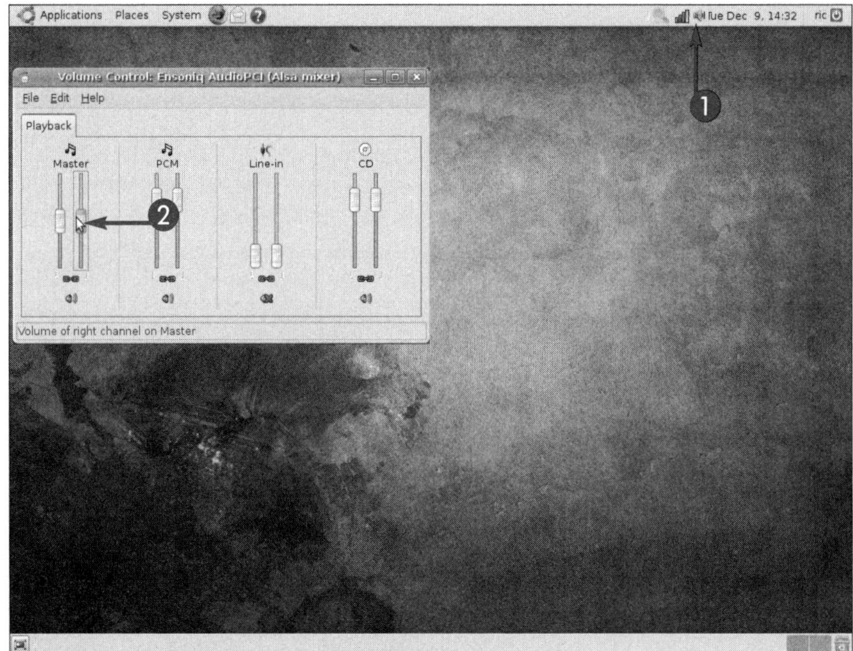

ADD A CHANNEL TO THE VOLUME CONTROL APPLET

3. Click Edit.
4. Click Preferences.

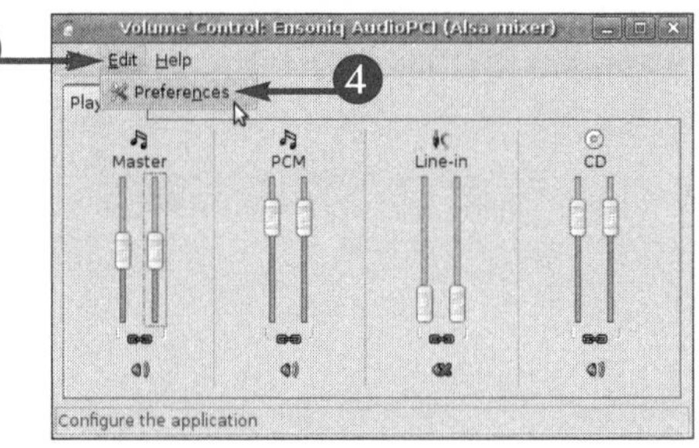

The Volume Control Preferences dialog box opens.

5. Click the check box of the channel that you want to add.

- The channel appears in the mixer application.

6. Click Close.

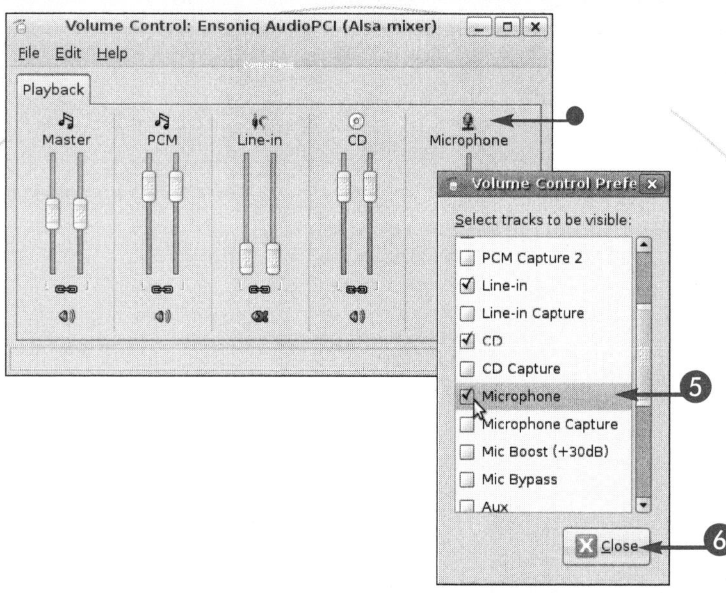

- You can now adjust the volume of the new device.
- You can click here to mute or unmute a channel.

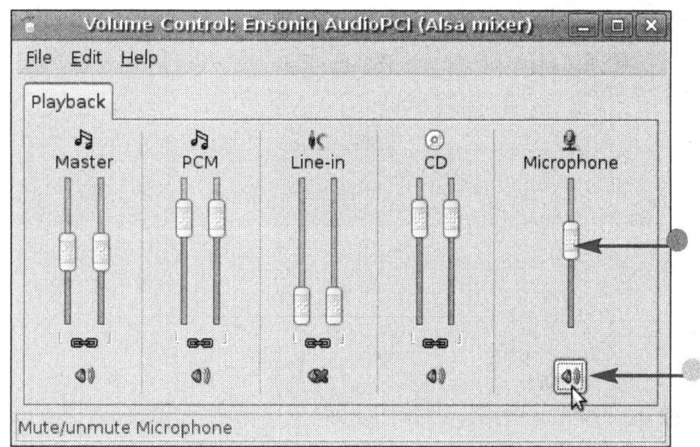

Extra

Ubuntu normally recognizes the multimedia keys on your keyboard. When you press your volume up or volume down buttons, you will see an onscreen display showing the current volume setting. This corresponds to the setting for your default mixer track, which is set under Sound Preferences. If your multimedia keys do not work, you can re-map them using the Keyboard Shortcuts application found under System Preferences. In the Keyboard Shortcuts dialog box, select the action that you want to re-map. Then, when the shortcut column entry says "New accelerator," press the new key that you want for the shortcut. The dialog box will notify you and prevent you from assigning a key twice.

The volume control contains sliders for all the channels provided by the sound card. One channel is the pulse code modulation or PCM channel. *Pulse code modulation* is a technique to convert durations of a simple on/off cycle into varying voltage levels for output by a speaker. Because computers are very good at turning on and off a switch, this has evolved to be the main way that sounds are synthesized. Therefore, this typically controls many of the normal sounds generated by your computer, that is, the beeps, bells, and warnings you hear while working.

Add or Remove Applications

Probably at some time during your first month of use of any operating system, you will realize that there is an application that you need that was not part of the initial installation. You can use the Add/Remove Applications program to quickly locate and install applications. Or if you want to remove an application that is already installed but you do not need or want, you can remove it just as quickly and easily.

When the Add/Remove Applications program launches, it first verifies if the list of available applications is up-to-date. It may ask you to reload the list if you have an Internet connection available. It then presents you with categories of applications, a search box to find a specific application by name, and an option box to limit the available applications to those supported by Canonical or third parties, or any package known to the Ubuntu system. This interface is similar to but much more friendly than the Synaptic Package Manager, and it allows for a more palatable selection of the applications and even a popularity indicator to show you how often others request the same program to be installed.

When you install new applications using the Add/Remove Applications program, the system takes care of the minute installation details, including all dependencies.

If you have installed an application that you do not want, or one came with the distribution that you do not need and want to remove, you can simply uncheck the box next to the application in the Add/Remove Applications program and then apply the change. The program will verify that you want to delete the program and then remove it properly from your system.

Add or Remove Applications

1. Click Applications.
2. Click Add/Remove.

   The program launches.

Note: *The Add/Remove Applications program may ask you to reload your list of available software if it is not up-to-date. Reload if needed and provide your password if needed.*

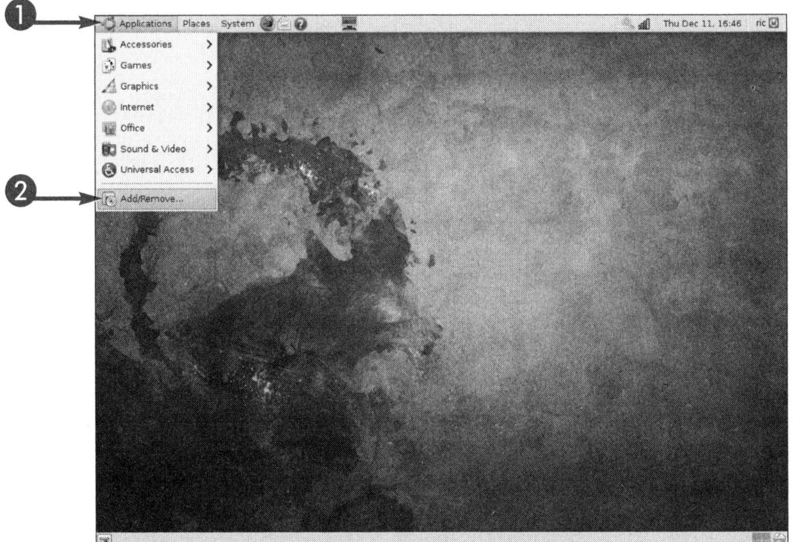

3. Click the category of application that you want to search for.
4. Click the check box next to the application that you want to install.

Note: *To remove an installed application, uncheck its box.*

5. Click Apply Changes.

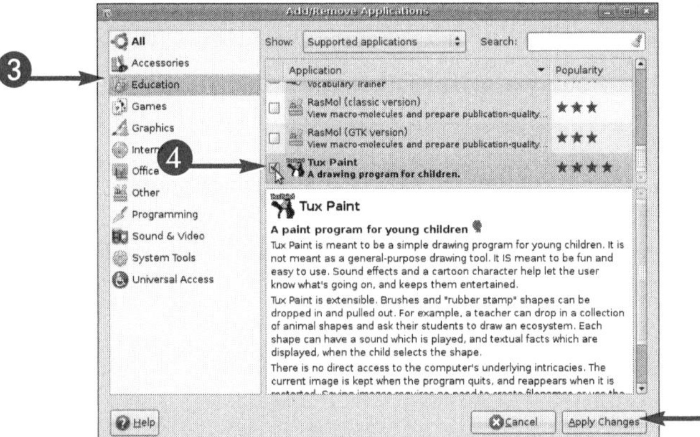

A dialog box appears, asking you if you want to go ahead with your installations and removals.

6 Click Apply.

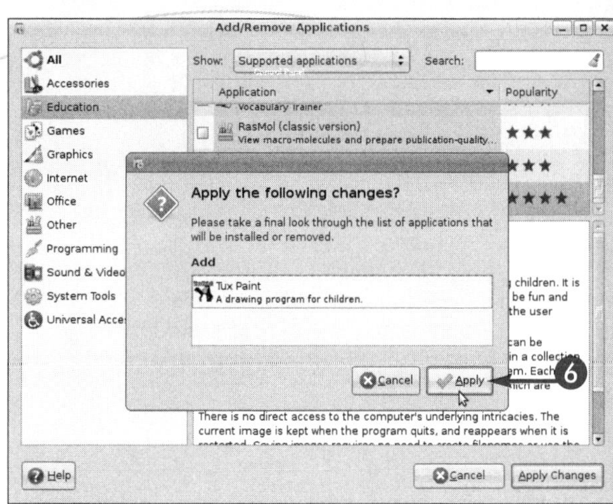

The application is downloaded and installed.

7 Click Close.

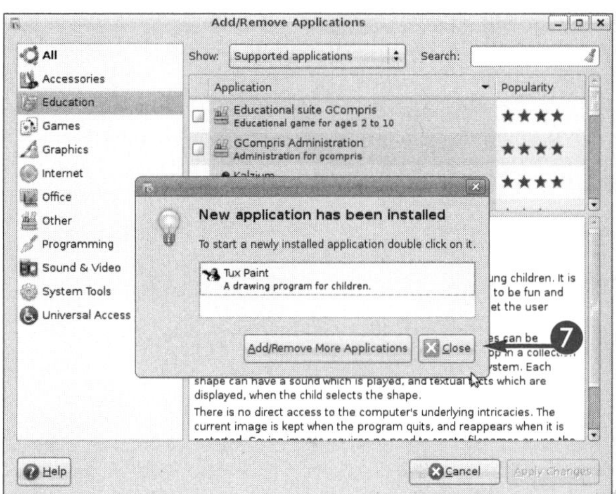

Extra

The Add/Remove Applications dialog box is a good place to browse through the catalog of applications available to you via the Ubuntu repositories. If you have heard that there are not enough applications for Linux to be a viable desktop operating system, a quick survey of the applications in this program will show you otherwise. Take a quick tour and see if there are any applications that suit your particular computing needs. There are of course many entertainment packages available for Ubuntu. Games range from 2D run and jump games such as SuperTux to 3D downhill skiing/belly flopping with Extreme TuxRacer. Many office productivity applications also exist as well — including three different office suites. There are also some industrial-strength tools such as full-blown databases, genomic analysis, and project-management tools for power users.

Installation of these applications is easy and quick if you have a fast connection. Keep in mind that although many applications will be available on the Ubuntu CD, not all applications will be available if you are not connected to the Internet.

Do not be afraid to install an application and take it for a test drive. After all, this is free software, so if you do not like it, you can just uninstall it.

Keep Your System Up-to-Date

No software is perfect. This altruism is what hackers prey upon. To keep them at bay, you must keep your system patched. In the world of the always-connected Internet, this has become a paramount necessity. Fortunately, for the same reason, it becomes relatively painless. You can keep your system up-to-date with the Update Manager and the Update Manager applet. The Update Manager applet keeps you notified when new versions of the software you have installed become available. By simply activating the applet from your main panel, you can see what is new and install the updates effortlessly. Most software updates do not even require a reboot or for you to log out of your session to take effect.

The applet's default behavior is to show you all pending updates based on your settings. This then gives you the opportunity to approve or deny the installation of these updates. The applet also enables you to check for, show, and install updates on-demand. On the right-click menu, you can launch the Synaptic Package Manager and access the Preferences dialog box. With Synaptic, you can install additional software. With the Preferences dialog box, you can change settings such as the frequency of checks for new software, the default action to perform when the applet finds new software, and the types of updates you plan to subscribe to. For example, you can set security-related changes to be installed automatically or specify that all updates should be automatically downloaded in the background for installation after you verify them. The various types of updates are those that are security related, and thus highly recommended, regular feature or bug-fix-related updates, any pre-release updates, and finally back-ported changes from a later release.

Keep Your System Up-to-Date

1. Click the Update Manager applet.

   The Update Manager appears.

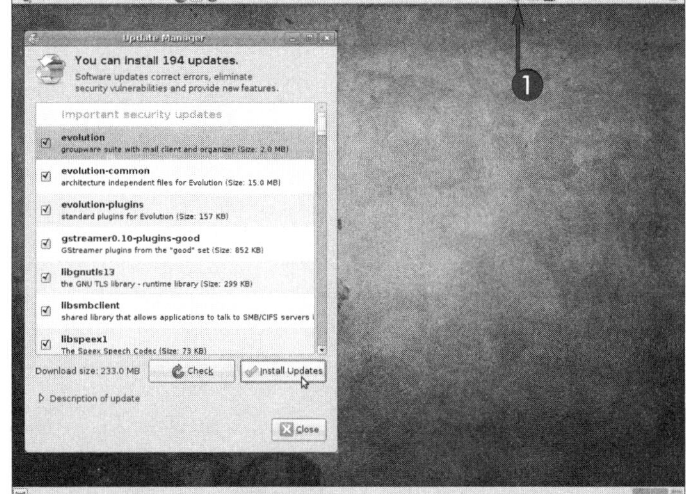

You are prompted to enter your password.

2. Type your password.
3. Click OK.

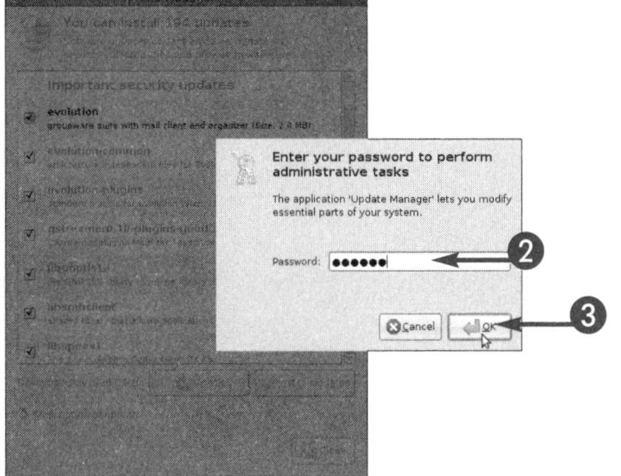

- The system downloads the updates.

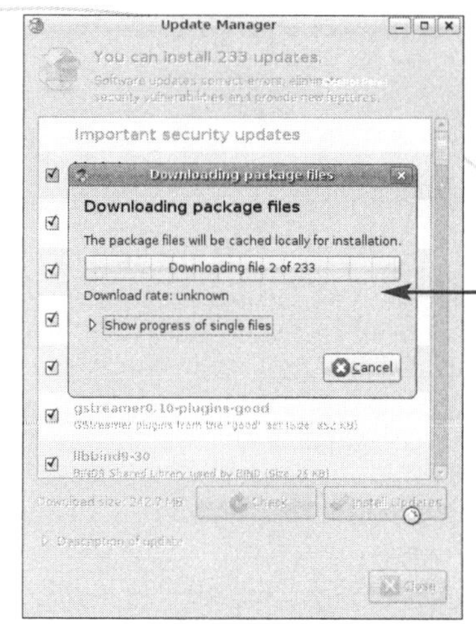

- The system then installs the updates.

4. Click Close.

   Your system is now up-to-date.

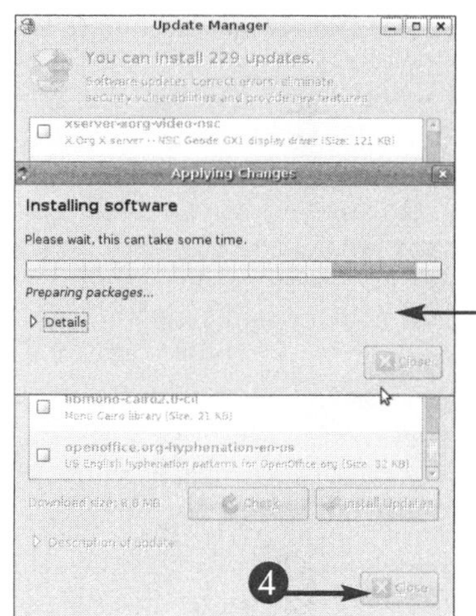

Extra

For additional information on any particular change, check the Description of Update area of the Update Manager dialog box. The first tab shows why the change was included for update by Canonical, with a link to more details in some cases. The second tab shows the general description of the software involved.

There is also a toggle to show notifications on the right-click menu of the Update Manager applet. This enables you to turn off the balloon notifications that sometimes get in the way while you are trying to work.

At the bottom of the Update Preferences dialog box, there is a Release Upgrade option, which enables you to select if you want to see upgrade options for the entire operating system and whether you want only the long-term support (LTS) editions or regular releases of the operating system.

Regular releases are on six-month increments to allow for the ever-changing landscape of new features available in open-source software. These releases are supported for 18 months and are meant for those who are willing to update more frequently and are not bothered by the shorter duration of support.

Understanding the Linux File System Structure

The Linux file system owes its structure almost entirely to earlier UNIX operating systems. These systems all operated under the philosophy that everything was a file. Files and programs were of course files, but the metaphor did not stop there; in fact, all manner of input/output (I/O) was considered a file. Consequently, Linux can use file system semantics for devices such as terminals, modems, sound cards, and video cards. Even interprocess communication, FIFO (first-in-first-out) queues, and parameters of the running kernel can be accessed using these same, well-defined operations. With everything being a file, there needed to be a structure for the organization of all the items, given their elevated significance to the underlying operating system.

All entries in the Linux file system follow a hierarchy. This hierarchy consists of a list of files and directories that constitute a tree structure. The *root,* or most parent directory of the file system, binds all the subdirectories and files together so that there is a navigable path from any point on the file system to any other point. Navigating from this root, you can locate almost any file or device.

Additional storage volumes are not designated as an alternative root directory or drive letter; rather, they are "grafted" onto the tree that exists within the Linux file system. The way that this is accomplished is by mounting these additional volumes on top of empty directories in the root file system. These empty directories are known as *mount points.* Once mounted, the contents of the new volume appear as a set of files and directories within that mount point directory.

The basic organization of the file system breaks down along the lines of that which can be shared among systems versus that which cannot, and that which changes frequently versus that which does not. The rationale for the first criteria is that items that can be shared should live in the same physical storage, and that storage may not be local. For example, the directories containing the user's files may be shared across multiple machines within a network by keeping them on a remote file server. System-specific configuration files, however, should not be shared, and consequently are usually stored locally to the machine. Because the two are kept separate, the number of mount points that are necessary to maintain is reduced. The rationale for the second criteria is that items that do not change frequently will not need to have the same backup requirements as those items that are changed more frequently or are even completely dynamic. For example, the kernel and bootstrap files change much less frequently than the items on a user's desktop.

The Root Directory

/bin

The /bin directory contains the most essential programs for system operation. It contains the programs for attaching additional file systems, inspecting and changing the organization of the file system structure, viewing the contents of files, and managing running processes.

/boot

The /boot directory contains the kernel and associated files needed by the boot loader to allow the system to boot.

/cdrom

/cdrom is not a real directory but a link to the /media/cdrom mount point.

/dev

The /dev directory contains all the device file entries. These are used to communicate with the system's hardware.

/etc

The /etc directory contains system-specific configuration files. These files direct the operation of the system during bootup, specify the default configuration of user applications, and specify the settings for any services.

The Root Directory *(continued)*

/home

The /home directory contains all the home directories for the users of the system. For each user of the system, there is a corresponding subdirectory named the same as that user's login.

/lib

The /lib directory contains the core libraries for the system. The modules for the kernel are also included in this directory.

/media

The /media directory is the root for mount points of removable media.

/opt

The /opt directory is for optional applications not included in the distribution of the operating system.

/proc

The /proc directory contains entries that represent settings in the kernel, devices recognized by the kernel and drivers, and running processes.

/root

/root is the home directory for the superuser. This user is commonly referred to in UNIX parlance as *root.* This user's home directory is not on the /home volume because during system maintenance, the home directories may not be mounted.

/sbin

The /sbin directory contains binaries that are critical for system maintenance and booting. This is essentially an extension of /bin, but with more of a slant toward system administration.

/tmp

The /tmp directory is used for temporary files. Although this may sound like a trivial role, on a system that considers everything a file, it is anything but trivial. In Linux, tremendous amounts of temporary files are created, so you need to allocate enough space for it as well as speed in the form of a fast access volume.

Types of Special Files

Symbolic Links

Symbolic links are indirections in the file system. When a program goes to open a symbolic link, it will be redirected by the operating system to the file or directory that the link refers to instead. When a symbolic link is applied to a directory, the navigation into the given directory still shows the traversed path instead of the physical path.

Hard Links

Hard links are essentially a cross-linking in the file system. The same file or directory is made to exist in two places in the file system directory structure. You can only do this within one physical volume as both entries refer to the same underlying allocation of the disk.

FIFO

Named for the first-in-first-out queue it represents, FIFO is a special type of file that stores information written into it and allows later reading in the same order that the information was received. Unlike a normal file, FIFO will not return the end of file or EOF marker until one is written into it. Thus, any reading program will sit and wait for more data or until the EOF marker is written into the file. Sometimes these files are also referred to as *named pipes.*

Block and Character Special Files

Block and character files are used by the operating system to associate drivers and other kernel-level entities with the file system so that programs can open, read, and write to them using the semantics for files.

Sockets

Sockets are used for interprocess communication. They do not actually use the file system to buffer the information but transfer the data via a buffer in the kernel. The file system is merely used as an addressing scheme so that multiple processes can locate and open the connection. The semantics for their use are different than files due to this difference in implementation, and they bear more of a resemblance to their network counterpart, Internet sockets.

Configure Nautilus File Browser Preferences

You can customize the way that the Nautilus File Browser shows you the files within the file system to your tastes. The browser allows for multiple configuration options. These options are all accessed via the File Management Preferences dialog box. Each tab in the dialog box corresponds to a category of preferences that you can choose from.

The Views tab enables you to change the type of view to either a grid of icons or a simple list with columns for different attributes of the files listed. You can also change the defaults for the size and layout of the icons in the Icon view or the size of the items in the List view.

The Behavior tab enables you to configure how the File Browser handles requests for actions. You can set the File Browser to open files with a single or double-click. This allows you to make navigating in the File Browser more like a Web browser versus the more traditional double-click metaphor with desktop systems. Also, you can configure whether to open files in a new window, known in GNOME as *spatial mode.* The default mode, Browser mode, is to keep the same window open and update its contents as you browse through the file system.

The Display tab allows you to change the details displayed next to icons. The attributes allowed are the same for icons as they are for the columns in the List view, so no detail is lost if you are using the Icon view. The detail displayed does vary depending on your zoom level within the File Browser. The format of the date can also be specified to your tastes. Formats range from very formal to relative terms like "yesterday at 11:00 AM."

Configure Nautilus File Browser Preferences

1. Click Places.
2. Click a location to open a folder.

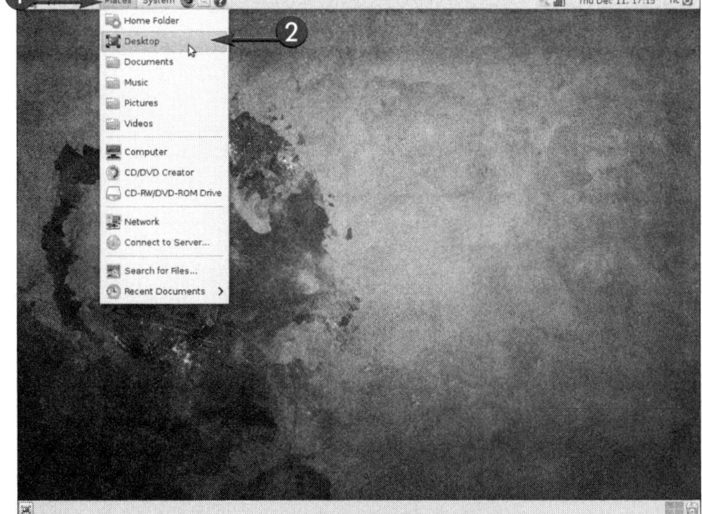

The File Browser window opens.

3. Click Edit.
4. Click Preferences.

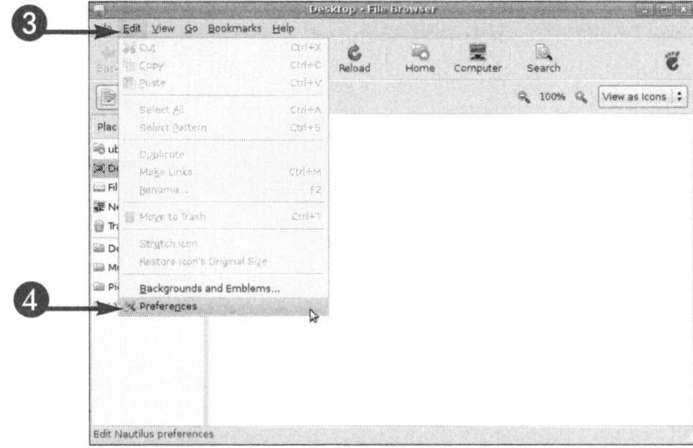

The File Management Preferences dialog box opens.

5. Click View New Folders Using and click the default view that you want.
6. Click here and select the default zoom level.
7. Click Behavior.

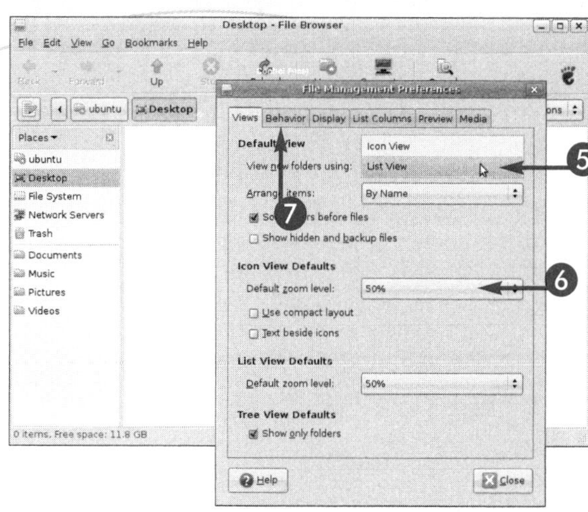

The Behavior tab is displayed.

8. Click how you want executable text files to be handled.
9. Click the options that you want for the Trash.
10. Click the Display tab.

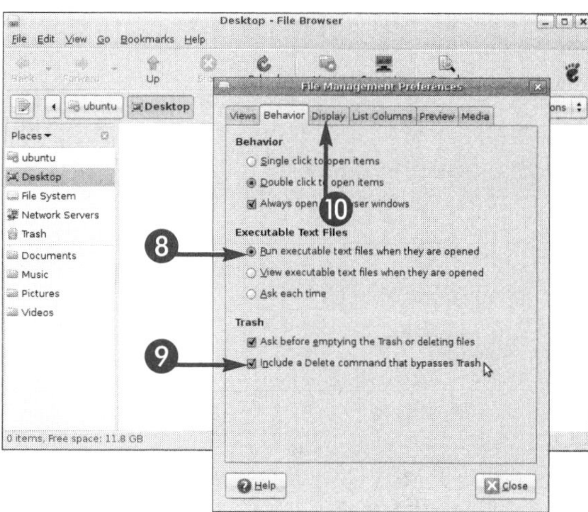

Apply It

For the minimalist, the following settings will give you a quick, light file-browsing experience. First put the View New Folders Using setting to List View. List view allows more files to be shown in a more compact way and to be located more quickly. Then set the List View Defaults setting to 50% or less. The smaller you can get the information to be listed and yet still be readable, the quicker you can find the file you are looking for. Then, on the Preview tab, turn off all previewing by setting all the selections to Never. This keeps the browser from wasting time reading in parts or complete files to make decisions on which preview applications to use and then generating the previews themselves. On large directories with hundreds or thousands of files, this can make a huge difference in the time to render the files within the File Browser. On the Media tab, you can set all the options to Ask First. This prevents the browser from having to do detection of the content and launch applications for media when that action may not be required immediately upon detection of the files.

continued

Configure Nautilus File Browser Preferences (continued)

The List Columns tab enables you to change the attributes to be displayed in columns next to the files in List mode. The list of attributes are those of the file system itself, such as last modified date, last access date, and the ever-present name, size, and type variety of information. But it also includes MIME type, which can be useful to sort files on, especially because Linux-based systems do not use the file suffix to determine the type of a file.

The Preview tab enables you to change the way the icons for document or image files are shown. For instance, you can even show the first lines of text from a text file in the icon for text files. The default performance behavior is to only preview files on a local file system. This keeps the File Browser from trying to retrieve large amounts of information from a remote server just for previewing purposes. Also, there is a file size limit on previewable files to keep the File Browser from having performance issues when large files are encountered.

The Media tab allows for configuration of the default application to be launched when new devices, or media, are connected to the system. It handles this by the type of media or content added. There is a default set of actions that come with Ubuntu, which work pretty well for most types of media. Options for changing them are to simply do nothing when the new media is detected, to open the folder where the new media can be found on the file system, or to ask the user what to do.

Configure Nautilus File Browser Preferences *(continued)*

The Display tab appears.

11. Click Format and select the date format that you prefer.
12. Click List Columns.

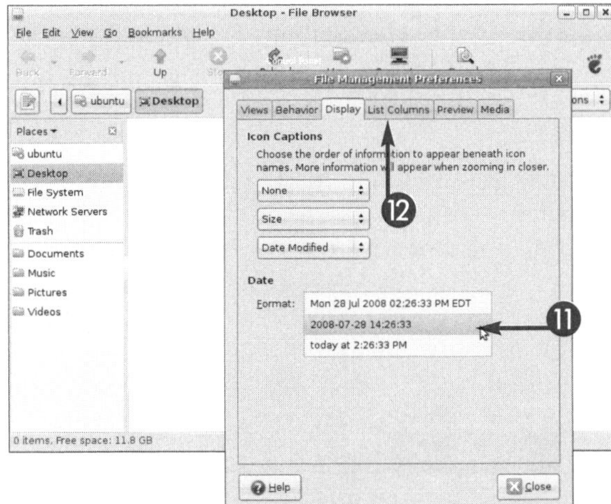

The List Columns tab is displayed.

13. Click the information that you want shown for the List view.
14. Click Preview.

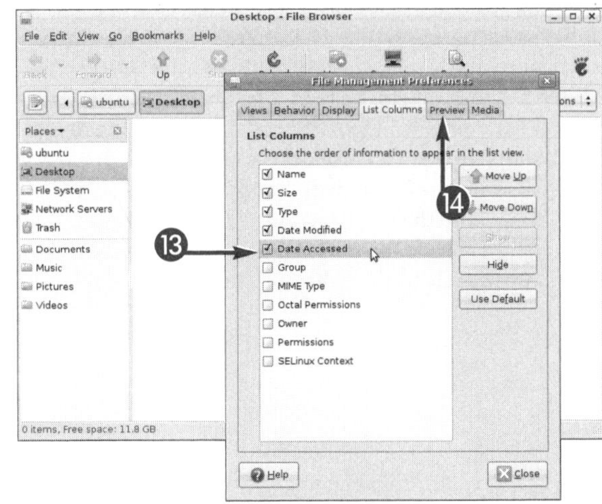

The Preview tab is displayed.

15 Click Only for Files Smaller Than and choose the maximum size of files to be previewed.

Note: *It is a good idea to go with a small file size here.*

16 Click the Media tab.

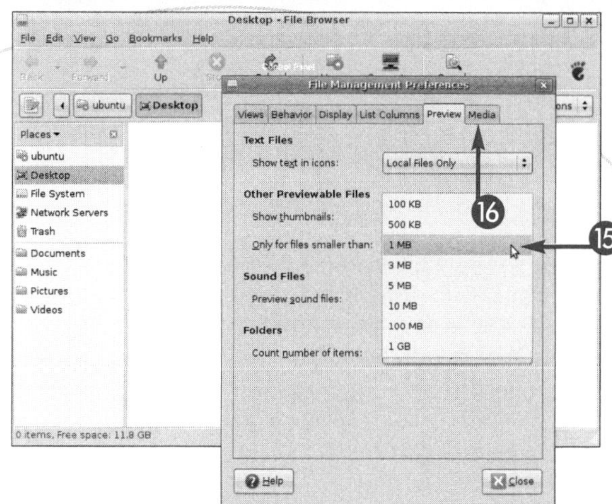

The Media tab is displayed.

17 Click Never Prompt or Start Programs on Media Insertion.

Note: *This is the recommended way to handle media. You can, of course, make other choices on this tab.*

The entire tab grays out with the exception of the check boxes.

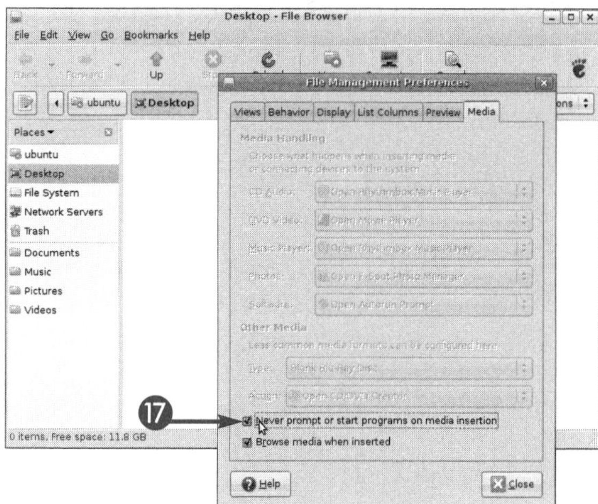

Extra

There are several other Web browser-like features of the File Browser that will help you as you make your way through the file system. The Back and Forward buttons should look familiar from the Web browser metaphor. The Up button is definitely a file browser–only addition. This button takes you to the parent of the current folder within the hierarchy of the file system. The next button is again familiar from the Web browser and is quite new to the file browser paradigm — the Stop button. If there is a particular operation within the File Browser that is taking an inordinate amount of time, you may cancel the operation by clicking Stop. The Reload button refreshes the window, showing any new details or details that have changed since the last time the window was drawn. This is not always necessary as the File Browser periodically checks for changes and reflects them on its own. Then there is the quick link to the user's Home directory and a quick link to the Computer folder, which shows a view of not only the root file system but the other available storage volumes that have yet to be mounted.

Create, Rename, and Manage Folders

Files have a tendency to proliferate on a system during use. This being the case, you will want to organize these files in some fashion. You can organize your files into groupings using directories within the file system. These directories are referred to as *folders* within the GNOME environment.

For example, the GNOME system allows for assignment of graphical icons to the folders. There are a standard set of decorative emblems that can be added to the default image for a folder.

You can also attach notes to folders or any file type item. This enables you to annotate the file with any comments you may want to keep about the contents.

You can open a folder's Properties dialog box to adjust the file permissions for it, allowing for read, write, and execute priveleges to be assigned. You can also change the group that the folder belongs to.

If you want to allow others to read or write to your folder from the network, you can share the folder.

From a folder's context menu, you can create an archive in various formats. The archive can be compressed or not depending on the format chosen. The ar and tar formats are simple uncompressed archives. The .zip format is the famous Phil Katz compressed archive format. This format is quite possibly the most popular archive format in history. Then there are jar, ear, and war formats, which are derivatives based on the pkzip format, and compressed variants of the tar format. The .tar.bz2 is simply a bz2 compressed tar file. The .tar.lhma is the Lempel-Ziv compression algorithm applied to the tar archive. The .tar.gz, sometimes named .tgz, is the gzip format applied to the tar archive.

Create, Rename, and Manage Folders

1. Right-click the desktop.
2. Click Create Folder.

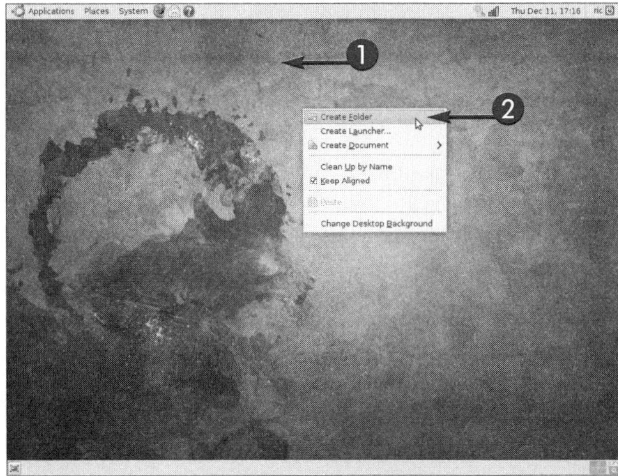

A new folder appears.

3. Type a new name.

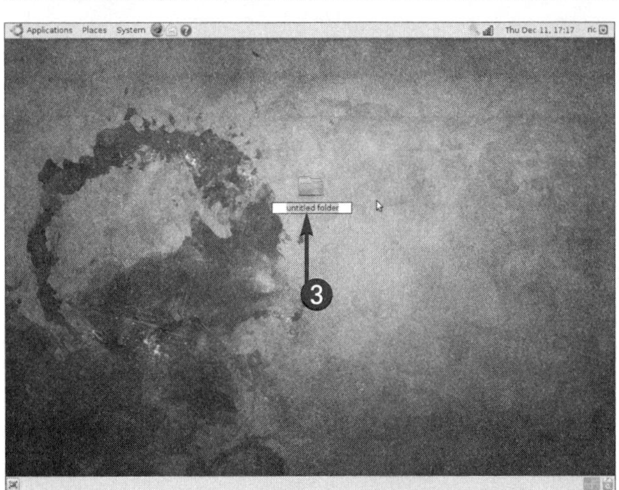

4 Right-click the folder.

5 Click Properties.

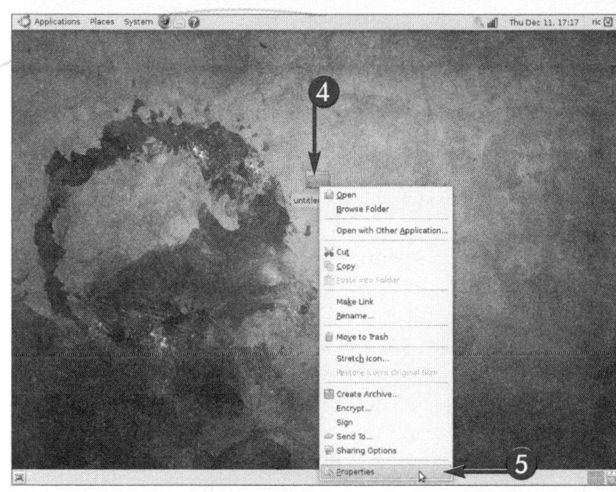

The folder's Properties dialog box appears.

6 Click the Emblems tab.

7 Click the check box for an emblem.

- An emblem appears on the folder icon.

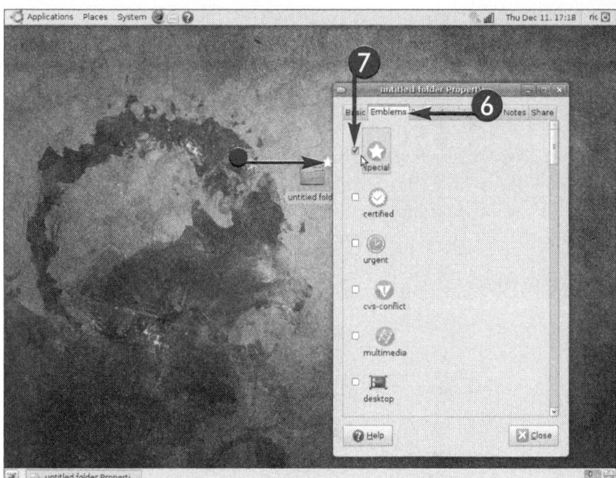

Extra

In order to quickly rename a file or folder, you can select it with the mouse and then press F2. This will show the title of the folder highlighted, and therefore editable. At this point, you can just type over the existing name.

To quickly delete the folder, select it with the mouse and then press Delete. This will take the file and place it into the Trash folder.

To create a custom icon for your folder, you can go to the folder's Properties dialog box and click the icon of the folder on the Basic tab. Then you are presented with a dialog box to select a new image file. Once selected, the image will become the icon for the folder.

If you find yourself traversing too many directories, you can also create a link in the file system. Simply right-click the folder you go to frequently and then select Make Link. This will create a symbolic link in the file system, allowing the one folder to show up two different places in the file system.

Browse to and Open Files and Folders

One of the first things that you will need to do with the file system is to be able to navigate within it. In order to do so, you will need to use the Nautilus File Browser. The File Browser offers a rich interface with many features. One feature of note is the side pane, which defaults to displaying quick navigational aides to commonly used directories as well as any bookmarks you make. Another feature is the Address bar, which defaults to displaying buttons for each level of the directory hierarchy that you have traversed. In addition to the familiar Web-browser Forward, Back, Stop, and Reload buttons, there is also the Up button, which can be used to navigate toward the root of the file system. There is also a Search button on the main toolbar that enables you to search the filenames of the directories below your current location.

Double-clicking any folder opens it and presents the view of the file system from that folder's location on the file system hierarchy. Double-clicking while holding down the Shift key opens the folder in a new window.

Double-clicking a file opens up the file using the default application for that file type. If there is no default application assigned to that file type, you will receive an error. If you know of an application that can open the file, right-click the file and then click Open with Other Application. This launches a dialog box that enables you to choose or specify the application to open the file.

Browse to and Open Files and Folders

1. Click Places.
2. Click Home Folder.

The File Browser opens.

3. Double-click the folder that contains the file that you want to open.

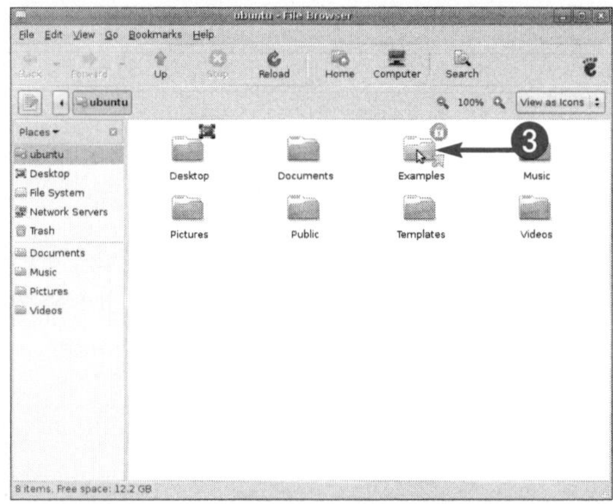

The folder opens, showing the files within it.

4 Double-click the file.

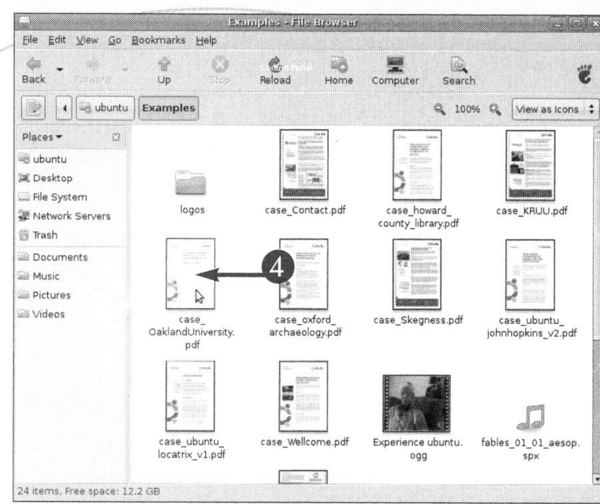

The application associated with the file launches and shows the contents of the file.

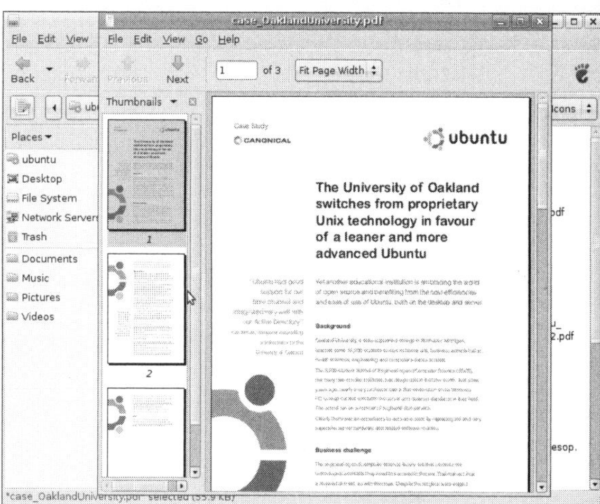

Extra

Clicking , just below the Back button, enables you to type in the directory path that you want to view. This feature also includes automatic directory name completion, in which the operating system attempts to finish the names of directories as you type. When it does this, you can press Tab to accept the directory name.

You can magnify or shrink icons within the File Browser by clicking or , respectively. Additionally, pressing Ctrl and rolling the mouse wheel adjusts the zoom.

You can stretch the size of any icon by clicking Edit ➔ Stretch Icon and then dragging one of the corners of the handle squares that appear around the icon.

You can mount other file servers or FTP sites by clicking File ➔ Connect to Server. You will then be prompted for your authentication information and the connection details. After all of these are populated, clicking Connect will bring up a dialog box prompting for your password for the remote file server. After entering that, you will be presented with a window showing files from the remote file server.

Find Files with the Nautilus File Browser

You will need to search for files. This is the inevitability of the information age. Fortunately, Ubuntu makes that easy. There are no less than three different subsystems for finding files on your system. The one covered in this section is the search built into the Nautilus File Browser. With this integrated tool, you can find files on your computer. While fairly elementary, this search feature is useful because it is deployed in the most common place you would need to search for or filter files. Additionally, searching can filter files down to only the ones on which you want to operate. This is particularly convenient if you are using the click-and-drag metaphor for moving files or copying files to another location.

When you click the Search button, the Location area of the file browser will change to a Search prompt. When you fill in this Search prompt with part of the filename that you want to search for or a common prefix or suffix that you want to filter on, you will receive a listing of just the files that match within that current working directory and subdirectories of that directory. The current working directory is determined by the directory you were browsing before you clicked Search. After the results are displayed, you can reload them or add additional filter criteria by using the options in the highlighted section of the results window. Filter options are available for filetering by content type or by location. Any number of filters can be applied, and they are additive, so the results of the first filter are then subsquently filtered by the next filter, and so on.

Find Files with the Nautilus File Browser

1. Click Places.
2. Click Home Folder.

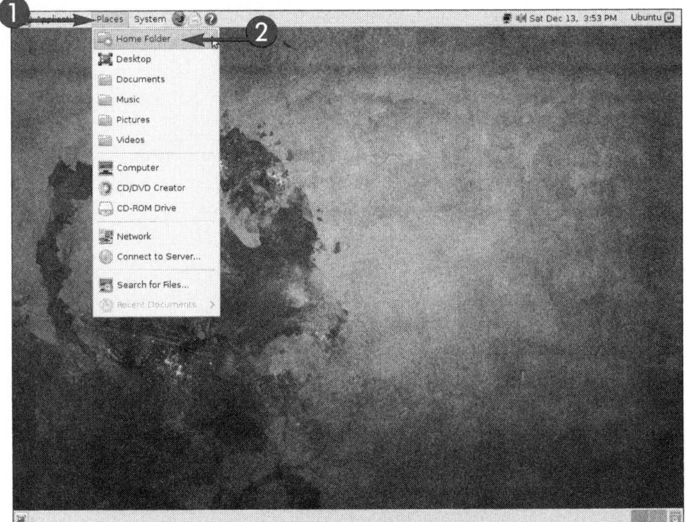

The File Browser opens.

3. Click Search.

- The Location bar becomes the Search bar.

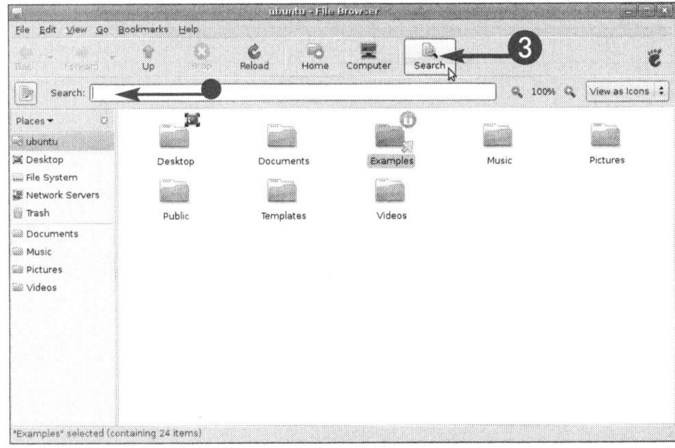

4 Type in part of the text of the filename that you want.

The files matching that partial filename are displayed in the File Browser.

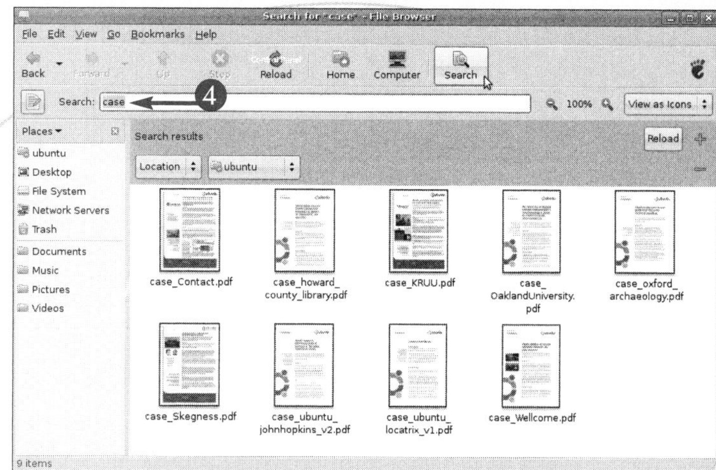

5 Refine the search by adding additional partial filename information.

The remaining matching files are displayed.

6 Double-click to open the file that you want.

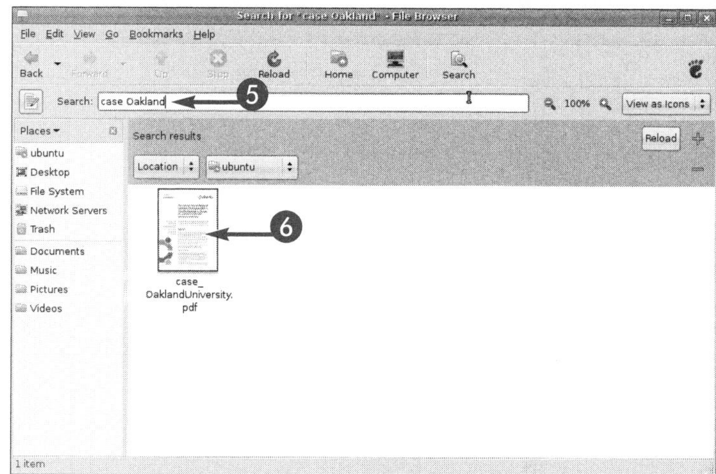

Extra

Sorting can be another fine way to find files in the browser window. By using the List view for the File Browser window, you can sort on any of the displayed columns. This allows you to see files by not only their last modified date or last accessed date, but by any of the other attributes shown by the File Browser. One particularly useful option is the MIME type. Because Ubuntu does not rely on the file extension to determine the type of the file, this is important since it will allow you to see this non-obvious, but very relevant, aspect of the file.

Also, under the Edit menu is an option to select files by pattern. This is a fairly powerful way to select specific files. Although this is not a recursive search, it can save a lot of time selecting a set of files versus holding down the Ctrl key while selecting them one by one.

The patterns accepted by the Select by Pattern option are not full regular expressions but do accept the generally accepted wildcard symbol * for matching any number of characters and ? for matching a single character.

Delete Files and Folders

Although disk space has been considered cheap in the recent decade, there is never enough to go around. You will come to a point where for either storage or organizational reasons, you want to get rid of files. This is a relatively simple task within the File Browser. Because the task is so frequent, there are several ways to achieve it. The first is the Delete key. Always be sure to have the file or folder you want to delete actually highlighted before pressing this key. Fortunately, there is still a last line of defense to protect you if you have not verified this. That defense is the Trash applet.

The Trash applet sits in the tray region of the panel and allows you to fetch back files prior to their final dispatch into oblivion. Because the Trash will continue to accumulate files until such a time that you "empty" it, checking it periodically is a very good idea. You can empty the Trash folder directly from the Trash applet or from the Trash folder in the File Browser window. When you empty the Trash, the system will give you a final warning before disposing of the files. The Trash is the first place to look if you discover that you are nearly out of disk space. Retrieving files from the Trash applet is fairly straightforward, needing only opening the Trash folder and then dragging or copying/pasting your file back to where you want it to be.

Another way to delete files is to use the context menu presented on a file or folder. The most graphical of the methods of deletion is to drag a file to the Trash applet.

Delete Files and Folders

DELETE A FILE OR FOLDER

1. Click Places.
2. Click Home Folder.

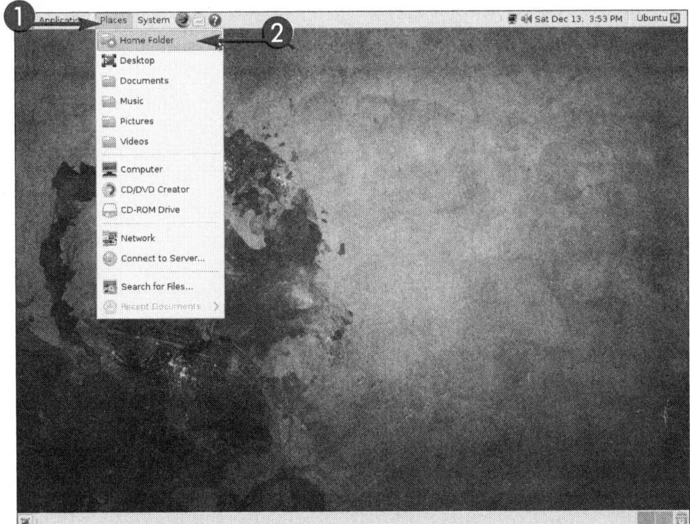

The File Browser opens.

3. Right-click the folder that you want to delete.

Note: *If you want to delete just a file, open the folder containing it and right-click the file.*

4. Click Move to Trash.

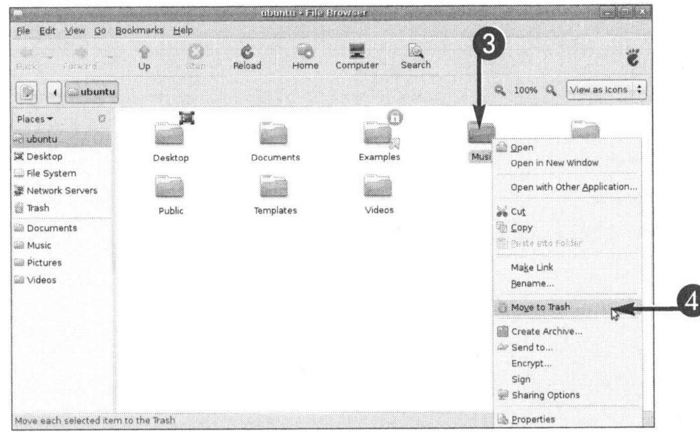

5 Click Trash.

- The deleted folder is now in the Trash folder.

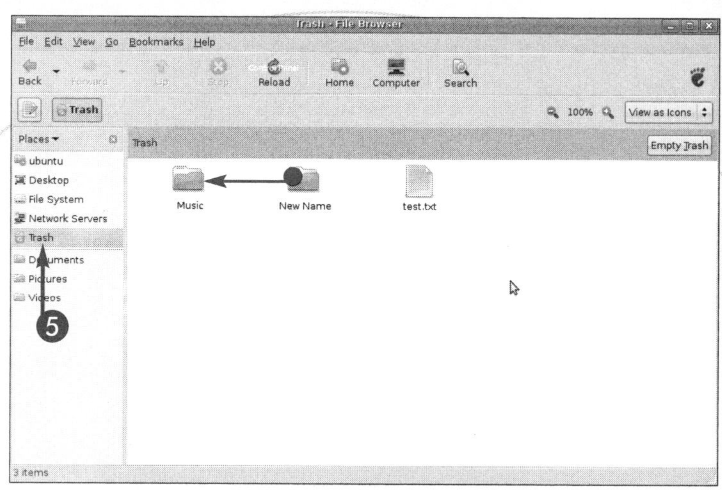

RETRIEVE A FILE OR FOLDER FROM THE TRASH

6 Drag the folder back to its original location.

The folder is restored.

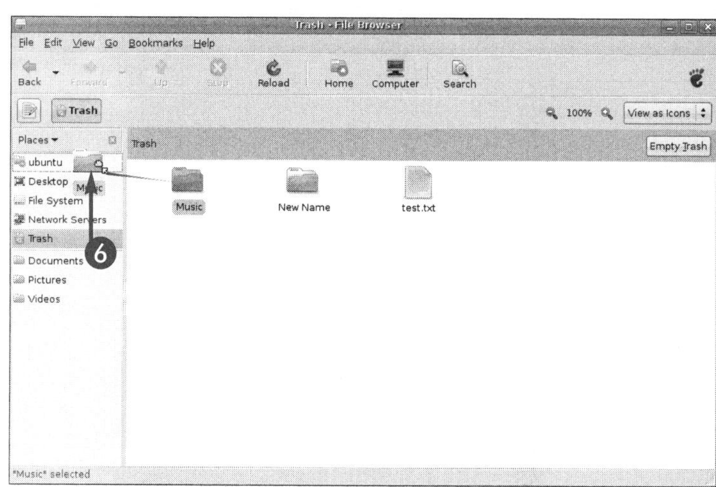

Extra

After files have been deleted, they are fairly irretrievable. This is due to the default file system of ext3 that is used on Ubuntu. Ext3 is an extension of the ext2 file system that supports the journaling of changes so that the file system can be recovered to a consistent state after a system crash. Part of this extension, however, actually destroys some of the data that would need to be used to recover files after deletion. If you need to retrieve files back from an ext3 file system after deletion, you will want to look at the Foremost tool (http://foremost.sourceforge.net/), which can locate files on a hard drive via a technique called *data carving*. Data carving is a process of reading the data from a disk, in a relatively raw form, until the header of a file is found. Then the length of the file is deduced and the contents copied off to a safe location.

Of course, the safest way to make sure that you do not lose your files to an inadvertent file deletion is to back your files up regularly.

Copy and Move Files and Folders

After you have downloaded files, saved attachments, and authored documents, you can move or copy them about at your leisure to organize them in a way that makes sense to you. As with deleting files, there are several ways to do these two common operations. The reason for the multiple ways to perform them is that they are so common that their quick, easy access is essential for productivity. The two common metaphors used by the File Browser for copying and moving files are the visual metaphor and the cut-and-paste metaphor.

In order to copy a file or folder from one location to another using the visual metaphor, you can drag the file from one File Browser window to another while keeping the Ctrl key pressed down. This also works when dragging the file between a File Browser window and the desktop.

The moving of a file or folder using a visual metaphor is even simpler. Just drag the file from the File Browser window — with no additional keys pressed — and then drop the file onto either the desktop or another File Browser window.

Using the copy-and-paste metaphor, you copy a file by simply using the Copy command in one File Browser window and the Paste command in the other File Browser window.

Using the cut-and-paste metaphor, you can move a file by simply using the Cut command in one File Browser window and the Paste command in the other File Browser window.

Copy and Move Files and Folders

MOVE A FILE OR FOLDER

1. Click Places.
2. Click Home Folder.

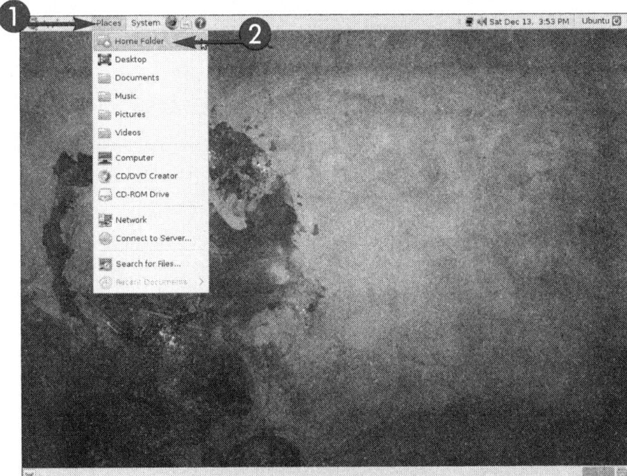

The File Browser opens.

3. Drag the file or folder to the desktop or another File Browser window.

The file or folder appears in its new location.

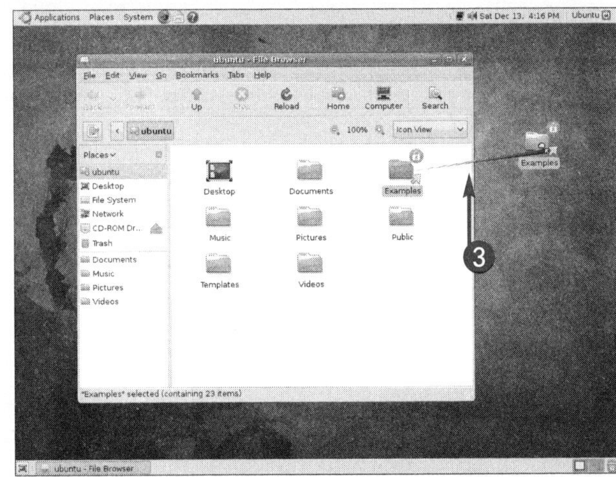

COPY A FILE OR FOLDER

4. Right-click the file or folder.
5. Click Copy.

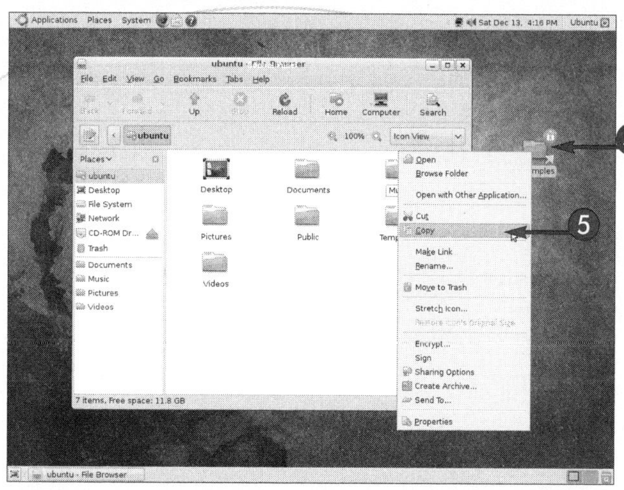

6. Right-click in the File Browser window showing the location where you want a copy.
7. Click Paste.

   The file or folder is copied to the new location.

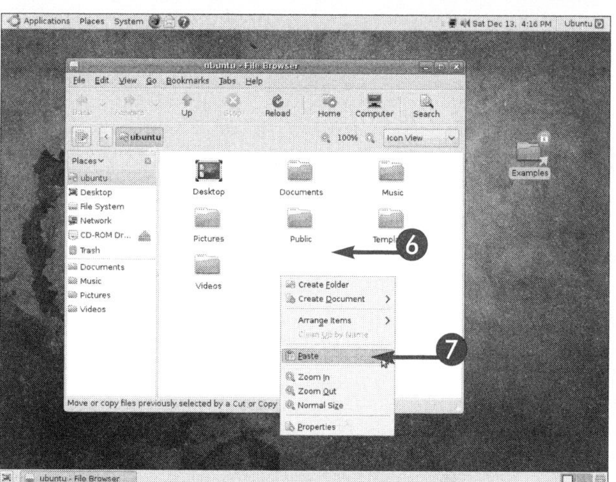

Extra

When you copy files, it does not matter whether you are copying from one disk to another disk, as a new allocation of space will be made either way. This is not the case with moving files. When you move a file or directory, if you are not moving from one physical disk to another, the allocation of the disk space remains the same, but the entries in the parent directories involved change. Essentially, the disk allocation of the file or folders being moved is transferred to the new directory. This holds true until the allocation crosses the boundary to a different disk. The allocation cannot simply be transferred because the allocation does not apply on the new disk. In this case, the files are copied to the new, target disk, and then the files on the original disk are deleted. When they are deleted from the original, they are not copied to the Trash, so they cannot be retrieved. This makes it very important to not stop move operations when they are taking place between disks. Although it is unlikely that you will lose files, you can easily end up with a split between the directories. This appears as if half the files are on one disk and half on the other. While this is not particularly dangerous, it can be tedious to clean up.

Access Recent Files

With all the spreadsheets, text documents, compressed archives, portable document files (PDFs), drawings, databases, and images floating around on your system, it is not unthinkable that you may forget the name of a file that you have recently opened or exactly where you opened it from. That is when you will want to use the Recent Documents list under the Places menu. This list shows what files you have recently accessed. This list is populated as you open different types of files on Ubuntu. The interesting thing about this list is that the applications themselves can draw from it to populate the list of recent files within their own menus. This is a very different approach than what is done with many other operating systems. The main advantage of this is that, theoretically, if you clear the list of recently opened documents from the centralized list, you clear it from all the applications that are derived from that list. This would be a boon for the security of this type of information. This feature is obviously very useful, but it does have a downside as well. Anyone who gains casual access to your computer for even a few moments while you are not looking, or even over your shoulder while you are talking with them, can see the filenames of your most recent work. Even if they cannot log into your machine, if they have physical access to it, there are techniques that, if directed to seek out a specific file, can retrieve the file quite readily. So, like many features for rapid access to information, there is a cost. Although the GNOME team has tried to balance this risk by allowing for a centralized clearing of this type of information, keeping the information around for any length at all introduces the possibility of revealing sensitive information.

Access Recent Files

ACCESS A RECENTLY USED FILE

1. Click Places.
2. Click Recent Documents.
3. Click the name of the recently used file that you want to open.

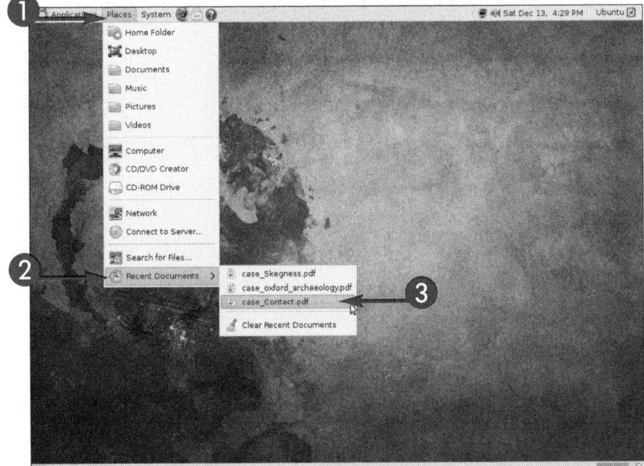

The file opens in its associated program.

CHECK THE RECENTLY USED FILES IN AN APPLICATION

4. Click File.
5. Review the list of recent files in the application.

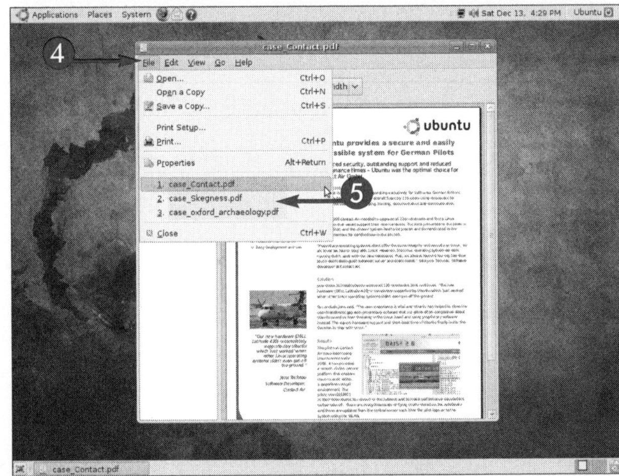

CLEAR THE RECENT DOCUMENTS LIST

1. Click Places.
2. Click Recent Documents.
3. Click Clear Recent Documents.

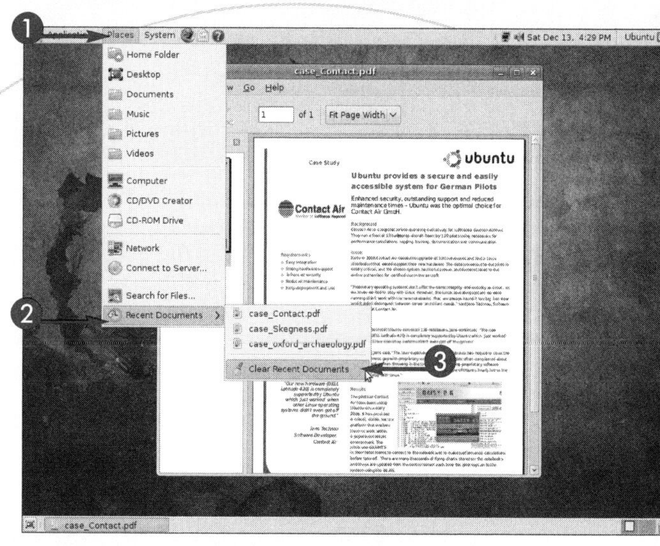

A dialog box appears, asking you to verify that you want to clear the list.

4. Click Clear.

The Recent Documents list is cleared.

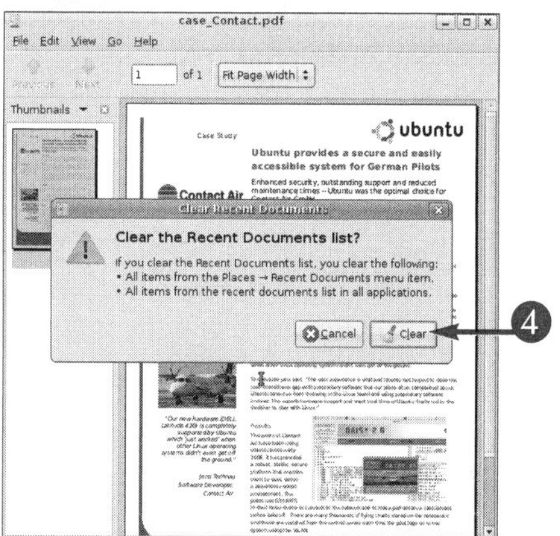

Extra

As mentioned earlier, there is an inherent risk in keeping information such as your Recent Documents list around. At this time, there is no setting within the GNOME environment to stop this automatic recording of your File Browser activity. Although this has been requested quite a few times in recent history on not only the Ubuntu forums but also the GNOME forums on the Internet, the capability is simply not currently available. If you want to eliminate the recording of this information, you will need to make the file that this information is stored in unwritable in some way. The GNOME code makes that a bit difficult, however. If the system cannot open the file for read/write purposes due to permissions, it will simply change the permissions. So a hack is needed. The following, when typed in a Terminal window, will stop GNOME from automatically reinstating its will over the user's:

```
$ rm $HOME/.recently-used.xbel
$ mkdir $HOME/.recently-used.xbel
```

Using a USB Flash Drive

If you want to get data onto or off of your Ubuntu machine without going across a network drive or server, you will likely need to use some form of flash media. The most common flash media today is the USB flash drive, sometimes referred to as a *thumb drive* due to its thumb-like shape. These drives are almost completely ubiquitous at this point, but they are really the latest in a long chain of removable media. They are different in implementation from all the previous removable media in that they are not part of a mechanical drive. Flash drives have true random access and extremely high reliability. They are actually a highly nonvolatile memory circuit. This type of memory requires no power to retain its contents, versus the much faster, but very volatile, memory used to support the computer's main processor. Because it is memory, however, it is faster than the previous magnetically, or optically, driven storage mediums.

When you connect a USB drive to Ubuntu, you will be presented with a new icon on the desktop. This icon will indicate that the file system of the USB flash drive has been mounted and is available. Depending on the contents of the drive, you may be presented with additional applications or options derived from your media-handling settings, discussed in the section "Configure Nautilus File Browser Preferences." For example, if you have digital pictures on the drive, you may be presented with a Preview dialog box from F-Spot Photo Manager that prompts you to add the photos to your collection.

Using a USB Flash Drive

USE A USB FLASH DRIVE

1. Insert the USB drive into a USB port.

- The USB drive icon appears.

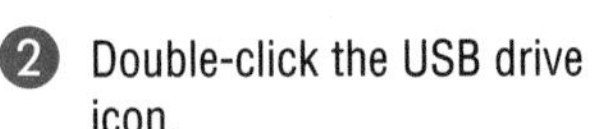

2. Double-click the USB drive icon.

   The File Browser opens the USB drive.

Note: *If you have files on the USB drive, you can copy them to your hard drive. You can also place files on the USB drive by copying and pasting them. See the section "Copy and Move Files and Folders."*

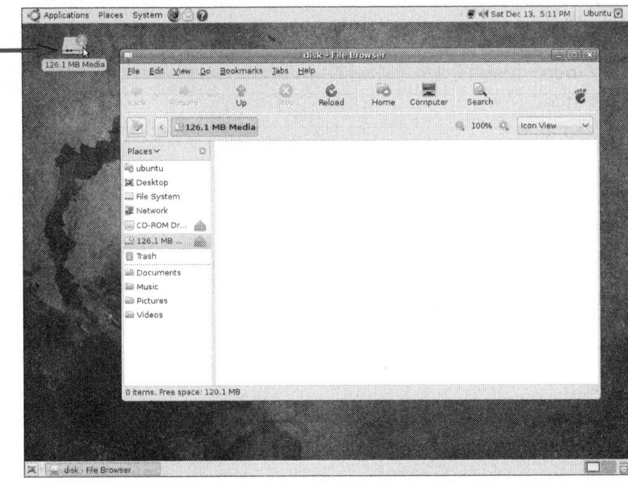

CREATE A NEW FILE ON THE DRIVE

3 Right-click in the File Browser window.

4 Click Create Document.

5 Click Empty File.

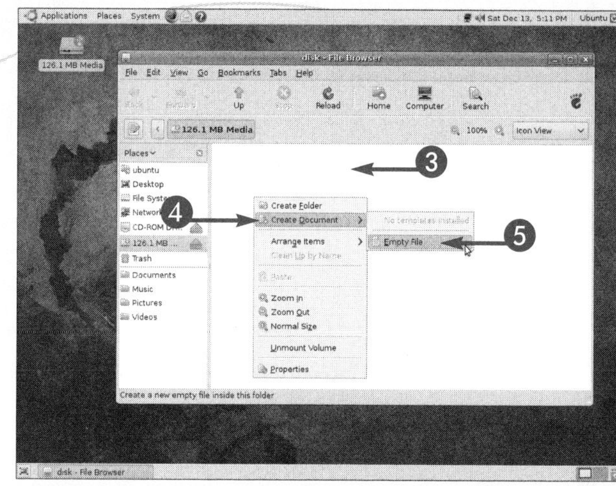

A new file appears on the USB drive.

UNMOUNT THE USB DRIVE

6 Right-click the USB drive icon.

7 Click Unmount Volume.

The USB drive icon disappears.

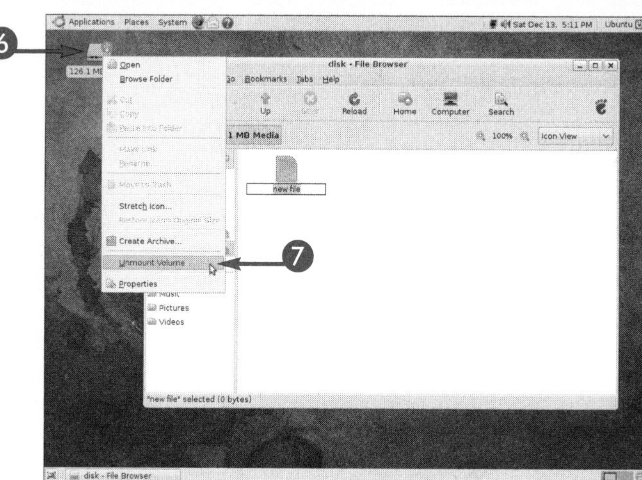

Extra

In the early days of computing, memory was far more scarce a commodity than storage on magnetic media. Information was often written to the disk immediately during a save operation. As the need for processing speed increased and the cost of memory became less expensive, this immediate write became far less common. In order to increase performance, the write operations were frequently cached, either by the operating system itself or the drive, to allow for successive writes to be more efficiently written to the drive in a block. This caching of writes, however, plays havoc when either the machine suddenly is powered off or the media in the drive becomes unavailable before the write operation can be flushed out to the magnetic media. This is why modern systems always require a proper shutdown, whereas older systems could simply be just shut off. This is especially important with removable media, where the write operation is cached, and you can in fact remove the storage medium from the system at will. The proper procedure is to unmount the volume before removing it from the port.

Encrypt a File

To prevent sensitive information from being seen by others if your laptop or machine is somehow lost or stolen, you will want to encrypt your files. Fortunately, encrypting your files is a fairly straightforward activity on Ubuntu.

Pretty good privacy, also known as *PGP,* is the default encryption engine for GNOME and consequently Ubuntu. PGP is a public-key form of encryption popularized in the encryption of email, although it can be used for encrypting any data. In PGP, the public key is bound to an identity, either an individual or organization. In order to send something securely to that entity, you use his or her public key as the key to encrypt the data. This public key is a cryptographic key, generated by that entity, and then distributed via publication to a key server. The entity you are sending information to holds the other half of the key, which is known as a *private key.* This key is used to decrypt the information. This type of technique is called *asymmetric-key encryption* because there are two keys used, one to encrypt and one to decrypt.

The first thing you must do to encrypt a file is to choose a PGP key. If you have not created a PGP key yet, refer to Chapter 6. After you have selected the key to use, you will be prompted to supply the passphrase for it in order to use the private key. When this has been entered, the process continues and when finished supplies you with a copy of the original file that has been encrypted and has the .pgp extension.

Encrypt a File

ENCRYPT A FILE

1. Right-click the file to encrypt.
2. Click Encrypt.

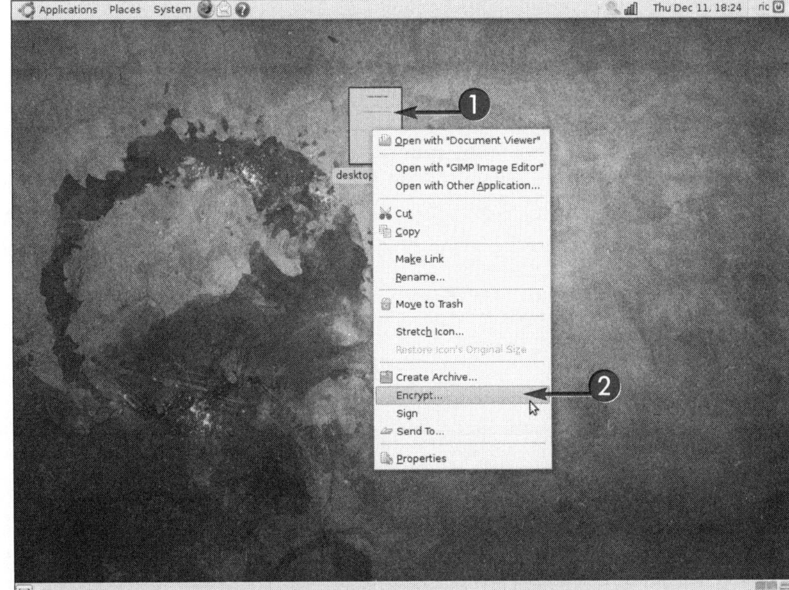

The Choose Recipients dialog box appears.

3. Click the check box next to the key that you want.
4. Click OK.

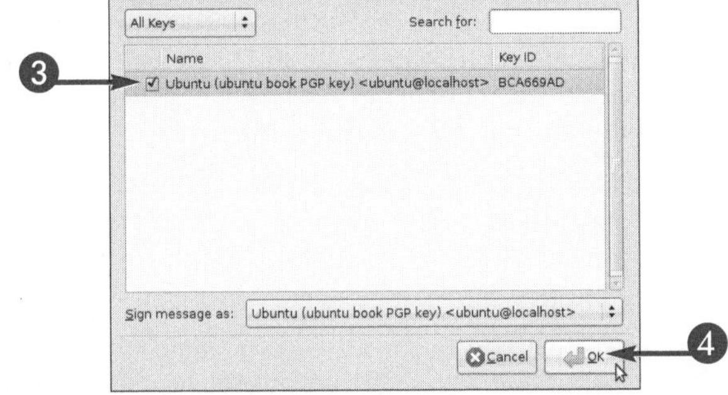

You are prompted to provide a passphrase.

5 Type in your passphrase.

6 Click OK.

The file is encrypted.

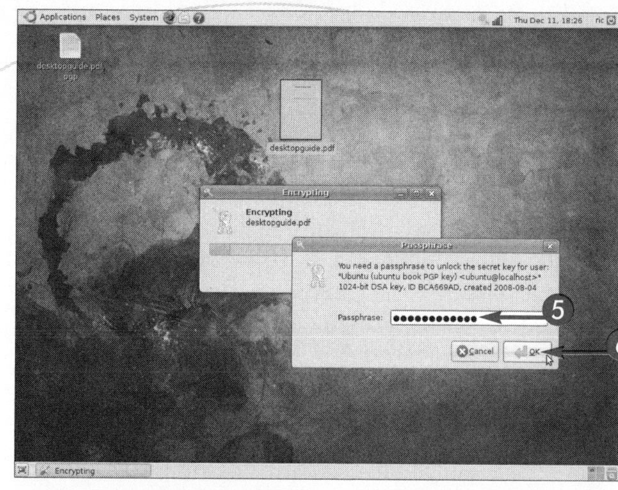

- The resulting PGP encrypted file appears.

Extra

One popular form of encryption for exchanging information in the early days of the Internet was ROT13. This was a simple rotation cypher in which all the letters of the alphabet were rotated 13 places forward, with the carry-over starting back at the beginning. This allowed for content that may have been offensive to be sealed via this low grade of encryption, and thus the viewer had to actively decode it in order to view it, thereby accepting the fact that the material might prove provocative. The interesting feature of this technique was that encrypting two times ended up with the original file due to the 13 character offset.

The encryption algorithms of today bear startlingly little resemblance to this simple cypher. They are based on deep mathematical principles and are constantly in an evolving state. The precept of most of the encryption work today revolves around mathematically-difficult-to-solve problems. As computing power increases, however, these problems slip more and more into the realm of possibility to be solved. So stronger, more advanced problems keep being devised, and the older encryption techniques become outdated and retired.

continued

Encrypt a File (continued)

When you want to retrieve your encrypted information, you will need the private key and your passphrase.

Many times when talking about encryption, you will hear the term *brute-force attack.* This term refers to the number of tries a simple-minded attacker or program thereof would have to systematically go through, one by one, to find the password or passphrase. Obviously the longer the password or passphrase is, the more tries it will take.

You may have noticed the term *passphrase* being used instead of the more common *password.* The use of a *passphrase* instead of *password* stems from the fact that the techniques for cracking passwords using brute force have improved to include dictionaries of words, as humans usually choose a word or name for a password. By limiting these brute-force tries to words that are in the dictionary and thereby more probable to be chosen as a memorable password, they allow the attacker to arrive at the correct password in fewer tries. When you use a phrase instead of a single word, you greatly increase the number of tries needed as each word then complicates the attacker's number of possible choices.

Choosing an appropriate passphrase can greatly increase the security of your private key. Generally, the longer your passphrase is, the better your security. As with passwords, adding additional characters not necessarily part of the standard alphabet will increase security as well. You must, however, ensure that it is something that you can remember. If you lose your passphrase, you will no longer be able to decrypt the information in your files, and the files will essentially become lost forever.

Encrypt a File *(continued)*

DECRYPT A FILE

1. Right-click the file to be decrypted.
2. Click Open with "Decrypt File."

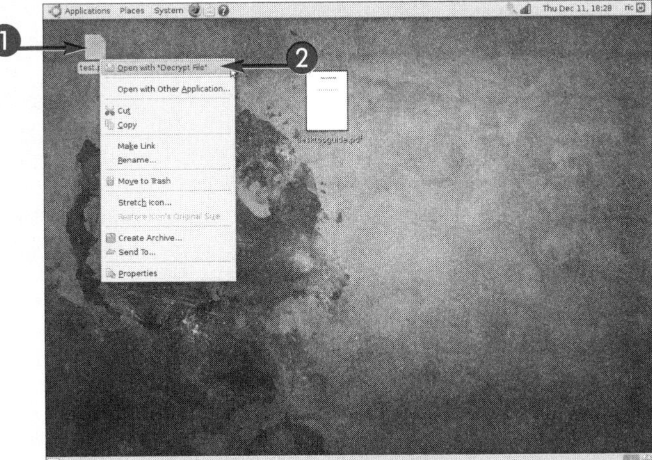

You are prompted to provide the passphrase.

3. Type in the passphrase.
4. Click OK.

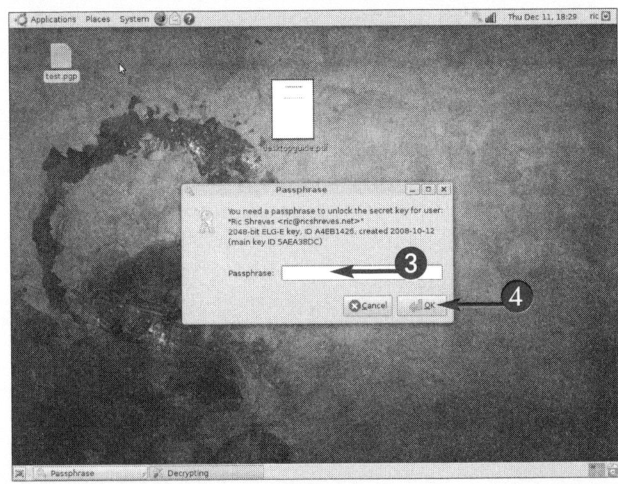

The file is decrypted.

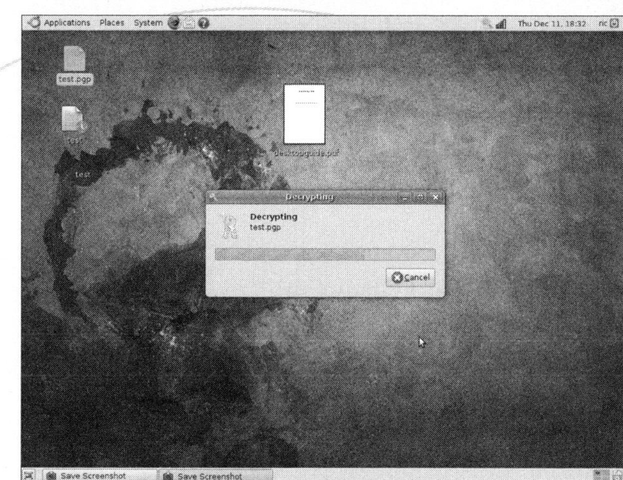

- The decrypted file appears after the process is completed.

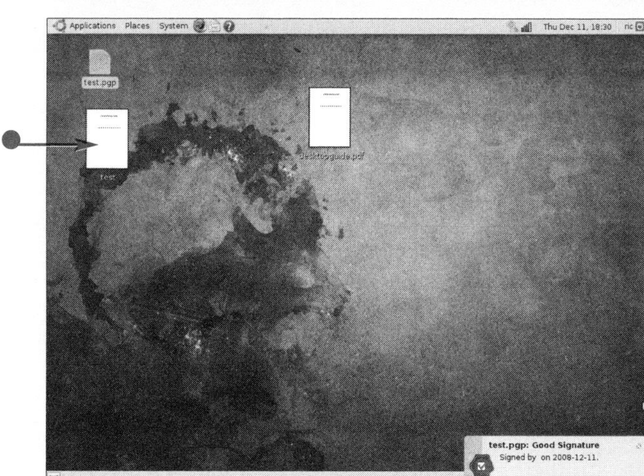

Extra

Although the focus of this section has been on asymmetric encryption, it is important to understand the use of symmetric encryption as well. Symmetric encryption involves the use of a single, shared, secret key that is used for both the encryption and decryption of the file or stream of data. Because the key itself is used for encryption and decryption, both parties need to have a copy of it. In order to keep it secret, the key must be distributed in person or through some other secure method that cannot be compromised.

Another variant that is widely used is the cryptographic hash. This allows an entire file or stream of data to be analyzed and produces a fairly unique numeric fingerprint that is very difficult to fake. This technique is used to validate the veracity of a file as containing the content the original provider intended. It allows you to do this by letting you check the published fingerprint hash from a known good source versus the one derived from the file you have obtained.

Although public-key cryptography is versatile, it is also computationally intensive. Because symmetric encryption does not rely on intensive, mathematically-difficult-to-solve problems, it is more efficient computationally.

Manage File and Folder Permissions

To ensure that your files are not viewed by others who may be using the machine, you can change the permissions for the files. Because Ubuntu, and all Linux and UNIX variants, are designed to be multiuser, ample facility is provided. Security is based around two different concepts: The first is the trust classification of the requestor, and the second is the permissions granted to that trust class for the file.

The trust classification is based on three different roles. The most trusted of these roles is the user role. This is the owner of the file. The second trust level is the group role. This is a named grouping of users. Any given user can belong to multiple groups. Then there is the other role. This role corresponds to any user. By manipulating the memberships in groups, you can share files among the members of the group.

The permissions allowed to any of these roles is broken into three basic permissions. The primary permission is the read permission. This allows a specified role to examine the contents of a file. The next most frequently used privilege is the write permission. This allows a role to create, delete, or modify a file. The last permission is the execute permission, which allows a given role to execute the file. The file may or may not be a binary executable, however. If a text file has the appropriate header information describing the appropriate script-handling binary, it can be executed, causing the binary to launch with the contents of the script fed into it as input. Additionally, the execute permission is required in order to enter a directory. Read permission alone is not enough to actually move the current directory into a folder if you do not have the execute permission.

Manage File and Folder Permissions

1. Right-click the file whose permissions you want to set.
2. Click Properties.

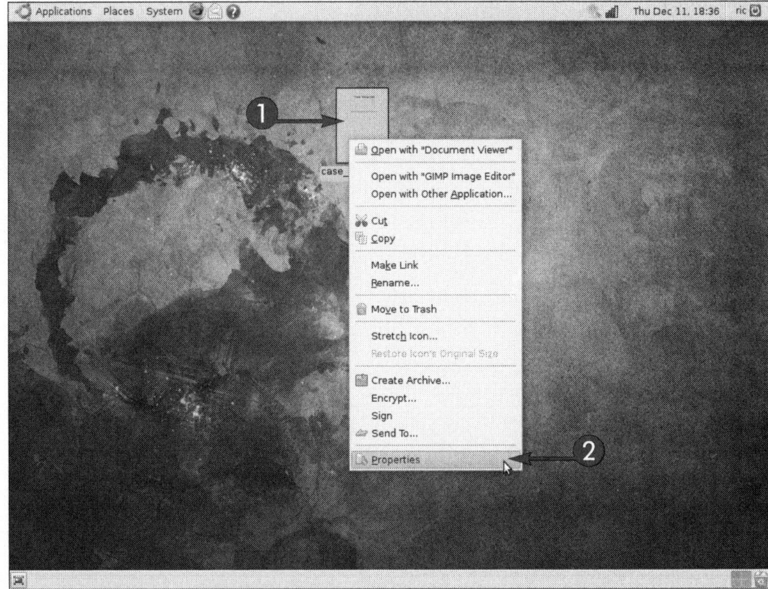

The file's Properties dialog box appears.

3. Click Access under Owner and select the level of access that the file's owner may have.

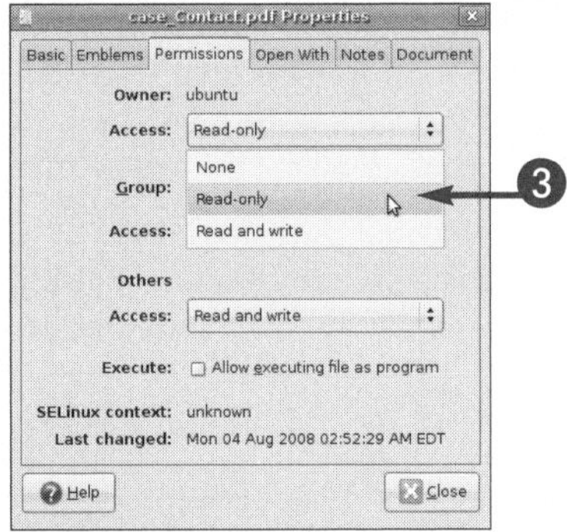

4 Click Group and select a group to specify access for, such as admin.

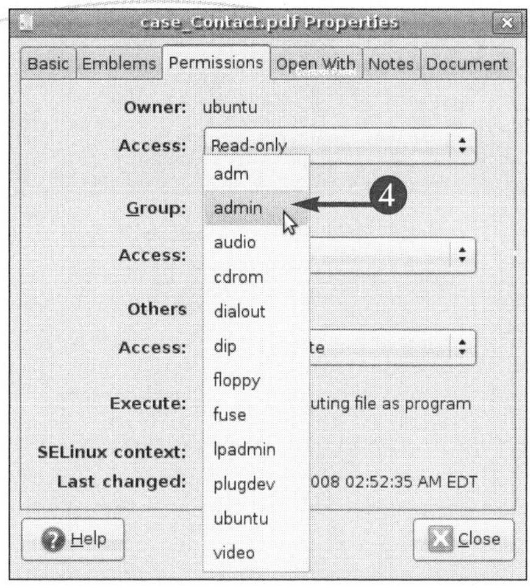

5 Click Access under Group and select that group's level of access.

6 Click Access under Others and specify the level of access that all other users may have.

7 Click Close.

Your permissions are set for the file.

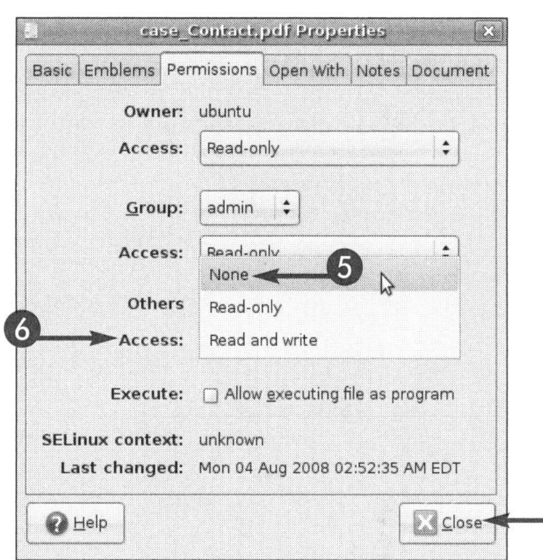

Extra

There are lesser-used additional types of permissions for files and directories within a UNIX-type file system. The first of these is the set-user-id flag, which allows a file to be executed by a member of a group or other as if he or she were the file's owner. This is usually done by a specific service account or even the superuser, thereby delegating the capability to run certain functions as a more privileged user. The set-group-id privilege is used on a directory for setting the group ID to that of the current directory for operations on that directory or its entries. This is especially useful for shared directories; by setting the group-id flag on a directory, all files created within that directory will maintain the group setting of the directory rather than the primary, or first, group in the user's group membership list. There is also a permission called the "sticky-bit" that is mostly obsolete, as it used to cause a file not to be flushed from memory and thus "stick." It also has the meaning that a file with this permission set cannot be deleted by other users even if they have write permissions to the containing directory. This is useful in shared directories such as /tmp.

Adjust the System Appearance

Although Ubuntu certainly has a nice look right off the installation CD, you can bend its appearance to your will. The term *personal computer* itself implies that this type of configuration is an extension of the user's needs and preferences. These preferences not only enhance the aesthetics of the computer interface, but also can make significant performance differences. In the case of some of the themes designed for the visually impaired, it can make all the difference in being able to even use the computer at all.

The Appearance settings are broken down into several areas. The primary area is the Theme area. The Theme area offers a number of predefined themes that vary on the styling of the user interface controls, colors for the windows, the input boxes, the selected and unselected items, and the tooltips. Other variables on the theme are the styling of the window border decoration, the icon set, and the mouse pointer image.

With so many things available to change within a theme, the included set of themes do not cover all the possibilities. You can build your own theme from the variations described here by using the Customize option. In the Customize dialog box, you are presented with all the possible variations, split out on different tabs. On each tab is a selection of options within that type of theme variability.

In addition to the themes allowed in the base installation, you can also use the Install button to add theme kits downloaded from the Internet. These allow for even more variation, within the limits of the GNOME desktop components.

Adjust the System Appearance

1. Click System ➔ Preferences ➔ Appearance.

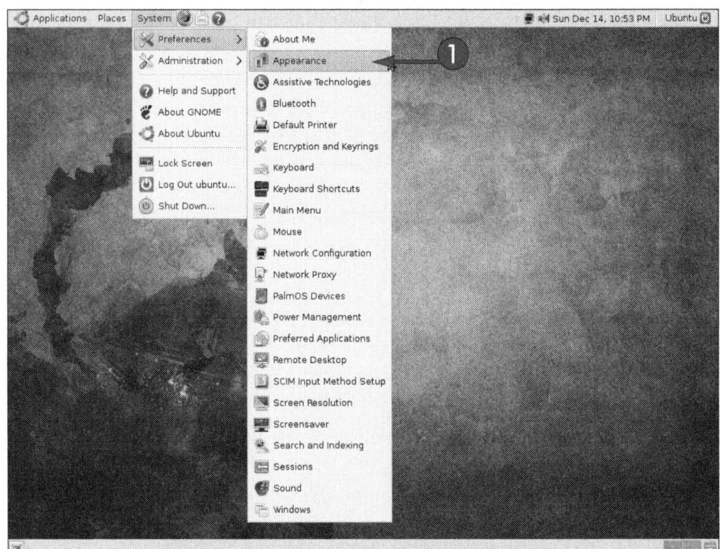

The Appearance Preferences dialog box appears.

2. Click a theme to try it out, such as Human-Clearlooks.

The theme changes to the one that you chose.

3. Click Customize.

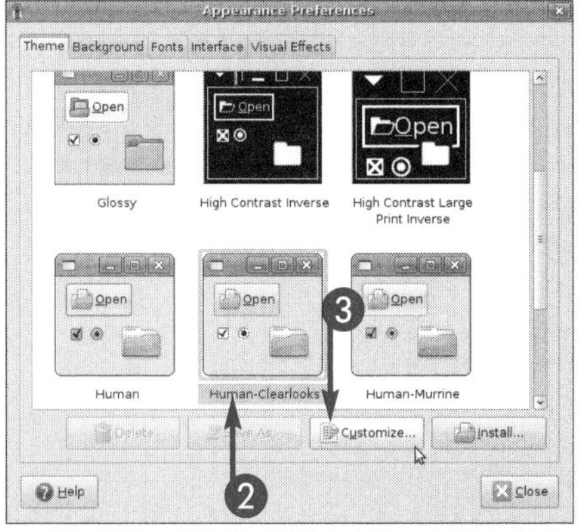

The Customize Theme dialog box appears.

4. Click Window Border.

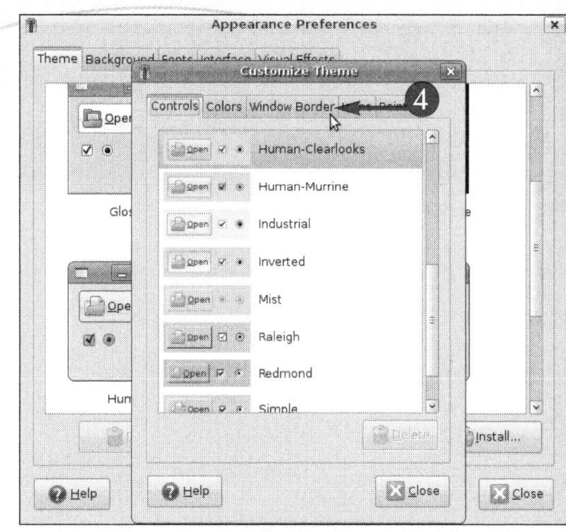

The Window Border tab appears.

5. Click a window border to try it out, such as AgingGorilla.

The window decorations change to your selection.

6. Click Close.

7. Click Background.

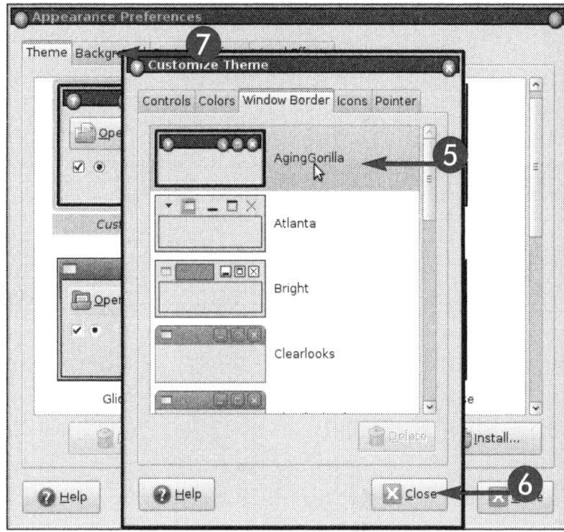

Extra

Installing themes is pretty easy. First you go to a theme site such as http://art.gnome.org/themes. Then you find a theme you like and download it to a location on your computer. After you have downloaded the theme, which is usually packaged as a compressed tape archive file (.tar.gz or .tgz), you simply click the Install button on the Theme tab of the Appearance Preferences dialog box. Navigate to the theme file in the Install dialog box, and the installer will add the new theme to the gallery of themes for you to choose from. This same method works for all of the theme items. You can also subtheme items such as icons, pointers, and control decorations this way. Although there are certain limits to how far you can modify the interface, some of the themes provide a very nice option for the eye-candy enthusiast. The site mention earlier is by no means the only source of themes for GNOME. Be sure to check out the themes area of http://themes.freshmeat.net as well. As you sample different themes, you may also want to go and look at how to author your own. A tutorial for doing that can be found at http://developer.gnome.org/doc/tutorials/metacity/metacity-themes.html.

continued

Adjust the System Appearance (continued)

The next major Appearance category is the background image. GNOME allows for using almost any image type for a background and enables you to center, stretch, or tile the image across the surface of the desktop. If you do not want to use an image, you can also use a solid color or even a gradient from one color to another. The gradient can be applied in both horizontal or vertical directions.

By modifying the settings on the Fonts tab, you can tailor the appearance of virtually all text. Also, you can adjust certain aspects of how the text is rendered, including anti-aliasing. *Anti-aliasing* is the technique of creating a smooth transition from the background color of text to the foreground color to reduce the pixelation. The brain smooths together similar colors, so avoiding an abrupt color change makes text appear clearer.

On the Interface tab, you will find settings that change the way the menus and toolbars are rendered by the GNOME applications. Additionally, you can configure whether you will have editable menu shortcut keys. This setting allows you to change the shortcut keys displayed on the right of many options within the GNOME interface. This includes features such as cut and paste, which are typically bound to the Ctrl+C and Ctrl+V keys. Although this can make it easier for you to do certain tasks, it is always a good precaution to double-check that the keys you plan to use for a new shortcut are not already used.

The final tab is the Visual Effects tab. This tab enables you to adjust the added visual effects that can be displayed by the desktop environment. This includes animated menus, fade in and fade out of windows, and various other eye-candy features.

Adjust the System Appearance *(continued)*

The Background tab is displayed.

8. Select a background image.

The background changes.

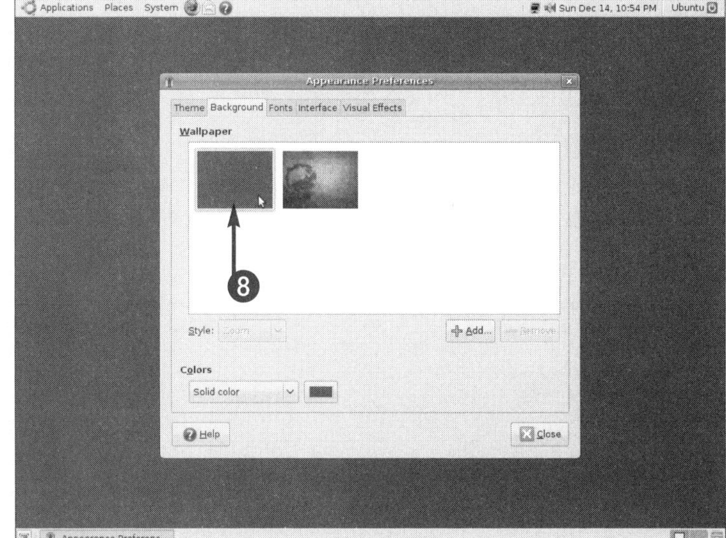

9. Click Fonts.

The Fonts tab is displayed.

10. Choose the font settings that you want, such as clicking Subpixel Smoothing (LCDs).

11. Click Interface.

The Interface tab appears.

12 Click the selection box and adjust the text/icon settings for menus.

13 Click Visual Effects.

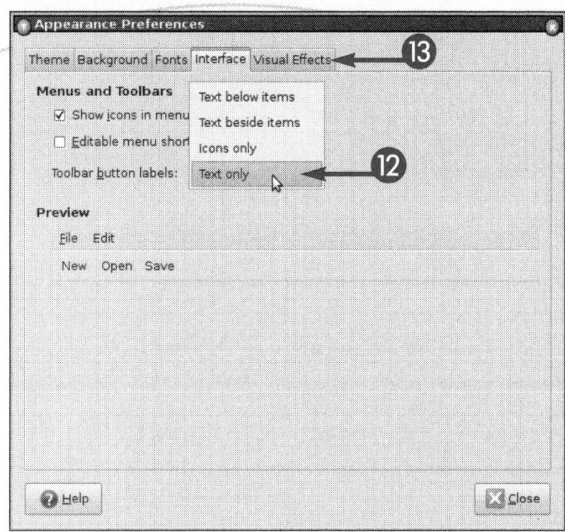

The Visual Effects tab appears.

14 Select your preference for the level of visual effects.

15 Click Close.

Your Appearance setting changes are applied.

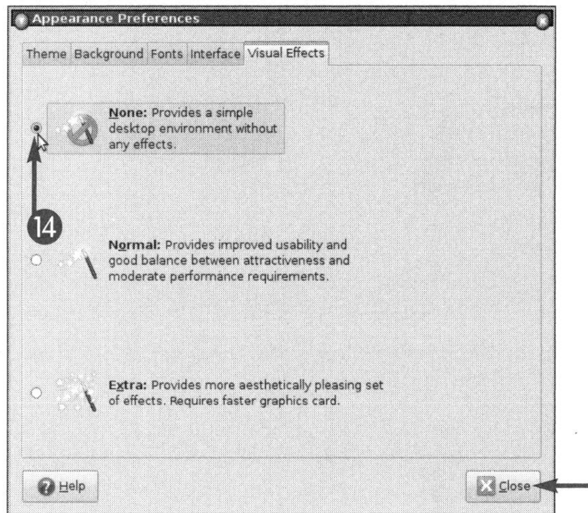

Extra

The Extra setting of the Visual Effects tab can additionally be augmented by using the Advanced Desktop Effects settings application, which is not installed by default. This application, along with the alternative Compiz Fusion window manager, can generate dazzling effects. The most notorious of these effects is the Desktop Cube effect plug-in. This plug-in causes the entire desktop/workspace to pull back from the screen and rotate as one of the faces on a cube. Each of the other faces around the perimeter of the cube (four sides) show the other workspaces. Whichever workspace is closest to facing the user when the plug-in is deactivated becomes the new active workspace. Additional plug-ins allow for the cube to become semitransparent and show gears spinning in the interior of the cube. And this is by far not the only trick that the Compiz Fusion window manager can accomplish. This display manager is based on OpenGL and as such can produce stunning effects not possible without tapping the advanced rendering engines of today's modern video cards. Although none of this increases the usefulness of the operating system, it does make for an impressive display of graphic capability and flexibility.

Set the Default Printer

You can set your default printer from a list of available printers using the Default Printer application. Historically one of the weaker areas of UNIX-like systems, the printing capabilities of modern Linux systems have all the capability of any other OS. The advent of PostScript support within the drivers of Linux printing subsystems have allowed the OS to tap into the capabilities of most modern printers. For a period in the mid-to-late 90s, there was a movement to drive the control logic of the lowest-end printers into the driver software, and this did present a problem for Linux printing, as the software drivers supplied by many manufacturers did not run on Linux-based operating systems. This incompatibility has largely been alleviated due to much diligence by the open-source community to reverse-engineer the protocols involved, and to build relationships to foster cooperation by the hardware manufacturers. Today, drivers exist for most of the printers sold. Modern Linux printing subsystems can drive printers of various types from the common desktop bubble jet to the most sophisticated of commercial printing operations. As always, it is a good idea to check to see if your printer is supported by the drivers. You can do so at www.linuxprinting.org/printer_list.cgi, which contains a database of printers and a rating of their compatibility with Linux.

The Default Printer application is rather simple in design and function. It displays a list of the configured printers available on the system and allows you to choose which one you want to use. Alternatively, you can have it detect and set your default printer preference to the same as the system's default printer.

Set the Default Printer

1. Click System ➔ Preferences ➔ Default Printer.

The Default Printer dialog box appears.

2. Select the printer that you want from the list.
3. Click Set Default.

Now when you print from any application, this printer will be used.

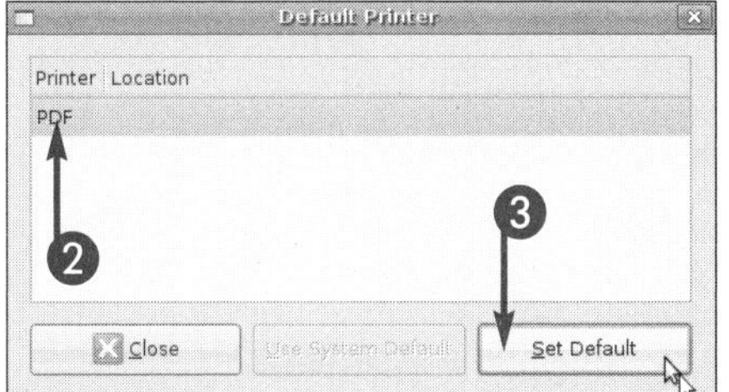

Adjust the Screen Resolution

Adjusting your screen resolution is likely to be one of the first things you will want to do on a new system. *Resolution* refers to the number of pixels, or displayable dots, on your screen. This measurement is usually given by the notation of number of pixels in the x-axis versus the number of pixels in the y-axis. As resolution increases, the processing power needed to move all the pixels around increases. For this reason, with a slower graphics card, you can expect better performance by lowering the number of pixels.

The *refresh rate* refers to how fast the pixels on the screen are redrawn. This is usually very tightly coupled with the capabilities of not only the video card but also the monitor you are using. For example, a typical cathode ray tube (CRT) monitor has available refresh rates from about 56Hz to 85Hz. This is significant because the fluorescent lights in an office can flicker at 60Hz and cause eye strain. If you adjust the refresh rate higher than that of the lights, the flicker is reduced and thereby the resulting eye strain as well. With liquid crystal display (LCD) screens, the refresh rate is usually set to 60Hz, but the technology behind LCD screens does not generate the same strobing effect because the crystals that make up the pixel locations do not completely deplete their illumination with each refresh cycle.

You can easily adjust the resolution after the system is up and running using the Screen Resolution application. This application displays the current resolution and refresh rate that the display is running. It also allows you to change those settings to anything allowed by the detection process.

Adjust the Screen Resolution

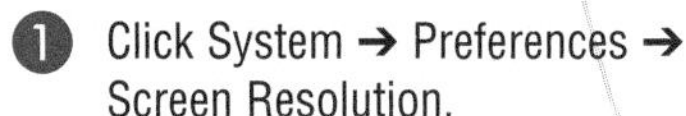

1. Click System ➔ Preferences ➔ Screen Resolution.

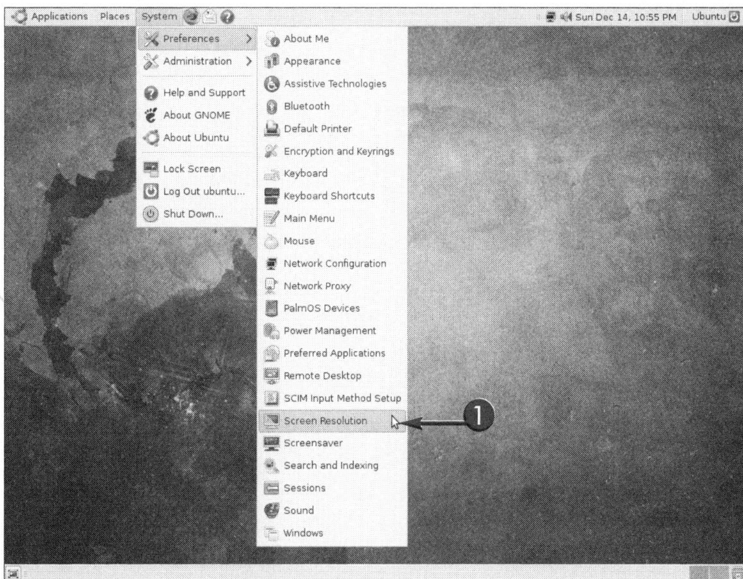

The Monitor Resolution Settings dialog box appears.

2. Click here and select the resolution that you want.
3. Click here and select the refresh rate that you want.
4. Click Close.

Your resolution settings are applied.

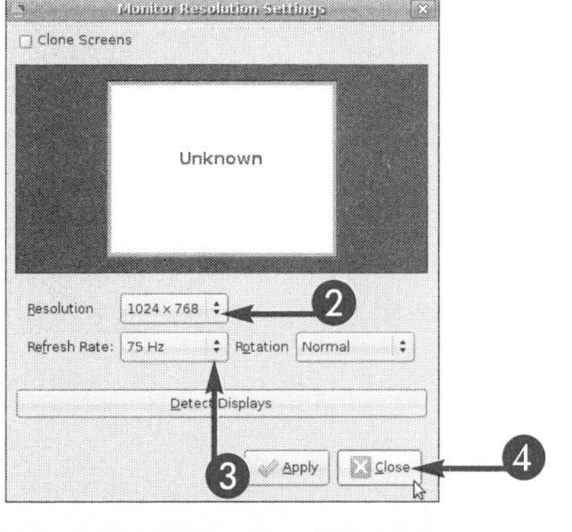

Change the Screensaver

One of the frequently modified settings on a personal computer is the screensaver. The screensaver originally was created to cause the computer to display a changing image on the screen so that the contents of the current desktop were not "burned" into the phosphors of the display. Modern CRT displays do not suffer nearly as much as older monochrome displays but still can be burned by continuous image display in such applications as kiosks and electronic advertisement signage. LCD monitors never suffered this vulnerability and are quite incapable of having this type of hysteresis.

The Screensaver Preferences dialog box enables you to change the screensaver that your computer will use when idle. It also allows you to set a blank screen or a random screensaver as your choice. When you are selecting a screensaver, the currently selected "hack," as it is sometimes termed by the Linux community, will be displayed in a small window of the Screensaver Preferences dialog box. By flipping through the items in the list, you can find a screensaver that you want to use. Whichever screensaver is selected when you close the dialog box will then be used whenever the machine is determined to be idle. You can adjust the period of inactivity that determines whether the machine is idle as well. You may also completely disable the screensaver activity by clearing the Activate Screensaver When Computer Is Idle check box. It is advisable, though not always completely convenient, to enable the locking of the screen when the screensaver is activated. This helps to secure your computer from use by others when you step away.

Change the Screensaver

1. Click System ➔ Preferences ➔ Screensaver.

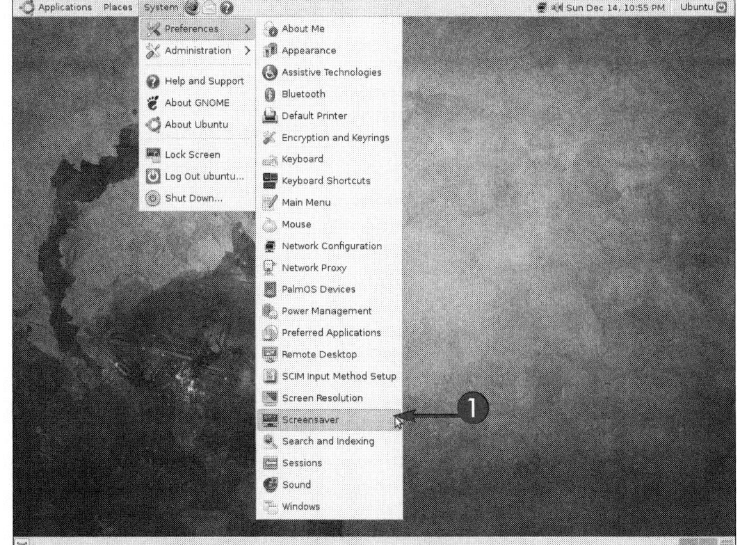

The Screensaver Preferences dialog box appears.

2. Select a screensaver.
   - A preview of the new screensaver appears here.
3. Click Preview.

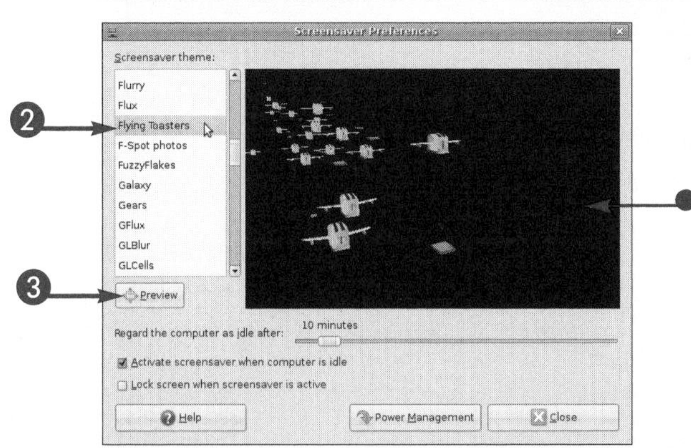

The new screensaver is previewed full-screen.

4 Click Leave Fullscreen.

You are returned to the Screensaver Preferences dialog box.

- Optionally, you can click Lock Screen When Screensaver Is Active to protect your computer.

5 Click Close.

Your new screensaver will appear when your computer is idle the set number of minutes.

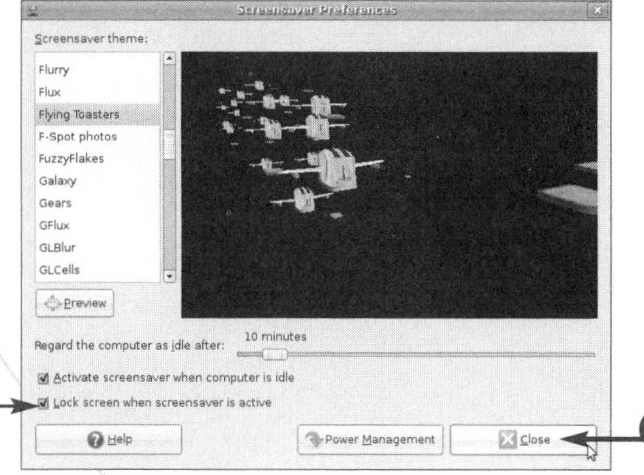

Extra

Even in their earliest forms, screensavers became a point of personal expression. One of the first companies to sell screensavers was After Dark, with a product line initially launched for the Macintosh computer system, which due to popularity was ported over to the Windows platform. One of the screensavers installed by default on Ubuntu pays homage to this ancestor by imitating its Flying Toasters theme.

Ubuntu ships with over 80 screensaver hacks. Although 80 may sound like a large number, there are many, many others available. In the package repository, there are two additional packages that you can install and get more screensavers. At a command prompt in a terminal window, type the following:

```
sudo apt-get install xscreensaver-data-extra xscreensaver-gl-extra
```

This will launch the package manager and install the new screensavers. Be sure to accept any prompts during the installation. After the installation completes, you can close the terminal window. Now you should have over 200 available screensavers in your Preferences dialog box.

Change the Mouse Preferences

Because the movement and clicking of the mouse is so important to many tasks in a visual interface, the settings for that input device need to suit the operator's preferences. You can change the options related to the mouse and its associated actions with the Mouse Preferences application. With this application, you can change the handedness of the mouse, thereby switching the right and left buttons to accommodate use on the opposite side of the desk and for the opposite hand. You can also activate a mouse-location tool, which proves especially handy when working in low contrast situations such as bright light, where the pointer may not be easy to discern from the background.

You can also adjust the pointer speed of the mouse. The first of these options is the Acceleration setting of the mouse pointer. This option controls the rate of movement across the screen as a function of how fast you move the mouse across the mouse pad. This means that the pointer will move farther if you move the mouse faster. The other Pointer Speed option is the Sensitivity option. This option adjusts the scaling factor of the mouse movement to the number of pixels movement of the mouse pointer on the screen. Caution should be exercised with either of these two Pointer Speed controls because they may make the mouse unusable if you adjust them too severely.

The Drag and Drop option controls how far an item must be dragged with the mouse to be considered a drag-and-drop operation.

The Double-Click Timeout option determines the length of time between a first click of a single-click and the start of another single-click. If another click is within this threshold, it will be considered a double-click.

Change the Mouse Preferences

CHANGE THE MOUSE SETTINGS

1. Click System ➔ Preferences ➔ Mouse.

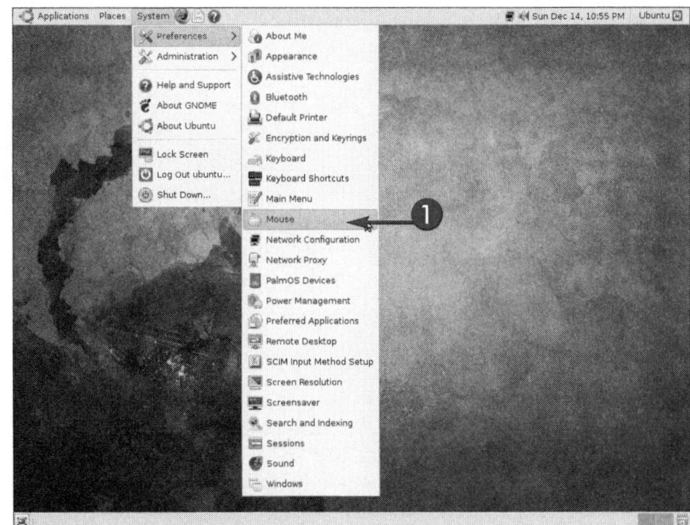

- The Mouse Preferences dialog box appears.

2. Change the settings according to your needs.
3. Adjust the Double-Click Timeout setting to your preference.
4. Test the double-click timeout by double-clicking the light bulb.

Note: *If you do not like the double-click speed, readjust the setting and test it again.*

5. Click Accessibility.

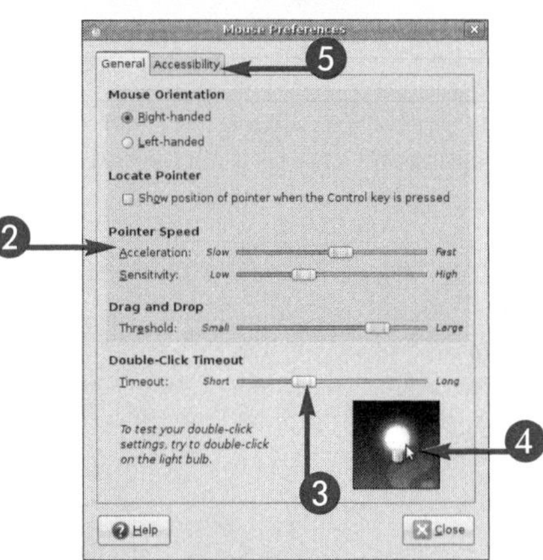

SET A DWELL CLICK

Note: *See the Extra for information about dwell clicks.*

The Accessibility tab appears.

6 Click Initiate Click When Stopping Pointer Movement.

7 Click Choose Type of Click Beforehand.

8 Click Show Click Type Window.

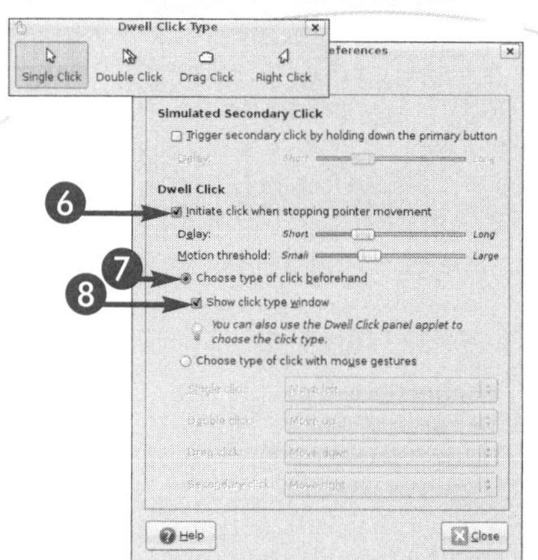

The Dwell Click Type window appears.

9 Dwell on one of the click type window icons.

The click type activates.

10 Dwell somewhere else on the screen.

The specified click action occurs. In this example, a right-click menu is activated.

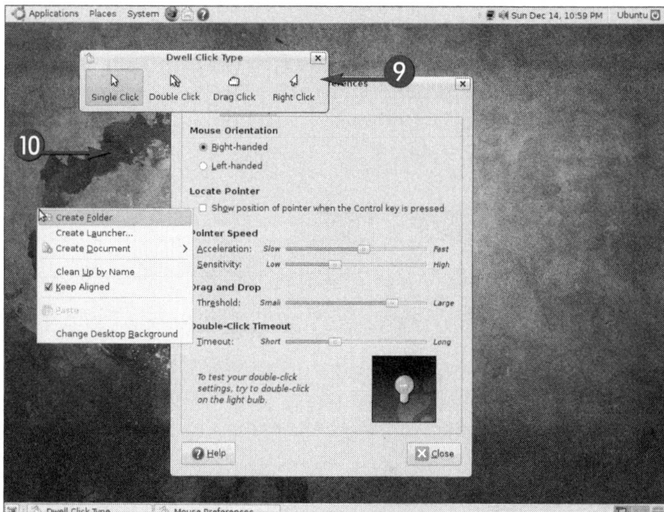

Extra

The Accessibility options tab allows you to activate features for alternatives to multiple buttons on the mouse. This functionality requires that assistive technologies be enabled; see the "Access Assistive Technologies Controls" section later in this chapter to learn how to enable them. There are two types of alternative click functionality. One is based on holding down the click and enables you to simulate the right-click. The second function, a *dwell click,* is more versatile and is based on the cessation of movement of the mouse. It will watch the mouse, and when the mouse stops, it will initiate the specified type of click. The selection of the click action can be made with the Dwell Click Type window or with a panel applet called Dwell Click, or even a mouse gesture. The Dwell Click Type window enables you to select the action for the next dwell click. The Dwell Click applet operates similarly to the Dwell Click window but resides in the panel and thus does not obscure any content on the screen. The Mouse Gestures options allow you to make a motion with the mouse to indicate your intention, and each of the four different actions can be associated with different gestures of the mouse.

Adjust Power Management Settings

Tweaking the power settings is essential for laptop installations. If you are using a laptop, you can change your power settings using the Power Management Preferences application.

The battery life of a laptop computer can be enhanced by the proper adjustment of these settings. Depending on the machine, the backlight of the display can use from one to over three watts of power. Add to that the power draw of the LCD and the graphics chips, and you total up to a fair portion of the idle power consumption for a laptop. Setting the display to go to sleep after a very short amount of inactivity causes practically no real loss of function but buys you extra battery life every time it activates. The default is 40 minutes, but commonly used values on laptops can be in the range of 1-5 minutes.

If the machine is inactive for several minutes, it can further reduce power by going into a sleep mode, only drawing power for keeping the memory refreshed. During this cycle, the hard drive and processor shut down and essentially wait for some activity to "wake" them up. Waking up usually only takes a few seconds, and you are brought back to the exact point at which the machine went into sleep mode. This is a drastic reduction in the power consumption, and the laptop can usually run for at least two times your normal battery life while in standby — and often even as much as four times your normal battery life. So, if you are only using your computer intermittently while away from power, you can dramatically extend your usage by having the computer in sleep mode when inactive.

Adjust Power Management Settings

1. Click System ➔ Preferences ➔ Power Management.

   The Power Management Preferences application appears.

2. Adjust the inactivity interval after which to put the machine to sleep.
3. Adjust the inactivity interval after which to put the display to sleep.
4. Click General.

   The General tab appears.

5. Adjust the actions for the power and suspend buttons according to your preferences.
6. Click Close.

   Your power settings take effect.

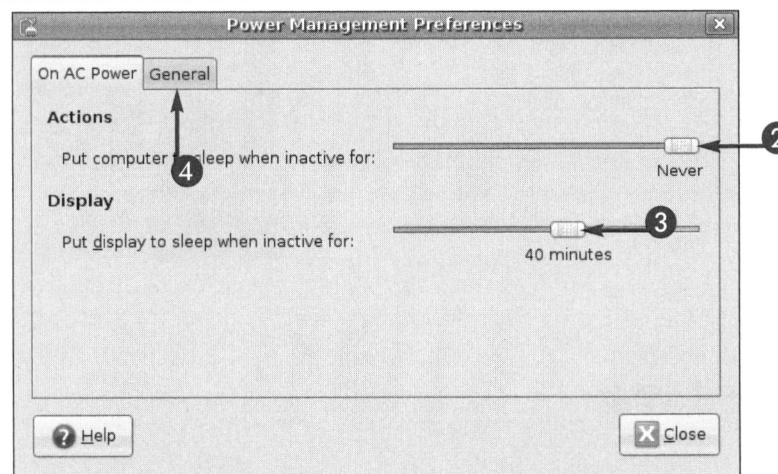

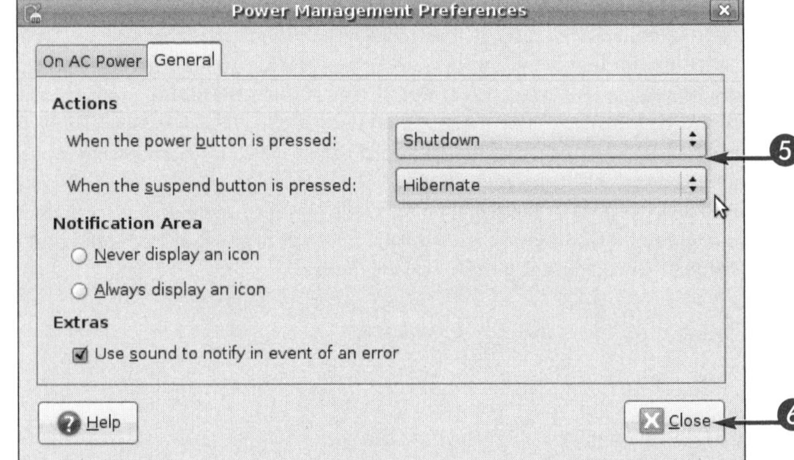

Change Keyboard Shortcuts

If you have been using a computer for a long time, you have no doubt become accustomed to certain keystroke shortcuts to accomplish tasks. You can configure your old favorite shortcuts using the Keyboard Shortcuts application.

The interface for this application resembles more a Properties dialog box or the key bindings from a game program. There is a list of actions grouped by the type of action to be taken on the left and the shortcut key associated with the action on the right. When a row is highlighted, the right column displays "New Accelerator," and you simply press the new key.

The three categories of key bindings are Sound, Desktop, and Window Management. The Sound category primarily deals with multimedia controls such as volume and interacting with media players.

The Desktop category deals with general tasks at the desktop level — including locking the screen, activating searches, and launching certain common applications. The Window Management category is the most expansive, due in part to the built-in multiple workspace support. There are key bindings available for essentially every way you may want to manipulate a window on a workspace or across workspaces.

The default keystroke shortcuts will accommodate most activities without need for adjustment, but as there are variances among keyboards, the multimedia keys may need to be adjusted to fit your particular hardware.

Keep in mind that shortcuts can be applied to application launchers as well. Additional key configurations within the Nautilus File Browser can also be made to customize keystrokes within that application.

Change Keyboard Shortcuts

1. Click System ➔ Preferences ➔ Keyboard Shortcuts.

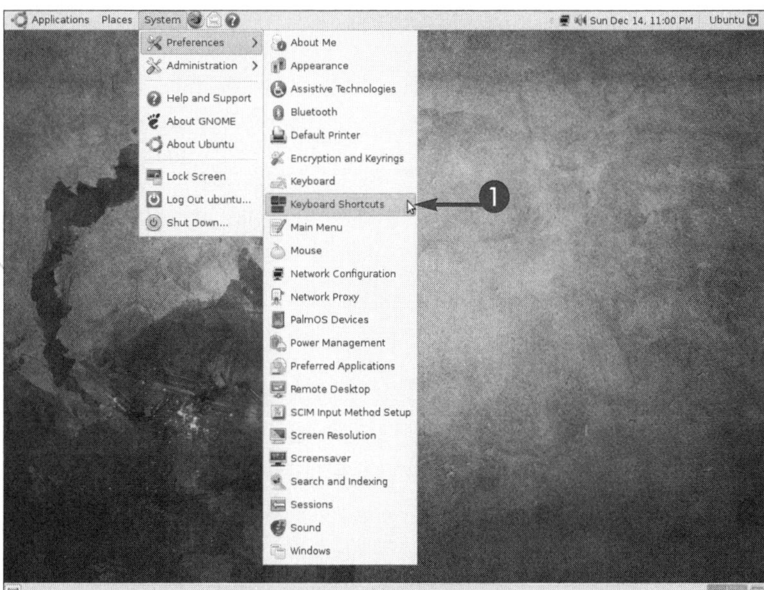

The Keyboard Shortcuts application appears.

2. Click the action whose keystrokes you want to change.
3. Type the new keys.
4. Click Close.

The new keystrokes are bound to the action.

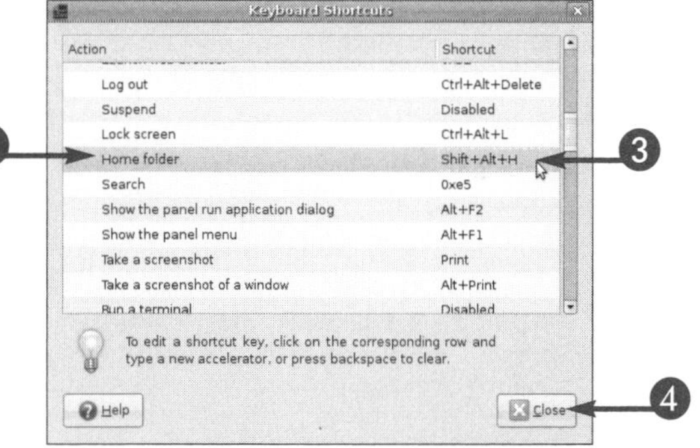

Modify the Main Menu

The main menus of the Ubuntu system are configurable. You can change them to suit your tastes or for specialized deployment scenarios in which you do not want all the functions of the operating system readily available to casual users.

The menus are categorized by two major divisions by default. The first category is Applications and includes all the programs that a user may run in the normal course of using the computer. The second category is the System category, which includes the preferences applications and the administrative applications. The preferences applications are typically things that users would configure to customize the desktop environment to their tastes, whereas the administrative applications are more systemwide settings that may affect all users.

The Main Menu preference application enables you to customize the main menus. This includes adding new menus and submenus. It also includes adding, deleting, and modifying existing items in the menus. You can also add separators to menus to indicate a grouping of like applications within a single menu. The menus can contain other menus. When creating a new menu, you can also include a comment parameter that will be displayed when the menu is hovered over with the mouse pointer. The order of the menu items can also be manipulated up or down as preferred.

The items within the menus are all standard launchers and take the usual name, command, and comment parameters.

Modify the Main Menu

1. Click System ➔ Preferences ➔ Main Menu.

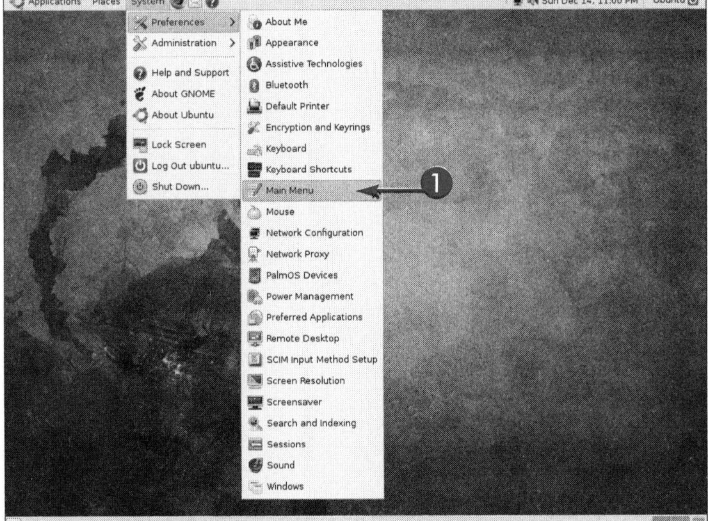

The Main Menu application appears.

2. Click a menu to modify.

The contents of the menu are displayed.

3. Click New Item.

The Create Launcher dialog box appears.

4 Type a name for the new menu item.

5 Type the command for the new menu item.

6 Enter the comment that you want to use.

7 Click OK.

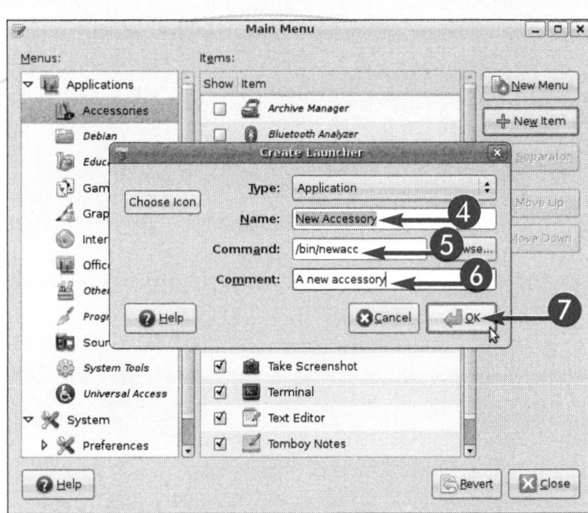

- The new item is inserted into the menu.
- You can also add a new menu or a separator or move items up or down.

Apply It

If you are not the type to use icons on the desktop or panel to launch your applications, you may want to take this opportunity to enhance your menu system to accommodate yourself. Start by launching the Main Menu preference application. Click New Menu and add a menu named Favorites to the top of the items under the Applications menu. Then click New Separator and add a separator at the Applications menu level so that you can distinguish them from the default items on the Applications menu. Then find any applications that you use frequently and add them to the Applications menu. Sort them as you like for the easiest possible access. For example, you may want to sort some to the top so that you can see them more easily or to the middle or bottom so that you can get to them extra quickly. Now you have rapid access to the applications that you use the most without cluttering up the desktop or the panel. Keep in mind that you can layer the menus as well, if your list of favorites gets too long to readily use on one menu.

Adjust Network Proxy Settings

If you are within a corporate network or use an ISP that requires you to use a proxy server, you can use the Network Proxy Preferences application to direct your Internet traffic through the appropriate server.

Proxy servers take the requests from your computer and retransmit them on your behalf out of your local network and out onto the public Internet. This additional complexity allows for all the Internet traffic from a local area network to be handled by a special machine that has been configured with special security features. Additionally, it can provide caching of frequently requested content. Another common usage of the proxy server is to control the Web content that can be reached by the users. This can be filtered by either the content itself or the domains and IP addresses available to be contacted, or both.

There are three major options for configuration of the proxy settings. The first is the Direct Internet Connection option. This option means that no proxy is used, so all requests made go directly to your default gateway and then get routed out to the Internet. The second option is Manual Proxy Configuration. You can set the same proxy for all protocols or an individual proxy server and port for each protocol. To be able to appropriately set these up, you will need to get the server name and port numbers for each protocol to be proxied from your network administrator. The final setting is the Automatic Proxy Configuration setting. This takes care of almost all the work of setting up the proxy configuration, with the exception that you need to know where to point the autoconfiguration URL. Again, you will need to get this information from your network administrator.

Adjust Network Proxy Settings

1 Click System ➔ Preferences ➔ Network Proxy.

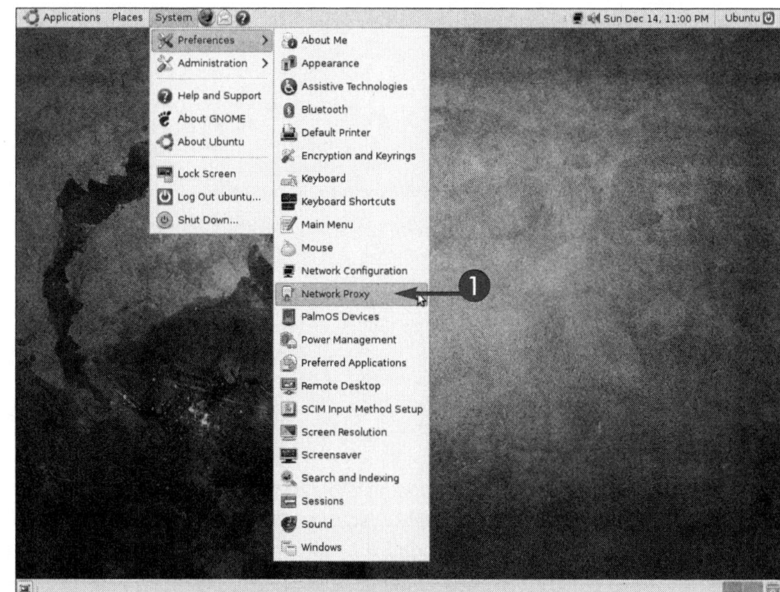

The Network Proxy Preferences application launches.

2 Click Manual Proxy Configuration.

3 Type in your local domain's proxy hostname and port.

4 Click Details.

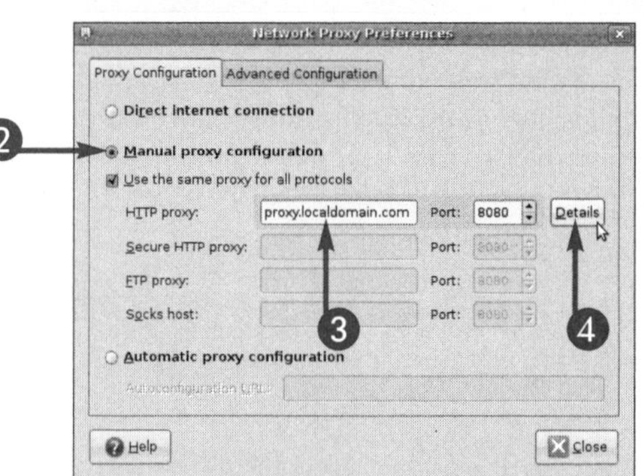

The HTTP Proxy Details dialog box appears.

5. Click Use Authentication.
6. Type in your username for your company's proxy.
7. Type in your password for your company's proxy.
8. Click Close.
9. Click Advanced Configuration.

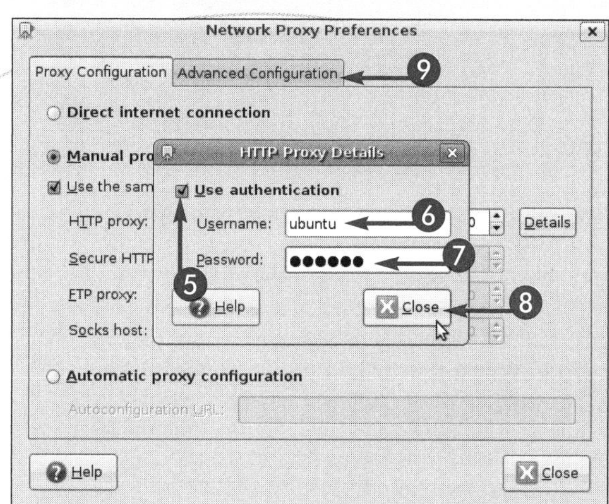

The Advanced Configuration tab appears.

10. Type in the name of your local domain.
11. Click Add.

Now when you connect to your local domain, the proxy will not be used.

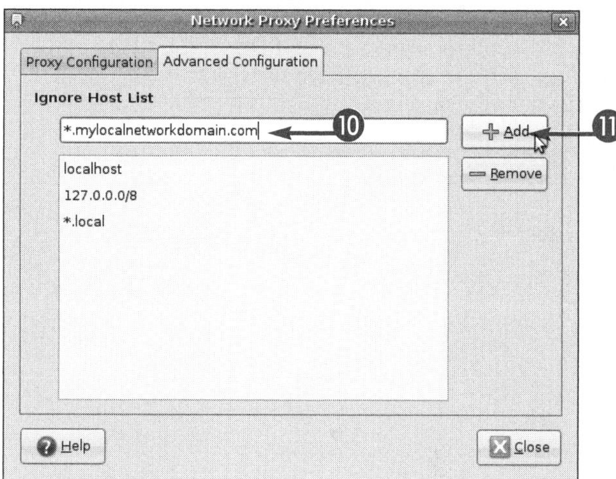

Extra

There are advanced settings for proxy configuration, or rather proxy avoidance. The only setting on the Advanced Configuration tab of the Network Proxy Preferences application is a list of hosts that you do not want to use the proxy in order to connect to. The items in this list can be a simple hostname, a set of hostnames using an asterisk as a wildcard for terms within the domain hierarchy, or an IP address. There are examples of each of these types of specifications in the list by default, and these should not be tampered with. The IP addresses specified may also use netmasks to allow for specifying ranges of IP addresses. The masking notation is in the form of the number of lower order bits of the IP address to ignore. For example, a "/8" at the end of a masked address indicates that the final octet of the IP address should be ignored and any address that matches on the first three octets of the IP address will not use the proxy server.

Manage Session Preferences

If you have special programs that you want to start every time you log into your account, you can specify them by using the Sessions Preferences application.

The Sessions Preferences application is used to configure applications that start when a new session is initiated. A *session* in this context is the child processes spawned from logging into an account from the login screen. When you log in, not only does the core GNOME desktop start but also any applications you have specified. Some of these are subordinate settings of the core applications, whereas others are fully standalone applications that are relatively unaware of whether you are using GNOME or another desktop environment such as KDE. Still others are applets that require services from the GNOME desktop environment but are not merely parts of the GNOME desktop environment.

The Sessions Preferences application presents the user with three tabs. The first tab, Startup Programs, enables you to add or remove the standalone or applet applications to or from your session. The Current Session tab allows you to see and modify the programs that are part of the GNOME desktop environment that are running. This enables you to modify the startup style as well. The Normal style allows for simple startup when the session starts. The Restart style makes the process persistent while the session is active, thus re-spawning the application if it is closed or killed. The Trash style means that the application will not start when a session starts. The final style is Settings, which starts with low startup order and usually is used for storing settings for GNOME and session-managed applications. The last tab, Session Options, enables you to record and automatically restart the currently running applications on the next session startup.

Manage Session Preferences

1. Click System ➔ Preferences ➔ Sessions.

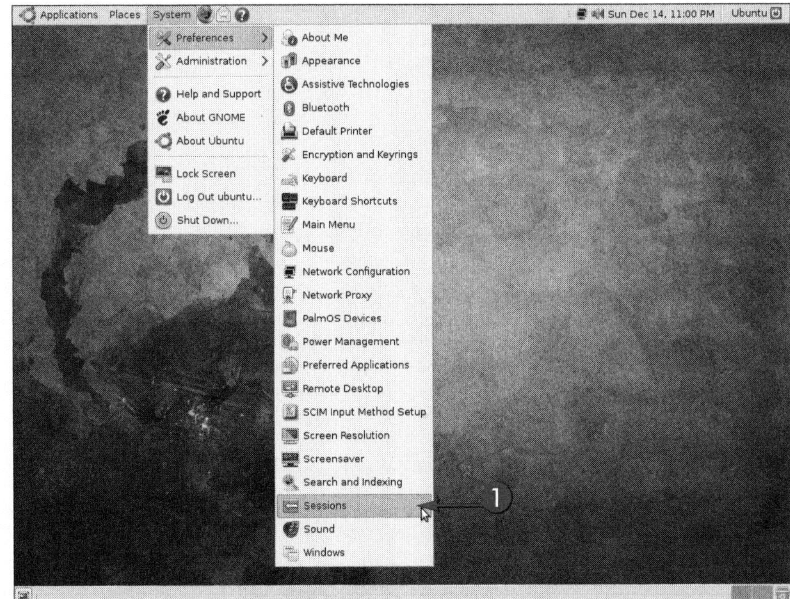

The Sessions Preferences application appears.

2. Click the check boxes next to applications that you want to start when you begin a session.

Note: *You can turn off unused services by unchecking them.*

3. Click Current Session.

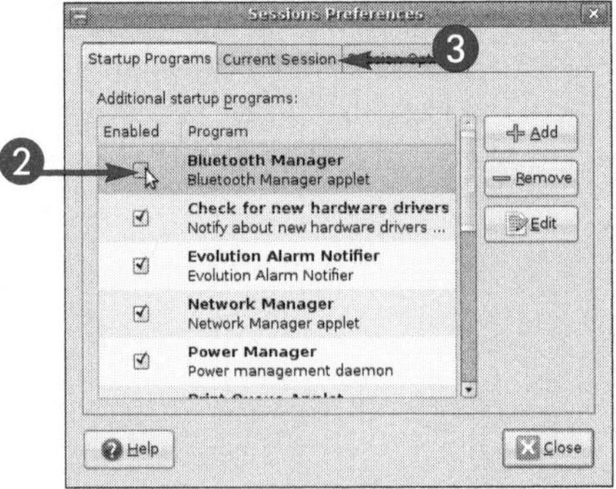

The Current Session tab is displayed.

4. If there is a service that you want to run continuously even if killed or closed, select it and change its startup style to Restart.
5. Click Session Options.

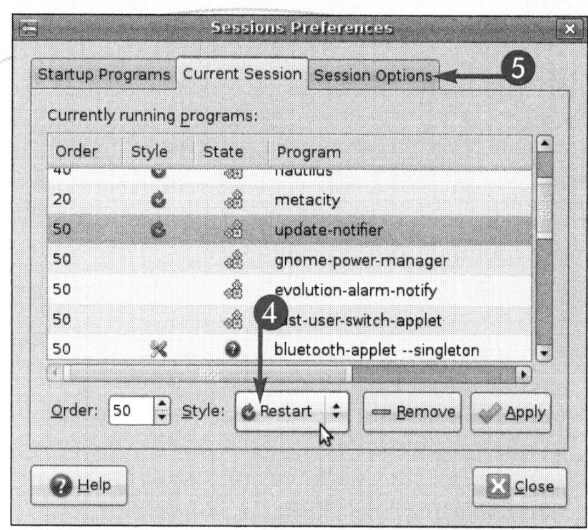

The Session Options tab is displayed.

- Optionally, you can click Automatically Remember Running Applications When Logging Out.

6. Click Close.

If you selected this option, the applications running when you log out will be restarted on the next session startup.

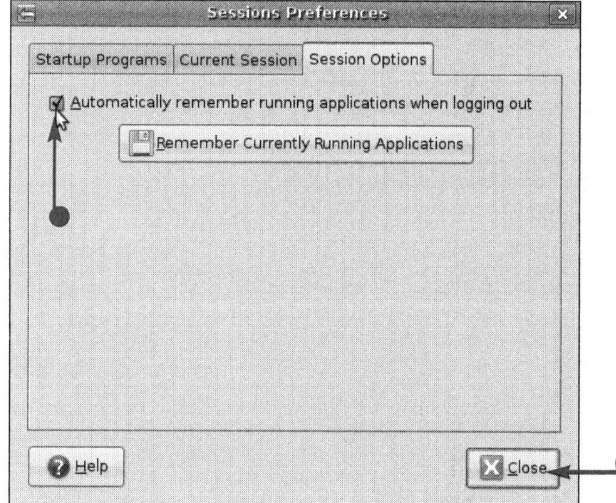

Extra

An example of the embedded type of session application is the fast User Switcher applet, which displays the current user in the panel and enables you to switch quickly to another user session. This is a built-in type of applet; although technically a separate executable, it is part of the desktop environment. An example of something that is started when a session is created but not part of the desktop is the Tracker program, which indexes the files and contents of files on your desktop. This indexing service does not need the desktop environment to run. This type of application does not even need the UI at all. In the middle ground is the Tracker applet, which provides an applet for the desktop environment to access the Tracker service's information.

Applications such as the Tracker that run continuously in the background handling tasks are usually referred to as *daemons*. This term was coined by individuals on MIT's project MAC and dates back to the early sixties. They related the term to a theoretical being suggested in a thought experiment by Maxwell on thermodynamics. The term *daemon* is derived from entities in Greek mythology who are used to mediate tasks for the gods.

Adjust System Sounds and Hardware

You can use the Sound Preferences application to adjust the hardware settings for your sound card.

The first tab is the Devices tab, which enables you to adjust which audio device or API you want to use to play back or record various types of audio. Typically, the Sound Events and the Music and Movies settings for playing back audio will be the same. An occasion where they may not be the same would be if you decided to use MIDI sounds for sound events and wanted to use a different device to render your MIDI sounds. Various devices may appear in the drop-down lists due to many cards having several drivers available under Linux. The most popular implementation is the Advanced Linux Sound Architecture, commonly referred to as *ALSA*. ALSA allows many of the modern features seen in other operating systems. Another popular sound subsystem is the Open Sound System, commonly known as *OSS*. Also on the Devices tab is the choice of what channel of the sound card will be controlled by keyboard volume controls. Primary choices for this would be either the Master volume or the Pulse Code Modulation (PCM) channel.

The second tab of the Sound Preferences application, Sounds, has a list of various system events and enables you to associate certain sound files with each event. Also, you can completely disable system sounds or disable software sound mixing, which, due to the design of the GNOME system sounds, will also disable system sounds.

The final tab is System Beep. It allows you to have a system beep or not and also to enable a visual signaling instead of an audible beep for system alerts. The choices for signaling are either flashing the window title bar or the entire screen.

Adjust System Sounds and Hardware

1. Click System ➔ Preferences ➔ Sound.

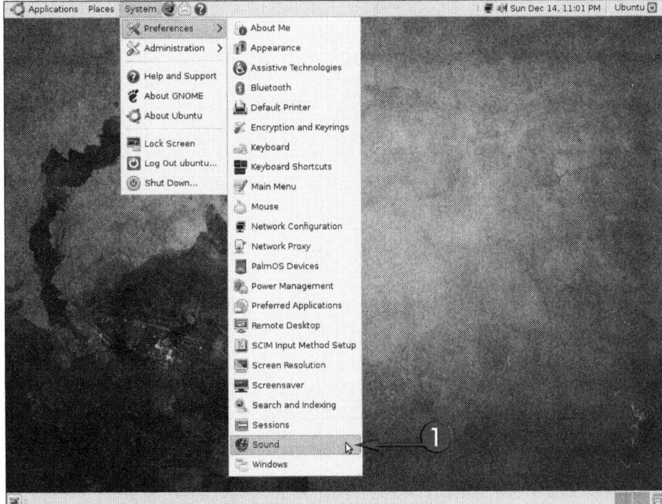

The Sound Preferences application appears.

2. Click Test.

A sound should play out of the speakers.

3. Click the track that you want the default mixer to control.

4. Click Sounds.

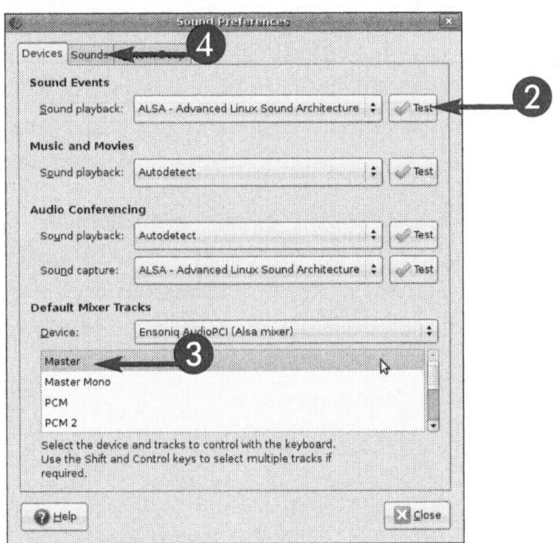

The Sounds tab appears.

5 Verify that Enable Software Sound Mixing (ESD) is checked.

6 Select a sound for an action.

- You can click Play to hear the sound.

7 Click System Beep.

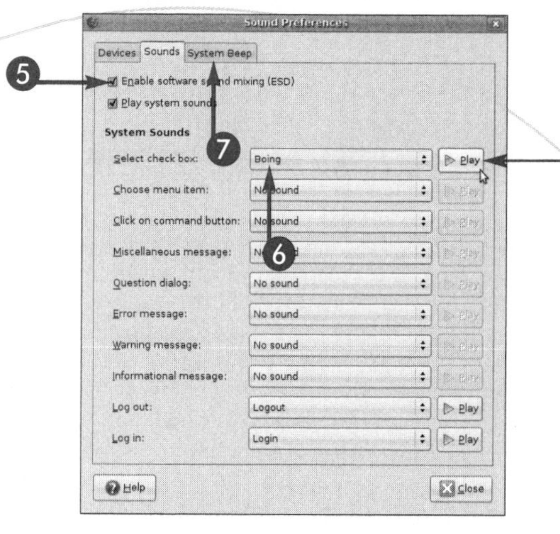

The System Beep tab appears.

8 Click Visual System Beep if you would like a visual signaling for a beep.

9 Click Close.

Your sound settings are applied.

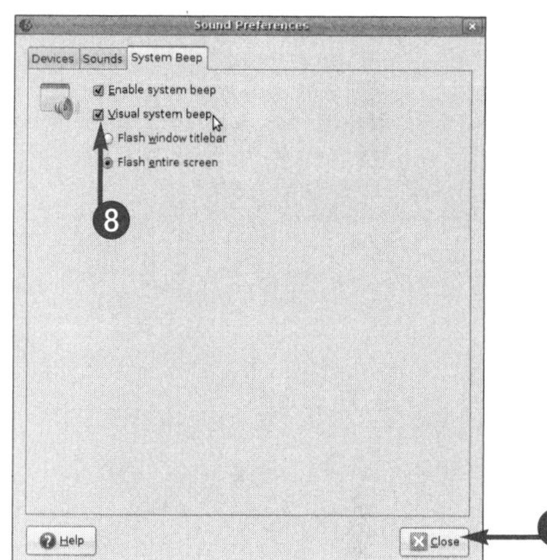

Extra

Open Sound System is a much older sound subsystem on Linux and thus historically has a much more diverse set of drivers for various and sundry sound cards. There are no true standards around sound cards, other than certain compatibilities with de facto standards due to the enormous success of the sound cards by Creative. That being the case, driver support for sound was always a challenge in Linux. The OSS drivers did not allow for more than one program to use the sound card at once, and from this lack of capability sprung up the concept of sound servers or daemons. These servers would accept requests to generate sound output and then mix them in software to form a single audio output to feed into the sound card. Because no one sound server became truly a de facto standard, application programmers had to link in multiple libraries to their code to allow for the various servers or forego the whole thing and just try to write to the sound device directly. This is why ALSA came to be. ALSA is an inherent set of drivers and a standard way to handle sound mixing, especially hardware mixing, which is available in many sound cards today.

Enable Remote Desktop Connections

Remote desktop access is a popular feature on modern desktops. This feature allows a user to connect to and control a desktop as if he or she were sitting in front of it from any network location. You can enable this feature using the Remote Desktop Preferences application. This application presents you with the option to allow other users to view your desktop over the network. A second check box allows you to grant access to actually control the computer remotely.

The lower portion of this dialog box allows for the very necessary addition of a password so that your desktop will not be wide open for anyone to view. If you plan to allow access to the computer remotely while you are not at the machine yourself, you will want to clear the check box requiring the system to ask you for confirmation before accepting connections. If you do not clear this check box, the remote machine would not be allowed to connect unless someone sitting in front of your machine clicked the prompt allowing the connection.

The second tab of this application allows you to set various security features. The first such feature is allowing only local connections. You can also select an alternative port to run the remote connection service on, which provides some security, albeit very little. Requiring encryption is always a good idea, but not enabled by default. You can also cause the screen to lock after a remote user disconnects from the desktop to prevent someone from accessing the desktop at the physically connected screen and keyboard after the remote user has disconnected from it over the network. Also, you can adjust the indication of whether the machine is being access remotely in the status area, either displaying continuously, only when someone is connected, or not at all.

Enable Remote Desktop Connections

1. Click System ➔ Preferences ➔ Remote Desktop.

   The Remote Desktop Preferences dialog box appears.

2. Click Allow Other Users to View Your Desktop.
3. Click Allow Other Users to Control Your Desktop.
4. Uncheck Ask You for Confirmation.
5. Click Require the User to Enter This Password.
6. Type a password.

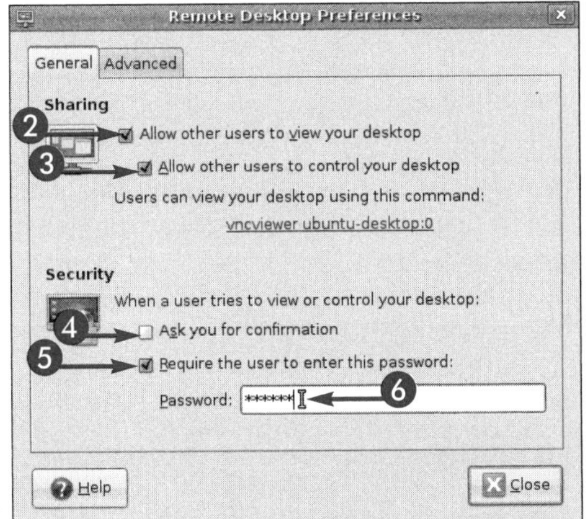

7. Click the Advanced tab.

   The Advanced tab is displayed.

8. Click Require Encryption.
9. Click Lock Screen on Disconnect.
10. Click Close.

    Your machine can now be accessed remotely.

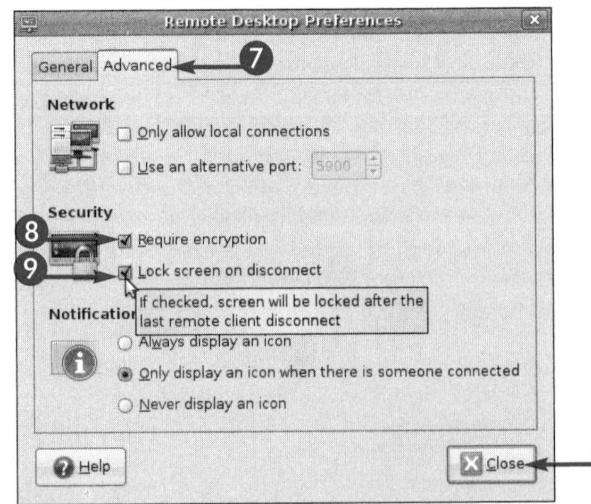

Set Up Bluetooth Preferences

Bluetooth devices such as wireless mice and wireless headsets are fairly common, and recent motherboards have even begun to incorporate Bluetooth adapters on board. Ubuntu supports Bluetooth adapters and devices, and using the Bluetooth Preferences application, you can adjust the services that you want to be running. There are four services available for customization: a service for audio devices such as Bluetooth headsets or speakers, an input service for devices such mice and keyboards, a network service for networking between computers or portable digital assistants (PDAs) at low speed, and a serial service for serial devices for data acquisition or synchronizing Palm PDAs. For the input and audio services, you can enlist available devices or add new ones.

On the General tab, you can specify whether to receive or share files from your Public folder, which is located in your home directory. The protocol typically used for these transfers is Object Exchange, referred to commonly as *OBEX*. This is actually an infrared transmission standard, but because Bluetooth has taken over some of the same types of uses that infrared devices served in the past, this protocol was adopted. A feature that is disabled by default and should remain so unless you have a specific need to enable it is the automatic authorization of incoming requests. This could present a security risk to your computer if enabled. The General tab also includes the option to automatically classify devices into one of the service categories by referring to a database of known hardware. Finally, the General tab has options for the notification in the panel of the current state of your Bluetooth devices and activity.

Set Up Bluetooth Preferences

1. Click System ➔ Preferences ➔ Bluetooth.

   The Bluetooth Preferences dialog box appears.

2. Click a service that you want to be running.
3. Set its status to Running.

   The service starts.

Note: *To stop a service, you can set its status to Stopped.*

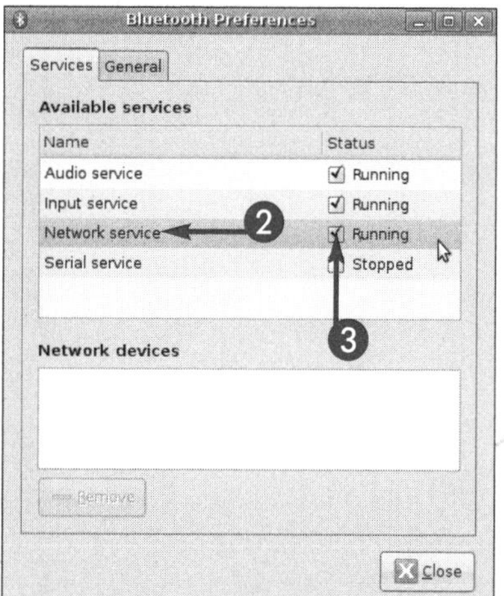

4. Click General.

   The General tab appears.

5. Click Receive Files from Remote Devices.
6. Click Share Files from Public Folder.
7. Click Close.

   The Bluetooth services that you chose will now be running.

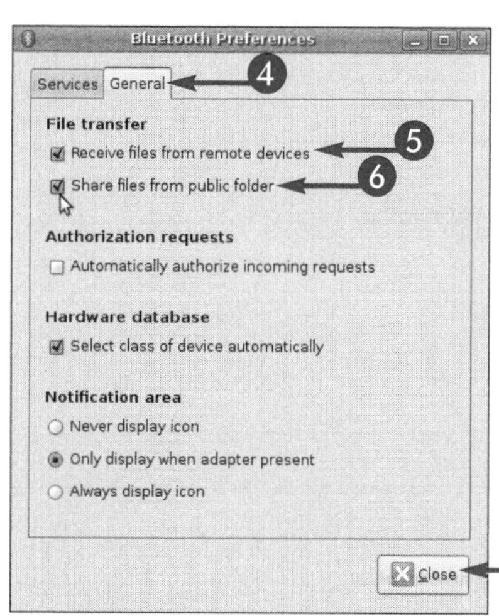

Set Up Encryption and Keyrings

The Password and Encryption Settings application controls how encryption will work during your session. With this application, you can manage critical elements of how encryption keys, passphrases, and the caching of them will be handled.

The application opens to the Password Keyrings tab, which enables you to manage keyrings. *Keyrings* are a way to keep all your passwords and encryption keys centrally managed and secure. There is a default keyring created with your account that will be used whenever you save a password within GNOME applications. This keyring is unlocked for your use when you log in using your password for Ubuntu. You can add keyrings to store information separately, change which keyring within which the application passwords for the session will be stored, and change passwords for keyrings.

The next tab is the Encryption tab. Here you can set a default encryption key to use when encrypting files, folders, or drives or sending either signed or encrypted email. Also, you can specify to always include a copy to yourself of any encrypted email that you send. This is useful since any email that you encrypt using the public key of the recipient of the email, you cannot decrypt. Only the recipient of the email may decrypt the text with their private key. By including yourself, a copy of the email is made for yourself and encrypted using your key.

The PGP Passphrases tab enables you to select whether to and how to cache passphrases in memory. This is useful if you have a lot of encryption going on and do not want to keep typing the passphrase in all the time.

Set Up Encryption and Keyrings

1. Click System ➔ Preferences ➔ Encryption and Keyrings.

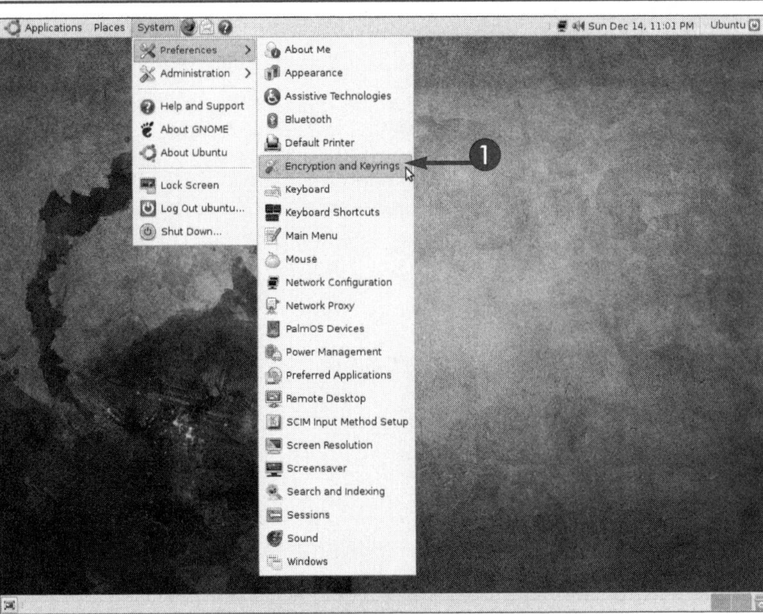

The Password and Encryption Settings application appears.

2. Click Add Keyring.

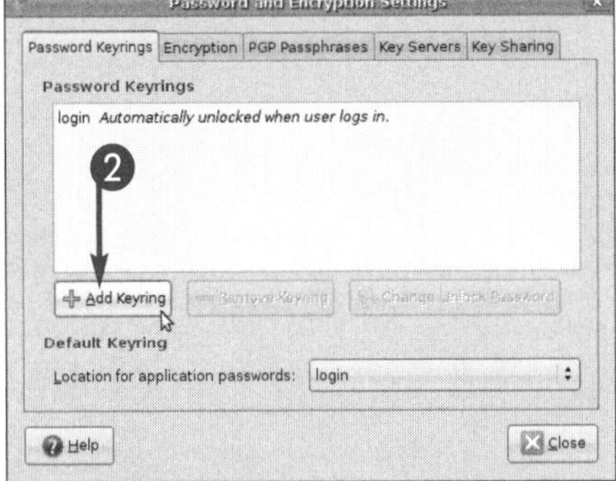

The Add Password Keyring dialog box appears.

3. Type the name for the keyring.
4. Click Add.

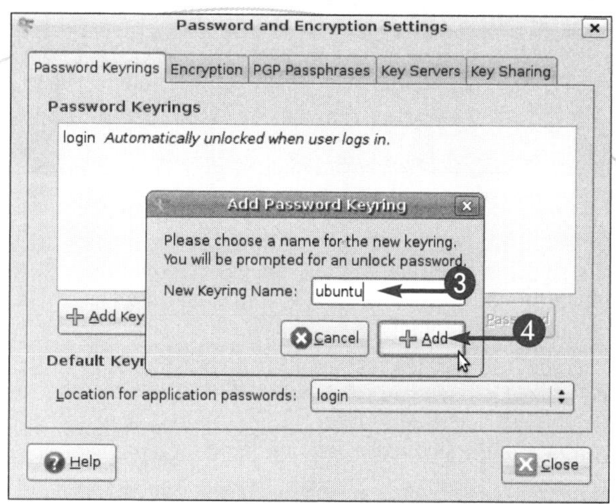

The New Keyring Password dialog box appears.

5. Type the password for the new keyring.
- The New Password Strength bar shows the strength of the new password.
6. Type in the new password again.
7. Click OK.
8. Click Encryption.

Extra

Like many things involving security, caching passphrases is a tradeoff. The passphrase, if kept in memory, is vulnerable to being found by a malicious program. So, keeping the passphrase cached as little as possible is the best practice. You can also select to show an icon in the status area so that you will know if you have any passphrases cached in memory.

Even if finding and extracting the passphrase from memory proves too difficult, an attacker could simply have a program wait for you to supply your passphrase and then, in the background, use the fact that the passphrase is cached to compromise your sensitive data.

Although this sounds a bit paranoid, one of the most dangerous types of malware is the *keylogger*. A keylogger is relatively low-tech. All it does is log your keystrokes and report them to the attacker via your Internet connection. When the attacker has your login and passwords for a site, say your online banking site, he or she can take control of your bank account. These types of attacks are very efficient in terms of effort involved in creating one, damaging to the victim, and unfortunately very common.

continued

Set Up Encryption and Keyrings (continued)

The last two tabs of the Password and Encryption Settings application revolve around the distribution of public keys. Although you would never distribute your private key, it is quite useful to share your public key widely.

The Key Servers tab enables you to publish your public key to centralized servers so that people who want to communicate with you securely can find your public key easily from one of these servers, encrypt the data using that public key, and then send the data to you. Because the data is encrypted with your key, only you can decrypt it.

There is, however, also the possibility of someone impersonating you and uploading a fake key into the key server. This is why keys can be signed. If you have people sign your key, they are attesting that the key they signed in fact belonged to the person whom the key identifies itself to belong to. The more signatures, theoretically, the more you can trust the key.

There are a few default key servers installed with Ubuntu, but you can add more if you want to use a different publisher for your keys. By default, your keys are not published to a server; if you want to publish them, there is a setting on the Key Servers tab to do so. Also on this tab, you can configure the encryption subsystem to automatically query these servers for the keys of people with whom you want to communicate.

The final tab is the Key Sharing tab. This is similar to the Internet-based key servers but is actually implemented with DNS protocols. This is implemented elsewhere under the name Zero-Configuration Wide-Area Service Discovery, Bonjour, or Rendezvous.

Set Up Encryption and Keyrings *(continued)*

The Encryption tab appears.

9 Click here and select a default key.

10 Click When Encrypting, Always Include Myself As a Recipient.

11 Click PGP Passphrases.

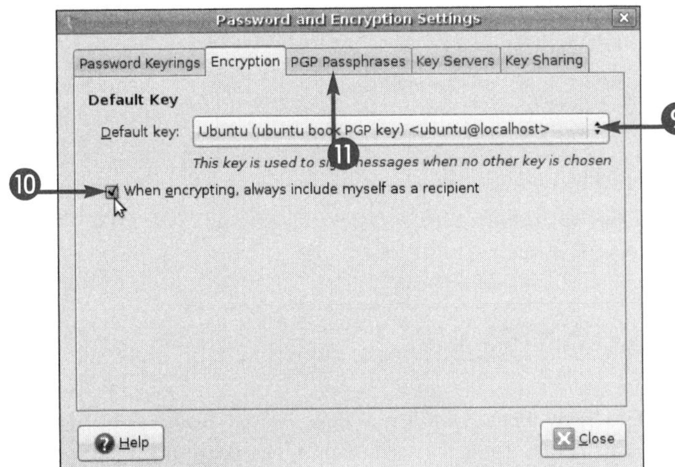

The PGP Passphrases tab appears.

12 Click Show Icon in Status Area When Passphrases Are in Memory.

13 Click Key Servers.

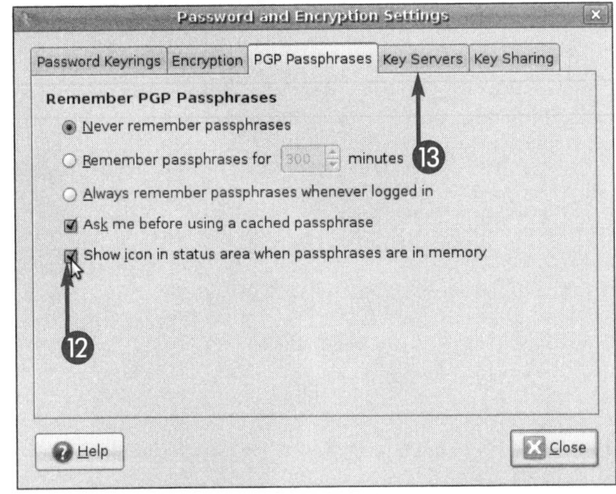

The Key Servers tab appears.

14. Click Automatically Retrieve Keys from Key Servers.
15. Click Key Sharing.

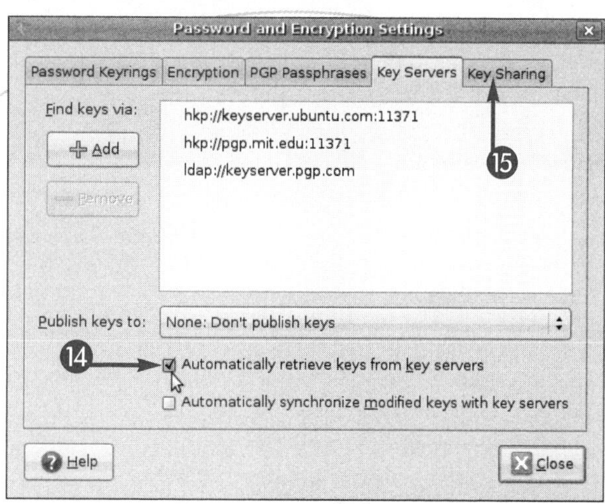

The Key Sharing Tab appears.

16. Click Share My Keys with Others on My Network.
17. Click Close.

Your encryption keyrings and passphrases are set up.

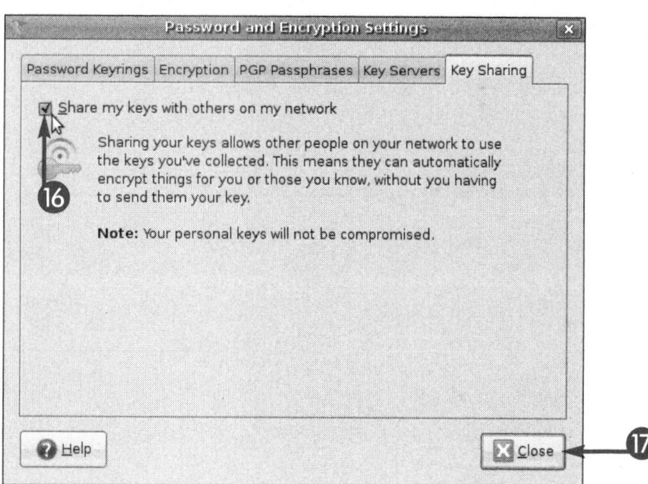

Extra

Key signing can be downright dangerous with people that you do not actually know. By signing someone's key, you are attesting that they are the people they purport to be. Out of the necessity to be very sure whose key you are signing, the key signing party was born. A *key signing party* is a gathering where everyone checks everyone's identification and then agrees to sign each other's keys. This signing usually takes place after the gathering. At the gathering, cryptographically-generated hashes of the public keys are exchanged, as they are more convenient for human purposes. Then the real public key is looked up by this hash value later, to be signed. Although it may be odd to think of in these terms, these events are somewhat social, where like-minded people, concerned about security on the Internet, discuss various aspects of digital security, privacy, and sometimes even public policy. Sometimes these are a good way to break the ice at users' groups meetings, due to the encouragement to interact.

Adjust Keyboard Settings

The absolutely most used input interface is the keyboard. You can adjust the preferences of how this critical input device functions by using the Keyboard Preferences application.

There are many different options for the keyboard. The General tab of the Keyboard Preferences application enables you to adjust the repetition of keystokes when a key is held down. This behavior is useful for navigation in documents or to produce a repeated series of characters. The adjustments around this functionality are the delay until the repetition begins and the speed at which the repeated keystrokes appear. Also, the General tab allows you to adjust whether and how fast the cursor blinks within active text fields.

The Layouts tab enables you to adjust the model and layout of the keyboard. Additionally, you can have a separate keyboard layout per window, thus allowing you to type in, say, Russian within OpenOffice Writer, while browsing the Web with Firefox using the default keyboard settings for the machine. You can switch keyboard layouts for such a purpose using the Keyboard Indicator applet.

The Accessibility tab allows you to enable or disable the ability to use keyboard shortcuts to turn on accessibility features such as slow keys and bounce keys. *Slow keys* is an accessibility feature to only allow long keystrokes that are longer than a certain duration. *Bounce keys* are quite the opposite in that the Bounce Keys feature filters out redundant presses of the same key within a certain period.

The Mouse Keys tab allows you to enable the use of the numeric keypad to control the mouse cursor. This can be handy if you are without a mouse for some reason.

The final tab is the Typing Break tab. This tab enables you to enforce a break from using the computer to give your hands a rest periodically.

Adjust Keyboard Settings

1. Click System ➔ Preferences ➔ Keyboard.

   The Keyboard Preferences dialog box appears.

2. Click and move this slider to set the cursor blink speed.
3. Click Layouts.

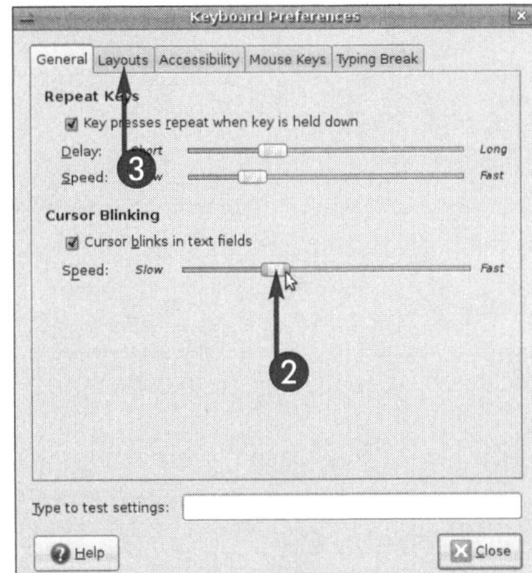

   The Layouts tab appears.

4. Click here and select the model of your keyboard.
5. Click Accessibility.

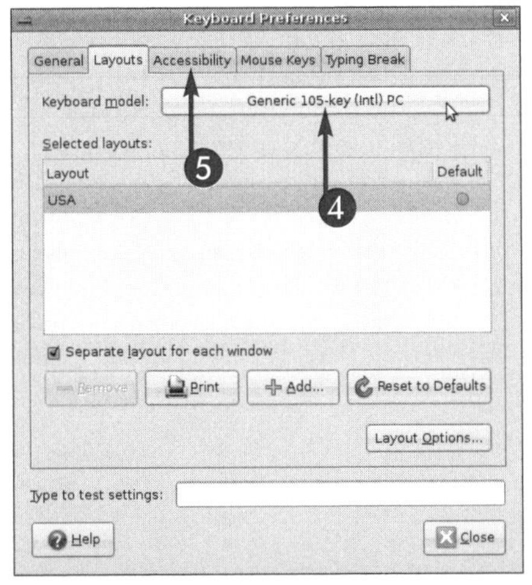

The Accessibility tab appears.

6. Click here to enable turning accessibility features on and off from the keyboard.

7. Click Mouse Keys.

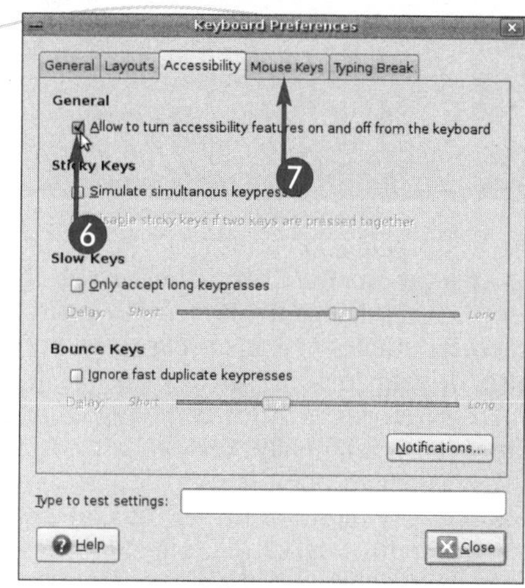

The Mouse Keys tab appears.

8. Click here to enable controlling the mouse pointer using the keyboard.

9. Click Close.

Your keyboard settings take effect.

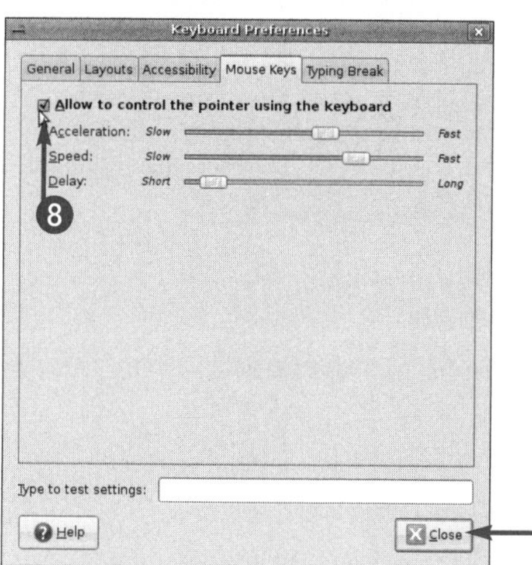

Extra

Although the predominant keyboard layout is the familiar QWERTY keyboard, there are others, and not just for internationalization. The very first typewriters had the keys all arranged alphabetically. Due to the mechanical nature of the first typewriters, the keys would stick and jam if they did not have enough of a time interval between strikes against the ribbon, allowing the first hammer to move out of the way before the next hammer hit. Consequently, the keys were rearranged physically to create less likelihood that two hammers would be in the strike zone at the same time. This evolved into the QWERTY keyboard we have today. Other competing layouts, predominantly the Dvorak layout, were based on the frequencies of certain letters within the English language. By placing the most popular letters on the middle row, also known as the *home row*, typing efficiency could be greatly enhanced. Although the Dvorak layout was more efficient, by the time the mechanical design issues were cleared up, the QWERTY keyboard had been cemented as the de facto standard, and the Dvorak layout remains more of an obscurity.

Set the Preferred Applications

The Preferred Applications settings specify the default applications used for various types of activity. The first tab of the Preferred Applications dialog box, Internet, enables you to choose what browser you want to use for your Internet surfing. On Ubuntu, the default is the Firefox browser, which is the predominant open-source browser. Additionally, this tab allows you to set your default email application, which by default on Ubuntu is Evolution. For either of these, you can also set a custom command as the application to handle these types. The %s in the Command box represents the path and filename of the file or URL you are opening.

The Multimedia tab enables you to pick the default application for the playing of music or video files. The default is the Rhythmbox music player, but as an alternative, the Totem Movie Player is also available.

The System tab allows you to pick the terminal emulator that will be launched by the desktop environment whenever you see the check box Run in Terminal or if you launch the terminal accessory application. This is a text window that allows command-line access to the operating system. The Execute Flag setting on this tab enables you to specify the command-line option that allows for passing a command to a terminal window. It varies by the terminal emulator.

The Accessibility tab allows you to pick the subsystems for accessibility and whether to start them up at the beginning of a session or not. The default visual accessibility subsystem is the Orca screen reader. Alternatively, you can specify just the magnifier options without the reader options. The Mobility section enables you to select options for alternative input, such as an onscreen keyboard.

Set the Preferred Applications

1. Click System ➔ Preferences ➔ Preferred Applications.

   The Preferred Applications dialog box appears.

2. Click here and select a Web browser.
3. Click here and select a mail reader.

- You can click Open Link in New Tab to have clicked links open a new tab in the browser.

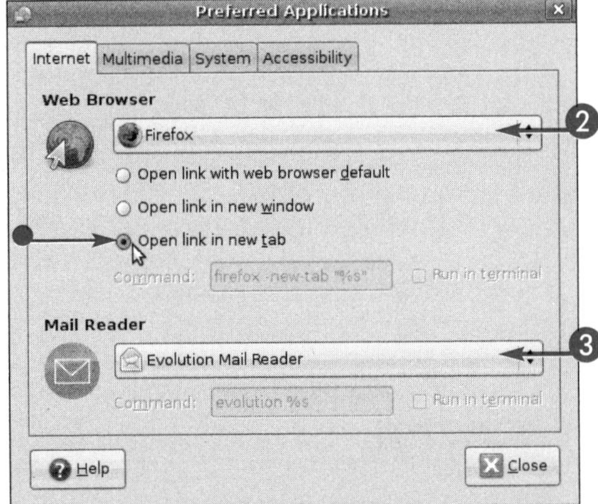

4. Click Multimedia.

   The Multimedia tab appears.

5. Click here and select a media player.
6. Click System.

The System tab appears.

7 Click here and select a terminal program.

8 Click the Accessibility tab.

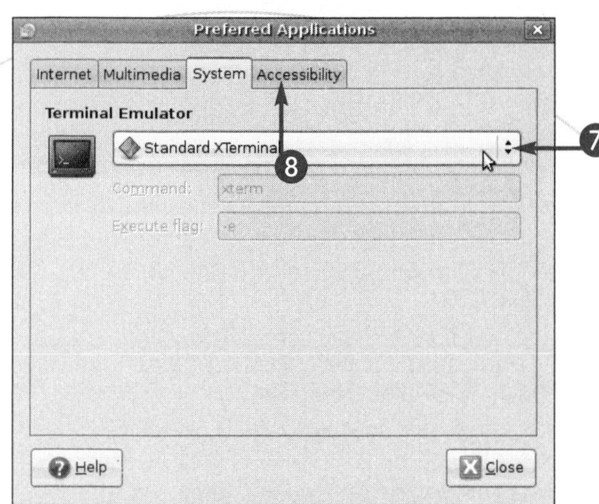

The Accessibility tab appears.

9 Click here and select a visual accessibility subsystem.

10 Click here if you want it to run at the start of a session.

11 Click Close.

Your default applications are set.

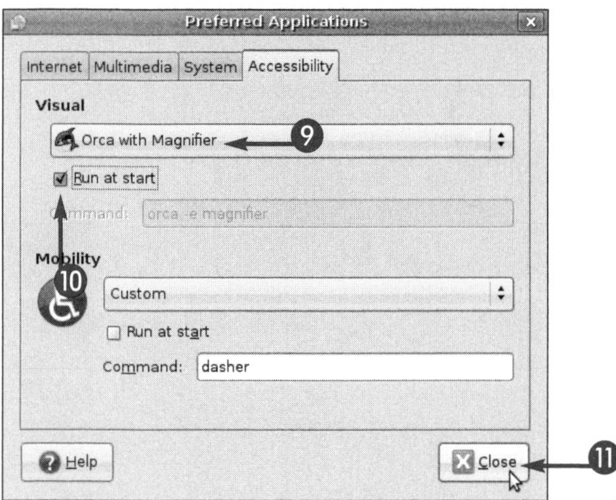

Apply It

You can create your own custom preferred application types by using the Custom setting of the selections in the Preferred Applications dialog box. But in order to launch the application with the appropriate parameters, you have to know a few key things: the command line of your application and the special token %s, which will be substituted by the media filename to open.

Here is an example: The command line for the multimedia player GMplayer looks as follows:

```
/usr/bin/gmplayer %s
```

Note that this player is not installed by default on Ubuntu, but it is readily available from the Applications → Add/Remove option of the main menu.

Change Personal Details with About Me

Changing your personal information is especially important on machines that have multiple users. You can change your personal information using the About Me application.

This application enables you to change details about yourself that an administrator may need to know or that may need to be used by various applications.

The Contact tab allows you to store all your common contact information, starting with email addresses and then telephone numbers for various places you might be reached. The final section of this tab can record all the various instant messaging logins that you have by protocol/platform.

The Address tab enables you to record home and work addresses.

The Personal Info tab enables you to record your personal Web page address, your personal Web log address, and the location of your published calendar on the Web. It also allows you to record various aspects about your current employment.

Also, the About Me application allows you to change your password. This is something that you should do periodically. First you must prove that you are in fact the owner of the account and not someone who happens to have found an unlocked session. You do this by providing the login password for the account and then authenticating. After that, you are allowed to enter a new password. New passwords have to be entered twice because the actual characters are never shown. Without this double entry, you might mistype the password and then have it changed to your mistake; this way, you could accidentally lock yourself out of your account.

Change Personal Details with About Me

1. Click System ➔ Preferences ➔ About Me.

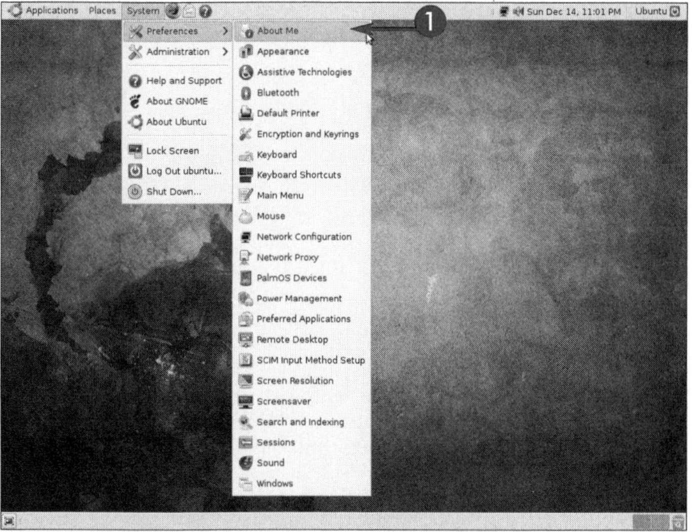

The About Me application appears.

2. Type in your contact information.
3. Add any instant messaging logins that you want to include.
4. Click Address.

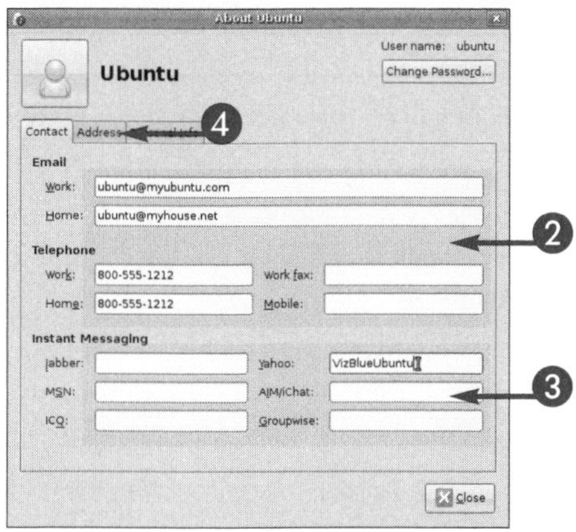

The Address tab appears.

5. Type in your address information.
6. Click Personal Info.

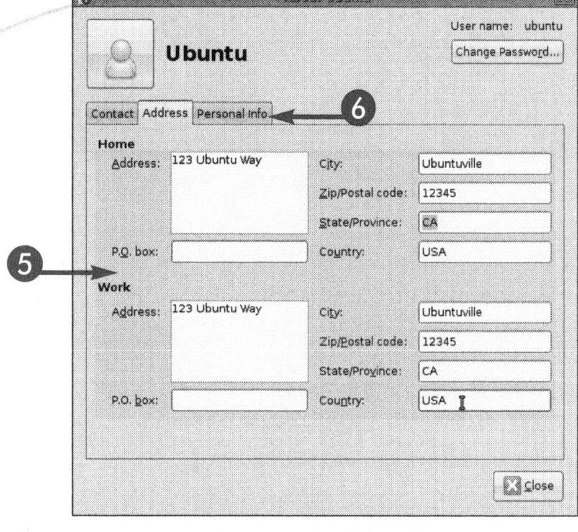

The Personal Info tab appears.

7. Type in any personal information that you want to include.
8. Click Close.

Your About Me information is saved.

Extra

Never give your password to anyone. This may seem a bit obvious, but it is almost always a common problem in work situations. Many times people will share a password with a coworker when they plan to be out or are already out and are being contacted to do something remotely. Although it seems that it may be fairly innocent, this can be somewhat catastrophic for you. This is because once you give your password to someone else, anything he or she does on the computer will look like it was done by you. This can lead to all sorts of mischief from simple email blunders to full-scale fraud. It is by far a better practice to request access be granted to perform a certain task rather than for you to forgo your own security by sharing a password. Additionally, changing your password often will help to keep your password safe. If someone is trying to use a brute-force attack against your account, he or she will have made a number of attempts to log in as you, hopefully failing. When you change your password, your account becomes a moving target and is thus harder to hack.

Access Assistive Technologies Controls

The Assistive Technologies application enables you to rapidly access the controls of all the various assistive technologies within Ubuntu from a single point. This application only has a few functions of its own. For most of its function, it directs you to the controls for areas such as the Accessibility tab of the Keyboard Preferences application, the Login Window Preferences application, and the Preferred Applications settings.

Assistive technologies allow persons with specific disabilities to use computers and applications on those computers either more easily or even at all. Ubuntu has several features in the default install that assist users with input to the computer or determining the output on the screen. For input, there is the onboard onscreen keyboard. This enables you to essentially type with whatever pointing device you have. Conversely, you can use the keyboard to move the mouse pointer using the Mouse Keys feature under the Keyboard Preferences application. For reading the screen content, the Orca application can perform text to speech of any window or the desktop.

The two settings that are actually part of the Assistive Technologies Preferences application itself are the Enable Assistive Technologies check box, which allows you to enable the assistive technologies within the GNOME desktop, and the Password Dialogs As Normal Windows check box, which enables you to use an onscreen keyboard with the gksu utility that asks you for your password to do administrative tasks.

Although assistive technologies are primarily aimed at users with disabilities, certain features such as the onscreen keyboard capability can help anyone to use a tablet PC properly.

Access Assistive Technologies Controls

1. Click System ➔ Preferences ➔ Assistive Technologies.

   The Assistive Technologies Preferences application opens.

2. Click Enable Assistive Technologies.
3. Click Password Dialogs As Normal Windows.
4. Click Preferred Applications.

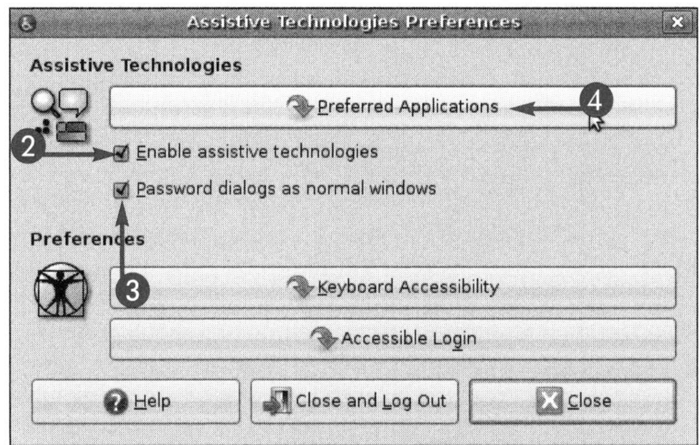

   The Preferred Applications dialog box appears.

5. Click Accessibility.

   The Accessibility tab becomes active.

6. Adjust the visual and mobility accessibility options.
7. Click Close.

   You are returned to the Assistive Technologies Preferences dialog box.

8. Click Keyboard Accessibility.

The Keyboard Preferences dialog box appears.

9. On the Accessibility tab, adjust the keyboard accessibility options.

10. Click Close.

    You are again returned to the Assistive Technologies Preferences dialog box.

11. Click Accessible Login.

Note: *If you are prompted for your password, provide it.*

The Login Window Preferences dialog box appears.

12. On the Accessibility tab, click Enable Accessible Login.

13. Adjust the accessible login options.

14. Click Close.

    Assistive technologies are now set up to be used.

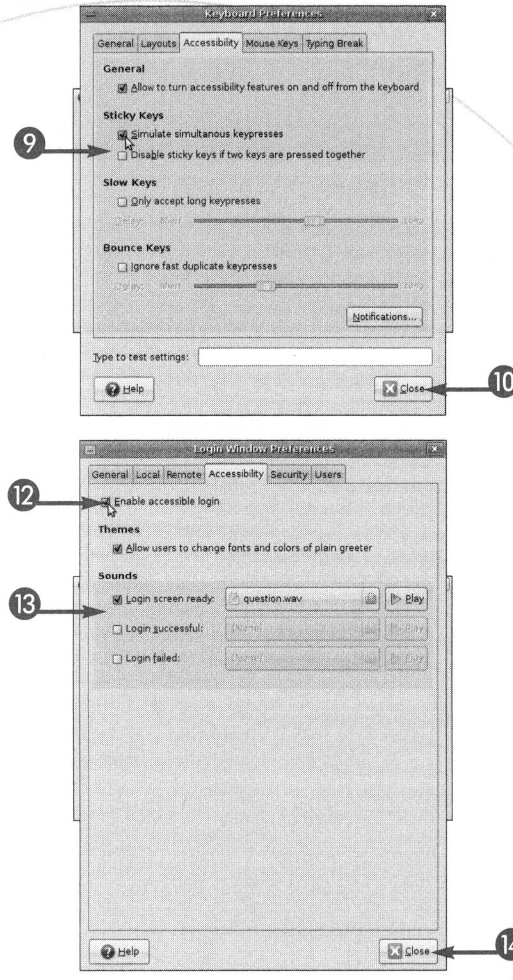

Apply It

To get an idea of what using a computer would be like for a mildly visually impaired person using the screen magnifier, you can start the magnifier manually to try it out without actually going through the configuration process for fully setting up assistive technology support. To launch the magnifier application, press Alt+F2 and type this command:

```
magnifier -m -f
```

Then click Run. This launches the magnifier in full-screen mode and follows the mouse around as you use the computer. The default magnification is 200%. To end the magnifier, press Alt+F2 and type this:

```
killall magnifier
```

Then click Run. This will kill all magnifier processes and return you to your normal display.

Using the magnifier full screen on a second monitor provides a very good magnifier solution, whereby a portion of the contents of one screen at normal resolution is magnified full screen on the second screen.

Configure PalmOS Devices

Connecting your PDA to Ubuntu is easy with the PalmOS Devices application. You launch the PalmOS Devices application, and it takes you into a wizard for gnome-pilot to configure the communication parameters. Over the course of the life of Palm devices, there have been many improvements in peripheral communication. The initial pilots used simple RS-232 serial communication ports. If you have a serial Palm or Visor, you can still communicate with it with an RS-232 cable or even infrared communication. But for most modern Palm-based devices, the communication method of choice is a USB cable. There are actually four options available to you: Serial, USB, IrDA, and Network. If you are connecting to a modern PDA with a USB connection, use the usb: Device option. If you forget to select this option, the wizard will attempt to connect with the older, serial USB /dev/pilot device, then fail, and then suggest the usb: Device option instead. The wizard also asks you whether the device has been connected to a PC before. Each Palm device gets a unique ID assigned to it the first time it is synced. This is to identify the device to the computer, and each device gets its own store for all the synced information. If your device has been synced with another machine, it will have this ID, and gnome-pilot will import the unique ID of the Palm device instead of creating a new one. Then it will allow you to set up a name for the device and finish the setup.

Configure PalmOS Devices

1. Click System ➔ Preferences ➔ PalmOS Devices.

   The gnome-pilot Settings application launches.

2. Click Forward.

   The Device Settings page appears.

3. Type a name for the sync device.
4. Click an interface type.
5. Adjust the device setting to match your hardware.
6. Adjust the transfer speed.
7. Click Forward.

   The PDA Identification page appears.

8. Answer the question of whether the PDA has been synced before.
9. Click Forward.

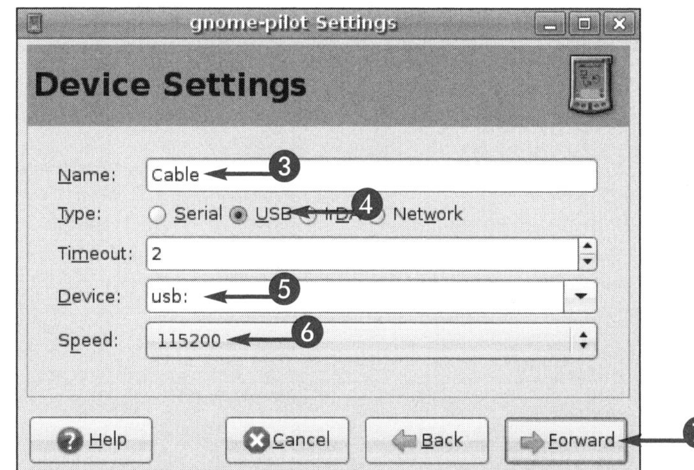

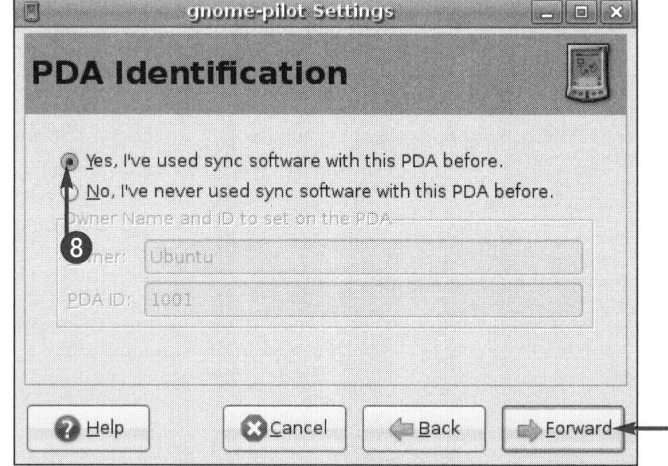

The Initial Sync page appears.

10. Click Forward.

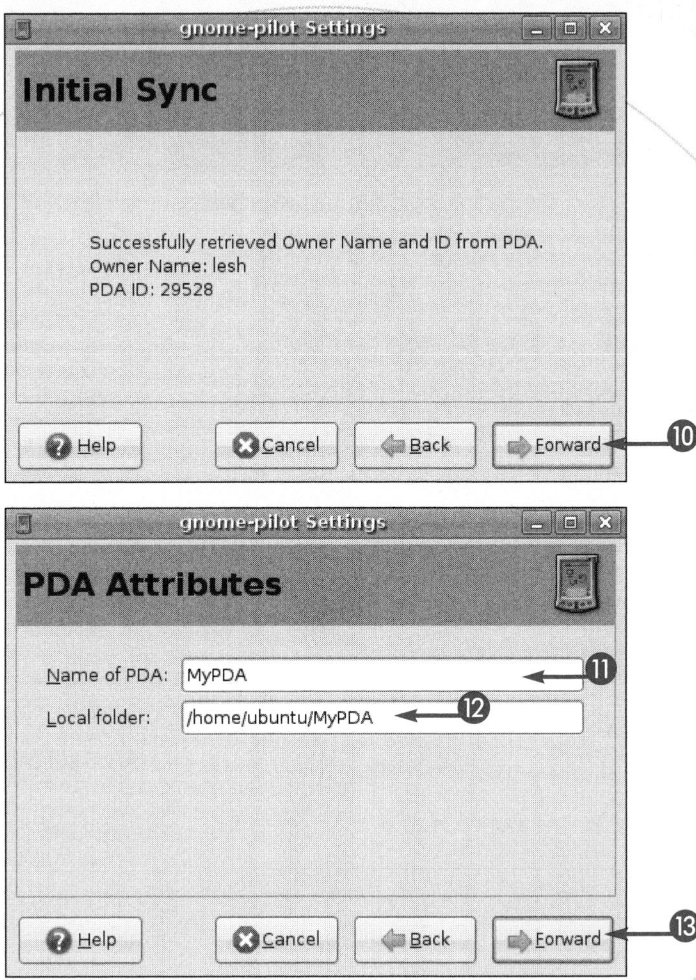

The PDA Attributes page appears.

11. Type a name for your PDA.

12. Type a path to a location to store your PDA information.

13. Click Forward.

Extra

In order to best use your pilot, you should add the Pilot applet to your panel as well. This applet enables you to restart the gpilot daemon, which runs in the background and waits for sync requests from your Palm device. It also allows you to initiate a restore operation to your device, should it lose all its information or have the information contained within it corrupted. The applet will change colors depending on the communication status of the gpilot daemon with your Palm device. If the daemon is not running, the applet will appear red and black. If the daemon is paused, the applet will be yellow and black. If the daemon is running but idle, it will be black and white. During a sync, the applet will appear green and black. Also during a sync, a dialog box will appear on the screen and show the progress of the sync.

continued

Configure PalmOS Devices (continued)

After setup, the gnome-pilot Settings window appears and allows you to enable any synchronization applications, also known as *conduits,* that you want to use. There are a number of conduits available — the most important of which is the Backup conduit, which keeps a selectable number of backups of your device on your PC. ECalendar is a conduit that synchronizes your Palm's calendar with the calendar of the Evolution application. The EMemos conduit syncs the memos of the Palm with the Memos feature of Evolution. The EAddress conduit syncs your Palm's address book with Evolution's address book. EToDo is the final Evolution sync conduit, and it syncs the ToDo list on the Palm device with Evolution's Tasks list. The Backup conduit shows that not all conduits interact with Evolution, although most of them do as Evolution is the default personal information manager (PIM) on Ubuntu. The MemoFile conduit syncs your memos from your Palm device to a set of text files in folders under your Home directory or any other directory that you choose to record your sync information to. Most of the conduits have a one-time action available under Settings that enables you to overwrite either the PC or the device with the contents of the other. This can be useful if your data in a given application becomes corrupted or if you simply want to revert to an earlier state. Additionally, many of the conduits have options of how the sync should happen, such as whether to overlay the information on the PC with the contents of the device each time, or vice versa, or a true sync via the merging of information.

Configure PalmOS Devices *(continued)*

The Success page appears.

14 Click Apply.

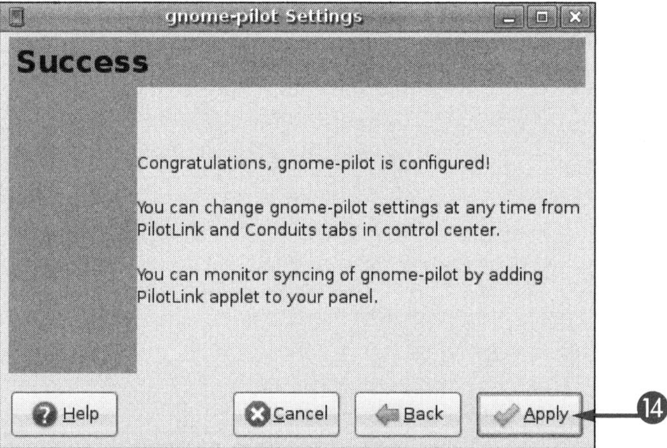

The gnome-pilot Settings dialog box appears.

15 Click Conduits.

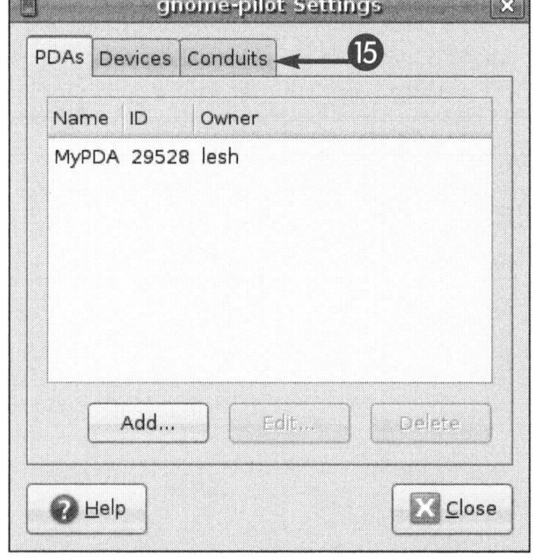

The Conduits tab appears.

16 Click a conduit to configure and click Settings.

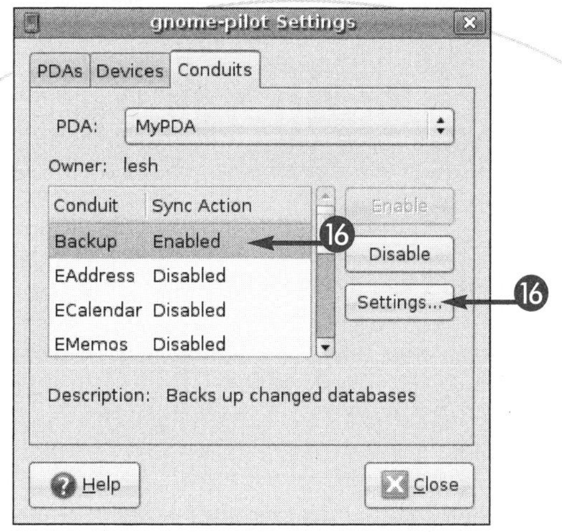

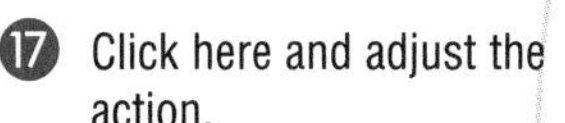

17 Click here and adjust the action.

18 Adjust the conduit-specific settings.

19 Click OK.

You are returned to the gnome-pilot Settings dialog box.

You can repeats steps **16** to **19** for as many conduits as needed.

20 Click Close in the gnome-pilot Settings dialog box when finished.

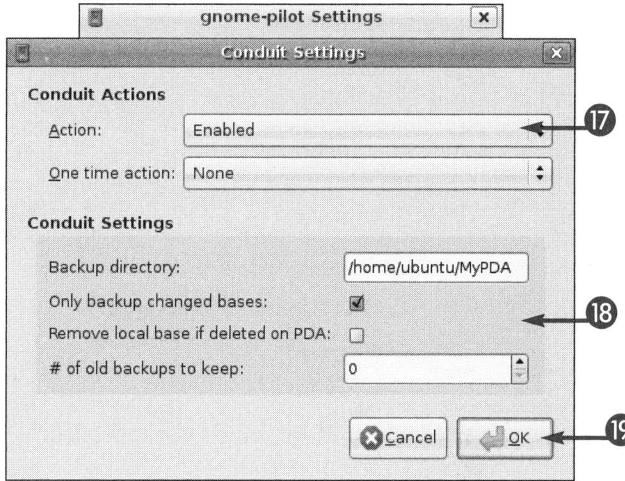

Extra

Although Palm devices in general have waned in popularity in recent years, they have remained strong among Linux users due to the early support within the operating system for Palm devices. Linux can also sync with Windows CE/ Mobile devices, but the support came about much later than for Palm devices.

Add to this the fact that Palm is investing in developing its next-generation OS based on Linux, and there is the high likelihood that Palm devices will be the PDA of choice for Linux users for some time to come.

If you do not want to rely on Evolution for all your PIM needs and want something more similar to the PalmDesktop shipped with your Palm device, you may want to investigate one of the work-alike packages available under Add/Remove Programs. JPilot and KPilot both resemble the original PalmDesktop application and allow for a tight integration with the Palm device.

Configure Removable Drives and Media

The Removable Drives and Media Preferences application enables you to modify the applications that automatically run when a removable device is connected to your machine.

The first tab of this application is the Cameras tab, in which you can specify commands to be run when various types of cameras are connected. The first camera type listed is digital cameras, which, when they are USB-connected, essentially present some sort of flash memory interface to the machine.

The second type of camera category is the digital video camera, which uses an IEE1394 interface also known more commonly as *FireWire.* Many video cameras with the miniDV cassettes have this type of interface.

The final camera type is the Web camera. These again are USB cameras, but they are built for continuous transmission of pictures to the PC and do not store any images themselves.

The second tab is the PDAs tab, on which you can configure the command that should run when a PDA device is connected to the machine. They break down into two types — the PalmOS type of device, which has support already built into the Ubuntu distribution, and the PocketPC type, which can be supported but does not come installed on Ubuntu by default.

The next tab is the Printers & Scanners tab, on which you can configure a specific command to run when you connect a printer or a scanner.

The final tab is the Input Devices tab. This enables you to fire up any special application that you want when a specific type of input device is connected. The categories of devices here are USB mice, USB keyboards, and tablets.

Configure Removable Drives and Media

1. Click System ➔ Preferences ➔ Removable Drives and Media.

   The Removable Drives and Media Preferences dialog box appears.

2. Enable actions for your camera devices.
3. Click PDAs.

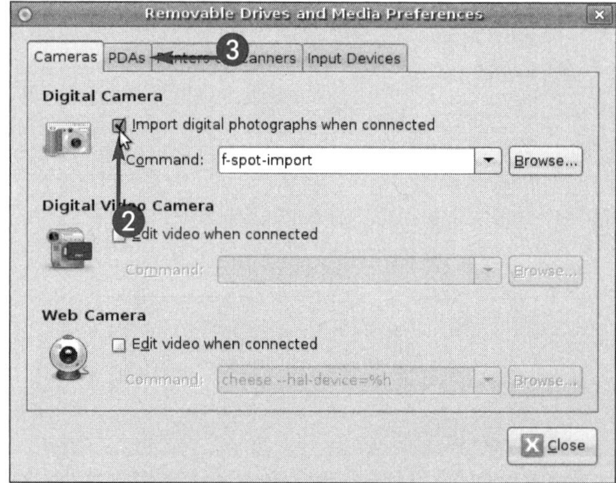

The PDAs tab appears.

4. Enable actions for your PDA devices.
5. Click Printers & Scanners.

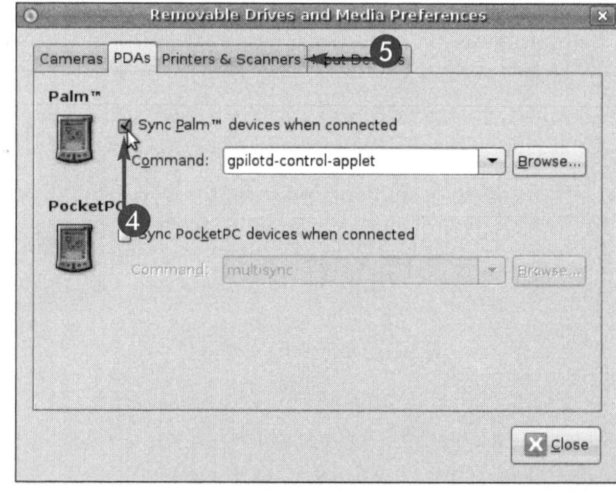

The Printers & Scanners tab appears.

6 Enable actions for your printer and scanner devices.

7 Click Input Devices.

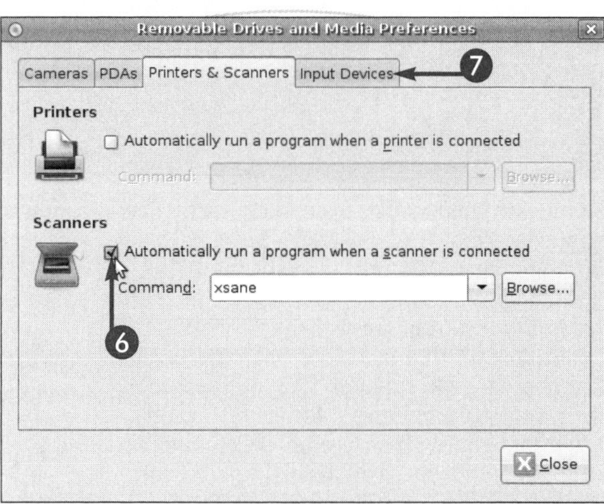

The Input Devices tab appears.

8 Enable or disable actions for your mouse, keyboard, and tablet devices.

9 Click Close.

Your removable devices will now interact with your machine as you have prescribed.

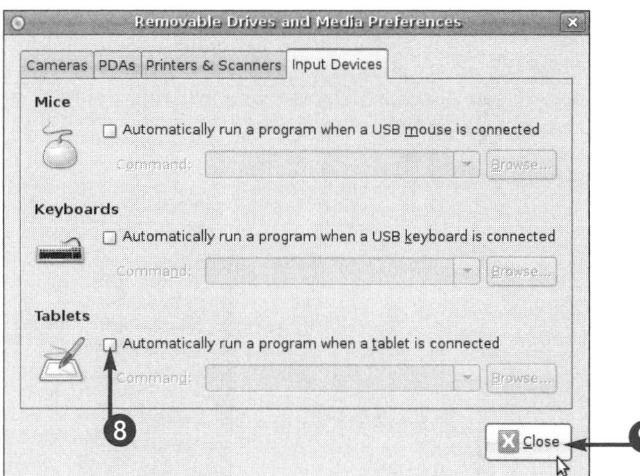

Extra

In some cases, there is no adverse effect from not using the settings in the Removable Drives and Media Preferences dialog box, but if you want a particular application to run whenever a device is connected, you will need this preferences application. You also may need to check that the prepopulated settings will work for you. The Digital Camera section of the Cameras tab, for example, has the F-Spot photo management application as the default when a digital camera is connected. This will cause it to launch and try to import the new photos into your photo library. Also, there is a default on the Web Camera section that will try to launch the Cheese photo/video application when a Webcam is connected. This is not enabled by default, however, with good reason. The Cheese application is not installed by default on Ubuntu.

The PDAs tab has defaults of running the gpilotd-control-applet when a PalmOS device is connected. This application allows you to configure the conduits that control synchronization with the PDA. The PDAs tab also includes a PocketPC default of multisync, which also requires installation of multisync on the Ubuntu system before it can work, as multisync is not installed by default.

Set Up SCIM Input Methods

To type Chinese, Japanese, or Korean character sets or special characters from European languages, you can adjust the SCIM settings with the SCIM Input Method Setup application. The interface of the SCIM application looks different from most of the GNOME preferences applications in that instead of tabs, the SCIM developers have chosen a file explorer–like interface to navigate between configuration areas. FrontEnd's Global Setup section presents you with a page on which you can specify the keyboard layout that you are using. You can choose whether to have the pre-edit string you are composing show in the client window or a separate floating window. And you can configure if the same input method should be shared across all applications or if each application should be able to have its own independent input method. Also, you can adjust the hotkeys that control how the input methods are activated and switching between them.

IMEngine's Global Setup section lists the installed input method engines; if you have not installed any specific language support other than English, the list will be quite sparse. On this screen, you can expand the list that is there and enable or disable the specific input methods. You can also select filters and hotkeys for the different IMEngines.

The Panel's GTK section enables you to configure the SCIM applet that appears in the status area of the panel. With this, you can enter the SCIM setup more easily and also reload settings after changes have been made. In this dialog box, you can also change aspects of the input window used for pre-edit information.

Set Up SCIM Input Methods

1. Click System ➔ Preferences ➔ SCIM Input Method Setup.

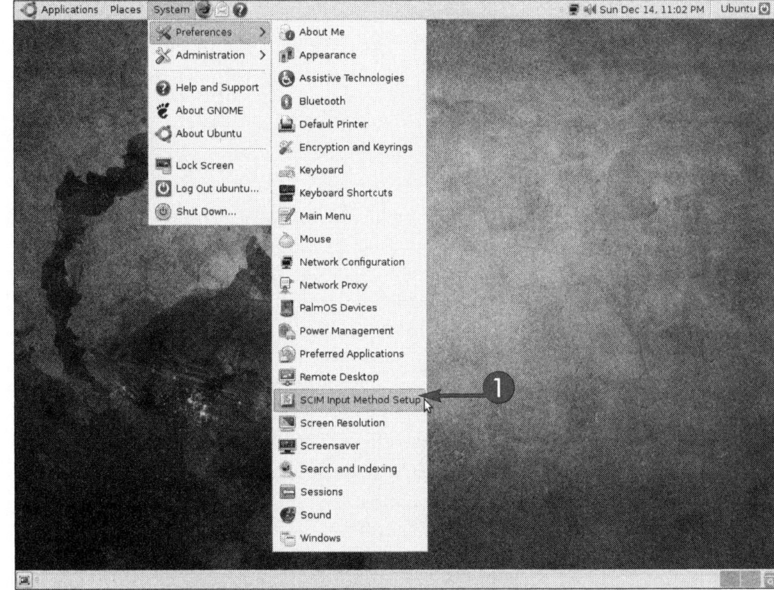

The SCIM Input Method Setup application launches.

2. Click Global Setup under FrontEnd.

The FrontEnd Global Setup page appears.

3. Click here and choose your current keyboard.

4. Click Global Setup under IMEngine.

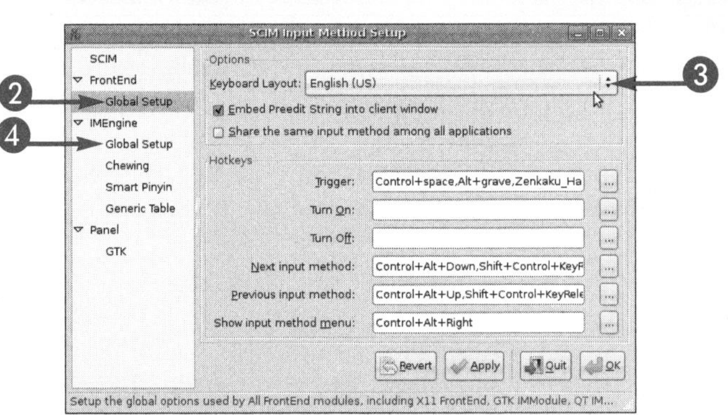

The IMEngine Global Setup page appears.

5. Verify that all languages you want to use are checked.

6. Click GTK.

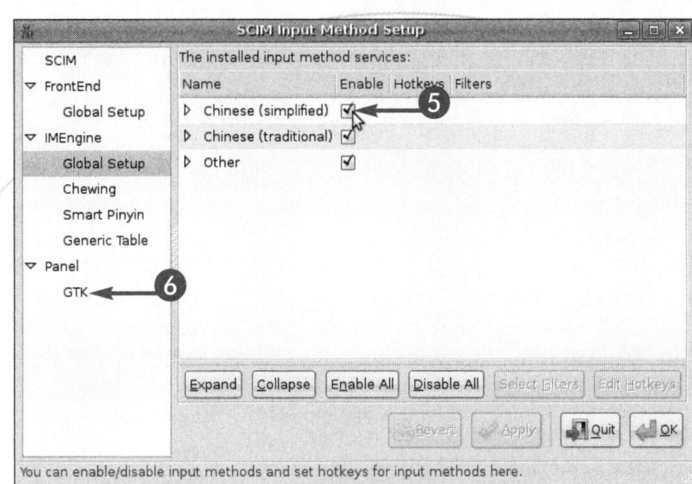

The Panel GTK page appears.

7. Change the options as needed.

8. Click OK.

Your SCIM settings take effect.

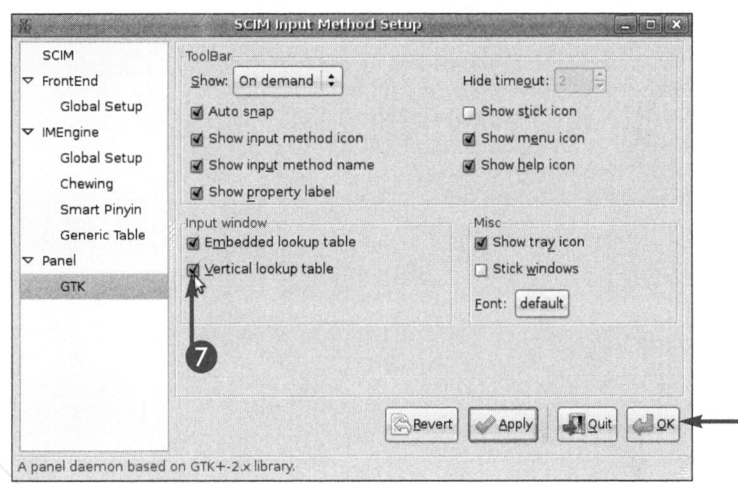

Extra

SCIM stands for Smart Common Input Method, and it is an effort to consolidate and componentize the various input methods available today. This allows for easier configuration of the input methods, as well as a more structured way to produce them for programmers, with the intention of making more input methods available. The need for this kind of consolidation comes from the distributed nature of the development within Linux. Various support mechanisms for alternative input methods have grown up independently with varying adoption based on the first sets of support they implemented. Over time, this has resulted in a patchwork of implementations, each with its own quirks and installation necessities. If the interface is consolidated, a programmer can make his application be able to support multiple different input types without having to code for each possible implementation. The result of using this type of interface is a much faster path to true internationalization of the application portfolio as a whole. Because one of the underlying tenets of Ubuntu is to have an operating system that is accessible to all peoples, it is no wonder that SCIM has been incorporated within Ubuntu.

Adjust File Search Indexing Settings

You can adjust the indexing and search preferences with the Tracker Preferences application.

The General tab's first setting is how long to delay before beginning indexing after startup. There are settings for whether indexing and watching file operations are enabled. When file operations are watched, modified files can be indexed immediately. There is also a selection for the stemming of words, in which *go*, *going*, and *gone* are instances of the same word. Finally, there are options for disabling indexing activities if your machine is on battery power.

The next tab is the Files tab, on which you can enable or disable the indexing of file contents, determine if thumbnails should be generated, and set whether to index directories that are not part of the base file system.

You can also specify which directories to index and watch or just to initiate a scan or "crawl" of your files on startup but not watch for changes.

On the next tab, Ignored Files, you can specifically exclude certain filenames or paths from being indexed. Ignoring certain files reduces the indexing time.

On the Email tab, you can enable the indexing of email in the Evolution email box.

On the Performance tab, you can choose the indexing speed and memory usage, which will affect the speed with which your index will be built. Index merging can be set to perform fast merges, but your system may operate more slowly during the merge process. Finally, you can adjust the amount of text to index within a given file and the maximum number of unique words to index.

Adjust File Search Indexing Settings

1. Click System ➔ Preferences ➔ Search and Indexing.

   The Tracker Preferences application launches.

2. Click here to change the index delay.

Note: *You can change the other General settings as needed.*

3. Click Files.

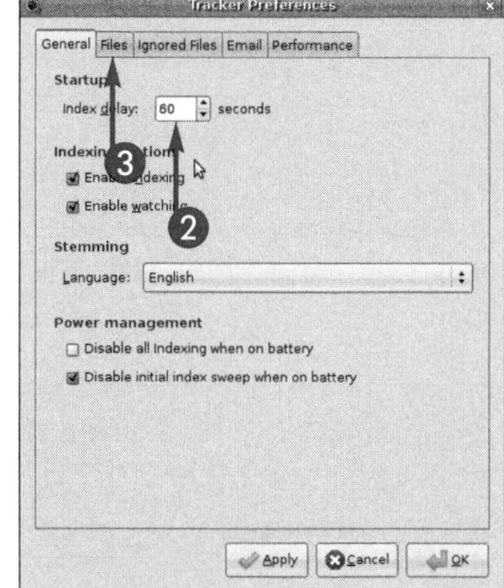

The Files tab appears.

4. Choose the file indexing options that you want.

5. Click Email.

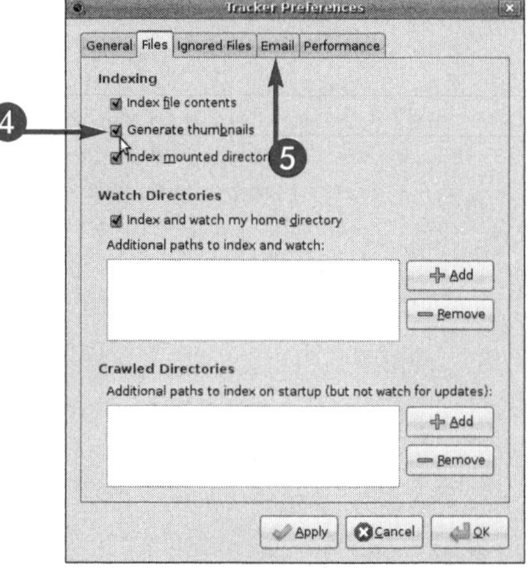

The Email tab appears.

6 Enable or disable email indexing.

7 Click Performance.

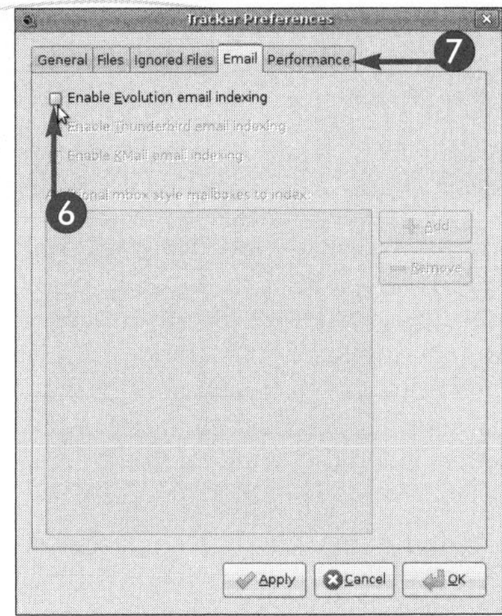

The Performance tab appears.

8 Change the Unique Words setting to index for better results.

9 Click OK.

Indexing will now be performed as you have prescribed.

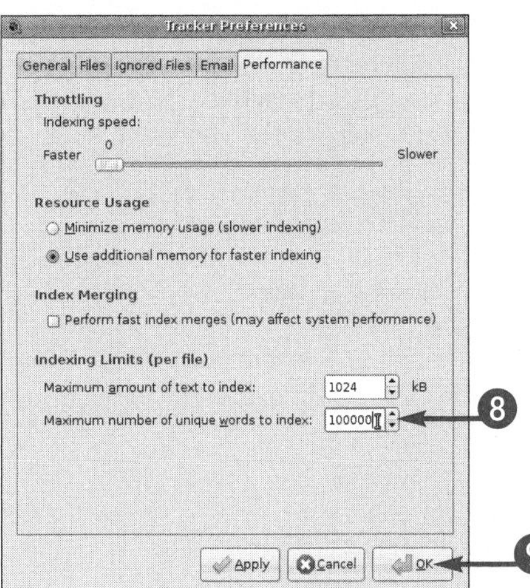

Extra

Why is desktop search so popular? With the vast amounts of digital content available to us each day, via Web pages, email, files and attachments, downloads, and purchased media content, it is very easy to misplace something on your computer. Average hard drive sizes increase each year, and the more they increase, the more we tend to fill them up. With a desktop search solution, you can essentially quit worrying about where you put a file and quickly locate a file by not only its filename but also its contents. This is a tremendous advantage because our brains work more on the semantic notions of what a piece of information was about, not necessarily the verbatim details of a filename. In fact, filenames can even be misleading with respect to the content of the file. By leveraging the power of the computer to sift through massive amounts of information and keep track of it all at a level of tedium that no human can, we can divest ourselves of the clerical task of where things are and focus on the task at hand.

Adjust Window Manager Behavior

The X Window system was designed from the ground up as a componentized set of services and applications consuming those services. A window manager is merely another application within X, which controls the position, size, and behavior of a window. You can adjust how the window manager that comes with Ubuntu works by using the Window Preferences application.

The default window behaviors on Ubuntu closely mimic the Microsoft Windows behaviors, which facilitates adoption of Ubuntu and switching between computers with different operating systems.

One traditional difference of window managers on UNIX/Linux systems was that the active window on X Window systems would normally be the window that the pointer currently rested within. This behavior is still available using the Window Selection setting. When enabled, a window will become active when the mouse pointer enters it.

The action taken by the window manager when a title bar is clicked is also selectable. Although the default is to toggle between maximized and normal window sizes, you can also have the window minimize when the title bar is double-clicked. You can also have a window "roll up" — the body portion of the window disappears, leaving only the title bar visible.

There is also a key combination in conjunction with using the mouse to quickly move a window. You can select the metakey to use to activate this function. The default is the Alt key. When you press the Alt key and click anywhere in a window, you can then drag it to a different location on the screen.

Adjust Window Manager Behavior

1. Click System ➔ Preferences ➔ Windows.

   The Window Preferences application appears.

2. Click here choose what behavior you want for a double-click of the title bar.
3. Double-click the title bar.

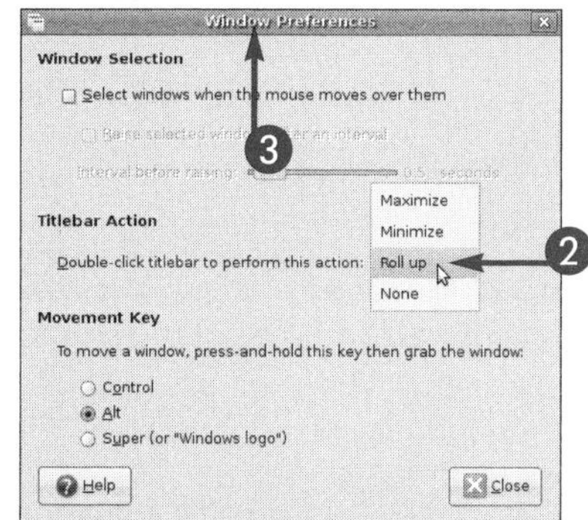

The new action is performed. In this example, the window is rolled up.

4. Double-click the title bar again.

The window returns to its former state.

5 Click here to have windows become active when the mouse pointer moves over them.

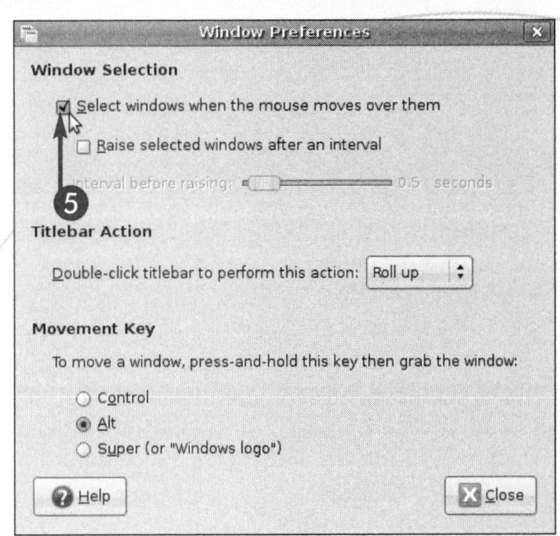

6 Launch another application.

7 Mouse in and out of the two windows to see the focus follow the mouse pointer.

8 Close both applications.

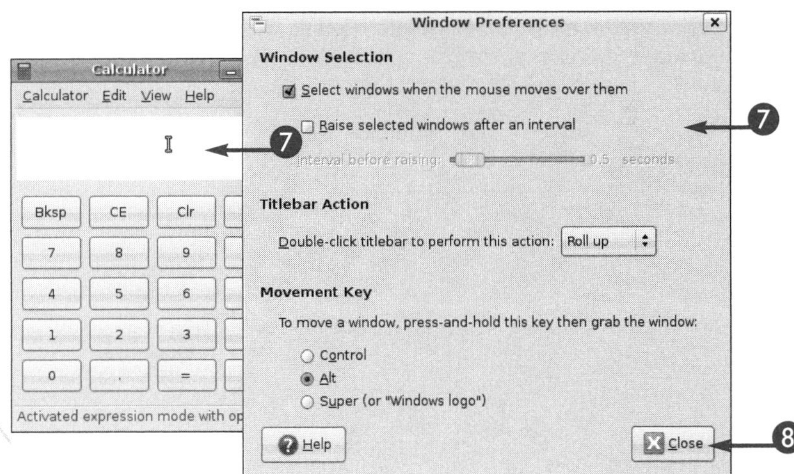

Extra

Ubuntu actually comes with two different window managers. The basic one is called *Metacity,* and it serves the window management role in a very traditional manner, keeping track of windows and providing the basics for moving, sizing, closing, and all the usual window management activities. The second window manager on Ubuntu is Compiz. Compiz offers all the eye-candy effects that are so popular in desktop environments today — animated menus, sliding effects, transparency, and much more. It is also the gateway to the infamous desktop cube effect, which takes four workspaces and places them on a 3D cube that you can rotate on your screen to switch between them. If you have not seen it, it is worth looking on YouTube for a video to see how it looks — for example, www.youtube.com/watch?v=Te8Kh4r5tCo. The cube effects are not installed on Ubuntu by default, but they are relatively easy to get running with the installation of a few packages. There are literally over a hundred plug-ins for different effects and behaviors to choose from after installing the Advanced Desktop Effects Settings package. If you are into eye-candy and having a tricked-out desktop, this is the package for you.

Adjust Authorizations

Ubuntu gives you the ability to control what the users of the computer can and cannot do with the system. The Authorizations utility enables you to tailor the privileges that each user has to help protect your system and your data.

The left pane of the Authorizations dialog box contains a list of various actions that can be performed from within Ubuntu. The right pane is blank until you select an option. When you click an action choice in the left pane, the details of that action appear in the right pane. The top of the pane, labeled Action, explains the functionality. The Implicit Authorizations section allows you to grant privileges automatically to users whenever certain conditions are met. The section at the bottom of the pane, labeled Explicit Authorizations, enables you to grant permissions to specific users.

You set implicit authorizations for an action by using the Edit Implicit Authorizations dialog box. In this dialog box, you select the condition under which certain permissions will be granted. You will have to enter your administrator's password to make the modifications. After you enter your password, click Authenticate.

You can set explicit permissions by clicking the Grant button and then selecting the name of the user from the Beneficiary drop-down list. If you want to add a condition to the permission, select one of the constraints at the bottom of the pane. Click Grant when you are finished.

Adjust Authorizations

1 Click System ➔ Administration ➔ Authorizations.

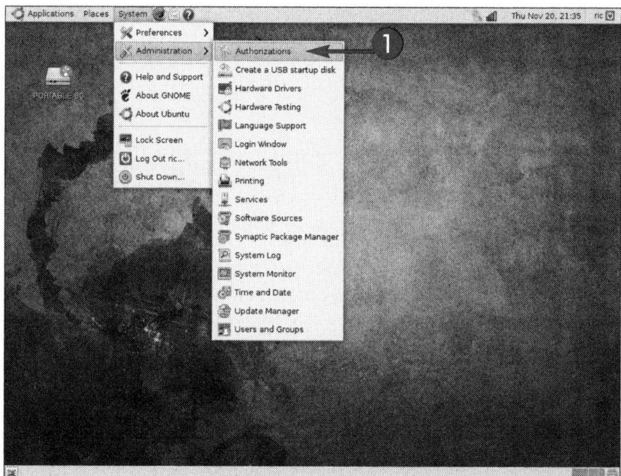

The Authorizations window opens.

2 Click the name of the action that you want to modify.

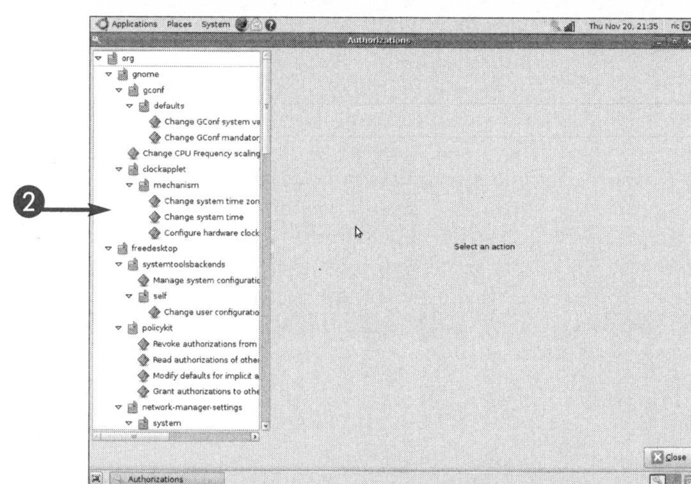

The action's details appear in the right pane.

3. Click Edit.

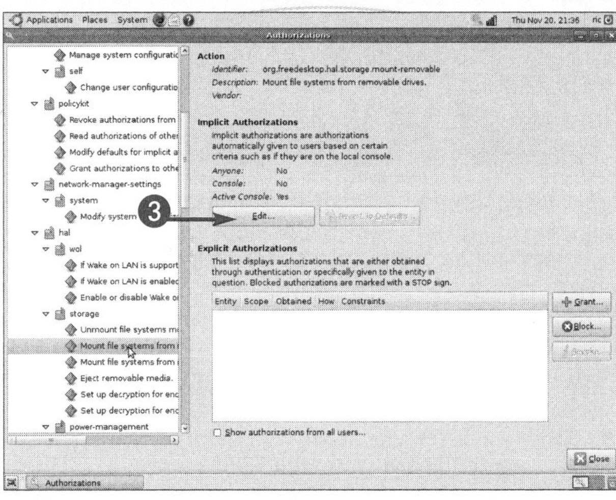

The Edit Implicit Authorizations dialog box opens.

4. Click here and select the condition that you want.
5. Click Modify.

Note: *You will need to provide administrative user authentication to authorize the modification.*

You are returned to the Authorizations window.

6. Click Close.

Your authorizations are set.

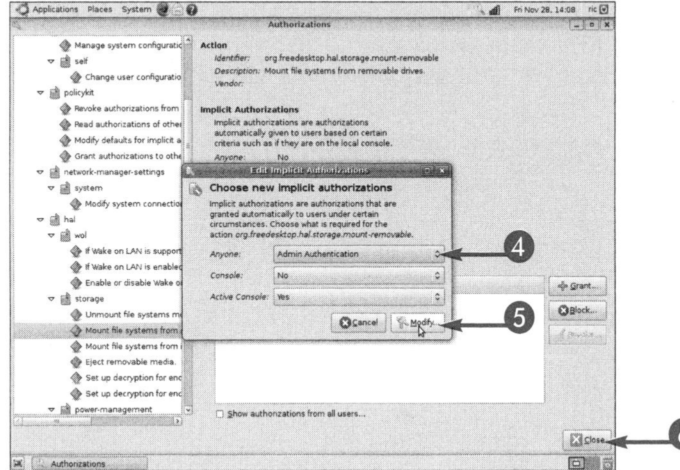

Extra

There is some overlap in functionality between the Authorizations utility and the Users and Groups utility that is discussed later in this chapter in the section "Add and Manage Users and Groups." Both applications are concerned with permissions to perform actions. The two utilities, however, come at the problem from different angles.

The Authorizations utility is task-focused. You work through the permissions process by selecting applications and discrete tasks that can be performed with that application. You then set permissions that are related specifically to that task.

The Users and Groups utility is user-focused. With Users and Groups, you select users and then place limits on what they can do with the system.

Speaking broadly, the Authorizations utility is narrower in its grant of privileges. The permissions you can control with the Users and Groups utility tend to be fairly broad, covering a range of tasks. In contrast, with the Authorizations utility, it is not uncommon to deal with a user's right to perform a single, specific task.

The other key difference between the two utilities is that the Authorizations utility enables you to grant permissions that are triggered by the presence of conditions that apply regardless of the identity of the user.

Participate in Ubuntu Hardware Testing

Ubuntu is a community-driven project, and you can help out by participating in hardware testing. The Hardware Testing application is really just a survey. It requires no technical expertise and takes only a few minutes of your time, but the contribution is valuable to the community.

The Ubuntu Hardware Testing application is designed simply to check whether the hardware on your system is working well and to report the results to the community where they form an ongoing survey of Ubuntu hardware compatibility.

All you need to do to participate is start up the Hardware Testing application and follow the steps. You do need to have an account at Launchpad (https://launchpad.net/) to use the application; if you do not have one, you can register for one for free on the Web site.

The Hardware Testing application gathers information about your system and then begins testing various common components. The first item to be tested is your display. You can answer each question of the survey, and you can provide comments in the provided boxes.

The application checks your video card, your mouse and keyboard, your network controller, and your Internet connection. At the end of the survey, the application asks you to type in your Launchpad ID, so have it ready. On the final screen, the application posts the results of the survey to the database maintained by Launchpad at https://launchpad.net/, where it adds to the ever-growing collection of data about Ubuntu.

Participate in Ubuntu Hardware Testing

1. Click System ➔ Administration ➔ Hardware Testing.

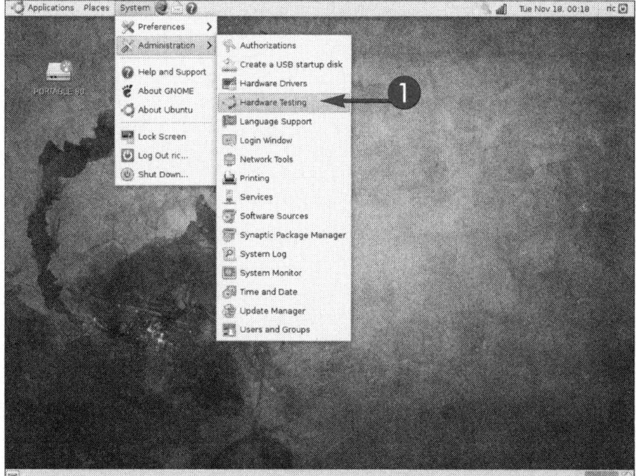

The system prompts you for your administrative password.

2. Type your password.
3. Click OK.

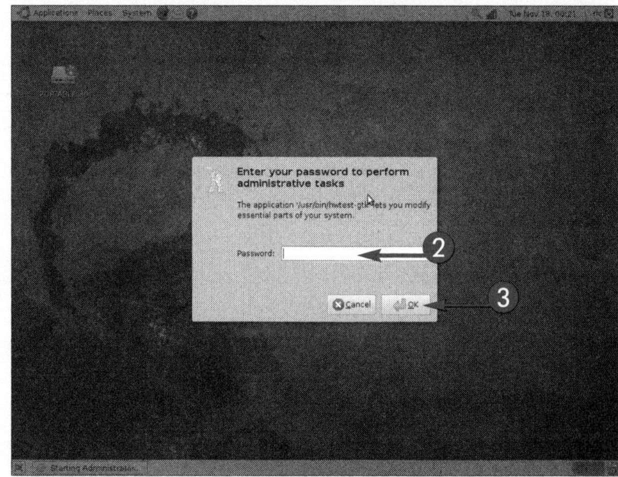

The Hardware Testing Welcome screen appears.

Note: *You will need an account on launchpad.net to complete this survey. Follow the link in the dialog box to obtain an account if you do not have one.*

4. Click Next.

The first step in the Hardware Testing survey appears.

5. Click to answer the question appropriately.
6. Click Next.
7. Answer each subsequent question and click Next after each one. On the final screen, click Finish.

The results of your survey are posted to Launchpad's database.

Extra

Launchpad is a noncommercial service whose purpose is to provide hosting and support services for open-source projects such as Ubuntu. You can use your launchpad.net ID to access all the features of the site.

Ubuntu uses launchpad.net for bug tracking, translations, and for a service known as *answers*. Answers allows you to post questions about Ubuntu that will then be answered by other members of the community, often members of the Ubuntu team. Before you submit a question, search the existing list of questions to be certain that the answer that you are looking for does not already exist. You can access the Ubuntu section of the answers service at https://answers.launchpad.net/ubuntu.

Similarly, if you think you have found a bug, search the bug tracking section of launchpad.net for reports of a similar problem. Reports often contain workarounds or solutions. If you cannot find your problem, please post the problem for the community to review. You can access the Ubuntu bug tracker at https://bugs.launchpad.net/Ubuntu.

Ubuntu is only one of over 1,600 projects that use launchpad.net. You can browse a list of all the projects from the launchpad.net home page.

Enable Proprietary Hardware Drivers

If your hardware or accessories require the use of proprietary drivers, you can add them using the Hardware Drivers utility in Ubuntu.

With Ubuntu 8.10, the vast majority of common hardware needs are met by preexisting drivers or by downloading additional open-source drivers using the Synaptic Package Manager. In those rare cases where the existing and open-source drivers do not cover your needs, you may have to install proprietary drivers from the hardware manufacturer.

The drivers are likely to come included with your hardware, typically on a CD. You will first need to get those drivers on to your Ubuntu machine by following the instructions included with the driver files. After the drivers are installed, you can enable them through the Hardware Drivers utility.

When you open the Hardware Drivers utility, the application scans your system in an attempt to locate any proprietary drivers. The Hardware Drivers utility's dialog box lists the available drivers. You can use the dialog box to enable any of the proprietary drivers in the list.

If, after you have enabled a driver, it does not seem to be working, you may need to restart your machine.

If no drivers appear in the Hardware Drivers window, either there are no proprietary drivers on your system or they have not been installed correctly.

Note that where there is an open-source alternative for the driver, you should consider using the open-source version, as the proprietary driver cannot be maintained from within Ubuntu or the Synaptic Package Manager.

Enable Proprietary Hardware Drivers

1. Click System ➔ Administration ➔ Hardware Drivers.

   The Hardware Drivers dialog box opens, and any available proprietary drivers are displayed.

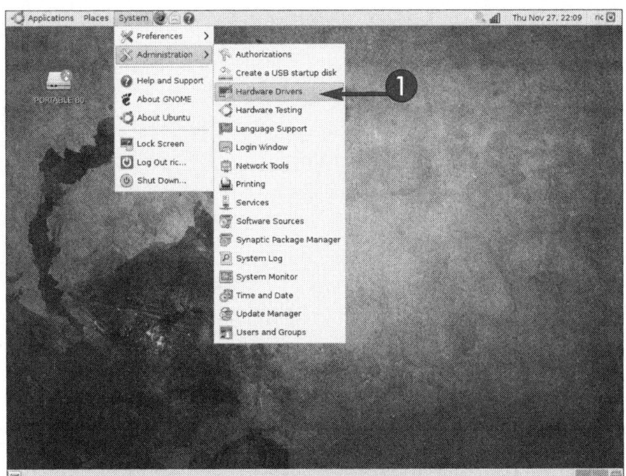

2. Click to select the driver that you want.
3. Click Activate to enable that driver.

Note: *This button says Deactivate, as in this example, if the driver is already activated.*

4. Provide administrative user authentication to authorize the change.
5. Click Close.

Note: *Depending on the driver, you may need to restart your computer to see the changes.*

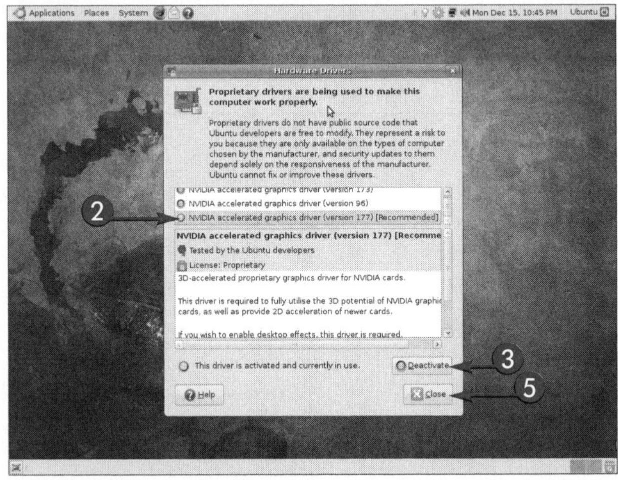

Add Additional Language Support

Your Ubuntu desktop can be configured to accept input in a large number of languages. Ubuntu supports the most common global languages; it is merely a question of enabling the language through the Language Support utility.

The default language support of your Ubuntu distribution depends on the variety of Ubuntu that was installed on your machine. Perhaps the most common is United States English, but it could be any of the other supported languages, as localized distributions exist for many languages.

If you want to change the default language or you need to enable support for other languages, you will need to use the Language Support utility. The Language Support utility first checks your system for installed language packs before it launches the Language Support dialog box.

To add support for additional languages, you select them from the list at the top of the dialog box. You can click Details to view the options for the language and choose whether you want to install all the options for that language. Note that the options change, depending on the language selected. At the bottom of the dialog box is an option labeled Input Method. If you want to use a complex character-based language, such as Chinese, you can use its option to enable the support to enter complex characters.

You can also change the default language for your system in the Language Support dialog box. The default language affects your navigation, your warning dialog boxes, and many of the items that you see in your interface.

Add Additional Language Support

1. Click System ➔ Administration ➔ Language Support.

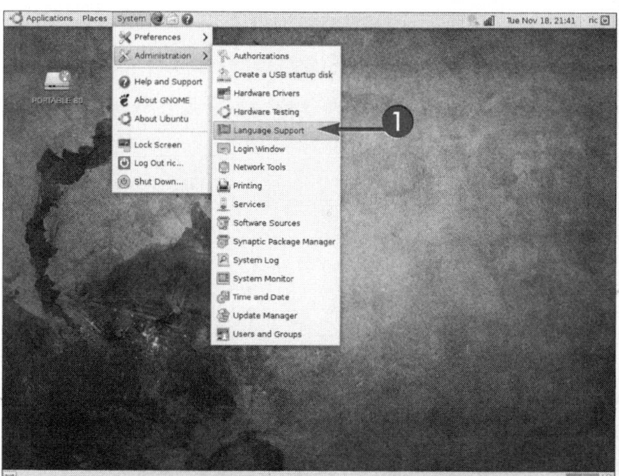

The Language Support window opens.

2. Click the languages that you want to add.
3. Click OK.

The chosen languages are downloaded and installed.

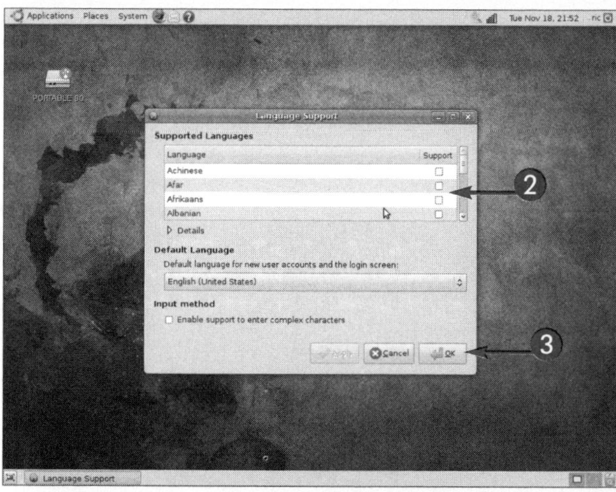

Change Login Window Options

You can change the appearance and behavior of your Ubuntu Login window with the Login Window utility.

Before you can make changes to the Login window's options, the system will prompt you for your administrator's password. Then you can change the options that you want in the Login Window Preferences dialog box. Across the top of the dialog box, you will see six tabs: General, Local, Remote, Accessibility, Security, and Users. The most important of these to the typical user are the Local tab and the Security tab.

The Local tab enables you to change the appearance of your Ubuntu login window. On this tab, you can select both the style and the theme used for the Login window. You can click the Add button to add additional themes to your system. The Menu Bar choices allow you to specify whether to make the bar visible. The final section on this tab lets you set a custom welcome message.

The Security tab makes it possible to disable the default login procedure or to increase your security by placing restrictions on who can log in. If you select the Enable Automatic Login option, you will bypass the login procedure and have your system start automatically at the start of a session. This is not recommended for security reasons, however. In contrast, the options under the Security heading on the Security tab enable you to place conditions on login that improve the system's security. You can increase the time specified for the login retry delay to make it harder for brute-force attempts to succeed at cracking a user's account.

Change Login Window Options

1. Click System ➔ Administration ➔ Login Window.

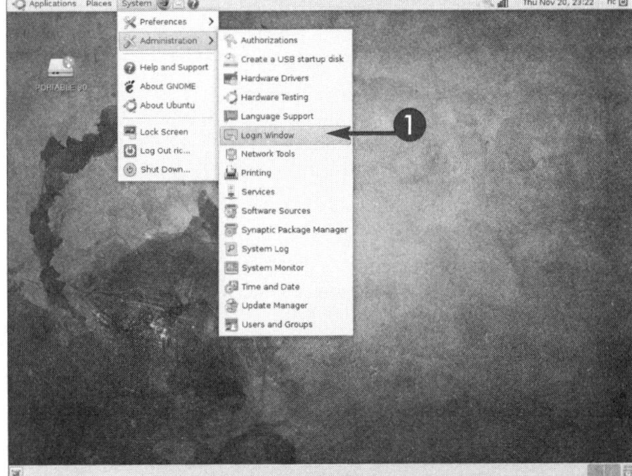

The system prompts you to enter your administrative password.

2. Type your password.
3. Click OK.

The Login Window Preferences dialog box opens.

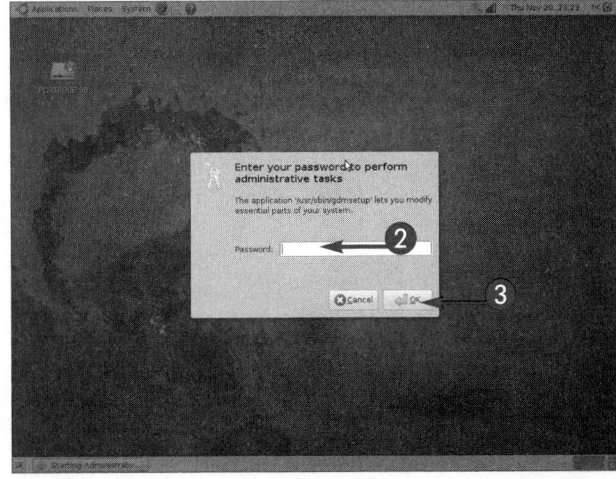

4 Click the Local tab.

The Local tab appears.

- You can set the style and theme using these options.
- You can use these check boxes to set different options for your menu bar.
- With this option, you can set a custom welcome message.

5 Click the Security tab.

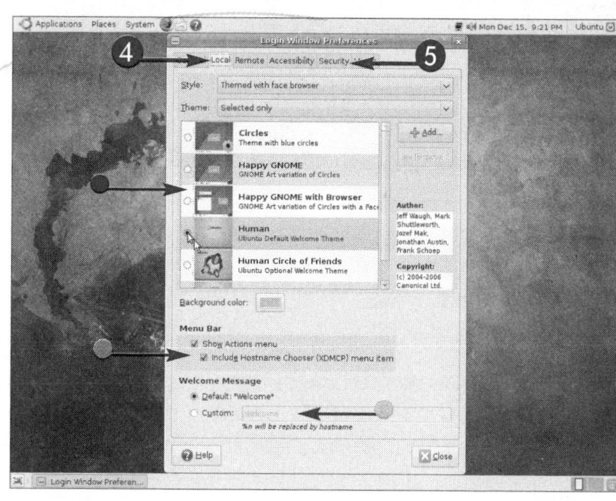

The Security tab comes to the front.

6 If you want to enable an automatic login, click here.

7 Click here and select the user whom you want to be able to log in automatically.

8 Set the Security options that you want.

9 Click Close.

Your changes to the Login window will be applied the next time you start a session.

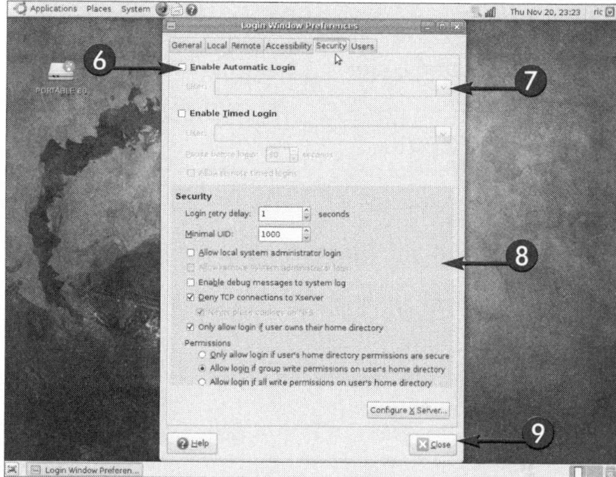

Extra

You may notice on the Local tab of the Login Window Preferences dialog box several options that reference the "face browser." The face browser option is one of the layout choices for your login screen, and it adds a useful functionality to the screen.

Face browser puts a small image of each of the users on the login screen. Users can log in by either clicking their icon or by typing their name and then entering their password. The images, which the system calls *face icons,* are selected by the user and kept in their home directory.

This feature adds a personal touch to the system, and when there are many users of a single machine, the feature is also a time-saver. The system tracks the user sessions and automatically orders the images with the most frequent users ranked at the top of the list. This helps ensure that users who log in often can find their accounts quickly. There is also an auto-complete function that tries to recognize the username as you type it in; this is also a time-saver and particularly useful if you have a long username.

Configure the Network

The Network Configuration utility enables you to set up and manage your various network connections.

In many cases, Ubuntu detects your network connections automatically or with very little help from the user. There are times, however, when you may need to adjust your settings or create a new connection; in those cases, the Network Configuration utility is there to help.

Before you can access the Network Configuration utility, you will need to type in your administrator's password. Then you will be able to use the Network Connections dialog box to adjust your network settings. The dialog box has five tabs: Wired, Wireless, Mobile Broadband, VPN, and DSL. Each of the tabs is intended to assist with a different type of connection, so it is possible that not all will be relevant to your situation. Use the choice that matches the type of connection that you need to manage.

The Wired connection tab displays your wired network; likewise, the Wireless tab displays all the wireless networks that are available in your area. When you try to make changes, the system will prompt you to request access to your keyring. You must grant access to proceed. Note that in some cases it may prompt you several times; you must grant access to each prompt.

The Editing connection dialog box displays the connection's name and its details. You can use this dialog box to adjust your connection settings and your security and access privileges.

Configure the Network

1. Click System ➔ Preferences ➔ Network Configuration.

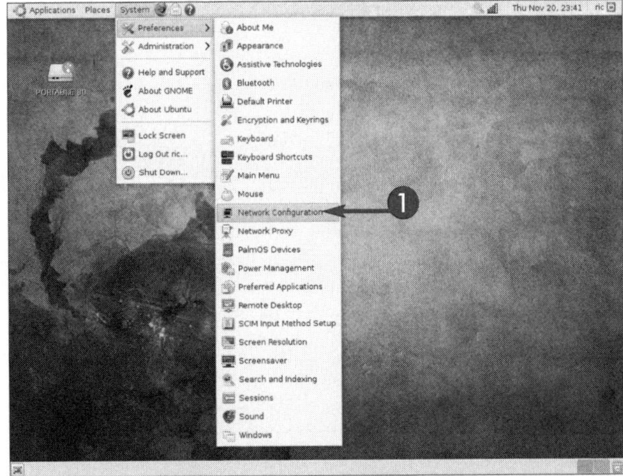

Note: *If prompted at any time during the following steps, type your administrator's password.*

The Network Connections dialog box opens.

2. Click the tab of the type of connection that you want to modify.

Note: *This example shows the Wireless tab.*

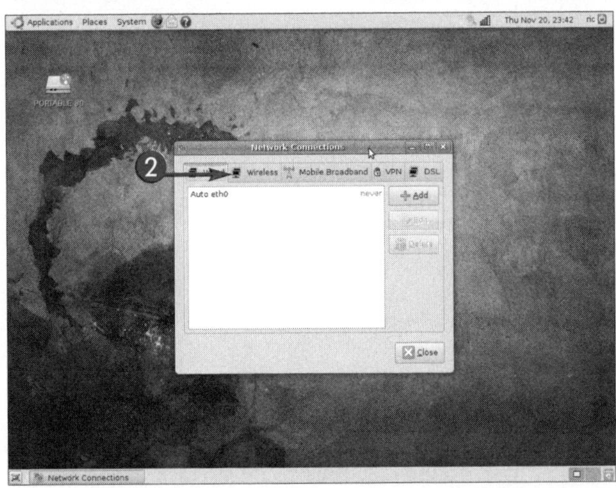

The tab comes to the front.

3. Click the name of the connection that you want to edit.
4. Click Edit.

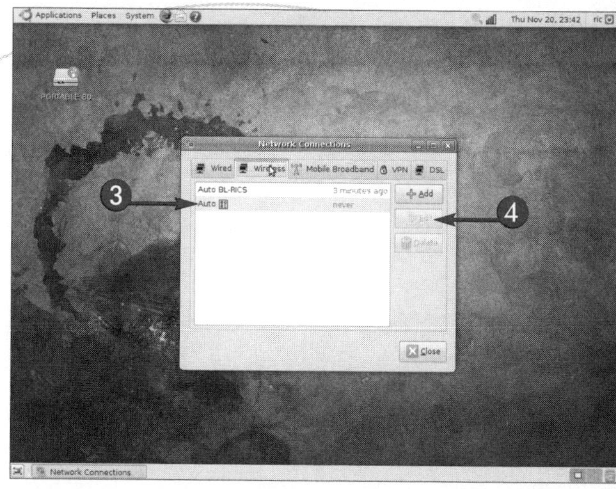

The Editing window opens.

5. Make your changes.
6. Click OK.

   You are returned to the Network Connections dialog box.

7. Click Close.

   Your network changes are applied.

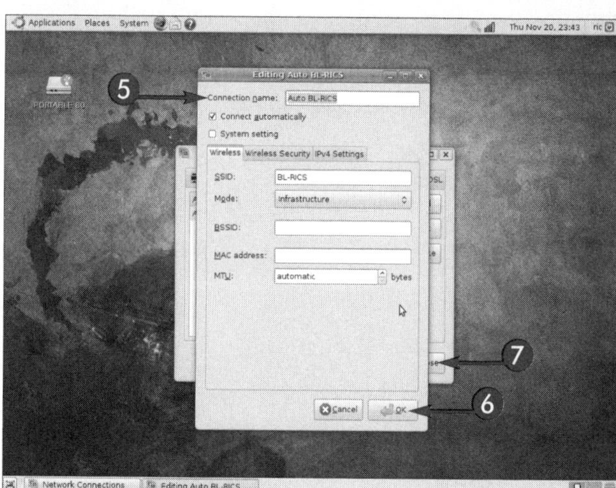

Extra

One of the most anticipated aspects of the Ubuntu 8.10 release was the promise of improved support for 3G. The release has not only delivered on the promise and but is widely viewed as having exceeded expectations.

The expanded 3G support in version 8.10 makes Ubuntu more usable for notebook computer users and others for whom mobile access is an issue. Intrepid Ibex provides 3G connectivity via a variety of options that help you maintain a connection seamlessly. You can use the built-in 3G modem, a dongle, your mobile phone, or a Bluetooth connection to another device. Juggling various modes of connectivity, fortunately, does not involve juggling your configuration; Ubuntu handles all of these options through a single interface in the system's network manager.

Users will find that the most common hardware is supported out-of-the-box. Simply plug in the hardware and the system will auto-detect it and begin searching for a connection. The system essentially treats a 3G connection as any other type of network connection. All of this can be managed through the tabs in the Network Connections dialog box.

Using the Network Tools

Ubuntu comes bundled with a number of tools that can help you learn more about your network connections and diagnose any problems that you may experience.

The collection of various tools comes in one handy utility called *Network Tools*. In the Network Tools window, you will see eight tabs across the top of the window. The first tab is labeled Devices. On this tab, you can find information about your various network connections, as well as your IP address and information about how much data has been moved over the connection. This information is extremely useful if you are trying to troubleshoot a network connection problem. You can use the Network Device drop-down list to change between your various types of network connections.

The next tab is named Ping and is useful in diagnosing problems with your Internet connection and in determining whether a particular Web site or computer is accessible. On this tab, you type in the name or the IP address of the Web site or computer that you are trying to reach by pinging it. The system will try five times to contact the site or the computer and will display the results of the efforts in the pane at the bottom of the window. The information will show not only whether the system was able to connect successfully, but also how long it took each time. You can click the Details button to see a bit more information about the ping test.

Using the Network Tools

1. Click System ➔ Administration ➔ Network Tools.

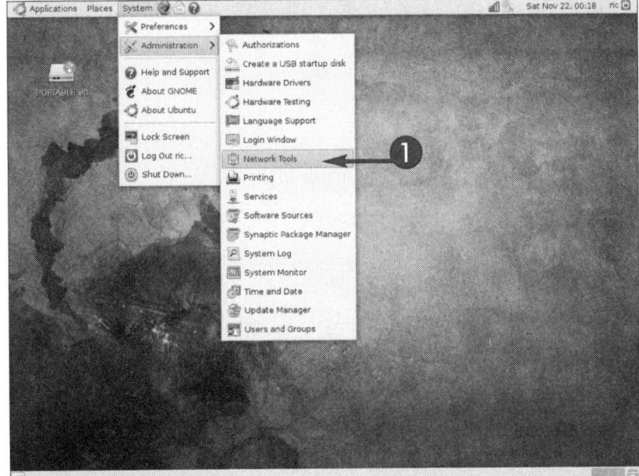

The Network Tools application opens.

- You can check the information about various network devices.

2. Click Ping.

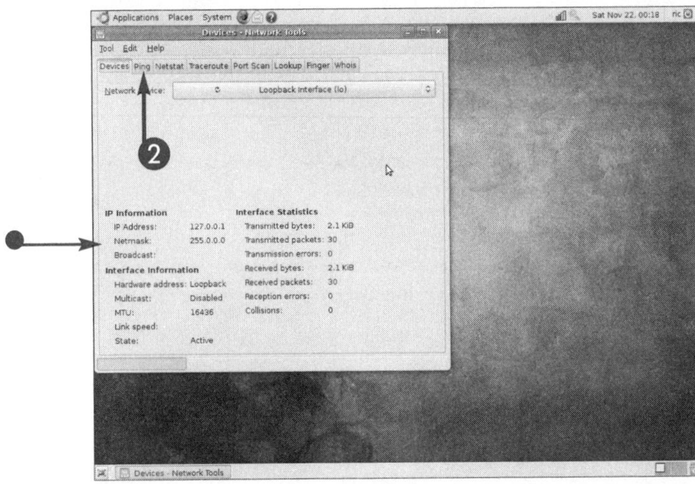

The Ping tab comes to the front.

3 Type the address that you want to test.

4 Click Ping.

The system will attempt to contact the address five times.

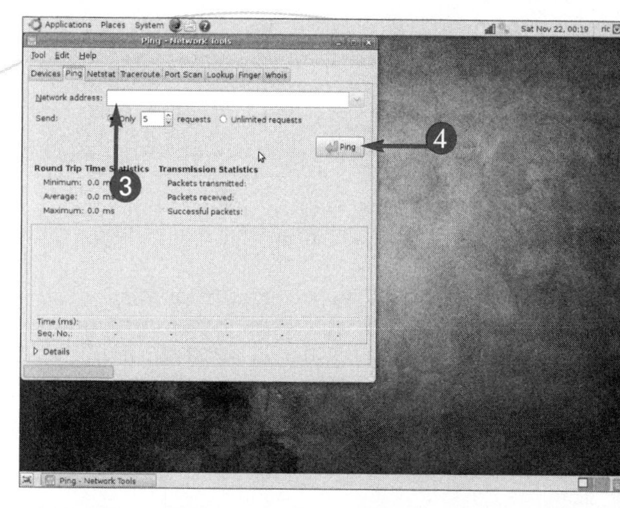

- The Ping test results are displayed.

5 Click the Whois tab.

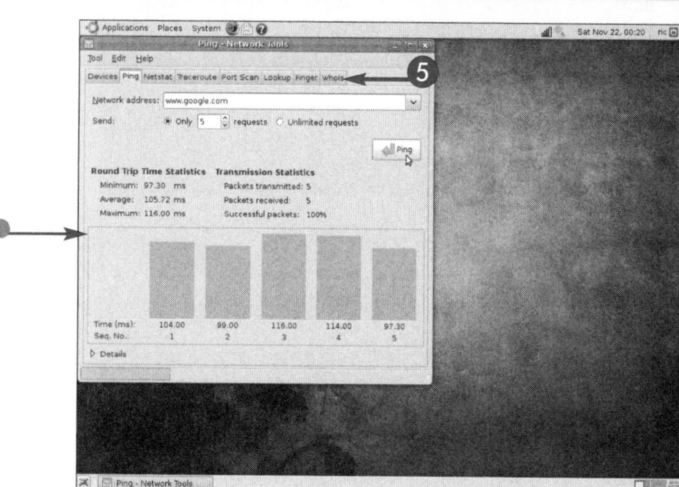

Extra

In addition to the Devices and Ping tabs, shown here, and the Whois and Traceroute tabs, discussed later in this section, there are other utilities built into the Network Tools application.

The Netstat tab actually holds three different functions: Routing Table Information, Active Network Services, and Multicast Information. This tab is useful for finding problems in network connections and provides insight into both incoming and outgoing connections. The Routing Table command helps you find information on how network traffic is routed between nodes. The Active Network Services tab tells you what network services, such as TCP or UDP, are being employed by the system. The Multicast Information control displays multicast group memberships for your machine.

On the Port Scan tab, you can search for open ports on systems. It will tell you the port number, the state, and the service.

Lookup is a research tool for learning more about an address. Use the drop-down list to select the information that you want to find.

Finger is used to find information about a user on a network. You need to know both the network name and the username.

continued

Using the Network Tools (continued)

The Network Tools utility can help you learn more about Web sites and about your connections to them.

The Whois tab of the Network Tools window is an easy way to learn more about a Web site. Whois information can tell you where a domain is registered, when it expires, where it is hosted, and even the name of the owner. In some cases, you will be able to obtain the contact information of the domain owner. When you request information about a site, the Network Tools window searches the Whois directory and, if an entry is found, displays the results in the main pane of the window. Note that this feature will only work if you are connected to the Internet.

Another useful tool is the traceroute function, which is on the Traceroute tab. You type in a domain name or an IP address and ask the Network Tools application to trace it. The utility will then try to connect to the address, and as it does so, it will show you the connections that it has to make to find its way to the server where the address is located. As it makes each connection, the utility will display the amount of time that each step takes. This is useful for several purposes. First, if you are having a hard time connecting to a specific site, this can tell you where the connection is having problems. By viewing the time information, you can detect where there are delays or a failure. Second, a traceroute can tell you where the server is located, including the name of the server and its IP address.

Using the Network Tools *(continued)*

The Whois tab comes to the front.

6 Enter the domain name that you want to check.

7 Click Whois.

The application queries the Whois database.

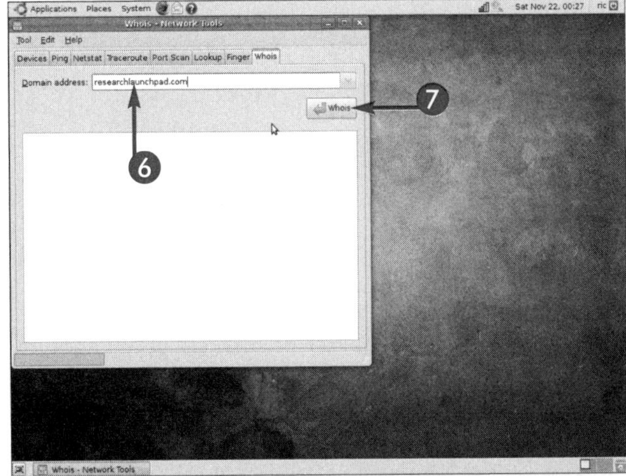

• The results of the Whois search are displayed.

8 Click Traceroute.

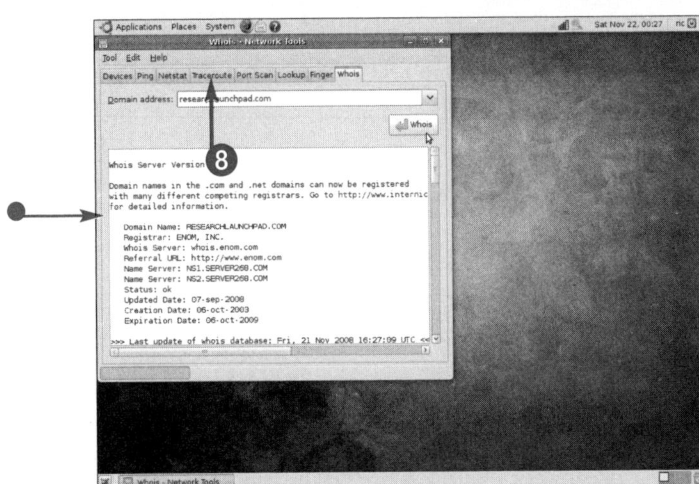

The Traceroute tab comes to the front.

9. Type in the network address that you want to test.

10. Click Trace.

The application will begin to trace the connection route to the address.

- The traceroute results are displayed.

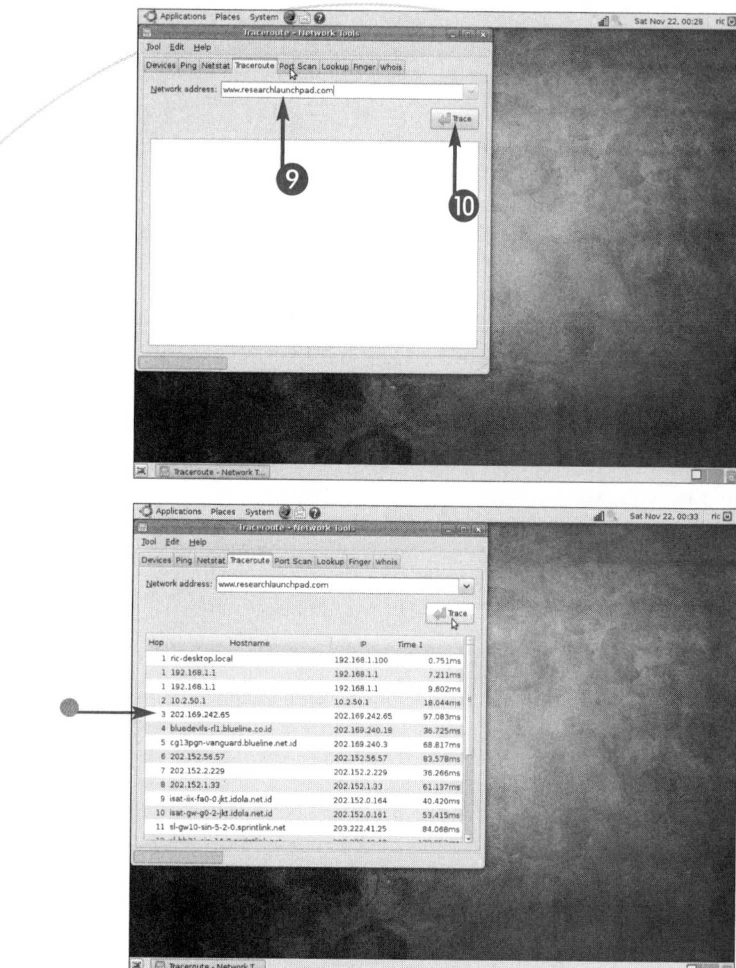

Apply It

A handy tool for monitoring your network activity is the Network Monitor application, which you can add to any panel.

Right-click a panel and select Add to Panel from the menu. The Add to Panel dialog box opens. Scroll through the list of items and select the one named Network Monitor. Click Add and the dialog box will close.

You will now have on the panel a visual aid tool to monitor your network connection. As data moves in and out of your computer, the small screens on the icon will flash. If your connection is dropped, a yellow alert triangle will appear on the icon.

Click once on the monitor icon, and the Connection Properties dialog box will open, displaying a General tab and a Support tab. The General tab shows the connection, its status, the incoming and outgoing activity, and if applicable to the connection, the signal strength. If you have multiple connections, you can switch between them by choosing from the Name drop-down list. Click the Support tab to view your IP information.

Add and Configure a Printer

Ubuntu provides excellent support for both local and networked printers, enabling you to easily detect and add new printers to your system.

To add a new printer, you first use the Printer Configuration window. If you have not yet set up any printers, the window will be empty. If you have set up a printer, it will be shown here. You use this window to access the New Printer window. This window lists the possible methods of connection for your device.

If your printer is connected directly to your machine by means of the parallel port, you click the LPT option. If the printer is connected to one of your machine's serial ports, you select the proper serial port number. You can modify the connection options if the default settings do not work.

If the printer is located on your network, you will need to click one of the other options. For HpjetDirect connections, you input the host name. If you have an IPP Printer on your network, you select the IPP option and enter the hostname. You can test the connection by clicking the Verify button. If you are using the LPD network protocol, you select the LPD option and type in the hostname or probe the network to find the printers automatically. If you have a printer on a Windows network, select the SAMBA option and enter the address and authentication.

Add and Configure a Printer

1. Click System ➔ Administration ➔ Printing.

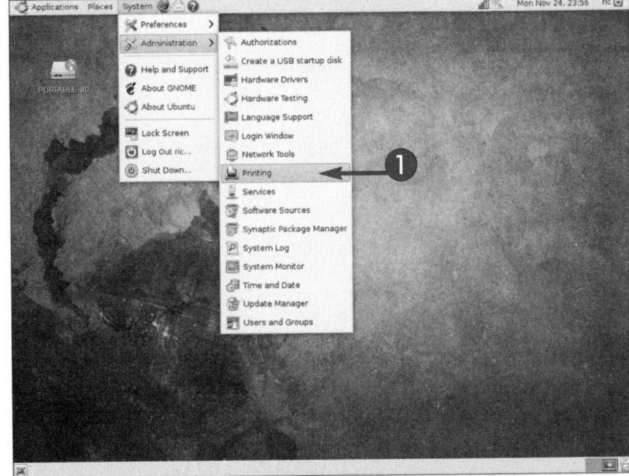

The Printer Configuration window opens.

2. Click the New drop-down arrow.

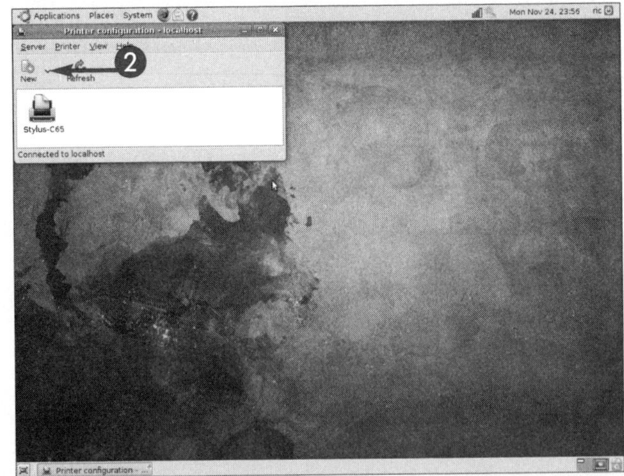

3 Click Printer.

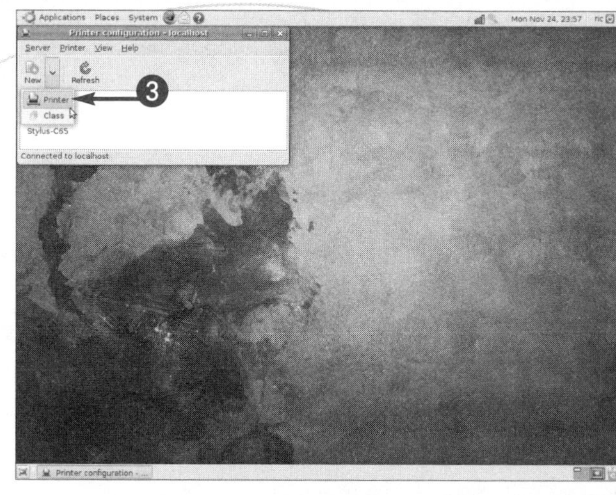

- The system searches for printers that need to be installed.

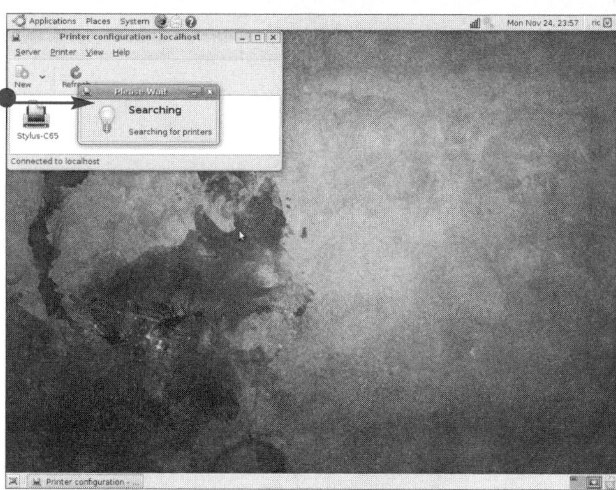

Extra

Ubuntu employs the CUPS system for handling print server duties. CUPS stands for *Common UNIX Printing System,* and it is widely considered to be an industry standard. One of the areas in which CUPS excels is in the handling of network printers.

In the Printer Configuration window, click Server ➔ Settings to view basic and advanced server settings. Note that you can configure CUPS to allow a local printer connected to your machine to be published to the network and used by other users.

If you are trying to reach a printer on the network from your machine, not only does the printer need to be added to your system, as described here, but you will also need to be connected to the network, and the printer needs to be turned on. If you have to turn it on and it does not appear automatically on your list of printers, click the Refresh button to refresh the list of printers.

If you have access to multiple networks, use the Server ➔ Connect option to select which network you want to use for print purposes.

continued ➔

Add and Configure a Printer (continued)

Printer configuration in Ubuntu 8.10 is often automatic, but the system also allows you to install drivers where needed.

After you have set up your connection type, the system will perform a search in an attempt to locate the necessary driver files automatically. If the driver is found, the system will complete the installation and return you to the Print Configuration dialog box where your printer will be ready for use. If the system cannot locate the driver by itself, you will see a screen that asks you to help.

The installer will ask you to select the printer by name, search for the driver on the Internet, or install a PPD driver from a disk. Choose the method that matches your situation. If you attempt to select the printer from the database, you must first select the printer's manufacturer and then click Forward. On the next screen, you will need to identify the specific model. If you want to supply the driver from a disk, you will need to point the system to where the file is located. After you have located the file, click it and then click Open, and the system will install the driver. Searching for a driver online requires you to identify the maker and the model and then search online. You must be connected to the Internet for this to work.

After the driver has been identified and installed, the system will ask you to give the printer a name and a description.

Add and Configure a Printer *(continued)*

If the system cannot find and install the new printer, the New Printer window will appear.

4 Click the connection type that reflects how your printer is connected to your computer.

5 Click Forward.

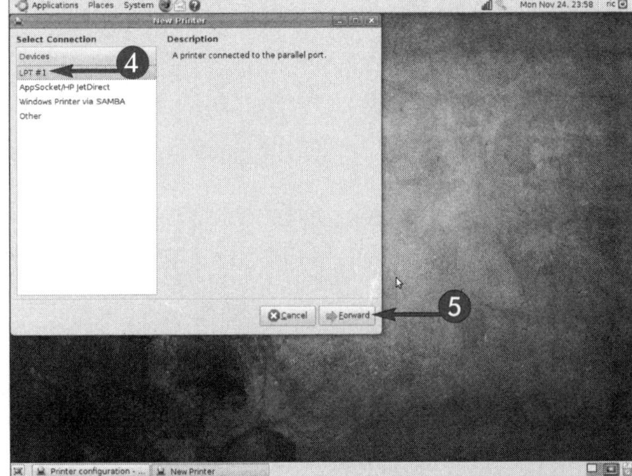

- The application will try again to find a printer on that connection.

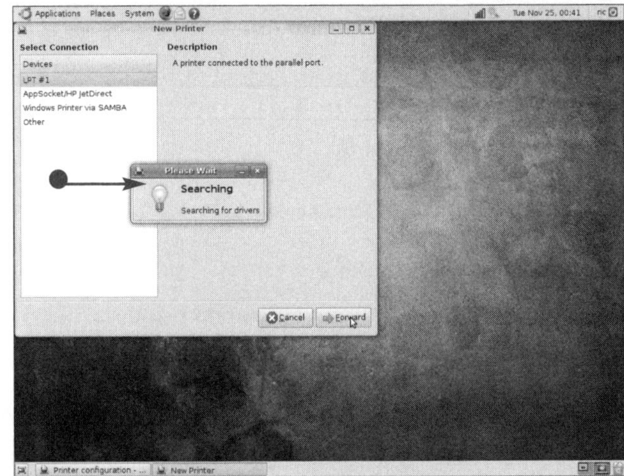

The final screen in the New Printer window opens.

6 Type a name.

7 Type a description.

8 Click Apply.

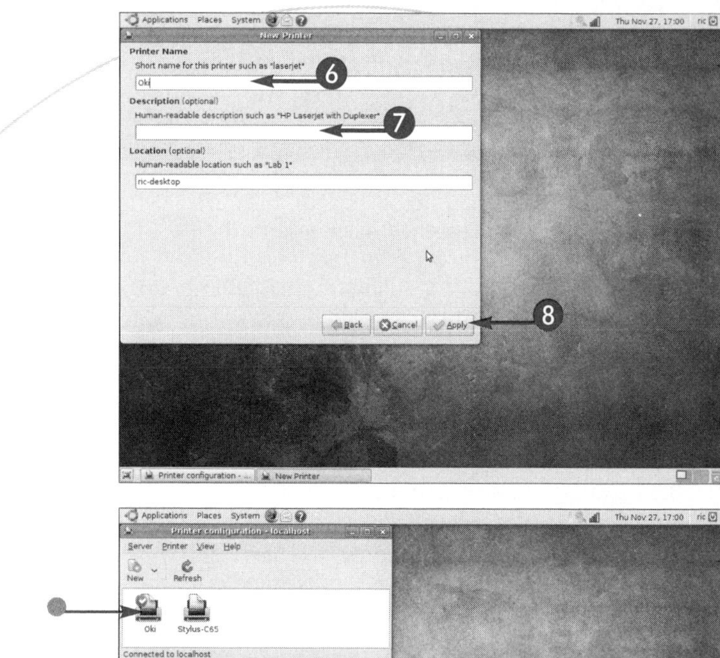

- The new printer appears in the Printer Configuration window.

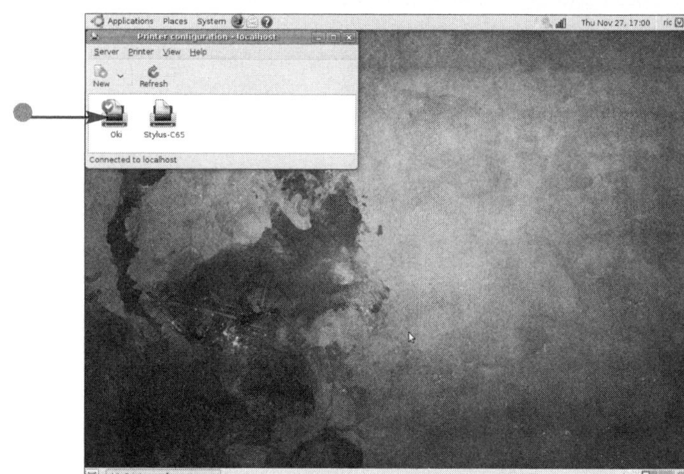

Extra

After a printer is installed on your system, you can access the configuration settings for that printer from the Printer Configuration dialog box. Double-click the name of the printer that you want to modify. The Printer Properties window displays all the configuration options for the printer. You can rename or adjust the location information without impact on the device. Changes to the URL need to be carefully considered, or the device may become unavailable.

If the printer is connected and turned on, you can use the Test and Maintenance options to verify that the device is working properly.

The Policies tab enables you to specify how the system will react to various conditions, such as errors. Access Control gives you a way to control the use of the device by other users. Printer Options contains a number of configuration settings that relate to basics such as paper size, print quality, and so on. Job Options lets you set defaults for the printing of documents. Using this tab, you can specify the number of copies to be printed, the orientation, and the dimensions.

Once you have the settings adjusted to suit your needs, click OK, and the settings will be applied.

Manage Startup Services

With Ubuntu, it is easy to control the software services that are launched when you turn on your computer. The Services utility makes it possible for you to configure the system and customize your computer to suit your particular needs.

To control your startup services, you need to use the Services utility. However, when you first open the Services Settings window, it will be locked. In order to add or remove your startup services, you must first unlock the window. To do so, you must enter your system administrator's password in the Authenticate dialog box.

After your identity has been authenticated, the Services Settings dialog box will be unlocked and ready for you to use. To turn a service on or off, click in the box next to the name. The changes will take effect the next time you start your Ubuntu system.

Note that if there are services you do not use, it is a good idea to disable them at startup. Reducing the number of services that run at startup will decrease the amount of time that it takes the system to boot up, and it will also save on system resources. Be conservative, however; if there are services that you do not recognize, do not disable them until you have done a bit of research, as those services may perform useful, though unobvious, purposes.

Manage Startup Services

1. Click System ➔ Administration ➔ Services.

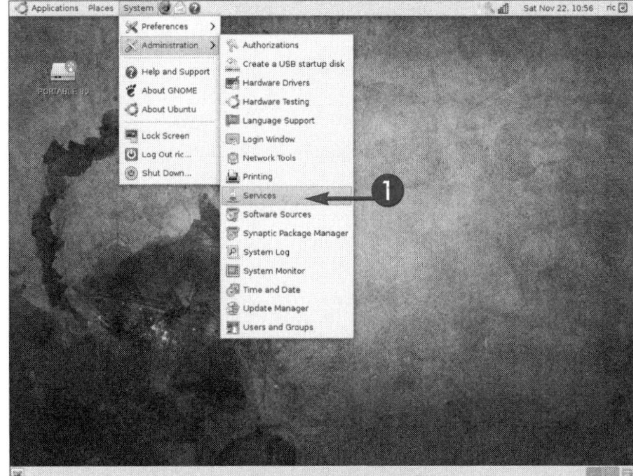

The Services Settings window opens.

2. Click Unlock.

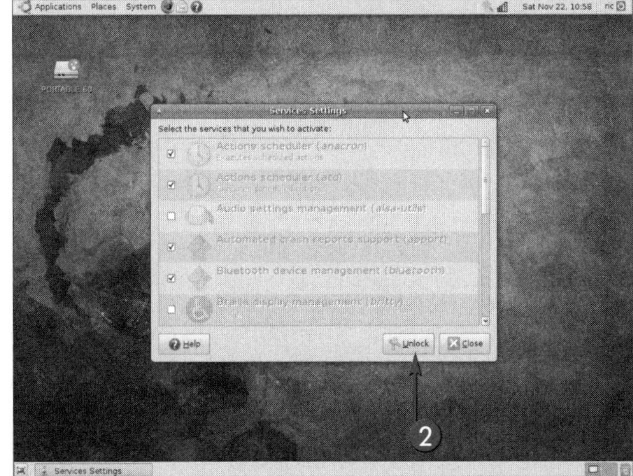

The Authenticate dialog box opens.

3 Type your password.

4 Click Authenticate.

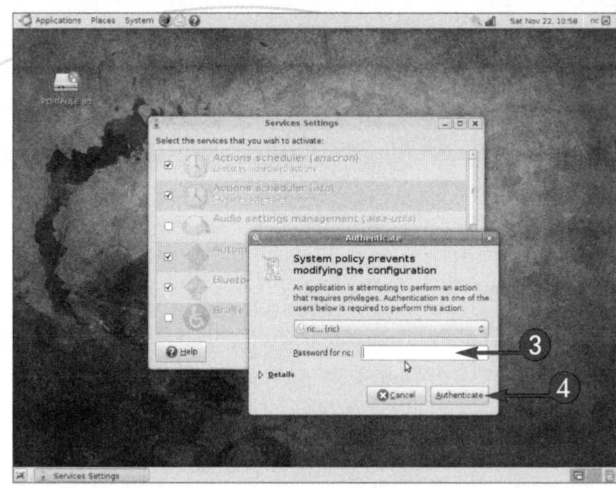

The Services Settings controls are unlocked.

5 Click to make changes to the items on the list.

6 Click Close.

The services that you added will launch the next time that you start an Ubuntu session. Any services that you disabled will not be launched at startup.

Apply It

There is an alternative application that can be used to manage your startup services. The application, known as BUM (BootUp Manager), can be installed via the Synaptic Package Manager. BUM is designed to perform the same task as the Services utility, but it offers more control and much more information.

Install BUM using the steps described in the section "Add Software with the Synaptic Package Manager" later in this chapter. You will need to be connected to the Internet to download this package.

After it is installed, it will appear on the Administration submenu under the System menu. Click BootUp Manager to launch BUM. The first time you start the application, it will take some time, as it scans the system and logs all the processes.

Once it is open, you can browse the services in the Summary tab and select or deselect those that you want. Click the Advanced check box, and the display splits into three tabs that provide a great deal of information about each service as well as a rundown of the startup and shutdown scripts.

Although the Services application is fine for basic configuration, if you want to really fine-tune the system, try BUM.

Configure Software Sources

The Software Sources utility enables you to control the type of software your system will download and from where. The utility adds important security to your installation and ensures that the system software you download is legitimate and secure.

As discussed later in this chapter in the section "Run the Update Manager," Ubuntu will automatically check for and even download system patches and upgrades. The Software Sources application gives you control over important aspects of that process and integrates with both the Synaptic Package Manager and the Software Update utility.

The Software Sources window shows five tabs: Ubuntu Software, Third-Party Software, Updates, Authentication, and Statistics.

The Ubuntu Software tab is key as it allows you to select what aspects of the Ubuntu system can be downloaded from the Internet. The Download From drop-down list lets you select the location that will be used for the download. Note that the system will automatically select what it thinks is the closest server to you, but you can change this option by using the drop-down list.

The Updates tab is also important; it enables you to select the type of files you will download. By default, the system is set to download only important security updates and recommended updates. The default configuration is perfect for most users. The Automatic Updates section enables configuration of the updates' functionality. Use the drop-down list to specify how often the system checks for updates and the check boxes below to specify the action that will be taken.

Configure Software Sources

1. Click System → Administration → Software Sources.

The system prompts you for your administrative password.

2. Type your password.
3. Click OK.

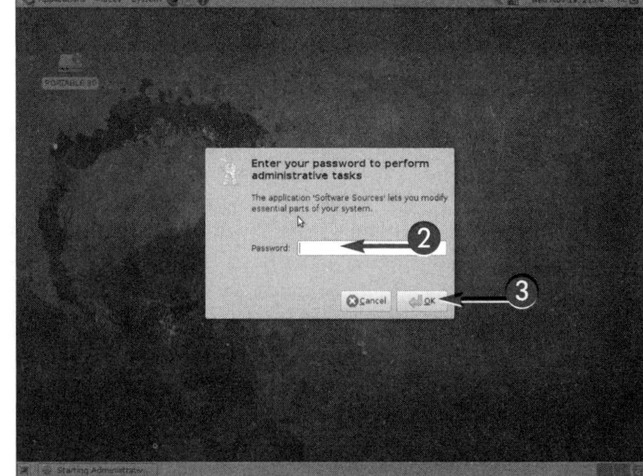

The Software Sources window opens to the Ubuntu Software tab.

4 Click to select what you want the system to be able to download from the Internet.

5 Click Updates.

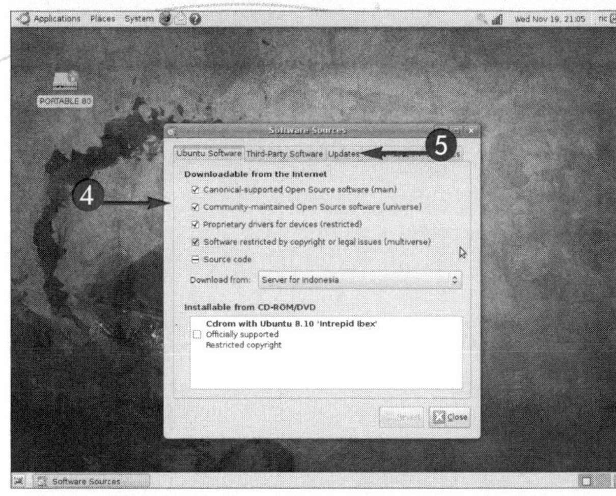

The Updates tab comes to the front.

6 Click here and select how often you want your system to check for updates.

7 Click Close.

Your system will download software according to your settings.

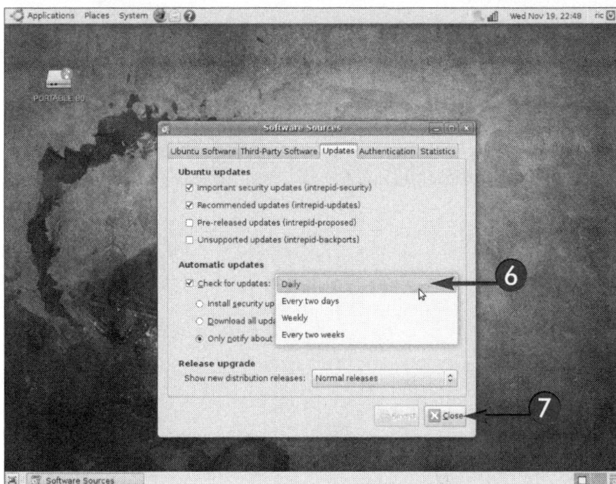

Extra

The other tabs in the Software Sources window are worth mentioning. The Third-Party Software tab enables you to select or add trusted sources for third-party software downloads. By default, only two are presented, and none are selected. Both of the default sources are archives from Canonical and are considered to be trustworthy. You can add additional sources if you need to.

The Authentication tab provides keys for verifying the correct source of the software. Do not delete the default keys. If you have additional keys, you can add them here.

The Statistics tab is optional and intended to help the Ubuntu community gather information about what software the users have found worthwhile and have installed.

Finally, there will come a day when the next version of Ubuntu is released and you will want to upgrade. You can upgrade manually by using a copy of the new system on a CD or a USB stick. However, there is a much easier way. On the Updates tab, go to the Release Upgrade section and select Normal Releases from the Show New Distribution Releases drop-down list. The system will notify you when a new release is out, and you can install it automatically.

Add Software with the Synaptic Package Manager

The Synaptic Package Manager helps you find, install, and manage the wide variety of additional components that can be added to your Ubuntu system.

Your Ubuntu desktop is the tip of the iceberg; there are many, many additional free and proprietary software packages you can install to extend Ubuntu. These packages can be found and installed via the Synaptic Package Manager.

The first time that you run the Synaptic Package Manager, it will also show you an introductory screen with basic instructions. When the Synaptic Package Manager window opens, you will note three panes: The top-left pane has a tree of categories used to help organize the packages. The top-right pane shows the contents of each category. When you click the name of a package in this pane, details about the package appear in the bottom-right pane.

To find a package, you click the category that you think it is in on the left and then click the application name on the top right. When the application details appear in the bottom pane, you should take special note whether you must install additional packages for your choice to operate properly. You can choose to install any application listed, or if there is a package that is already installed that you do not want, you can uninstall it. The right-click menu also has an easy link for downloading additional required packages, if any.

Note that the Synaptic Package Manager is associated with the Software Sources utility, discussed in the preceding section, "Configure Software Sources." Synaptic will only show packages that are available through the sources you have selected in the Software Sources utility.

Add Software with the Synaptic Package Manager

1. Click System ➔ Administration ➔ Synaptic Package Manager.

   The system will search for packages and update the package list.

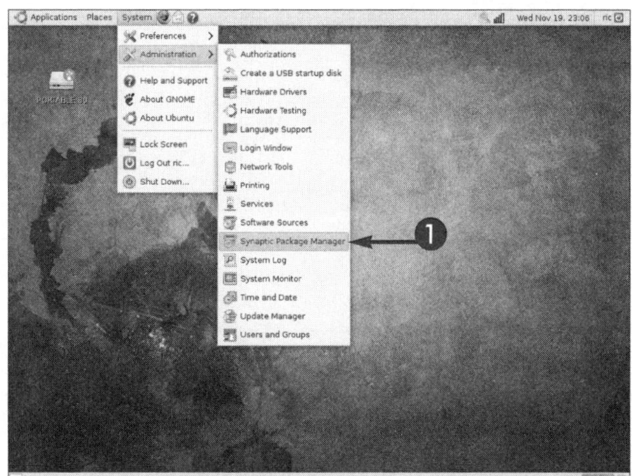

The Synaptic Package Manager window opens.

2. Click the category that you want to browse.
3. Click the name of an application to learn more.

- The details of the application package appear.

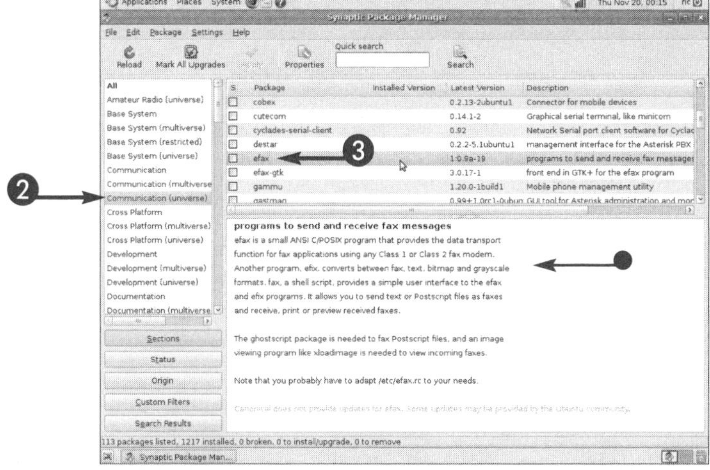

4 Right-click the application package's name.

5 Click Mark for Installation.

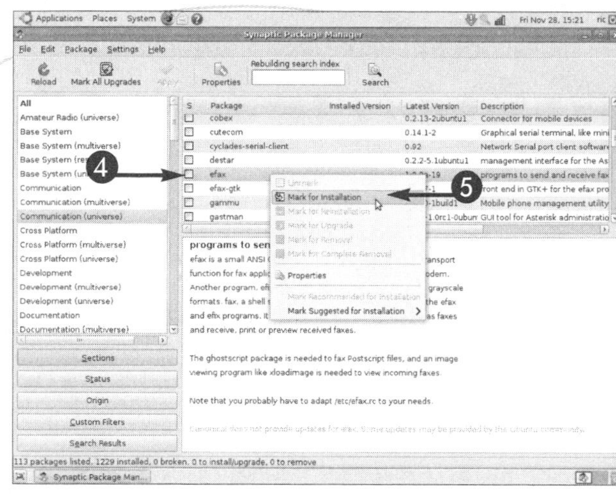

The Apply button becomes active.

6 Click Apply.

The Summary dialog box opens.

7 Click Apply.

The system installs the package.

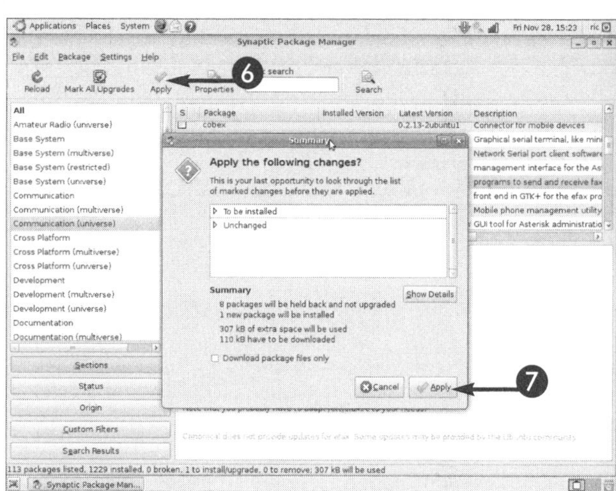

Extra

At the bottom of the left pane of the Synaptic Package Manager, there are five buttons. The buttons provide alternative ways to view the large collection of packages and can be used to help you screen and locate appropriate packages.

By default, the Sections button is active when you open the Synaptic Package Manager. The sections are displayed at the top of the left pane. Sections are essentially categories of packages.

The Status button lets you filter the packages catalog by their status. For example, you can use this to locate quickly all installed packages on your system.

Click the Origin button to categorize the packages by their source.

The Custom Filters button triggers the display of filters that are available in Synaptic. Filters sort and group the packages using a variety of useful categories. The default set of filters includes broken packages and upgradeable packages. Note that you can create your own custom filters by selecting Filters from the Preferences menu and then specifying your criteria.

Search Results provides you with an alternative view of the results of your searches.

Review the System Logs

The System Log Viewer built into the GNOME desktop makes it easy to view a record of system events and helps to diagnose problems with your system. Although you can access the same information by reviewing the text log files, the data presented in the System Log Viewer is easier to read and simpler to find.

The System Log Viewer has three panes in the window. The top-left pane shows you the various log files. The bottom-left pane shows you a calendar indicating the dates of the logs. The main window on the right contains the contents of the log file itself.

You can select any of the logs in the left pane to see their contents. You can access additional log files by using the Open Log dialog box, which displays the various log files the system has saved throughout the recent history of your system. You can select the one that you want to view and then open it in the System Log Viewer.

Log files can be very long and are notoriously hard to scan and review. If you are looking for a specific reference, you can make the task more manageable by using the Filter control, located under the View menu. When you select Filter, a search box will appear beneath the main pane. As you type in the box, the active log file's contents will be filtered to restrict the view to only those lines that contain the string you have entered.

Review the System Logs

1. Click System ➔ Administration ➔ System Log.

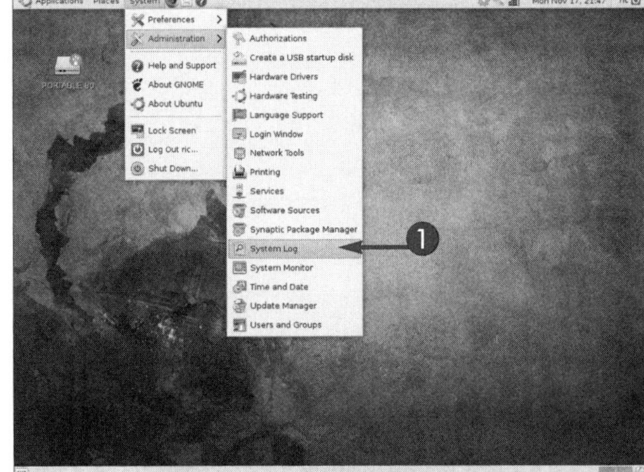

The System Log Viewer opens.

- If the log that you want to review is in the list, you can click it, and its contents will appear on the right.

2. Click File ➔ Open.

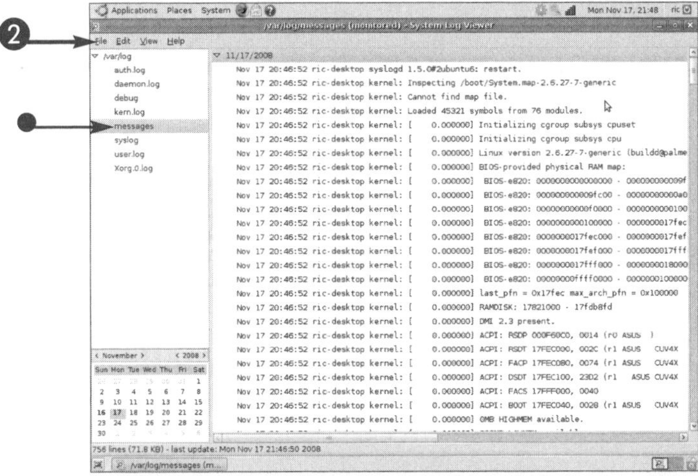

The Open Log dialog box appears.

3. Click the log file that you want to view.
4. Click Open.

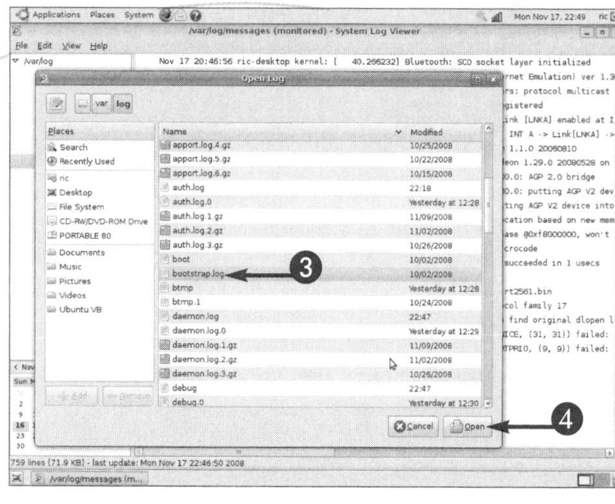

- The log file appears in the Viewer window.

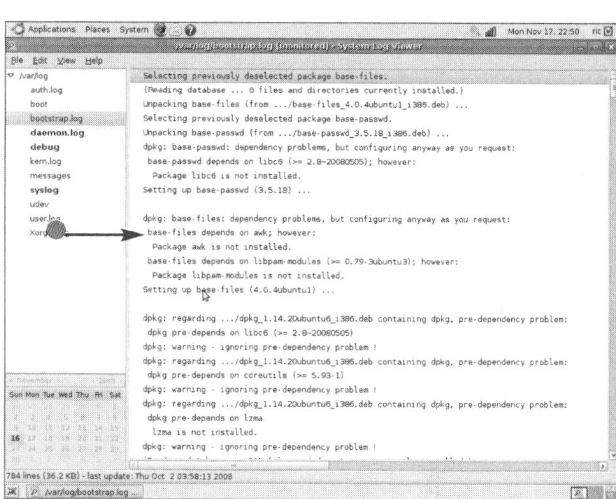

Extra

The default System Log application is quite good and thorough. It will suffice for the vast majority of users. If, however, you are a developer or you have a special need for a more advanced application, you can find several in the Synaptic Package Manager.

Open Synaptic, as discussed in the section "Add Software with the Synaptic Package Manager." Run a search for the term **log** using the Quick Search feature on the Synaptic toolbar. A number of search results will appear.

Among the search results, you will find log applications tailored to a variety of environments. There is one for the .Net framework, another based in Perl, one in Java, and one in C++. Some of these applications are quite powerful and provide feature sets that match or exceed the default System Log application.

Also of note is the log2mail application. Log2mail lets you set up a watch list for the log, and when a string is found matching your watch list, an email is sent to the address you specify. This is a particularly useful way to keep track of and manage your machines remotely.

Observe System Performance with the System Monitor

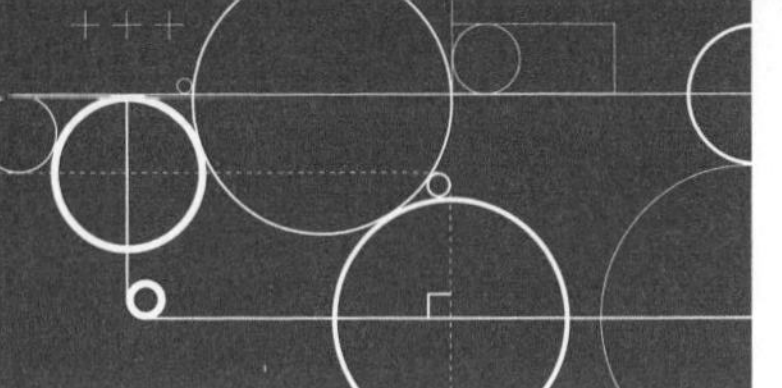

The System Monitor provides valuable insights into your Ubuntu system's performance and helps you isolate and deal with problems. Not only does this application provide useful information, but it also can help you prevent and recover from hardware and software crashes.

When the System Monitor application opens, you will see four tabs at the top of the window: System, Processes, Resources, and File Systems. The default view is the Resources tab, which gives you a real-time look at what is happening with your system. The top line, labeled CPU History, shows the load on your CPU. The Memory and Swap History section tells you about memory usage. The Network History chart at the bottom gives insight into the network activity, if any, of your computer.

The Processes tab lists all the active processes in the system. The chart shows the process name, along with its status, its CPU and memory usage, and several other statistics of less importance. You can sort the list by clicking the column headings.

The System tab displays information about your system, including your Ubuntu version, your Linux kernel, and your available disk space.

The File Systems tab provides a summary view of information about all the disk drives on your computer. This tab is useful as it gives you a quick view of all the drives on the system, along with their free space.

Observe System Performance with the System Monitor

1. Click System ➔ Administration ➔ System Monitor.

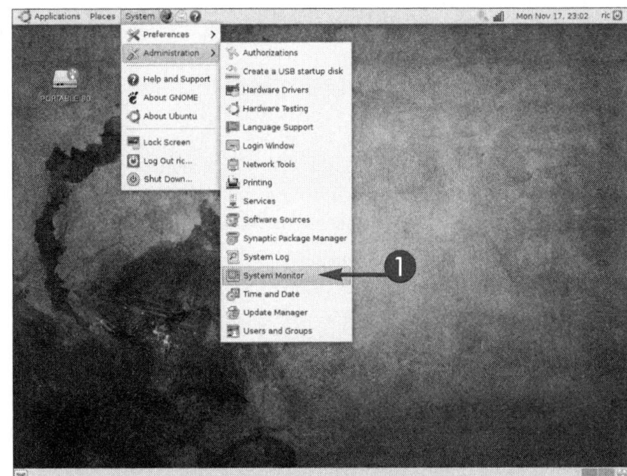

The System Monitor opens to the Resources tab.

2. Check out the information to see your system's CPU load, memory usage, and network activity.
3. Click the Processes tab.

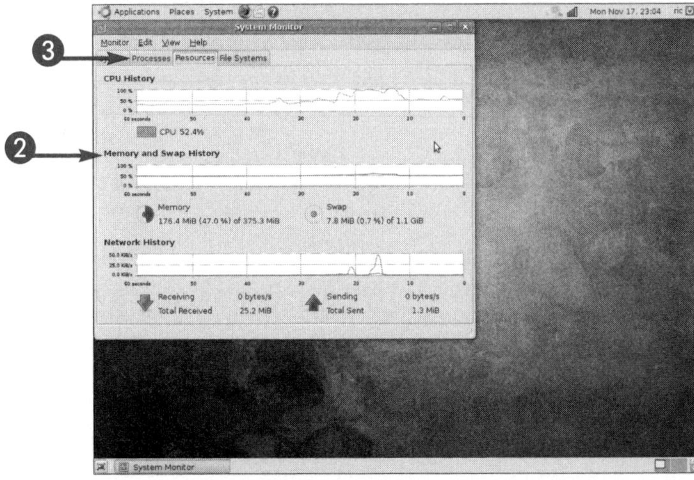

The Processes tab comes to the front.

4 To stop a process, first right-click it.

5 Click Stop Process.

- The process will be suspended until you click Continue Process.

6 Click the System tab.

The System tab comes to the front.

7 Check out the information about your version of Ubuntu, RAM and processor, and available disk space.

8 Click here to close the window.

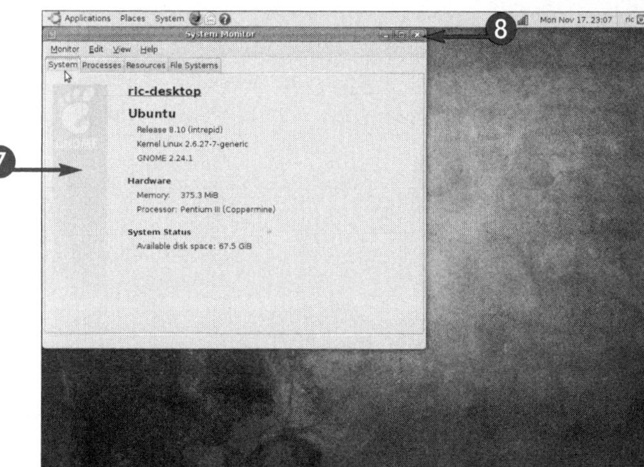

Apply It

If you have a piece of software that has failed and is causing you problems, you can use the Processes tab to locate and disable the software. You will want to do this when a piece of software will not close or has frozen and ceased to operate properly.

View the list of processes on the Processes tab and look for the name of the software that is causing the problem. Right-click the name of the process. If you are not certain if the process you have selected is the source of the problem, select Stop Process and view the impact on the system. If stopping the process does not solve the problem, the process is unlikely to be the cause of the problem. Choose Continue Process and look for another cause.

When you find the source of the problem, right-click it and choose End Process for an orderly shutdown of the process. If that fails, select Kill Process, which is a more abrupt cancellation.

The selective use of this feature makes it possible to regain control of your computer with a minimum of disruption.

Adjust the Time and Date

You can use the Time and Date utility on your Ubuntu desktop to adjust the time, date, and time zone.

Time settings can be adjusted from either the clock on your taskbar or from your System menu. Although adjusting settings from the top taskbar may be faster, lasting changes to the system are best executed from the Time and Date Settings application under the System menu.

The Time and Date Settings dialog box is used to control the system clock, and that means modifications require a user with administrator access. The application is initially locked. When you try to unlock it, the system will prompt you for the appropriate access credentials, that is, a proper username and password. After your credentials are authenticated by the system, the Time and Date Settings will be editable.

You can select your time zone by clicking in the Time Zone dialog box. You can click on a location on the map to set the zone, or you can use the drop-down list at the bottom of the dialog box.

In the Configuration drop-down list of the Time and Date Settings dialog box, you can select either a manual setting of the time or an automatic one, which will keep your system's time synchronized with Internet servers. Note that to use automatic synchronization, you must have the NTP support plug-in installed on your machine.

In the calendar at the bottom of the Time and Date Settings dialog box, you can select the current month, day, and year.

Adjust the Time and Date

1. Click System ➔ Administration ➔ Time and Date.

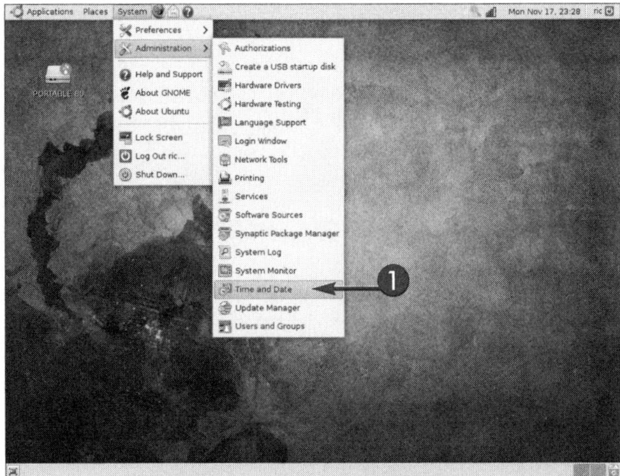

The Time and Date Settings dialog box opens.

2. Click Unlock.

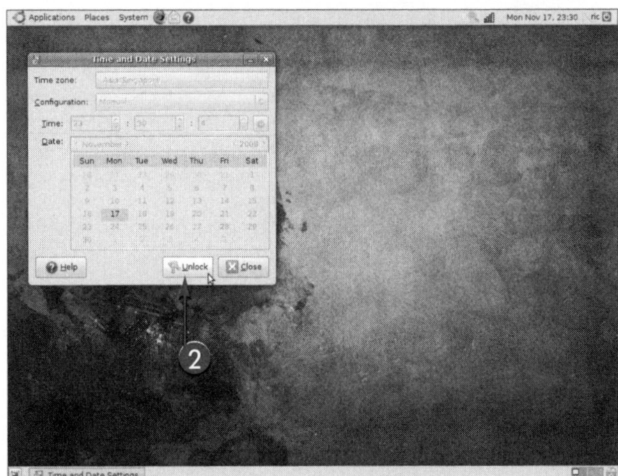

The Authenticate dialog box opens.

3. Type your password.
4. Click Authenticate.

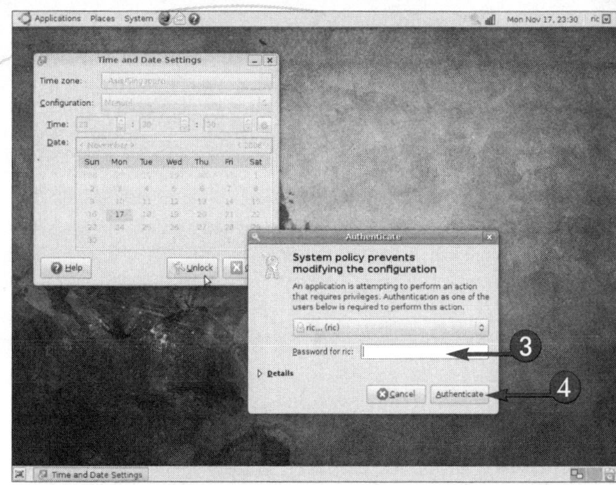

The Time and Date Settings dialog box is unlocked.

- You can click here to set your time zone.

5. Adjust the time and date.
6. Click Close.

The time and date are set.

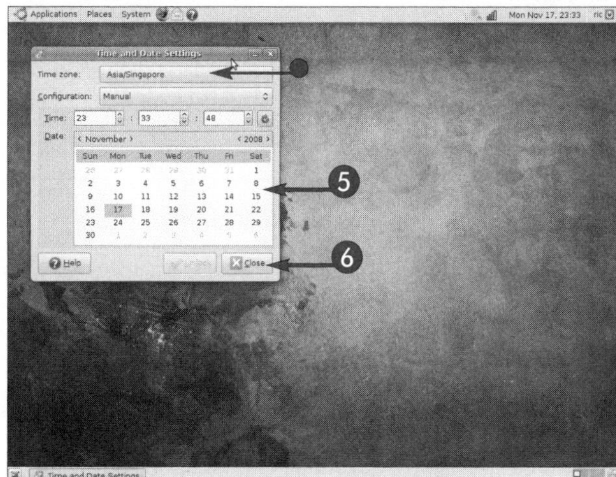

Extra

You can also adjust your time and date settings directly from the desktop by clicking the time and date that is displayed in your task panel. Click the time and date, and the application window will expand. Expand the window further by clicking Locations. Then click the Edit button to adjust your time zone and time settings.

Clicking Edit opens the Clock Preferences dialog box. On the General tab, set a 12- or 24-hour format and configure the display. On the Locations tab, set or edit your location. If your location does not appear, click the Add button. The Add dialog box lets you name the location and select a location from the drop-down list. You can even add your latitude and longitude if you want to. The Weather tab configures the measurement units that will be used for the weather data. Click Time Settings to set the time and the date. When you are finished, click Set System Time, and the Time Settings dialog box will close. Click Close in the Clock Preferences dialog box, and you are done.

Your new settings will appear immediately.

Run the Update Manager

Ubuntu makes it easy to keep your system up-to-date and secure with the Update Manager utility. The Update Manager automatically detects when new updates are available and helps you download and install them.

When you launch the Update Manager, it will automatically check for any outstanding updates for your Ubuntu system. For this to work, you must be connected to the Internet.

If any updates are found, the Update Manager will list them and prompt you to download and install them. You can click an update and then click Description of Update to learn more about an individual update.

If you choose to download the updates, the application will attempt to download the various update files to your machine. Then it will automatically install them. You will need to enter your administrator's password to authorize the application to install new updates to your system.

After the installation process is finished, the Update Manager will show that your system is up-to-date.

Note that Ubuntu also provides you with a visual notification in the event that there are updates available for your system. The indicator will appear on your taskbar at the top right of the screen. Clicking the notification will cause the Update Manager to launch.

If for any reason you do not want to download a set of updates, you can cancel the process by clicking the Close button and run the Update Manager at a later date.

Run the Update Manager

1. Click System ➔ Administration ➔ Update Manager.

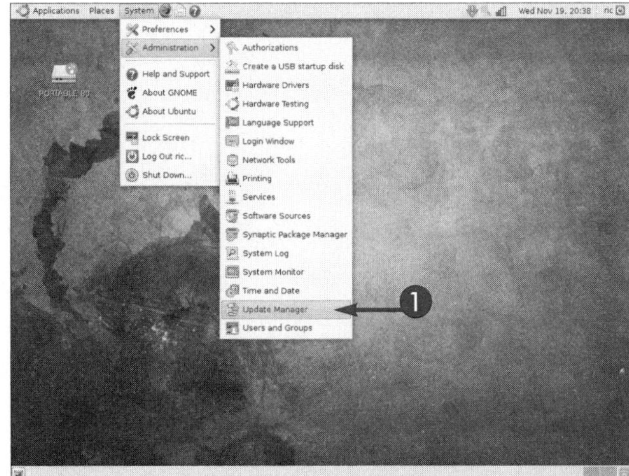

- The Update Manager opens and checks the system status.

Note: *For this to work properly, you need to be connected to the Internet.*

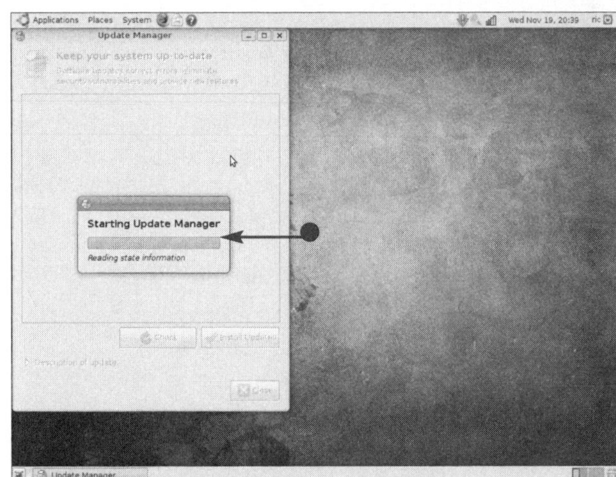

- The Update Manager displays a list of packages that need to be updated.

2. Click Install Updates.

   The system will connect to the Internet, download the necessary files, and install them.

- The Update Manager shows the system status.

3. Click Close.

   Your system is now up-to-date.

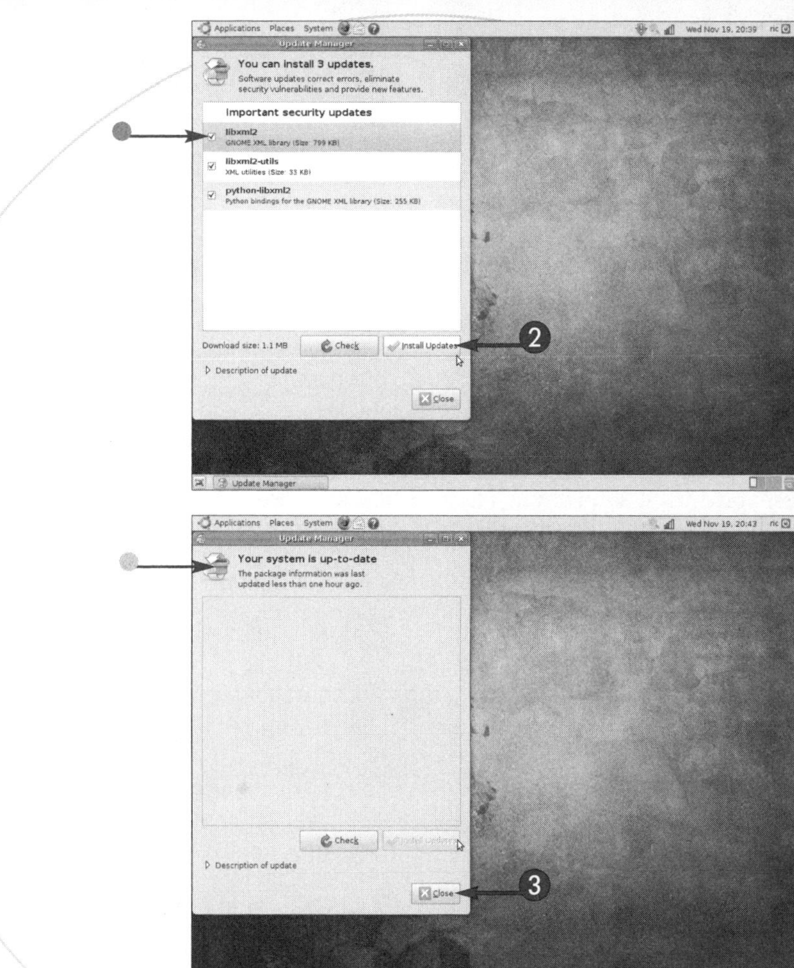

Apply It

The Ubuntu Update Manager will keep your packages up-to-date, but it does require an Internet connection to download the files. Although the Update Manager is certainly the easiest way to upgrade your system, if you do not have an Internet connection, you will need to explore alternatives.

Your first goal is to obtain the files for the update. Synaptic can help you manage this process. Open the Synaptic Package Manager and click File ➔ Generate Package Download Script. Save the file to a USB flash drive or other removable media and then remove that media from your computer. Next, you must go to a PC that is running Linux and has an Internet connection. Run the script and save the resulting files to your removable media. Disconnect the removable media and plug it back into your machine. Open the Synaptic package Manager. Click File ➔ Add Downloaded Packages and follow the steps.

If you want to conduct a full upgrade to a new version of Ubuntu, you need to obtain the files for the upgrade and burn the ISO to a CD. Insert the CD in your computer and follow the steps.

Add and Manage Users and Groups

Your Ubuntu system makes it possible to create new users and organize them into groups. With the Users and Groups utility, you can control the permissions of the users and grant or deny them access to different aspects of the system. The ability to limit access and set permissions is key to maintaining the security of your system and the integrity of your data.

When you first open the Users Settings window, it displays a list of all the users in the system. However, the window will initially be locked. Before you can make any changes, you must first unlock it. To do so, you will need to enter your password and be authenticated by the system. After you are authenticated, the controls of the Users Settings dialog box will be fully functional.

You can create a new user using the New User Account dialog box. You specify a username and an initial password for him or her on the Account tab. You can specify other details about the user on this tab, but those settings are optional. On the User Privileges tab, you set his or her privileges, granting or limiting the new user's ability to perform certain tasks with the system. On the Advanced tab, the choices are all optional.

Add and Manage Users and Groups

1 Click System ➔ Administration ➔ Users and Groups.

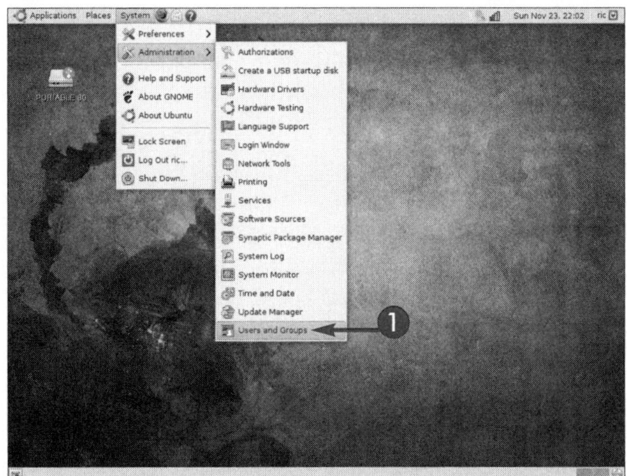

The Users Settings window opens.

2 Click Unlock.

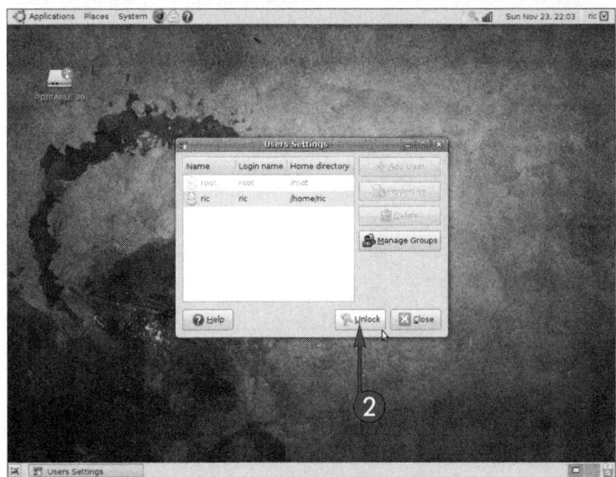

The Authenticate dialog box appears.

3 Type your password.

4 Click Authenticate.

The Authenticate dialog box closes, and the Users Settings dialog box will be unlocked.

5 Click Add User.

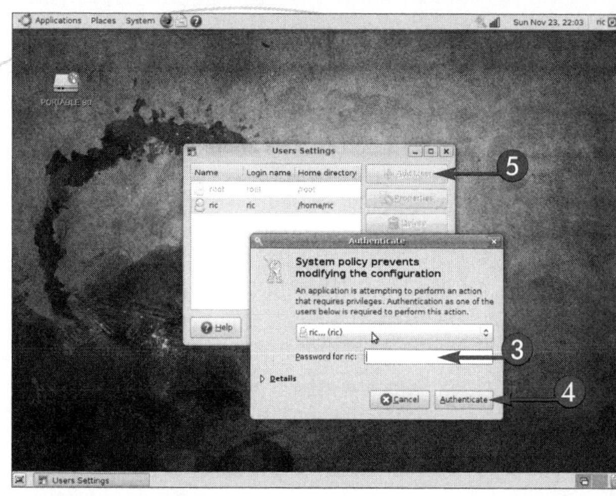

The New User Account dialog box opens.

6 Type a username.

7 Type a user password.

8 Type the password again to confirm it.

Note: *The other fields on this dialog box are optional.*

9 Click the User Privileges tab.

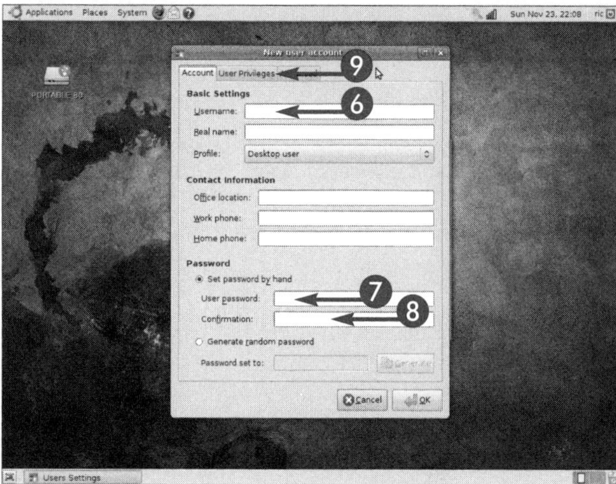

Extra

Permissions management in Ubuntu requires a combination of the options under the Users and Groups application and those of the Authorizations utility, discussed earlier in this chapter in the section "Adjust Authorizations."

In general, you should try to grant only those permissions that are actually needed by a user. Granting unnecessary rights opens up the system to compromise. When you view the Privileges tab of the New User Account dialog box, you will see that there are a number of options that are probably not relevant to all the users on your system. Does the user really need access to a modem? To a scanner? If not, disable those privileges. Most importantly, you will notice that one of the privileges is Administer the System. This is a very high-level grant of access to a number of powerful functions in Ubuntu. Only grant this access to trusted users. Ideally, you would have only one person on the system with these privileges in order to avoid problems and maintain accountability.

When a user is no longer going to be using the system, delete his or her account, if you have no compelling reason to preserve it. Unused accounts are one of the most frequent avenues of hacks on individual machines.

continued

Add and Manage Users and Groups (continued)

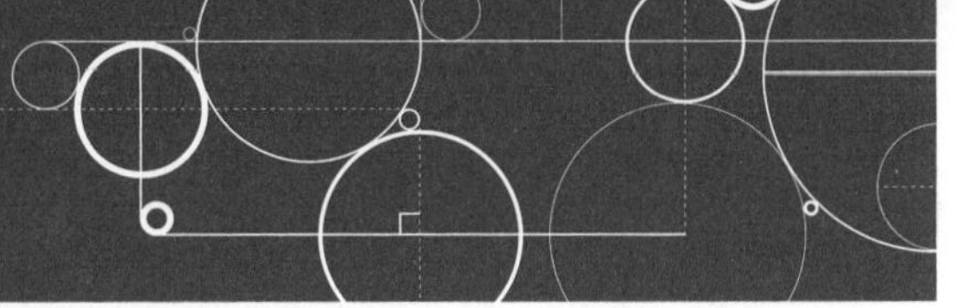

The User and Groups utility enables you to view and modify existing users and to organize them into groups.

Existing users can be viewed by clicking their name in the Users Settings window and then clicking the Properties button; this will cause the Account Properties dialog box to open. The Account Properties dialog box is identical to the New User Account dialog box discussed earlier in this section. You can make changes to the user's account in the Account Properties dialog box, including setting a new password.

You can delete a user by clicking his or her name and then clicking the Delete button in the Users Settings window. The system will ask you to confirm this action. Note that deleting a user will remove the account, but it will not delete any files that he or she has on the computer.

Groups are also managed from the Users Settings dialog box. Groups in Ubuntu are primarily for organizing users. They are very helpful if you have a large number of users on a machine. However, unlike some other systems, you cannot control privileges by group; rather in Ubuntu, you control privileges per individual user.

To work with your groups, you use the Groups Settings dialog box. You can add a new group, view a group's attributes, and delete a group by clicking the group name and then clicking the Delete button.

Group properties options are very limited. Essentially, you can only rename the group, change the group ID, or assign members to the group.

Add and Manage Users and Groups *(continued)*

The User Privileges tab appears.

10 Click the check boxes to set user privileges for the new user.

11 Click the Advanced tab.

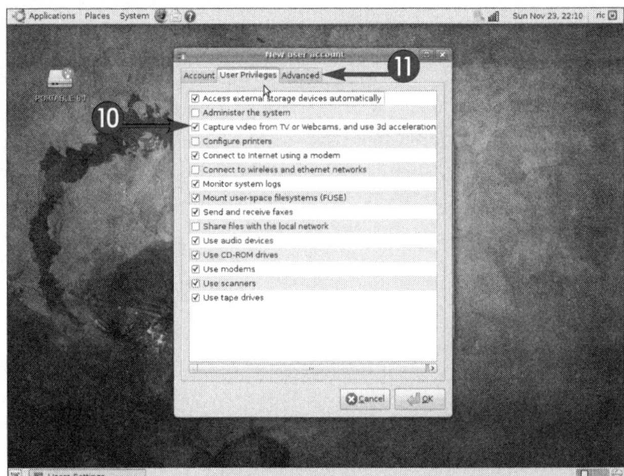

The Advanced tab comes to the front.

12 Adjust the settings that you want to apply to the new user, including specifying a main group, if needed.

13 Click OK.

The new account is ready for use.

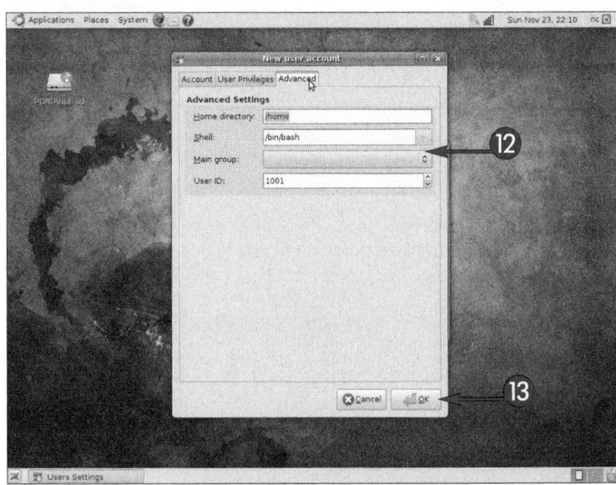

You are returned to the Users Settings window.

14 Click Manage Groups.

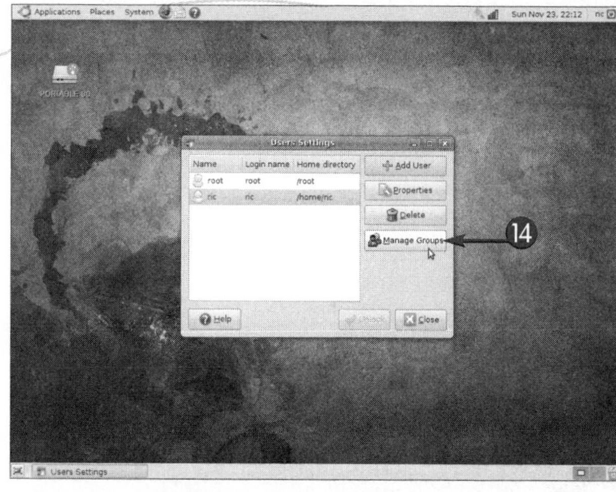

The Groups Settings dialog box opens, allowing you to review the eligible groups.

- You can click Add Group to add a group to the list.
- You can click a group and then click Properties to modify a group's settings.

15 Click Close.

Your user and group settings are applied.

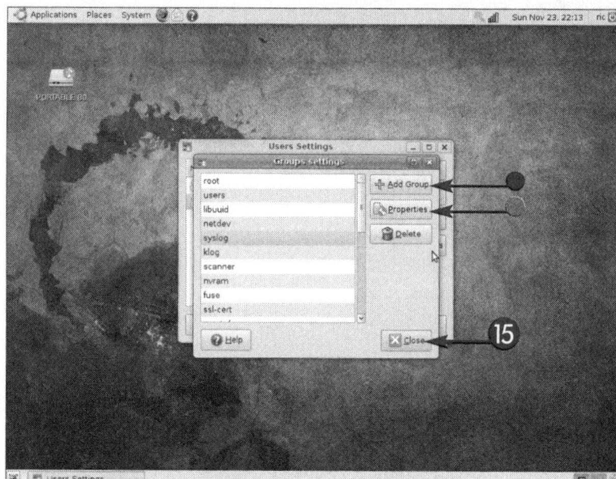

Extra

One of the nicest new features of Ubuntu 8.10 is guest accounts. In previous versions of the system, you could create guest accounts, but in Intrepid Ibex, they are available by default.

Guest accounts are a great way for you to allow someone else to use your system without having to create a full user account for them. Guest accounts are also very handy as the guest user cannot make changes to your system, and when the user logs out, the account is reset for the next user. Guests can use your computer to check their mail, surf the web, and so on, and when they log out, their history is removed from the system.

To give someone guest access, simply click the User Switcher located on your top panel. The first choice on the menu that appears is Guest; select that option. The system will switch to Guest mode, allowing the user to have limited access to the system. When the user is finished, he or she can log out, or you can switch back to your account. While the guest user is active, your session information is preserved.

Using the Calculator

The default GNOME desktop comes bundled with a powerful and flexible Calculator application that enables you to perform common mathematical operations. The calculator provides a range of features and can be used either in a very basic form or in any of three more complex modes. The four calculator modes are Basic, Advanced, Financial, and Scientific.

The Basic mode is a simple four-function calculator with no option to store values in memory. If you want to only add, subtract, multiply, or divide, then this is a fast, simple choice with a clean and uncluttered interface.

If you want more features, you can select one of the other three modes. The Advanced calculator provides many of the options that most people need, including the capability to determine roots and fractions and a memory function that can be used to store and recall values.

The Financial and Scientific calculators are more advanced still and include specialty functions, as you may expect from their names. The Financial calculator includes options for calculating interest and depreciation. The Scientific calculator includes a number of trigonometric functions such as sine, cosine, tangent, and logarithms.

After you start the calculator, you can freely change back and forth between the various modes by way of the View menu, which appears on the menu bar of each of the calculators. The system will remember the mode that you have selected, and the next time the calculator is opened, it will appear in the mode last viewed.

Using the Calculator

1. Click Applications ➔ Accessories ➔ Calculator.

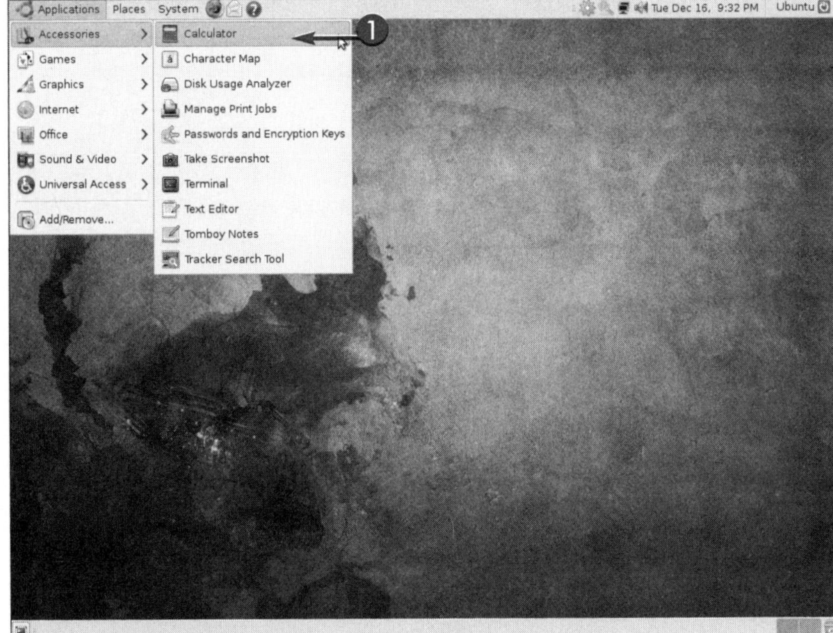

The Calculator application appears, by default in the Basic mode.

2. Click the keys to enter the calculation that you want to perform.
3. Click =.

- The result appears in the calculator's window.

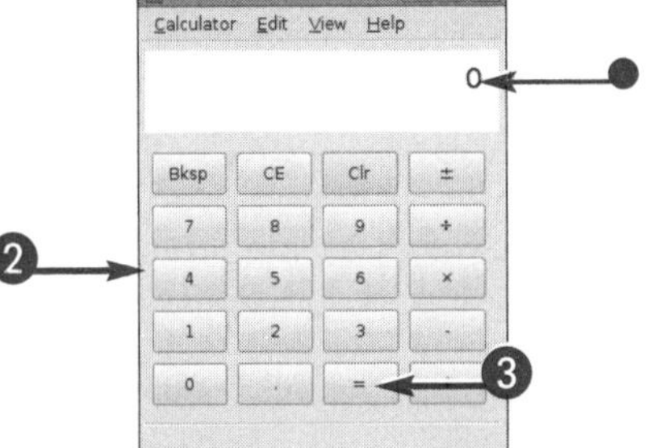

4. Click View.
5. Click the type of calculator that you want to open, such as Advanced.

   A confirmation dialog box will appear.
6. Dismiss the dialog box to proceed.

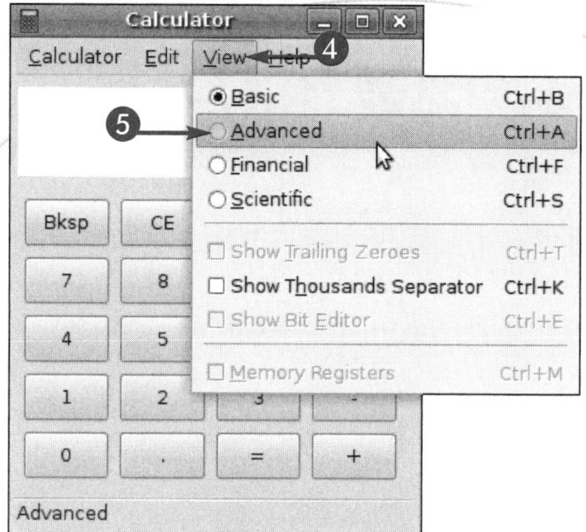

The Calculator changes to the mode that you selected.

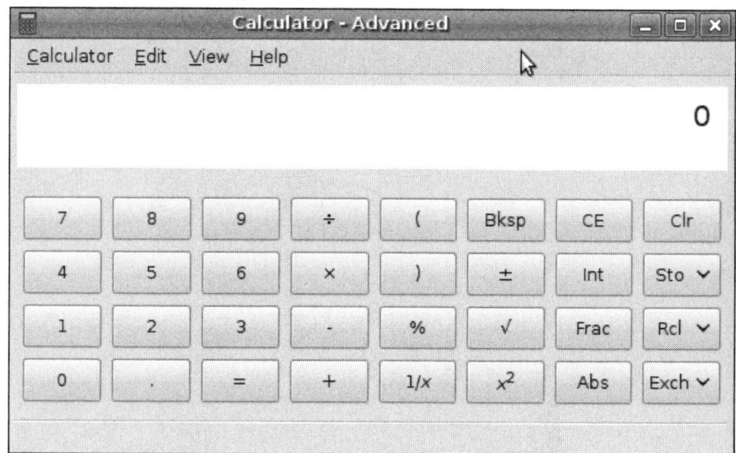

Extra

A full-featured memory function is available in the Advanced, Financial, and Scientific calculators. The Basic mode does not include a memory function. Data is stored and retrieved from the memory through the keys on the calculator. Sto stores a value, Rcl recalls a value, and Exch swaps, or exchanges, values.

The system supports ten memory slots, meaning that you can store up to ten entries in the memory simultaneously. You can select the memory slot to hold the value by clicking the Sto button and then selecting from the drop-down list that appears. When you click either Rcl or Exch, you can select from the values that you have stored in the various memory slots.

If you want memory data to remain visible on the screen, click View → Memory Registers; doing so will cause the contents of the memory slots to remain displayed on your screen as you work. Note that the contents of the memory will persist; you can close the calculator or restart the computer without fear of losing the contents of the memory.

Insert Special Characters with the Character Map

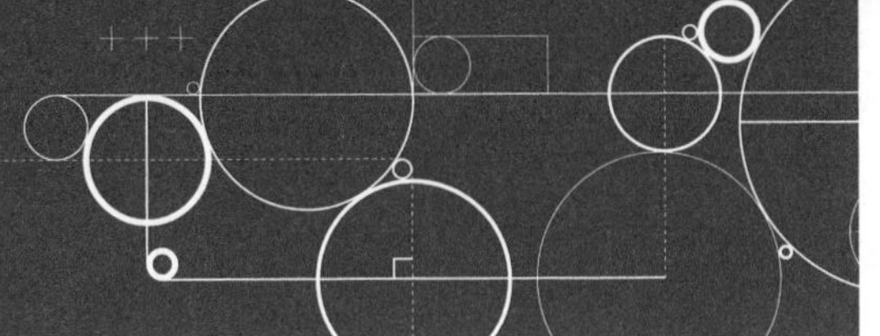

The Character Map window provides a way to access all the characters that are available in your system. This tool is most frequently used to find and insert into your documents characters that do not normally appear on your keyboard, such as the copyright symbol.

The GNOME Character Map application, technically known as *gucharmap,* is particularly powerful; it is based on the Unicode Character Database, which gives your system access to an incredible assortment of characters, including foreign alphabets, phonetic alphabets, and even Braille characters. Finding the right character or symbol in the midst of this huge assortment of options is where the Character Map application comes in handy.

You can browse the available characters and symbols by category, under the label Script, or you can search for key terms via the options under the Search menu. Given the wide number of options available, the search feature is particularly useful. Each character in the collection is accompanied by a description. You can search for the character you want by using common descriptive terms. So, for example, if you want to see what options exist for the Euro currency symbol, simply type **euro** in the Search box.

When you have identified the character that you need, use the font selection combo box to match the character with your document's font style. You can zoom in and out to view the character in whatever font size you choose.

Insert Special Characters with the Character Map

1. Click Applications ➔ Accessories ➔ Character Map.

The Character Map application appears.

2. Click Search ➔ Find.

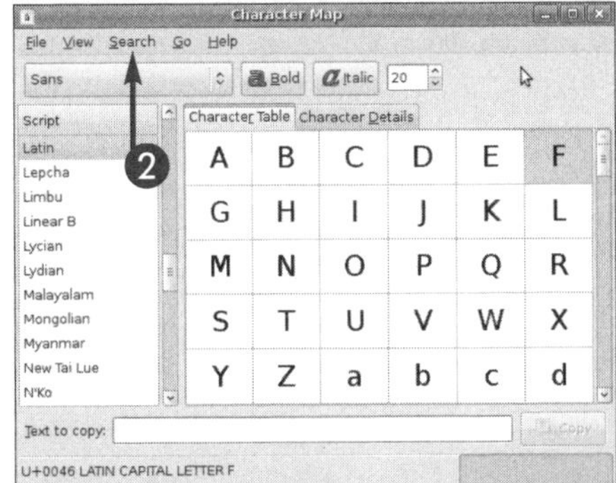

The Find dialog box opens.

3. Type your search term.
4. Click Next.

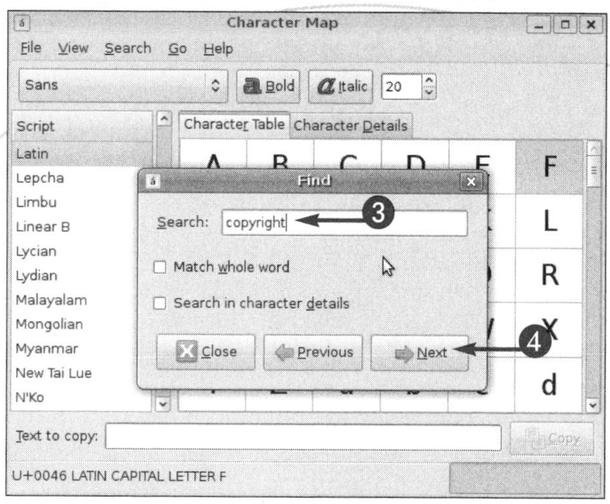

- The first search result is highlighted.

5. If the character is the one that you want, copy and paste it into your document.

Note: *Alternatively, you can simply click the character and drag it to your document.*

- If the character is not the one that you want, click Next to view other search results.

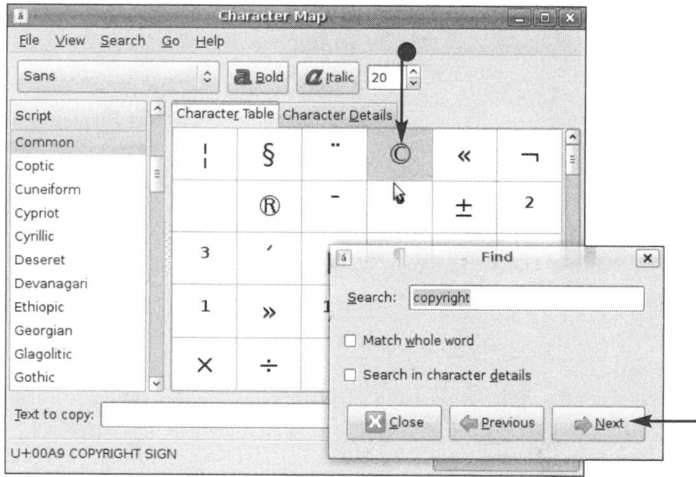

Extra

The Character Map application can also be used to help you learn more about the characters you see on your screen. The Character Details tab includes information about each individual character in the system. To use this tool, simply select a character and then click the Character Details tab to view the information associated with that character.

Although some of these details may seem rather esoteric, if you are a developer, you may find this information to be very useful. You can learn, for example, the character's proper name, its UTF-8 encoding, and its Unicode code point. Although a typical user may not have a great need for that particular feature, one closely related feature that is useful to everyone is the Character Map's capability to identify characters that you do not recognize.

If you have a document with an unusual character, simply open the Character Map application, select the character with your mouse, and drag it into the Character Map's window; if there is a matching character, it will be shown automatically. You can then click the Character Details tab to learn about that character.

Look Up Words in the Dictionary

Your Ubuntu desktop includes a built-in Dictionary application that enables you to quickly look up word definitions, pronunciations, and related terms. The default Ubuntu distribution supports English, Spanish, and Thai-to-English dictionaries, whereas regional distributions are sometimes bundled with additional languages.

The dictionary source files are located online, so the Dictionary feature is dependent on your having a working connection to the Internet. Without an Internet connection, the application will launch, but you will not be able to look up definitions. When you do have a working connection, you can type the word into the Look Up field. The results of a search will appear in the left pane of the Dictionary application's window, with the right pane showing a list of similar words. As the definitions are sometimes quite lengthy, the application is often easier to use if you enlarge the window a bit, or if you prefer, maximize it to occupy the full window.

Search results are saved in a history file that enables you to go back and forth using the commands in the Go menu. You can also print the definitions or save them for future reference. The Print and Save commands are both located under the File menu.

The system also includes a Dictionary applet that can be installed on the panel of your choosing, as discussed in Chapter 2. The applet is quite convenient, as it gives you instant access to a text field where you can enter a term and search for a definition without having to open the application.

Look Up Words in the Dictionary

LOOK UP A WORD

1 Click Applications ➔ Office ➔ Dictionary.

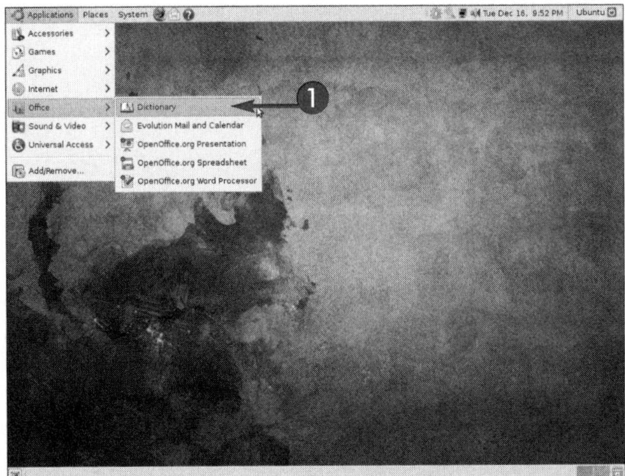

The Dictionary application appears.

2 Type the word that you want to search for and press Enter.

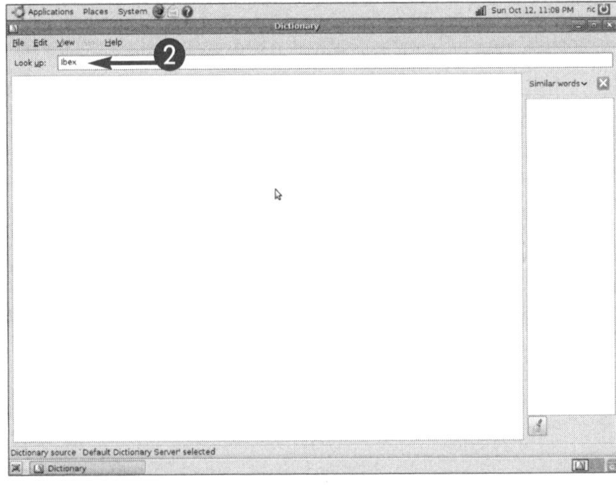

- The result appears in the left pane.

CHANGE THE SOURCE

3 Click View → Dictionary Sources.

- The optional dictionary sources appear in the right pane.

4 Double-click the dictionary that you want to use.

The chosen dictionary is now the source that will be searched.

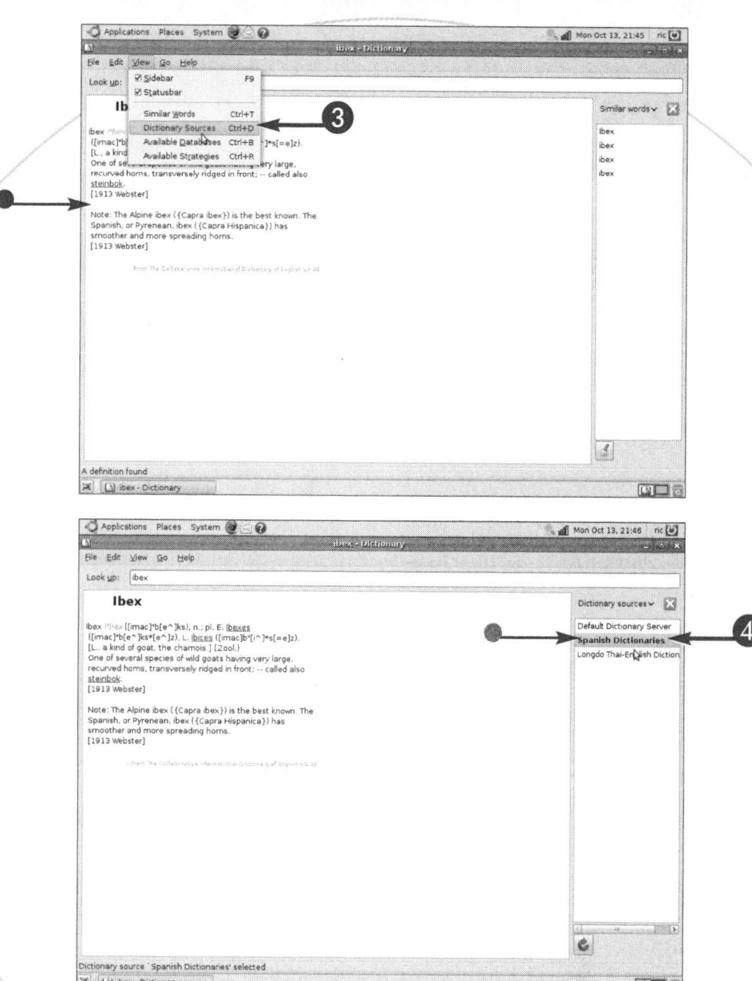

Extra

The system's default dictionary sources can be viewed from the Preferences dialog box, under the Edit menu. If you open the right pane of the Dictionary application, you can also select the dictionary sources from the list. The Preferences dialog box gives you the option to switch between dictionaries or to add or remove new sources.

The Ubuntu Dictionary application relies on the dictionary network protocol commonly known as *DICT*. You can add to your Ubuntu system any dictionary source that uses the DICT server protocol. For a list of alternative dictionary sources, try the Wikipedia page on the DICT protocol, which can be found at http://en.wikipedia.org/wiki/DICT.

Before you add a new source, take a look at the entries for the existing sources to determine what information is needed to list a new source. Given that the dictionary sources are not stored on your local machine and therefore do not take up any disk space, you should feel free to add as many sources as you like, and similarly, it is probably not worthwhile to delete any of the default sources in case you need them at some future point in time.

Find Out Where Memory Space Is Being Used with the Disk Usage Analyzer

Ubuntu is packaged with a tool that makes it possible for you to view the way the space on your hard drive is being used. The Disk Usage Analyzer provides insight into the space taken by all your various files and directories. If you find yourself running short of space on your hard disk, the Disk Usage Analyzer is a fast and easy way to find out what directories and files are taking the most space and where there may be opportunities for you to free up more space.

The Disk Usage Analyzer is a port of a Linux application called *Baobab* and is part of the Linux Utils bundle that comes with Ubuntu.

Once launched, the application waits for you to select an action to perform. You can scan all your system, or just a single directory, by selecting from the icons at the top of the screen. After you select an action to be performed, the application will start to index the target and display the results on your page.

The Disk Usage Analyzer window is divided into two regions. On the left side of the window is the list of the directories and files. On the right side is a graphical representation of the space allocation. You can select the way the chart on the right functions by using the drop-down list at the top right of the screen. The default display is a rings chart, but you can also view the results as a treemap chart. Regardless of which method you select, the data display is essentially the same, displaying the relative space taken by the various directories and their contents.

Find Out Where Memory Space Is Being Used with the Disk Usage Analyzer

1. Click Applications ➔ Accessories ➔ Disk Usage Analyzer.

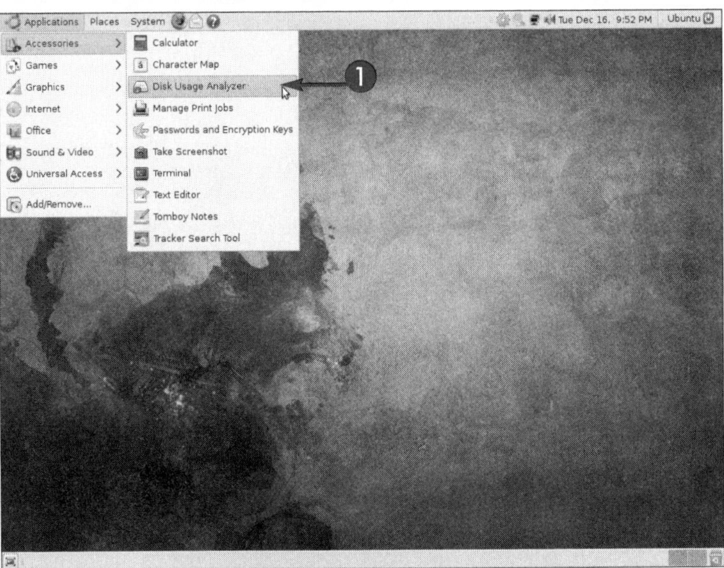

The Disk Usage Analyzer appears.

2. Click Scan Filesystem.

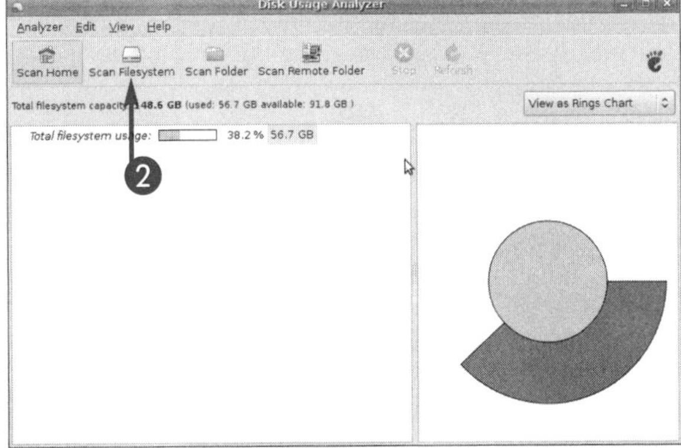

- The application scans your hard drive and displays the results.

3 Click here and click View as Treemap Chart.

- The right pane now displays the results in the Treemap Chart view.

4 Move your cursor over an area of the chart to see what space allocation it represents.

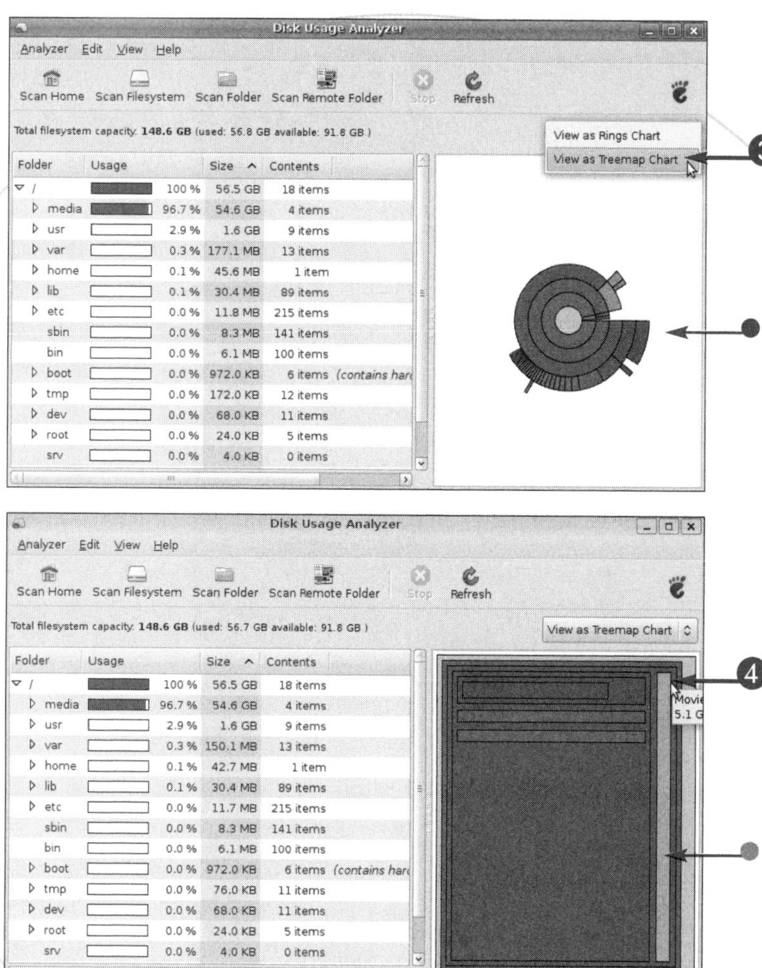

Extra

In addition to analyzing the contents of your local internal hard drive, you can also use the Disk Usage Analyzer utility to take a look at mounted drives and even remote drives not connected directly to your computer. To assess the usage of space on external drives connected to your machine, click the Scan Folder option and then navigate to the directory that you want to analyze. If you are seeking to analyze a drive that is not directly connected to your computer, click Scan Remote Folder.

The Scan Remote Folder option enables you to select the proper protocol to access the remote location: SSH, FTP, Windows share, HTTP, or any other custom connection type that you specify. After you have selected the protocol, type the address in the boxes provided and click Scan. If you have a valid connection to that server, the results will appear on your screen in the same fashion as they do for a scan of your local drive. At any time, you can update the display by clicking the Refresh button on the top toolbar.

Manage Print Jobs

You can check the status of your print jobs and make changes to them using the Manage Print Jobs application. Manage Print Jobs does just exactly what the name implies: It enables you to manage the printing of documents. You can use this application to view, pause, cancel, or restart your pending print jobs.

Typically, when you want to print a file, you will open the file with an application and choose Print from the menu, or you may click the application's Print icon. After you have done that, the print job is basically gone from your control; you can no longer control it from the original application. The Manage Print Jobs application is provided to overcome this limitation and give you more control over printing.

Any time you print a document in Ubuntu, the pending print job will be visible in Manage Print Jobs. The Manage Print Jobs window displays each job by name, along with the size, time, and status. By right-clicking a document on the list, you can choose to cancel or pause the job. You can also restart paused jobs by right-clicking and choosing Restart. Note that if you cancel a job, it is deleted from the queue. Canceling a job means that you will need to tell the system to print the file again using the other application.

You can use Manage Print Jobs to review a list of previously printed documents. You can also open a window that displays the printer's status by clicking View ➔ Show Printer Status.

Manage Print Jobs

1 Click Applications ➔ Accessories ➔ Manage Print Jobs.

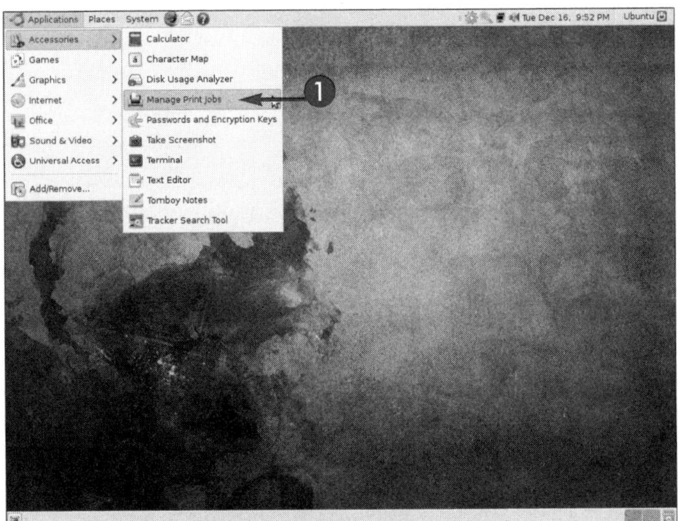

The Manage Print Jobs application appears, showing the work in progress.

- You can cancel or pause a job by right-clicking its name and then clicking Pause or Cancel.

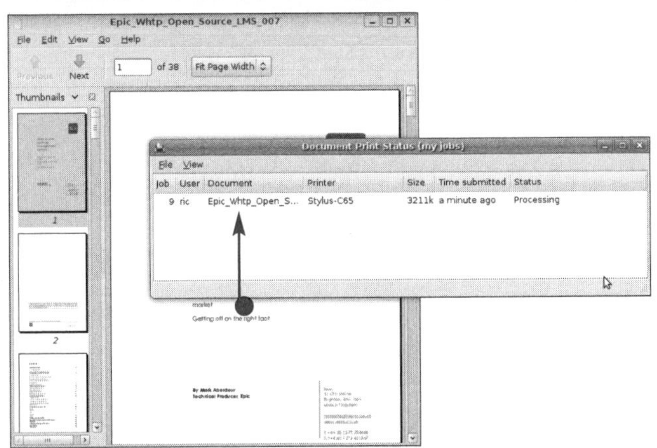

2. Click View ➔ Show Completed Jobs.

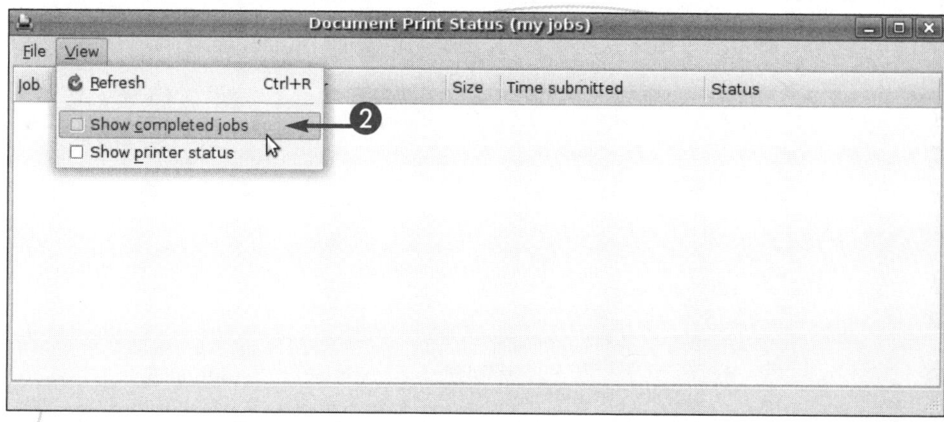

- A list of previous jobs appears.
- You can in some cases reprint documents directly from this list by right-clicking the document name and clicking Reprint.

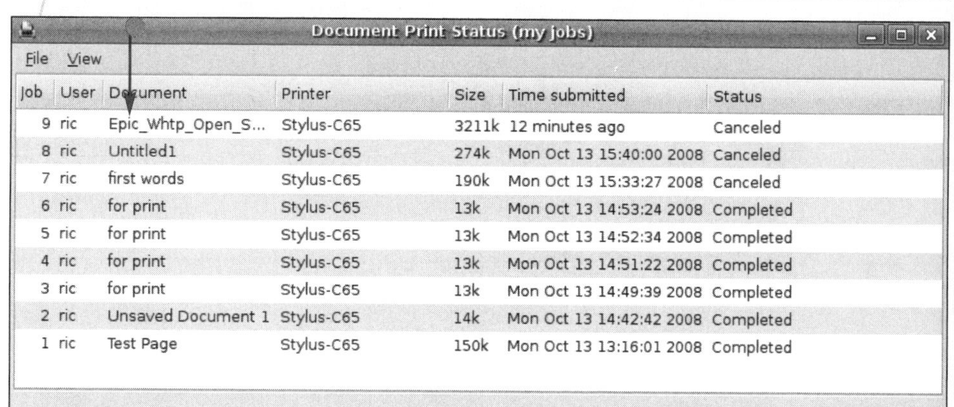

Extra

The Manage Print Jobs application comes in most handy when print jobs stall out due to the printer running out of ink or running out of paper. In those situations, the printer will typically pause the job automatically. Although some printers are pretty reliable about restarting the job when the problem is corrected, other printers require a little help. Going back to the original application that you used to request the print job may be an option when the printer's actions caused a warning dialog box to pop up. In these situations, it is best to use the original application to manage the print job. However, in many cases, the best way to get the printer to resume printing is through the Manage Print Jobs utility. Open it, find the job that has been paused by the printer, and then right-click and restart the job.

The application is also useful when a document has failed to print due to a serious application error. In those cases, it may be necessary to clear the printer queue. To do so, click the document name and cancel the print job.

Manage Passwords and Encryption Keys

You can use Ubuntu's Passwords and Encryption Keys application to create and manage both encryption keys and the passwords for your system. This application enables you to create and manage PGP and SSH keys and to keep up with the passwords used by your Ubuntu system applications. Readers who are familiar with GNOME may recognize this application; outside Ubuntu, it is known as *Seahorse.*

The first time that you launch the Passwords and Encryption Keys application, you will want to either import your existing keys or create new ones. The starting window for the application gives you both options.

The system supports the two most common forms of encryption keys: PGP and SSH. The PGP protocol, also known as *pretty good privacy,* is most useful for encrypting email or other files that you send to people. The Passwords and Encryption Keys application helps you manage those keys and use them easily in your Evolution email client.

The SSH protocol, also called *secure shell,* is primarily used for gaining secure access to a remote computer. SSH provides an alternative to traditional password login schemes but is not supported by all systems.

Both PGP and SSH involve the creation of two keys: a public key and a private key. These keys exist in pairs, and both are necessary, as discussed in Chapter 4. Collections of keys are known as *keyrings,* and as your collection grows, it can sometimes require a bit of management.

Manage Passwords and Encryption Keys

CREATE A NEW KEY

1. Click Applications ➔ Accessories ➔ Passwords and Encryption Keys.

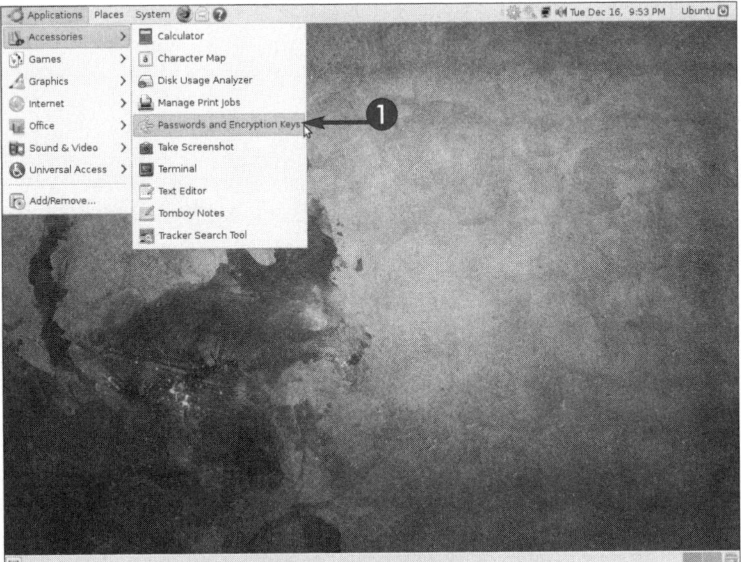

The Passwords and Encryption Keys application appears.

2. Click New.

- You can click Import to import your existing keys.

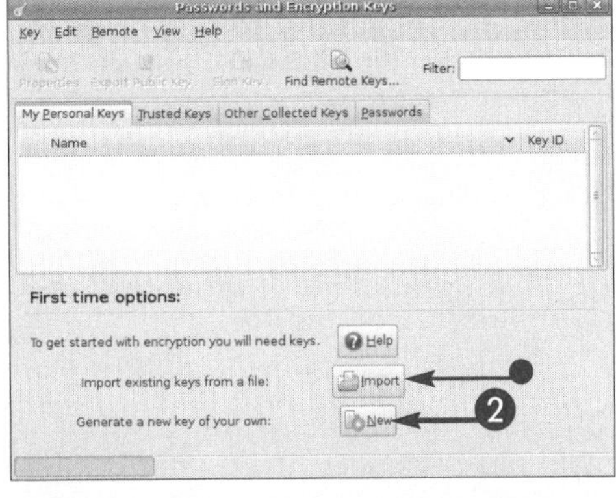

The Create a New Key dialog box opens.

3. Click the type of key that you want to create.

Note: *This example shows creating a PGP key, but the steps for an SSH key are similar.*

4. Click Continue.

The New PGP Key dialog box opens.

5. Type your name.

6. Type your email address.

7. Click Create.

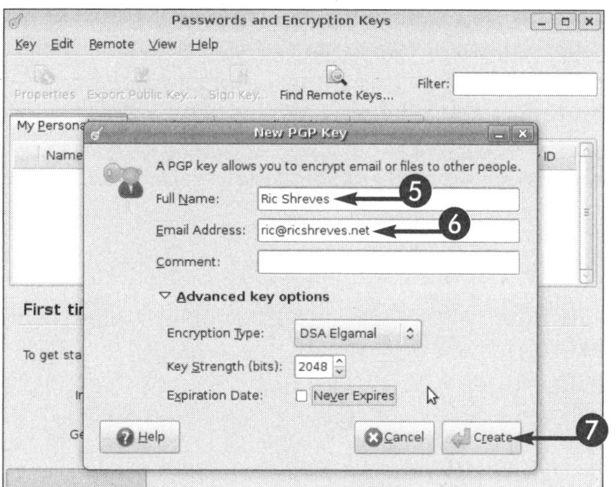

Extra

The Advanced Key Options section of the New PGP dialog box provides additional choices for creating a new key. The Encryption Type field specifies the algorithm that will be used to generate your keys. You can select from DSA Elgamal, DSA, and RSA. The DSA Elgamal option is the suggested choice.

The Key Strength option is important, as this sets the length of the key. Key length is expressed in bits. You can enter any value between 1,024 and 4,096. The higher the value, the stronger the encryption. Note, however, that the larger the value, the longer it can take for keys to be generated and otherwise processed. A value of at least 2,048 is recommended.

After creating a key, you can modify its expiration date. During creation, you can only specify if it will have an expiration date or if it will never expire. When the expiration date is reached, the key will cease to be usable. After the expiry date, you will need to either generate a new key or extend the expiry of the expired key. This field is optional; however, if you want to maintain a stronger privacy practice, you should set an expiration date. A good value for this field would be six months.

continued →

Manage Passwords and Encryption Keys (continued)

The Manage Passwords and Encryption Keys application can also help you keep track of your keys and passwords. Keys created elsewhere can be imported into the system in just a click, and similarly, the keys you have created, or previously imported, can be exported for use elsewhere.

The View menu contains a set of filters that make it easier to manage large keyrings. Using the choices on that menu, you can view keys by expiry, trust, or type of validity.

The Passwords tab plays a distinct but closely related role. The tab is concerned not with your public keys and keyrings, but rather with the passwords used by your local applications, such as your Evolution email client. On the Passwords tab, you will find a list of all your local system passwords. Double-click a password identifier on the list to open a dialog box. In the dialog box, you can view details about the password, including the application it is related to and the login it is associated with. On the Details tab of the dialog box, you can view the technical details associated with the password. The Applications tab tells you which applications have privileges to the password information. You can change a password on the Key tab. The password is shown in an obscured form, but you can clear that and read the password by clicking the Show Password check box.

To back up your keyrings, simply click Key ➔ Back Up Keyrings in the Passwords and Encryption Keys window. You will be prompted to name the archive and to select a location on your drive to store the information.

Manage Passwords and Encryption Keys *(continued)*

The Passphrase for New PGP Key dialog box opens.

8 Type your passphrase.

9 Confirm the passphrase by entering it a second time.

10 Click OK.

The Generating Key dialog box will appear as the system creates your key.

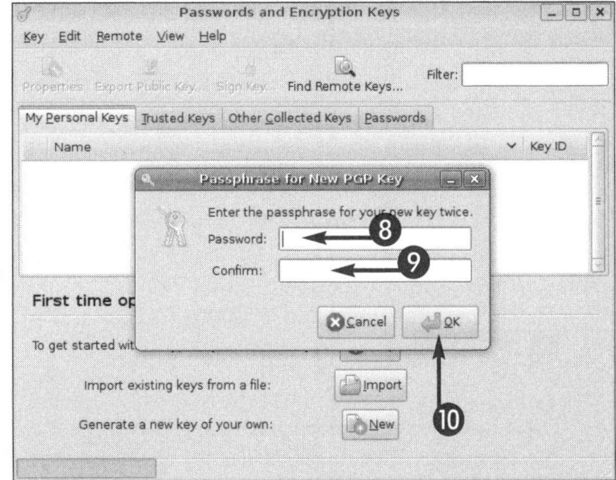

- After the new key is generated, it will appear in the Passwords and Encryption Keys window.

CHANGE YOUR PASSWORD

11 Click the Passwords tab.

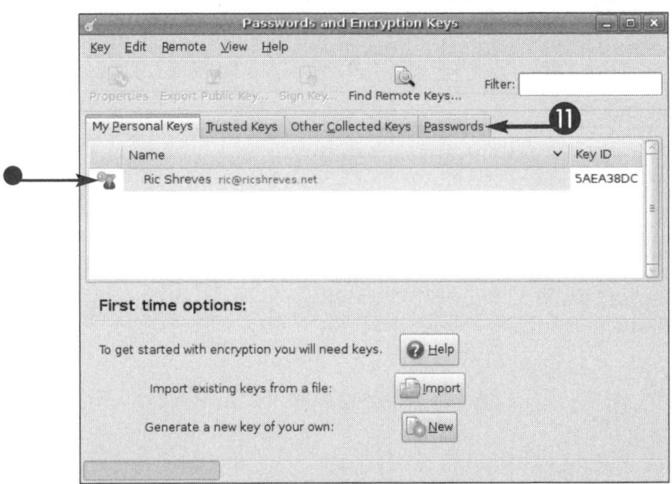

Your saved application passwords appear.

⓬ Click the entry that you want to change.

⓭ Click Properties.

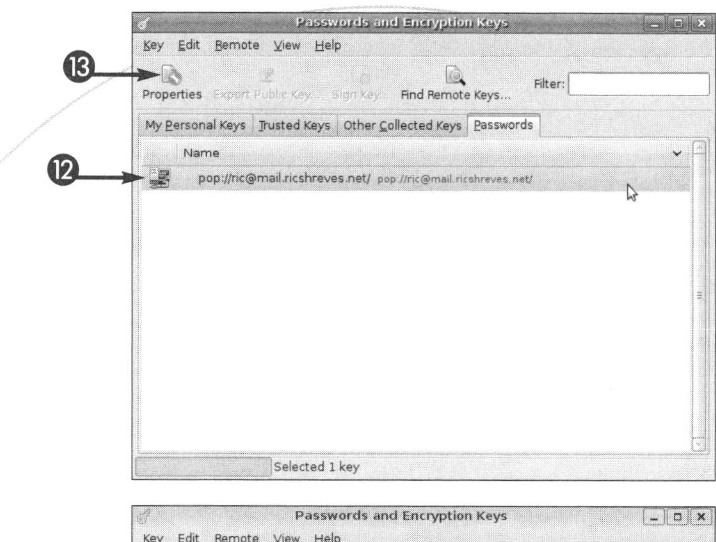

The entry's Properties dialog box appears.

⓮ Click Password.

The Password field is revealed in the window.

⓯ Type a new password.

⓰ Click Close.

Your new password has been saved.

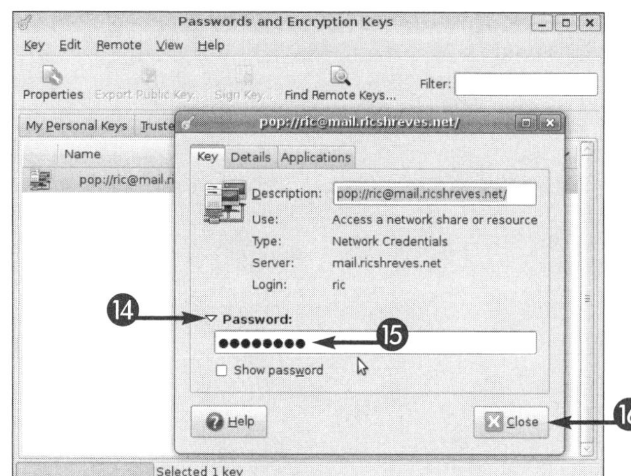

Extra

You can add additional identifiers to a key to both enhance its usefulness and make it more user-friendly. You can add a user ID by using the options on the Names and Signatures tab of the key's Properties dialog box. You access the Properties dialog box by right-clicking the key and clicking Properties.

A user ID typically consists of your full name and your email address. The Full Name entry does not technically have to be your complete first, last, and middle names, but you must enter at least five characters in this field. Note that using your real name will make it easier for people to find your key if it is published among others. Most people will find your key by searching against your email address, so make sure that you enter this information correctly in the provided field.

An additional option you may want to consider is adding a photo ID. You can embed one or more photos. The identities can be signed. Photos have to be in JPEG format and can be no larger than 240 x 288 pixels in size. The Photo ID option can be found in the key's Properties dialog box.

Capture a Screenshot

If you need to capture a picture of what is happening on your computer desktop, you can easily take shots of either the entire screen or of just an active window. The system gives you several alternatives for taking screenshots. You can even automatically add drop shadows and borders.

The fastest and easiest way to capture a screenshot is to use the Print Screen key that appears on the vast majority of keyboards. Pressing this key will result in the system taking a shot of the entire desktop and then prompting you for a name and a location to save the file. If you only want a shot of the active window, you can also do that from your keyboard by pressing the Alt key at the same time that you press Print Screen.

The Take Screenshot application, however, offers a few more options. The Take Screenshot dialog box lets you take shots of either the entire screen or just the active window. Additionally, you can set a delay that gives you time to arrange the elements on the screen or position your cursor. Take Screenshot also includes options to designate whether the cursor appears in the screenshot and to add effects to the image, such as a border or a drop shadow.

Screenshots taken by either keyboard shortcuts or the Take Screenshot application are saved in the PNG format. Image sizes are typically about 300KB to 400KB, and the dimensions tend to run at or a little larger than the actual size of the screen or window being imaged.

Capture a Screenshot

1. Click Applications ➔ Accessories ➔ Take Screenshot.

The Take Screenshot application appears.

2. Click to select the whole desktop or just the active window to capture.
3. Set a delay to the number of seconds that you want the application to wait before capturing, such as 3.

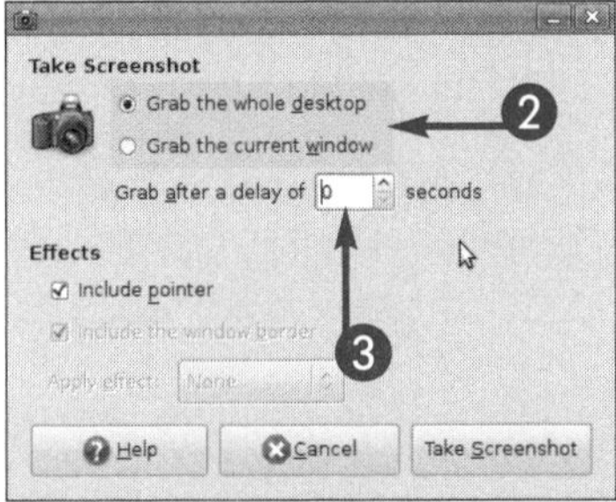

4 Click here and click Drop Shadow to apply a drop shadow effect.

- You can select other effects as well.

5 Click Take Screenshot.

The Take Screenshot application captures the screenshot.

The Save Screenshot dialog box appears.

6 Type a name for the screenshot.

7 Click Save.

The image is saved to your computer.

Extra

Taking a screenshot is a basic function, so perhaps it is not surprising that there are a number of different ways to get it done. The Take Screenshot application is certainly the most full-featured option, and using the keyboard shortcuts is certainly the fastest option; however, there are still other ways that you can capture all or part of your computer screen.

Those of you who are comfortable using the Terminal application can take screenshots directly from the Terminal. The command is easy enough to remember: just type **gnome-screenshot** at the Terminal prompt. The command also supports the same set of options as the Take Screenshot utility, including the choice between shooting the screen as a whole or just a particular window. You can also add borders or drop shadows.

If you expect to take screenshots often, consider adding a Take Screenshot button to one of your desktop panels, as discussed earlier in this book in Chapter 2. With the Take Screenshot button at your fingertips, you do not need to fumble around for a keyboard shortcut or an application — just click the button when needed.

Access the Command Line with Terminal

The Terminal application enables you to control your machine at the command line and opens up the system for power users. Virtually anything you can do in the normal desktop interface, you can do from the Terminal, if you know the right commands.

The Terminal application takes its name from its function: terminal emulation. With this application, you can access a UNIX shell to directly type in commands for your system to execute. This mode of operation, although very basic in terms of its interface, is all about power: When you need to work directly with your system, sometimes there is no substitute for having shell access.

Terminal supports the use of tabs to allow you to run multiple terminal windows simultaneously. You can open a new tab that will appear at the top of the window. Click the tab name to make it active. The tabs feature makes it easy to *multitask,* or run multiple processes simultaneously.

Another useful feature of Terminal is the support of multiple profiles. A *profile* is a set of configuration options for Terminal. You can create multiple profiles for users and customize the appearance of each one to help you keep track of them. You can also set a default command that runs automatically when the profile is opened, thereby allowing you to create accelerators for common tasks. To create a new profile, go to the File menu and select New Profile. The first profile you create will be based on the default profile, but thereafter you can model new profiles on any existing profile.

Access the Command Line with Terminal

1. Click Applications ➔ Accessories ➔ Terminal.

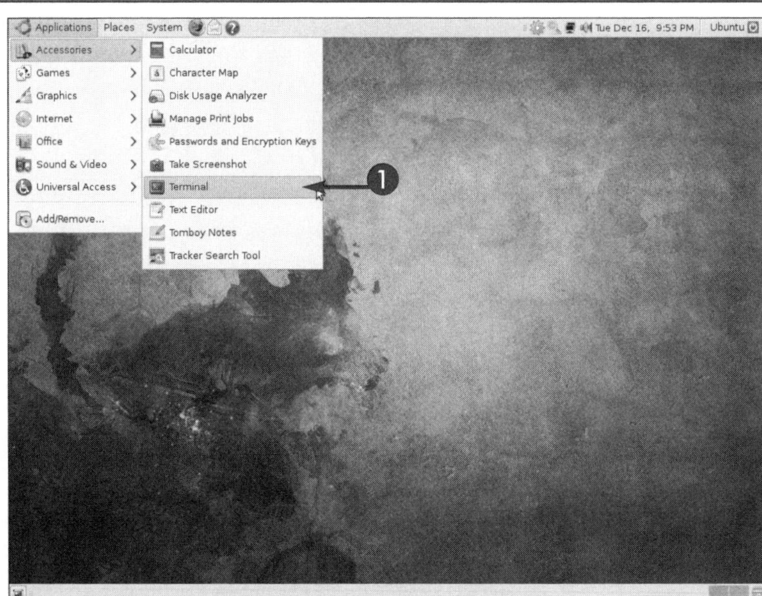

The Terminal application appears.

2. Click File ➔ Open Tab.

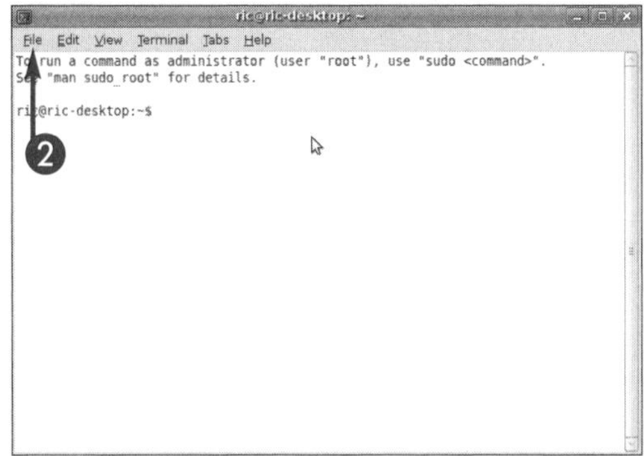

A new tab opens.

3. Right-click the new tab and select Set Title.

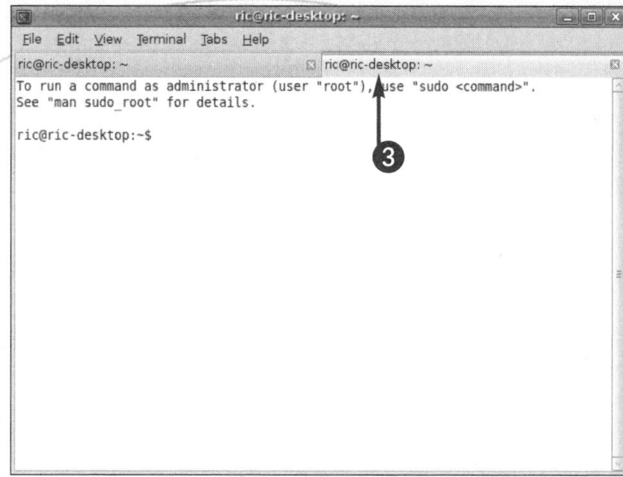

The Set Title dialog box opens.

4. Type a new name for the tab.

5. Click OK.

The title of the new tab will change to the value that you entered.

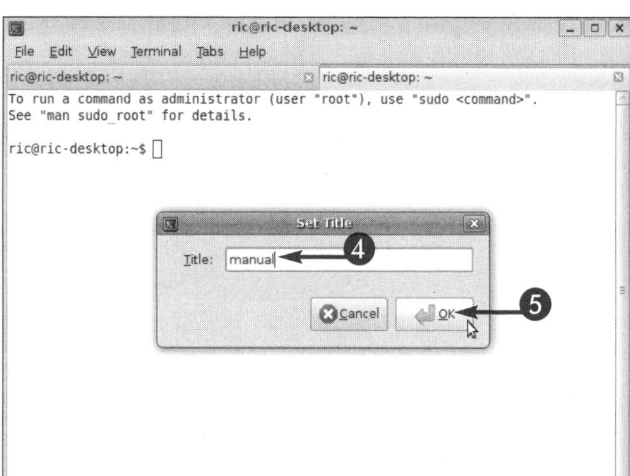

Extra

Using Terminal requires some familiarity with the syntax needed to enter the shell commands, and, of course, it also requires an awareness of the commands themselves. The list of available commands is very extensive and well beyond the scope of this book. A good place to learn more is the Ubuntu community documentation page "Using the Terminal," located at https://help.ubuntu.com/community/UsingTheTerminal. The page contains a quick reference to the most common shell commands.

If you are new to using shell commands, by far the best command to start with is the `help` command. When you execute the `help` command, the system displays a manual for you to reference. There are manuals for each command in the system. To access one of the help manuals, open the Terminal and at the prompt, type **man**, followed by the name of the command. An excellent place to begin is with the command `man man`, which will display the manual for the command `man`. Another good starting point is `man intro`, which will display the very useful "Introduction to Commands" manual.

Chapter 14 of this book contains more information on working with the command line.

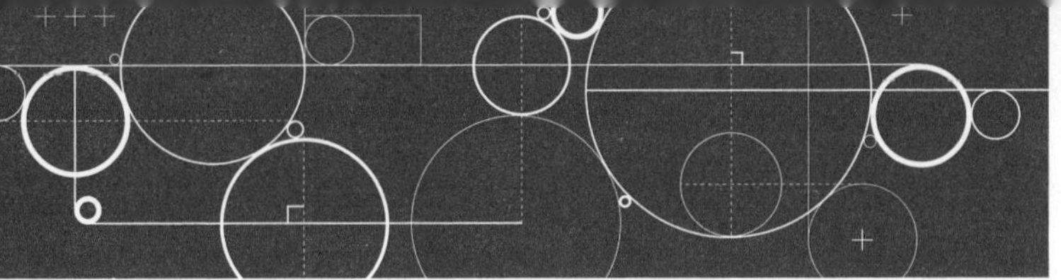

Edit a File with the Text Editor

The text editor bundled with your Ubuntu desktop is the powerful gedit application, which not only allows you to easily create and edit documents, but also gives you access to a wide variety of useful tools. By default, opening a text document in Ubuntu will also launch gedit.

If you are used to the functionality of editors such as Microsoft Windows's Notepad, you will find the Text Editor interface familiar, but the similarities really stop there. At its most basic, you can use the Text Editor to create or edit documents, but like more powerful word processors, you can also spell-check, find and replace text, and use tabs to control multiple documents.

Like other word processors, the Text Editor supports cut-and-paste editing using the buttons on the toolbar or keyboard shortcuts. You can also rearrange text by double-clicking to highlight a word and then grabbing it with your mouse and dragging it to where you want it to appear.

A spell-checker is available under the Tools menu. You can spell-check your text at any time, or if you prefer, you can switch on the Autocheck Spelling option. Autocheck Spelling can assess your spelling as you type and highlight words that it believes are questionable.

Also under the Tools menu is the Document Statistics option. Clicking Document Statistics will show you the number of lines, words, and characters in your document.

If you are working with code, explore the options for code formatting and highlighting in the Preferences dialog box, which is accessed from the Edit menu.

Edit a File with the Text Editor

1. Click Applications ➔ Accessories ➔ Text Editor.

The Text Editor application appears.

2. Type your text into the editor window.

3. Click Tools ➔ Check Spelling.

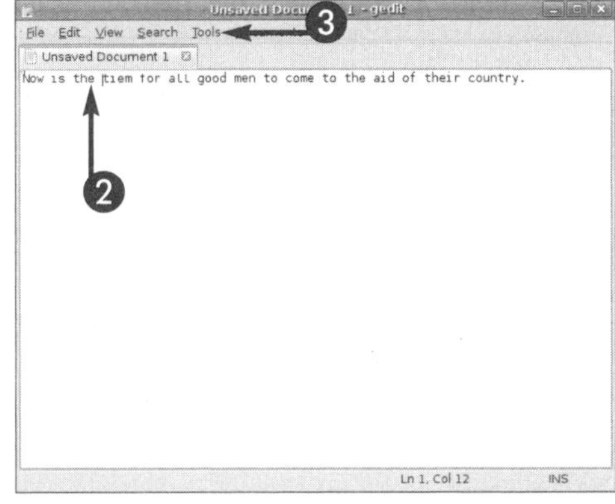

The Check Spelling dialog box opens and begins to check the document for errors.

4 Click Change to correct a spelling error.

5 Click Close when you are done with the spell-checker.

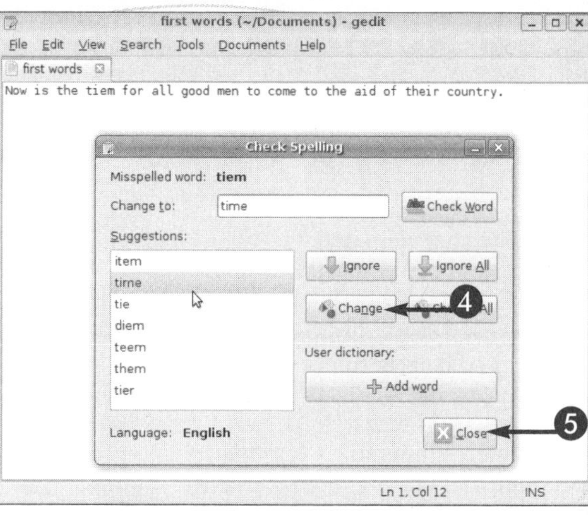

- The spell-checker changes the spelling to match the correction.

6 When you are finished with your document, click File ➔ Save As and provide a name for the file.

- The filename appears in the title bar.

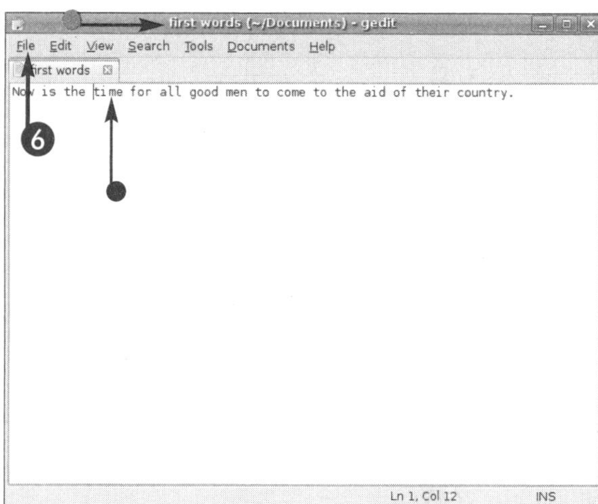

Extra

One of the things that makes the Text Editor such a useful tool is the fact that it supports plug-ins. Go to the Preferences option under the Edit menu. In the Gedit Preferences dialog box, select the Plugins tab. The Plugins tab displays a list of all the plug-ins installed on the system. A check mark next to the name of a plug-in tells you that it is enabled. You can see from the list that a number of the plug-ins are enabled by default; for example, the system uses plug-ins to provide the Document Statistics and spell-checker features. Other plug-ins provide formatting shortcuts and tools to help with code syntax.

Take note of the Snippets plug-in; this plug-in is not enabled by default, but you may find it to be useful. When Snippets is active, you are able to insert into a document short segments of text with just a simple keystroke. The system comes preloaded with a number of snippets, ready to use. You can also add your own snippets to the collection. All your snippets can be viewed and edited from the Manage Snippets option under the Tools menu.

Create Notes for Yourself with Tomboy Notes

Tomboy Notes enables you to make short notes to organize your ideas and thoughts. Although Tomboy Notes shines as a reminder system, its real potential lies in the ability to link notes together and to add in hyperlinks to Web sites, files, and even email messages.

The first time you launch Tomboy Notes, you will see two different windows: the Search All Notes window and the Start Here window. The Search All Notes window will become your standard interface into your Tomboy Notes collection. Start Here is intended to give you a quick introduction to the system and does so by showing you actual notes and links.

Although the Start Here note is a quick and easy way to learn the system, you should also feel free to just jump in and try it. Create a new note from the Search All Notes window. New notes appear in windows of their own, ready to go. The system automatically saves your notes as you work; you do not need to worry about losing anything.

After creating a note, you can automatically link it to another one using the Link button on the toolbar. When you have a collection of related notes, you can join them together by putting them into collections using the Notebook button on the toolbar. Notes can be searched as well, and the Tools menu gives you access to formatting and even spell-checking.

The Tomboy Notes application is one of those tools that makes you wonder how you lived without it. The linking power of the system is the key: Join together related concepts, ideas, and resources to create your own do-it-yourself Wiki.

Create Notes for Yourself with Tomboy Notes

1. Click Applications ➔ Accessories ➔ Tomboy Notes.

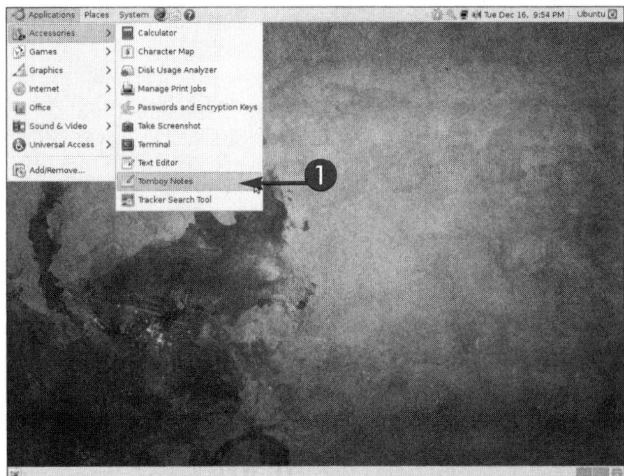

The Tomboy Notes application appears.

2. Click File ➔ New.

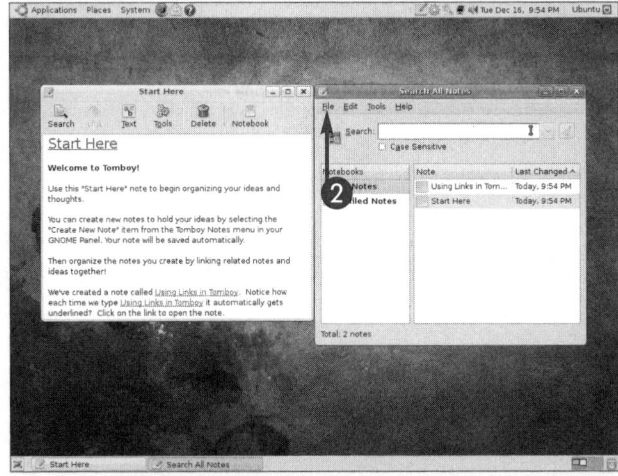

- A new note is created.
- You can type in any text that you want here.

3 Click and drag to highlight the text.

4 Click Link.

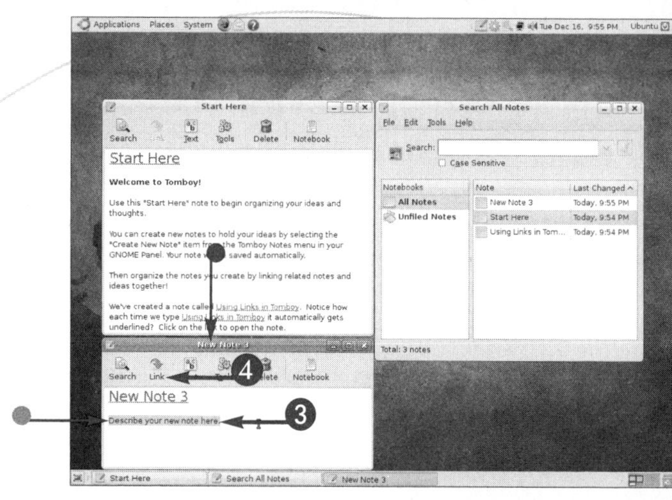

- A new note is created, and it is linked to the other note.

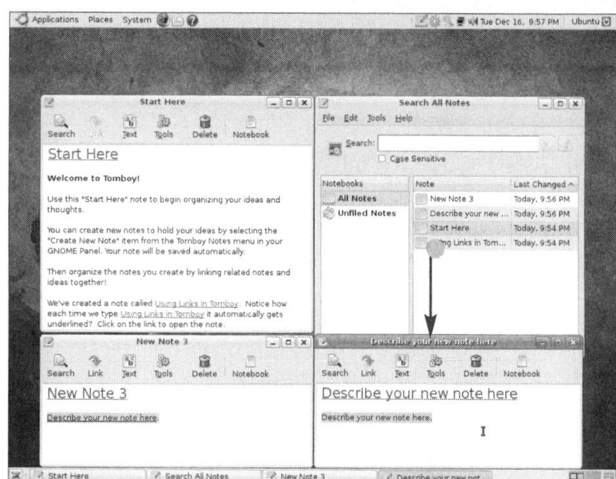

Extra

Like the gedit Text Editor, Tomboy Notes is extensible via the installation of plug-ins. To find out which plug-ins are already installed on your system, go to the Tomboy Notes Preferences dialog box, under the Edit menu, and click the Add-Ins tab. By default, you should see a number of plug-ins. One of the most helpful plug-ins is the Evolution Mail Integration plug-in.

The Evolution Mail Integration plug-in enables you to drag an email message from Evolution into a Tomboy Note. The note will automatically show the message subject as a clickable link. When you click the link, the email message will open, making this a useful tool for adding email messaging into your notes and notebooks.

In addition to the active plug-ins, you will see on the Add-Ins tab a number of items that are grayed out. To activate one, select it and then click the Enable button. Deactivating a plug-in works by selecting an active plug-in and then clicking the Disable button.

The Export to HTML plug-in is also quite useful. It allows you to convert notes to HTML format for use on the Web.

Find a File with the Tracker Search Tool

Tracker makes it easy to find things in your Ubuntu desktop installation. Tracker indexes all your data, and you can search for items using free text, like you would on a search engine such as Google.

The Tracker Search Tool window presents you with a basic Search box in which you can enter your query. The query results are drawn from your entire computer.

Tracker needs to be enabled before you use it for the first time. To turn on indexing, use the Search and Indexing feature under the Preferences submenu of the System menu. Select Enable Indexing and click OK.

After you click OK, Tracker will prompt you to re-index your hard drive. Confirm that and when it finishes, you are set up and ready to go. From now on, Tracker will keep track of any new files you add to the system, and it will even continue to re-index old files that it detects have changed.

When you run a search in Tracker, the results appear in the pane on the right, and the pane on the left groups the results into categories — for example, applications or documents. When you click a search result, a bottom pane gives you some brief information about it. Clicking on the plus sign in the search result description opens a text field where you can enter tags that the system will save and associate with the file; this makes it easy for you to label and group things in a fashion that is meaningful to you and helps you find those items more easily in the future.

Find a File with the Tracker Search Tool

1. Click Applications ➔ Accessories ➔ Tracker Search Tool.

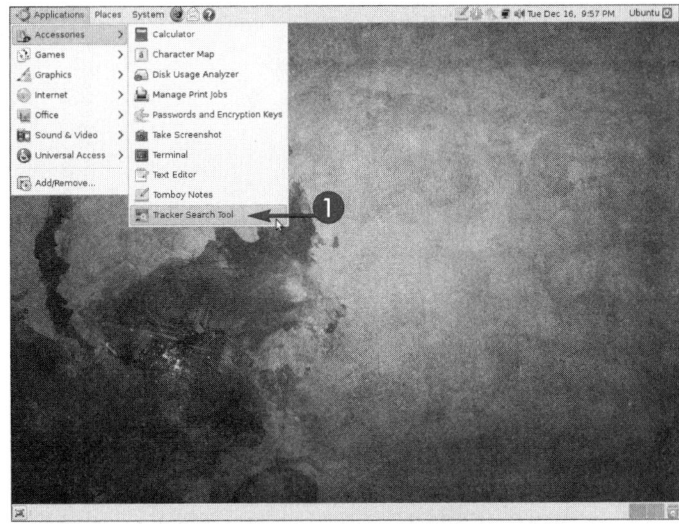

- The Tracker Search Tool application appears.

2. Type a search term.
3. Click Find.

- The search results, if any, appear.

4. Click the plus sign next to Tags.

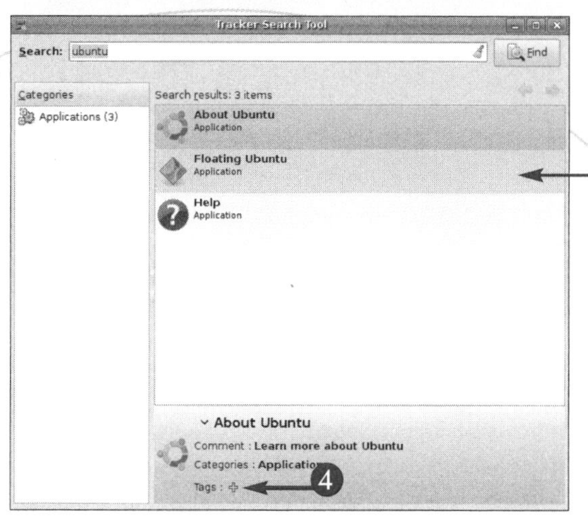

The Tags field is now available for typing.

5. Type any tags that you want, separated by commas.

The tags will now be associated with the item.

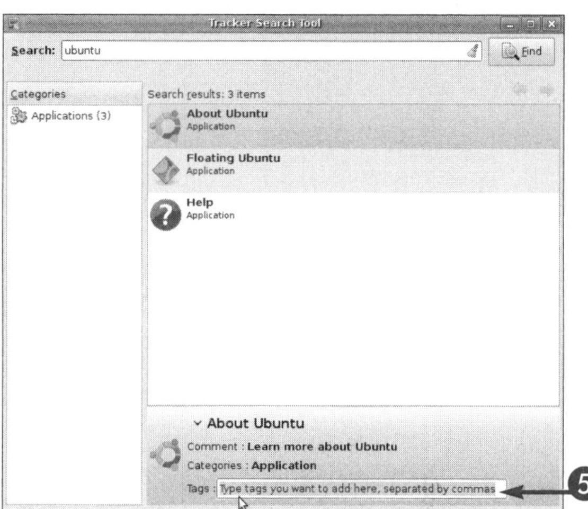

Extra

When indexing has been enabled, upon your next session start you will see the Tracker applet in the panel. This applet enables you to quickly access the Tracker Search Tool application by simply double-clicking. Additionally, you can access other options of Tracker and indexing services by right-clicking the applet. One option presented is the ability to pause the indexing service to avoid conflict with other applications. Another option presented enables you to force a re-index of your files to ensure the capture of new or recently modified files. Another option enables you to access a dialog box that sets the policy for automatic pausing of the indexing service when you are actively using the machine. The menu also contains an informational option to bring up statistics on how many files and the types of these files that are currently within the index. Also, you can access the Indexer Preferences dialog box through this menu. This is the same dialog box accessed by clicking System ➔ Preferences ➔ Search and Indexing.

Play Games

Ubuntu Linux Desktop comes bundled with a collection of 17 games of skill and chance. All the games can be played alone or against the computer, and some even support multiple human players.

The games vary from classics such as Chess to more contemporary games such as Robots. There are games of logic and skill, card games, and problem-solving games. Chess provides a number of popular options and can be networked for remote play. For traditionalists who prefer card games, there is a choice between FreeCell Solitaire and AisleRiot Solitaire. Whereas the former supports only one mode of play, the latter includes over 80 variations, including the popular Klondike and Canfield varieties.

For card lovers, there is Blackjack, the ever-popular 21. For those who prefer dice games, there is Tali.

Problem-solving games are the most numerous in the set. The Mahjongg game provides a large number of different variations in the game set, which can be combined to create numerous levels of difficulty. Four-in-a-Row, Five or More, and Iagno all bear a certain resemblance to each other. Each is rooted in games such as Reversi and provides variations that keep this style of game play fresh and interesting. Same GNOME is a matching game that is one of the easier in the set, but can still be quite fun.

For those who prefer mathematical games, the popular Sudoku is here. Tetravex is a math-oriented matching game that can be very challenging.

For sheer escapist gaming, there is Robots, Mines, Gnometris, and Nibbles, all basic spatial problem-solving games.

Note that most games are easier to use in full-screen mode.

Play Games

1. Click Applications.
2. Click Games.
3. Click the game that you want to play.

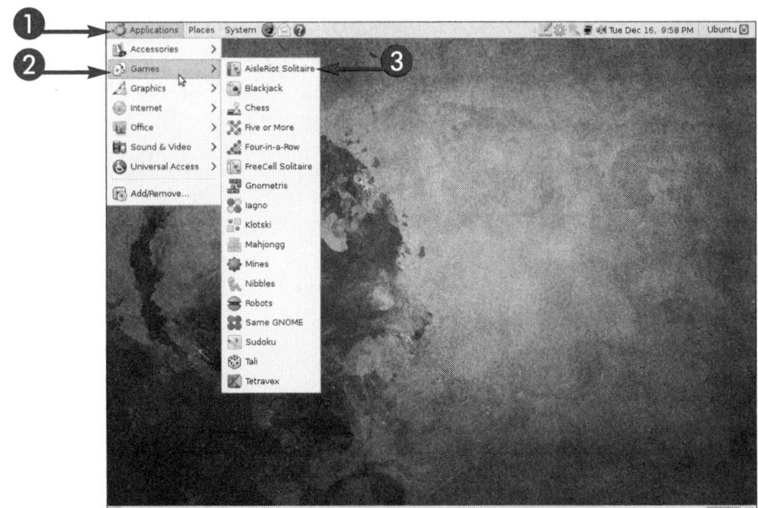

The game opens.

4. Click View ➔ Fullscreen.

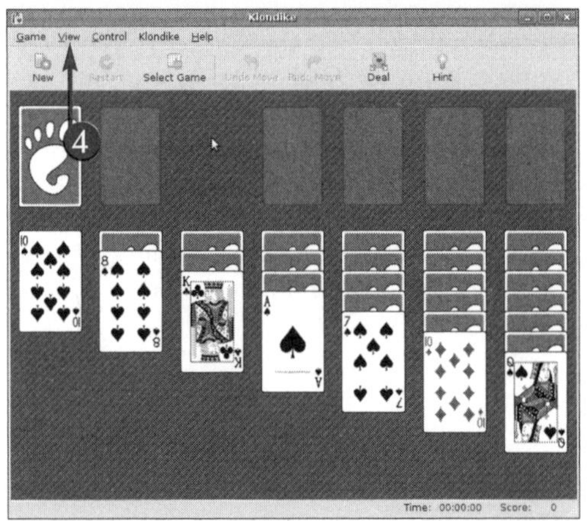

The game expands to fill the full window.

5 Play the game.

Note: *Different games have different options.*

- In AisleRiot Solitaire, you can change from the default game of Klondike to Canfield by clicking Select Game and choosing Canfield in the dialog box.

- In this example, the game board changes to display Canfield.

Apply It

The games bundled in Ubuntu are part of the GNOME Games pack. GNOME Games supports networked multiplayer gaming through the GGZ Gaming Zone at www.ggzgamingzone.org.

The following games currently support network play: Nibbles, Iagno, Four-in-a-Row, and Chess. According to the GNOME Games Web site, other games are currently under development and will be added to the program in the near future.

To activate this feature, you need to select Network Game from the game's menu. If you are connected to a network, you will see a connection dialog box that allows you to put in the server profile and user details. After you have successfully connected to the server, you will find an assortment of gaming rooms from which to choose. To play Nibbles, go to the Nibbles room; to play Four-in-a-Row, enter the room of the same name, and so forth.

When you enter a room, you can find other players, or you can host your own game and invite players to join. For a list of the current servers in the system, visit the GGZ site, above, or go to http://live.gnome.org/GnomeGames/Multiplayer.

Using the F-Spot Photo Manager

Photo-management software has recently sprung into existence to manage the deluge of images from the shift from film to digital cameras. Because high-density flash-based media can hold so many more photos than a roll of film, more pictures are being taken today than ever before. Added to that is the fact that these digital cameras are now incorporated into almost all cell phones.

A photo manager facilitates the import of pictures from media, enabling you to quickly and easily pull photos from your flash card or camera directly into a staging area for filing. With a photo manager, you can preview your images, determining what the subject of each picture is, and record information that will help to find or explain the image later. You can categorize and sort your images so that they can be retrieved with other pictures according to your own concept of how they should be grouped together. Photo managers also include some form of simple image manipulation so that you can touch up your pictures.

F-Spot is the photo manager for Ubuntu, and it provides all this functionality. When F-Spot launches for the first time, it will present you with a dialog box for importing pictures from a folder. This can be a folder on your hard drive, a CD, or a flash device. After you select the folder, a scan of it is begun. When the scan is complete, the main F-Spot window is shown, and thumbnails of any picture files within the folder and subfolders of it are shown in the preview area. These images are then available for categorization and commenting. When you add a comment to a photo, make sure that it is descriptive of the subject of the photo.

Using the F-Spot Photo Manager

IMPORT PHOTOS INTO F-SPOT

1. Click Applications ➔ Graphics ➔ F-Spot Photo Manager.

   The F-Spot photo manager application appears.

2. Click Import.

Note: If this is the first time you have opened F-Spot, the Import dialog box will automatically come up, so you will not need to click Import.

   The Import dialog box appears.

3. Click Select Folder.

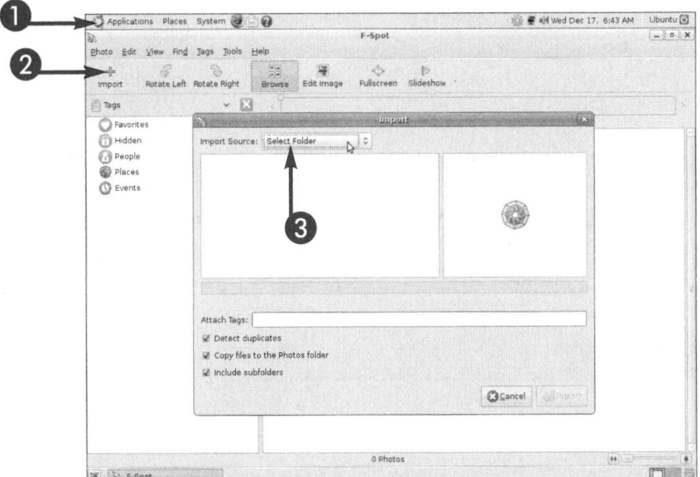

   Another dialog box appears.

4. Navigate to a folder to import photos from and click it.

5. Click Open.

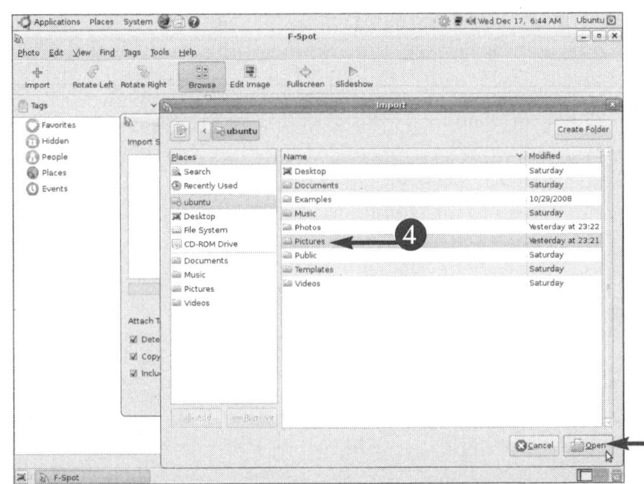

Photos are searched for and presented in thumbnails.

6. Click Import.

The import begins.

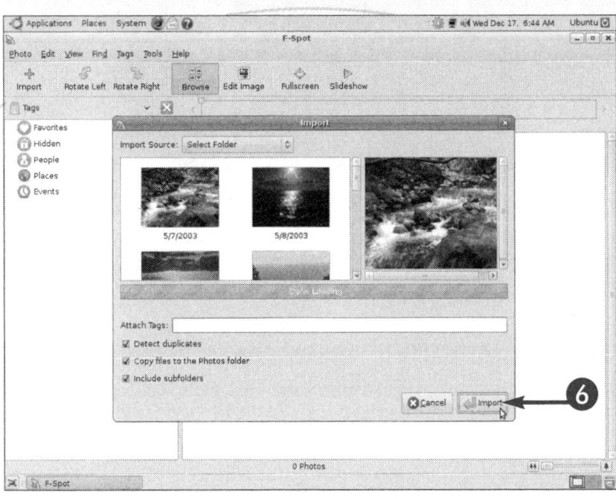

- The images are imported into the F-Spot gallery.

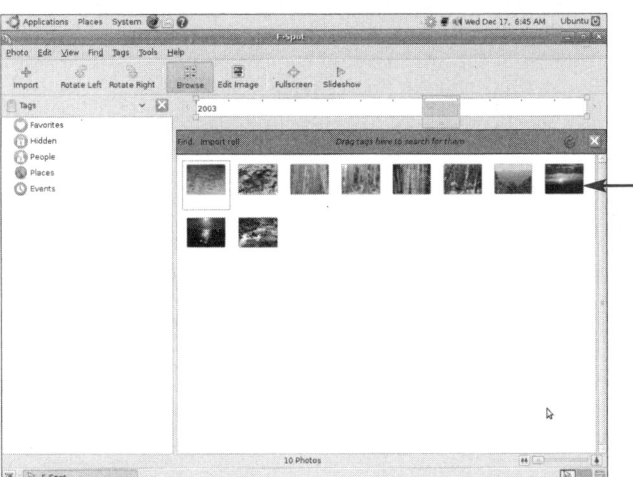

Extra

Tags are a relatively new way to sift through content. Many Web sites use tagging to categorize content. Tags are meant to be unstructured by nature and then shown as a tag cloud. A *tag cloud* is usually an alphabetical listing of the available tags, with each tag's font size determined by the number of items that possess that tag. Each of the tags in the cloud is a hyperlink, which when followed shows a second-level tag cloud for all the items that match the first-level selection. This is a more efficient way to organize information because not all people conceptualize the hierarchy of things in a similar manner. In fact, many viable hierarchies may exist for a given photo. For example, a picture may contain a 1957 Chevy and therefore be classified under "cars," but the same picture may also contain your Uncle Bob and thus be classified under "family photos." If you tag the photo with "cars," "1957," "Chevy," "uncle," "bob," and "family," the photo will show up under a hierarchy for "cars" and for "family photos." In fact, the cloud allows more rapid traversal to parts of the hierarchy because it shows multiple hierarchy roots simultaneously, and at each level.

continued

Using the F-Spot Photo Manager (continued)

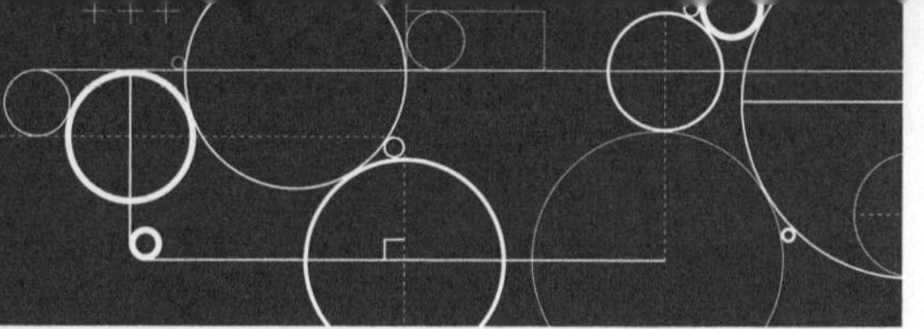

F-Spot gives you all the basic photo touch-up capabilities once requiring the magic of a darkroom. These touch-up tools are located in the sidebar and accessed via the Edit Image button on the main toolbar.

You can use the Crop tool to cut out unwanted parts of the picture around the edges to highlight the subject and remove distractions from the background. You can also use it as a means to re-center the subject mater of the picture.

The red-eye removal tool endeavors to remove the red glow that sometimes is produced by a person's retina as they look into the flash of a camera. Because this produces a fairly specific effect on the photo, and the red color is never similar to the surrounding eye color, the tool can usually fix this common photographic issue.

The Adjust Color tool displays a dialog box in which you can adjust the brightness, contrast, hue, and saturation, as well as white balance and the exposure of your picture. The Desaturate button converts a picture to black and white. The Sepia Tone button converts the image to sepia tones. This produces a nice old-time daguerreotype picture effect.

The Straighten tool helps when the camera was not level when you took your picture. This tool can rotate the picture back to level. The Soft-Focus Effect tool is very popular for portrait pictures; it causes the center of the photo to be clearly focused, while all the periphery is blurred.

The Auto-Color correction button is probably the most powerful of these tools. While not always perfect, it works very well for most pictures and improves pictures taken under low-lighting situations.

Using the F-Spot Photo Manager *(continued)*

CREATE A NEW TAG

1. Right-click an existing tag or anywhere in the Tags area of the sidebar.
2. Click Create New Tag.

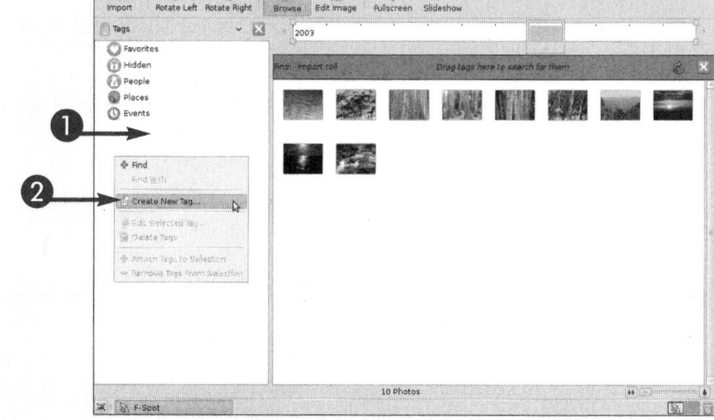

The Create New Tag dialog box appears.

3. Type in a tag name.
4. Click Create.

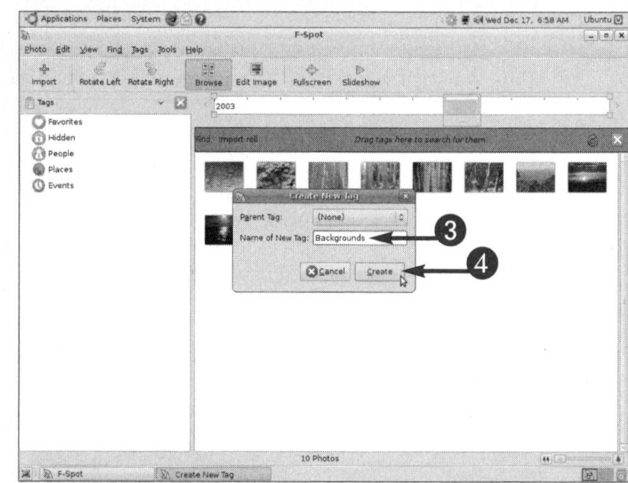

- The new tag appears in the list.

ADD A TAG TO A PHOTO

1. Right-click the photo to which you want to add a tag.
2. Click Attach Tag.
3. Click the tag that you want.

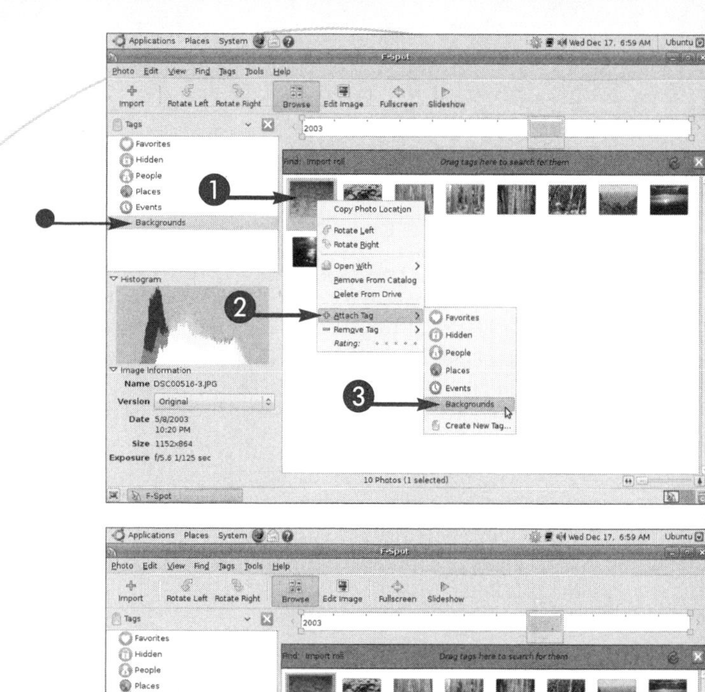

- The tag is added to the image.

Extra

Although tagging your pictures makes it easier to quickly find them, there is certain data that your camera will put directly into the photo information for you. This data is called *exchangeable image file format (EXIF)* data. EXIF data contains the date and time the picture was taken, the camera make and model with which the picture was taken, and the camera's orientation, aperture size, shutter speed, focal length, metering mode, and photo-sensitivity/speed. Some high-end cameras even have global positioning system (GPS) capabilities and record the geolocation coordinates of where the photo was taken.

Using the EXIF information, you can locate a picture quickly based on when it happened. This is a powerful tool, especially if you have a bunch of pictures of places that you have been multiple times. The tags for a given picture in such a case might be very similar, but by including date information, you can find only the matching pictures relating to a specific date range.

Edit Photos with GIMP

Graphic editing is accomplished in the open-source world with the GNU Image Manipulation Program, GIMP for short. This is a powerful, feature-rich application — so feature rich, in fact, that there are more than a few books written about it. In this section, you will learn the basics of starting up the application, loading an image into it, and using one of the many tools from the toolbox on that image.

When GIMP first launches, it may present you with a tip of the day. The fact that there even is a tip of the day should give you a hint at all the features packed into this one program. The initial tip is often the Welcome tip and can be dismissed after reading. The remaining windows are the main window, the toolbox, and the dock window containing various dialog boxes as tabs.

When an image is loaded for editing, it opens in a new window that is the work surface. The general sequence of events for editing is to select a tool from the toolbox, adjust any parameters in the lower pane of the toolbox, and then by using drag operations on the work surface, apply the tool as needed. The specific effects vary by tool.

The most frequently used tools are the selection tools. The selection tools allow you to specify a region of the image to apply certain tools to. For example, if you use the Lasso selection tool and draw an arbitrary boundary, you can then apply a tool such as the Area Fill or cut to just that selected area.

Edit Photos with GIMP

OPEN GIMP

1. Click Applications ➔ Graphics ➔ GIMP Image Editor.

   The GIMP application launches.

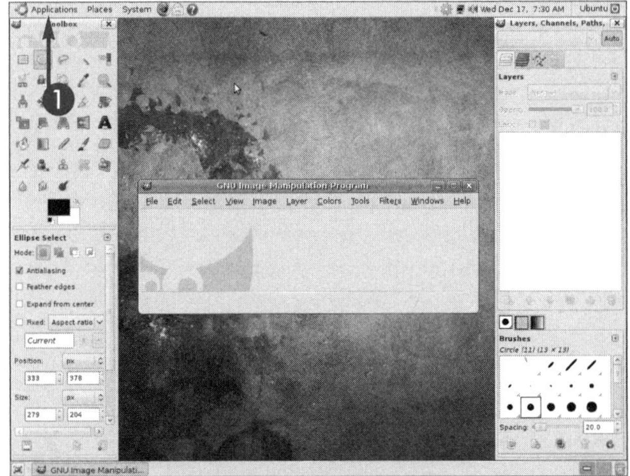

OPEN AND EDIT AN IMAGE IN GIMP

2. Click File ➔ Open.

The Open Image dialog box appears.

3. Navigate to an image to edit and click it.
4. Click Open.

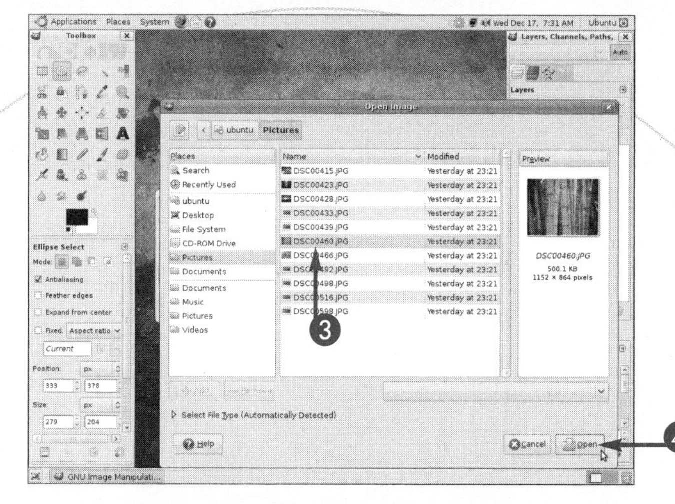

The image is loaded and appears in a new window.

5. Click a tool that you want to apply in the toolbox.
6. Click the image.

The tool is applied to the image.

Extra

Because the widget set that virtually all of GNOME is built on is so ubiquitous in GNOME, it is often forgotten that this set of widgets (GTK+) was originally developed for the GIMP project. It is a huge coup for a single project to spawn such reusable componentry within the software world, and the developers of the GIMP project should be lauded for this amazing accomplishment. GTK+ is so popular and successful that it is used as a cross-platform UI development platform with ports for Windows and Mac OS. GTK+ is written in C but has bindings for many languages, both compiled and interpreted. GTK incorporates several libraries to enable its work. GLib is the nuts and bolts of the internal processing, including the handling of structures for data and event-handling mechanisms, as well as multithreading. GTK+ also relies on the Pango library for text rendering, including internationalization. There is also the Cairo library, which aims to provide a 2D rendering system that can display consistent visual representations across multiple platforms. Finally, there are the ATK libraries, which provide hooks for accessibility throughout.

continued

Edit Photos with GIMP (continued)

If you plan on doing any serious editing within GIMP, you will need to understand the concept of layers within your image. Each image in the GIMP is composed of one or more layers that "stack" from bottom-most to top-most. When you are looking at the Layers tab of the dock, you can see each of these layers. Within this layer view, you can also rearrange the order, change the transparency, and even turn on and off different layers as contributing to the composite view. Careful manipulation of these layers allows the graphic artist to separate the details of the image into components so that they can be modified independently. The layers can be mixed together using various modes that change how the pixels combine as they stack to form a composite. A given layer can also be translated in any direction to center the layer as desired.

Also, layers have an interesting feature called *layer masks.* This is a mask image that controls the alpha channel, or how transparent a portion of the image will be. When using only layers, you have only the choice about how transparent the entire layer will be, but by using a mask, you can have parts of a layer be transparent and create all sorts of cool effects.

For example, if you want the edges of an image to fade to black, you create a black layer with a layer mask with a radial gradient. This will cause the black layer to be gradually more opaque as the radius increases, giving that centered blackout effect.

MAKE A SELECTION

1. With the image open that you want to make a selection in, click the selection tool.
2. Click and drag over a portion of the image.

   A region is selected.
3. Right-click anywhere in the image and adjust the selection.

APPLY A FILTER

4. Right-click anywhere in the selection and select a filter to apply.

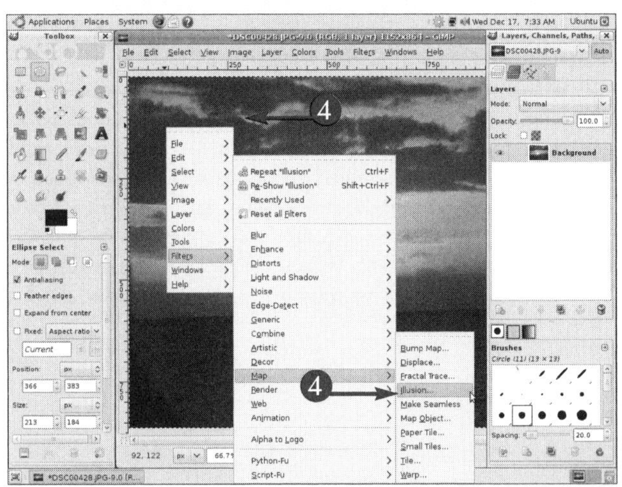

The filter options dialog box opens.

5. Adjust the filter parameters.
6. Click OK.

- The filter is applied.

Extra

GIMP includes a programmable scripting engine to author complex transformations of your image. This engine allows you to write scriptlets that are called *Script-Fu*. These scripts allow many of the common types of transformations provided by plug-in packs on packages such as Adobe's Photoshop. Some common effects are adding bevels to a layer, creating glass effects, and creating complex text logos. There are scripted effects that allow you to create an oil painting effect on your image. There are even plug-ins for creating animated images with rippling or wave effects. There is a standard set of these scripts included with the default installation of GIMP, and additional plug-ins can be found at http://registry.gimp.org/. The scripting engine was originally based on SIOD (Scheme in One Defun) but starting with version 2.4 TinyScheme. Additionally, in recent versions of GIMP, a new scripting capability has been included that is called Python-Fu, which allows you to use the full Python language from within a plug-in. If you have a repeated task that you want to automate, one of these two scripting capabilities will allow you to save a lot of time.

Scan Images with the XSane Image Scanner

Although most images are captured and transported digitally today, there is still a large cache of memories and information trapped in photo prints, negatives, and printed documents. In order to get this information digitized, you will need to scan them. In Linux, you use XSane to access and control a scanner device.

When you first launch XSane, it will scan the system for attached scanners. If it does not find one, you may need to configure your scanner manually. This should only be the case for older-style, parallel port based scanners or scanners with a proprietary interface card.

After XSane has found your scanner, it displays its main window. This window has many options, but it provides essentially a one-stop place for scanning your images.

The XSane dialog box allows you to enter a filename and select a type for the output of the scan. The types are essentially all image types, as well as PDF. Also, if you have multiple scanners, you can select which device to capture from. You also may specify if you want to only scan in various bit depths, which offer you a scan range from full-color to black and white. You can also select the DPI, gamma, brightness, and contrast for the scan. At the bottom of the dialog box are various buttons that allow you to adjust rather specifically certain corrections for the image. Below that, there is some information on the scanned image's size. The information is displayed in an equation format, as follows: number of pixels wide X number of pixels tall X number of bits per pixel. The resultant size in bytes, kilobytes, or megabytes is displayed after the equation in parentheses.

Scan Images with the XSane Image Scanner

SCAN AN IMAGE

1. Click Applications ➔ Graphics ➔ XSane Image Scanner.

   If this is the first time you have launched XSane, XSane scans your system and locates your scanner.

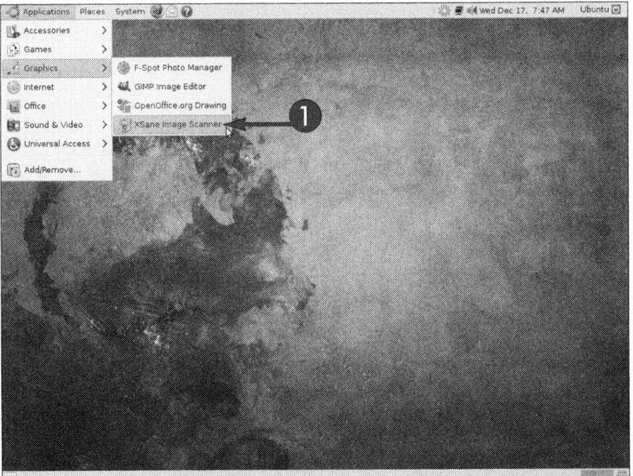

The XSane application appears.

2. Place the image that you want to scan on your scanner.
3. Click Acquire Preview.

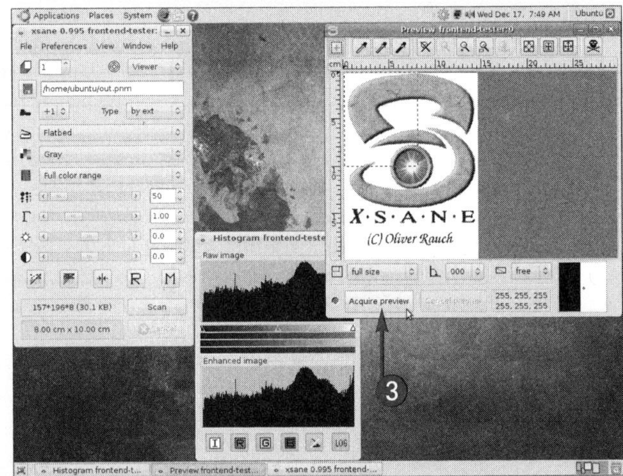

- The preview window is updated from the item to be scanned.

4. Click Scan.

   Scanning begins.

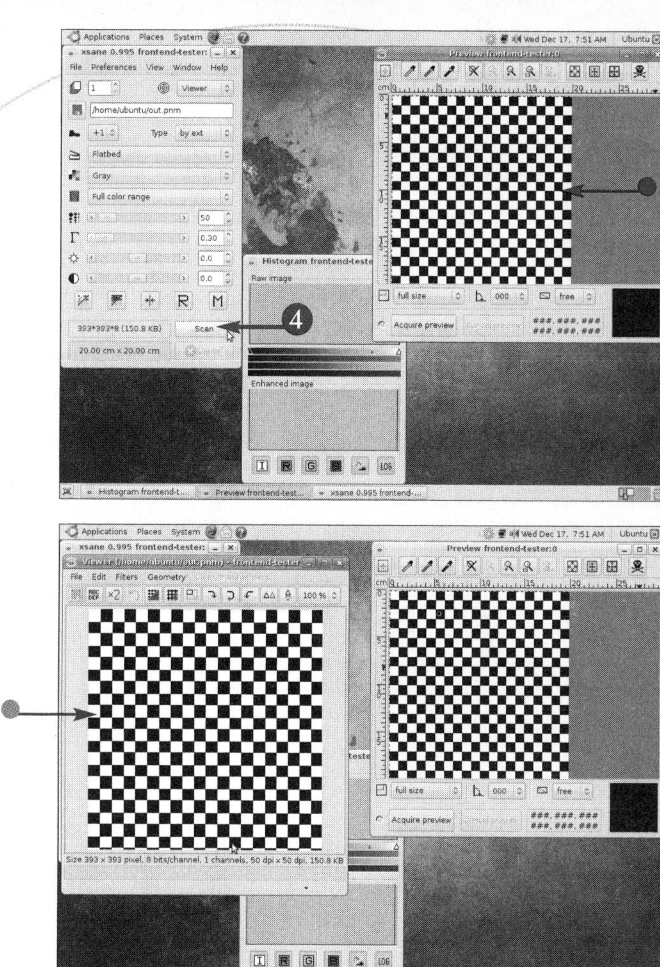

- The item is scanned, and a window showing the scan appears.

Extra

Scanners are complex pieces of equipment that enable you to capture a very high-resolution image of printed material. This is done by literally scanning a small camera, or set of cameras in today's scanners, across the surface of the subject. Because each picture is very small, the images all get assembled to produce a much larger image. These small images are of a very small area, and at normal capture resolution for a small camera. The high resolution of the scanner is accomplished by combining the normal resolution pictures taken of very small areas.

The mechanism itself is very similar to plotter technology in which the camera or camera bar is moved slowly across the surface along with a bright light that allows the camera to capture the image uniformly across the surface.

Most modern flatbed scanners use cameras that are very similar to those in cellular phones or digital cameras. These cameras are actually large arrays of photosensors on a chip that can be read out digitally to be stored in memory devices or streamed to a computer for further processing.

continued

Scan Images with the XSane Image Scanner (continued)

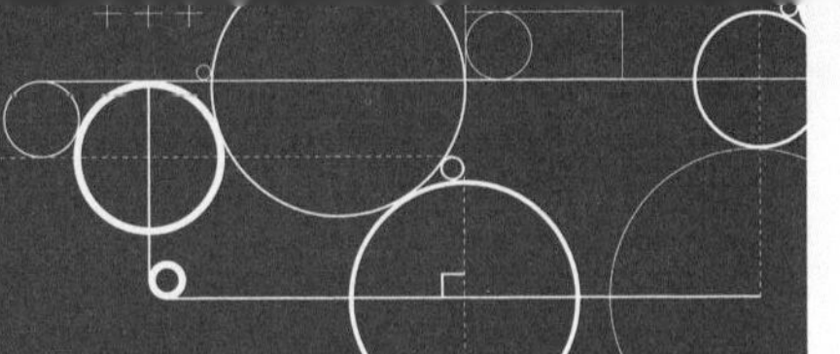

By changing the target of the scan, you can choose how XSane will handle the resulting scan. The Copy options allow you to specify a printer, and the image will be sent directly to printing to allow you to turn your scanner/computer/printer into a digital photocopier. Using the Multipage option, you can bundle several scans into one file. The types of files that allow multiple images are TIFF, PostScript, and PDF. The Fax option allows you to scan images and turn your scanner/computer/modem into a digital fax machine. Similar to the Multipage option, you can scan multiple images prior to the creation of the final fax message. By using the Email option, you can create an email and include the scanned images as attachments. If you just want the files scanned and dropped directly to a file, which is especially appropriate for batch scanning with an autofeeder attachment, you can select the Save option and have the files saved to the directory of your choice using an increment added to the end of the filename that you choose. There are options associated with all of these targets under the Setup option of the Preferences menu. One thing to be aware of is the resultant file size of your image settings. If the scan resolution is set too high on a full-page scan, you can create enormous files. Additionally, these files may take a very long time to scan and write to disk.

CREATE A MULTIPAGE PROJECT

1. Click the drop-down box and select Multipage.

The Multipage Project window appears.

2. Click Create Project.

A new multipage project is created.

3. Place the first image on your scanner.
4. Click Scan.
   - An image is added to the multipage project.
5. Important!: Click the Multipage Project window in order to scan additional pages.
6. Place the second image on your scanner.
7. Click Scan again.
   - A second image is added to the multipage project.

   You can repeat steps **3** to **5** for as many images as you need.

REORDER THE IMAGES IN THE PROJECT

8. Click one of the images.
9. Click either the Move Up or Move Down button.

   The ordering of the pages is changed.
10. Click Save Multipage File.

    The project is saved.

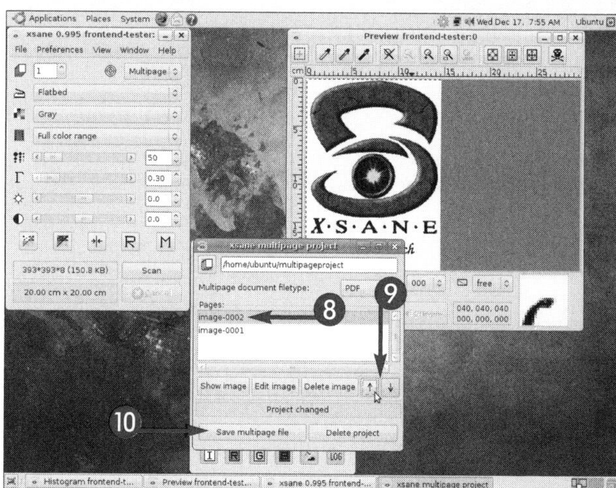

Extra

One very popular use for scanning is the conversion of printed text into digital text. This requires not only the capability to render the image of the original within the computer but to have the computer actually "read" the text from that image. Although computers can do many things much faster and with more accuracy than humans, this is not one of them. The signal processing of the human eye and visual cortex is completely unmatched in the computer world. So, whereas reading this page is trivial for you, to a computer, this is a very arduous task. Special software is needed to read the pixels of the document, determine where the letters are, correct for orientation, size variation, and all manner of distortions in order to identify a single letter.

There are several options for optical character recognition (OCR) on Ubuntu, but the one best integrated with XSane is GOCR (also known as *JOCR*). This application needs to be installed using the following line:

```
sudo apt-get install gocr
```

Make VoIP Calls over the Internet with Ekiga Softphone

You can use the Ekiga Softphone application to make phone calls over the Internet, to chat, and to have video conferences. The Softphone application makes it possible to call other computers at no charge and to call normal telephones at a nominal charge. You can even set up the system to receive calls from regular telephones.

The first time that you use Ekiga, you will need to set up your Softphone by following the steps in the First Time Configuration Assistant.

To use Ekiga Softphone, you will need a session initiation protocol (SIP) address. An SIP address looks like an email address, but it is unique and specifically suited to the Voice over Internet Protocol (VoIP). If you have an SIP address, enter it during the setup. If you do not have one, on step three of the configuration process, you can follow a link to get an Ekiga.net SIP account. If you are connected to the Internet, your browser will automatically open and take you to the Ekiga.net Web site. Follow the steps on the site to set up your account. There is no charge to create an SIP account. Make sure that you choose an appropriate name, as this is how other SIP users will find you.

After you have completed the steps in the First Time Configuration Assistant, you will be ready to use your Softphone. Note that you must be connected to the Internet to use this application. You will also probably want a headset with a microphone and earphones to conduct your calls. You will at a minimum need a microphone, speakers, and an audio card.

Make VoIP Calls over the Internet with Ekiga Softphone

1. Click Applications ➔ Internet ➔ Ekiga Softphone.

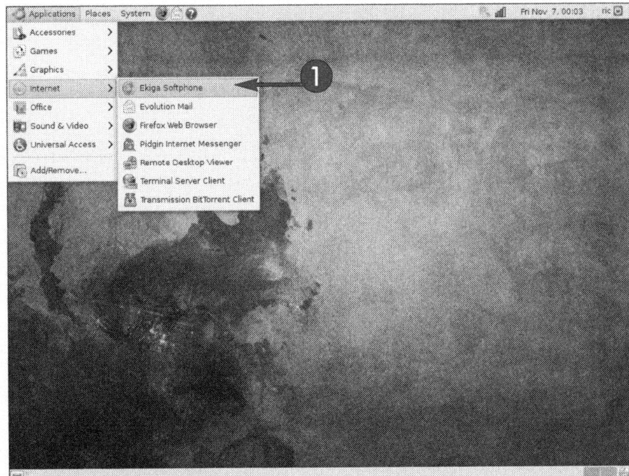

The First Time Configuration Assistant appears.

Note: *This only appears the first time that you launch the application. Follow the steps to set up the application.*

2. Click Forward.
3. Type your first and last names.
4. Click Forward.

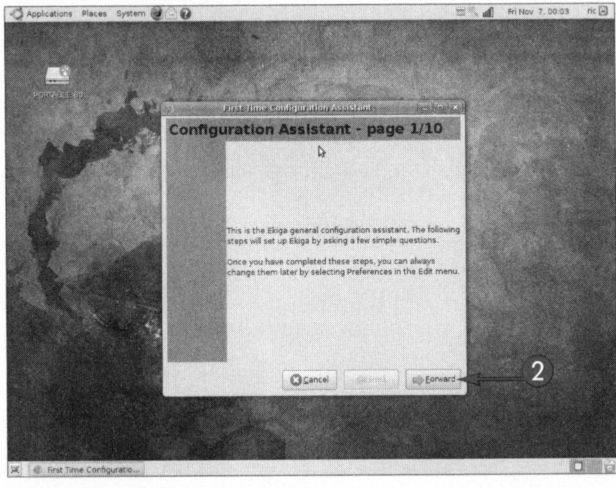

The third page of ten appears, on which you are asked for your SIP account details.

Note: *If you do not have an SIP account, you will need to get one to use Ekiga. You can click the Get an Ekiga.net SIP Account link to obtain a free account.*

5 Type your SIP username.

6 Type your SIP password.

7 Click Forward.

Note: *Follow the instructions in the assistant to complete the rest of the configuration.*

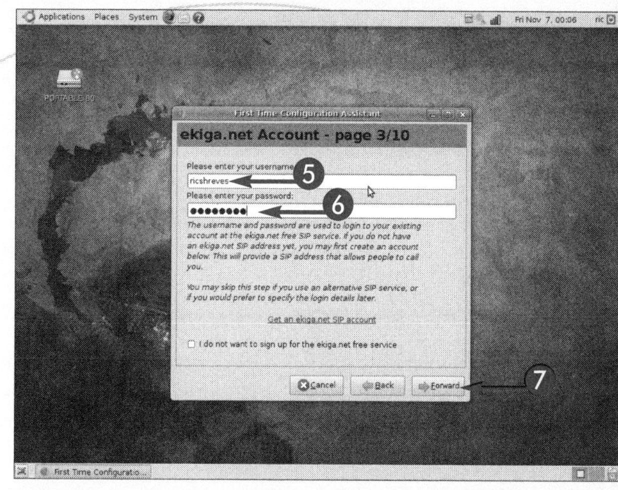

The Softphone interface appears after you complete the steps in the First Time Configuration Assistant.

Extra

Although you do not need a video camera to run Ekiga, make calls, or use chat, if you do have a Webcam installed on your machine, you can use it to make video calls. Ekiga uses plug-ins to detect your Webcam, and generally, any camera that is compatible with Linux will work with Ekiga.

To set up a camera, plug it into your machine and then run the Configuration Druid, which is located under the Ekiga window's Edit menu. One of the last steps of the configuration utility relates to video. It will enable Ekiga to use your Webcam.

To check the installation, click the Image button on the left side of the Ekiga window. If your camera is working properly, you should be able to see the image from your camera in the right pane in the Ekiga window.

To use video during calls, you will need to activate the video support for calls; to do so, click Edit ➔ Preferences. In the Ekiga Preferences dialog box, click Video Codecs and then check the box labeled Enable Video Support. Click the Close button, and you are ready to go.

continued ➔

Make VoIP Calls over the Internet with Ekiga Softphone (continued)

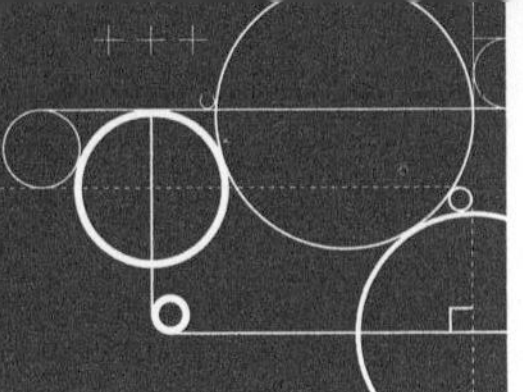

After your Softphone is set up and you have an SIP account, you can begin making calls. Calls to other computers require you to know the recipient's SIP address.

When you try to make a call to another SIP user on your Softphone, if the user is online and accepts the call request, the connection will be made, and you can talk normally. Note that you may hear some delay in the line, depending on the quality of the connection. Similarly, other SIP users can call you directly using your SIP address.

Note that you can also chat with other users who have SIP addresses. You can do so in a separate chat window.

To call a regular telephone using your Softphone, you must first contract with a service provider because these calls incur charges. If you have a contract with a provider, enter the details into the Accounts dialog box under the Edit menu. After the account is in the system, you can make a call using the regular phone number, preceded by **00**.

Receiving calls requires you to rent a telephone number. This can normally be done from the same company that provides contracts for making VoIP calls to a normal phone. The rates for this service can be quite low, depending on the country that you select as the basis for the number.

Make VoIP Calls over the Internet with Ekiga Softphone *(continued)*

8. Type the SIP address that you want to call.
9. Click the Connect button.

   The system attempts to connect to the address.

- A successful connection will show a confirmation message.

***Note:** At this point you should be able to speak to and hear the recipient through your microphone and speakers or headset.*

10. Click the Chat button.

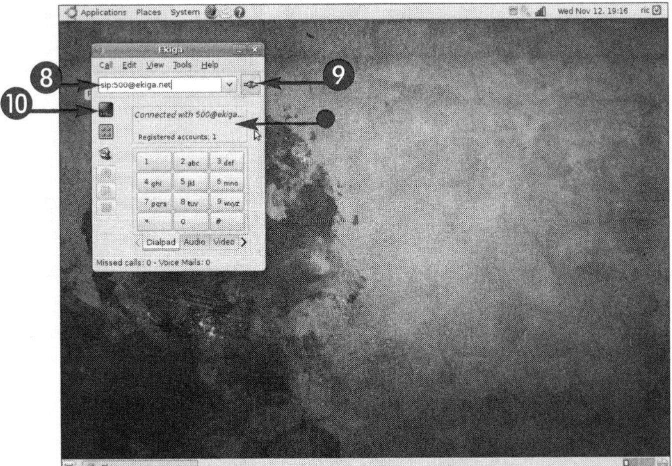

   A chat window opens.

11. Type your message.
12. Click Send.

   Your message is sent to the recipient.

***Note:** You will see your message in the pane above the text box, and you will also see in that pane the responses from the other party.*

13. When finished with your conversation, click Hang Up.
14. Click the close button.

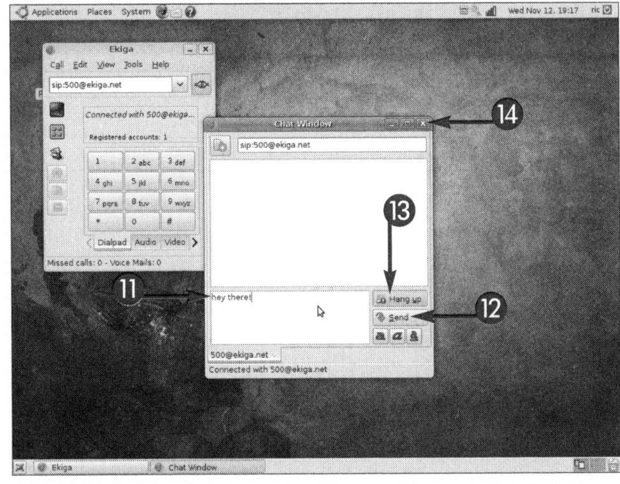

- When the call is over, the system goes into Standby mode.

15. Type the number of a normal telephone, preceded by **00**.
16. Click the Connect button.

    The system attempts to contact the telephone using VoIP.

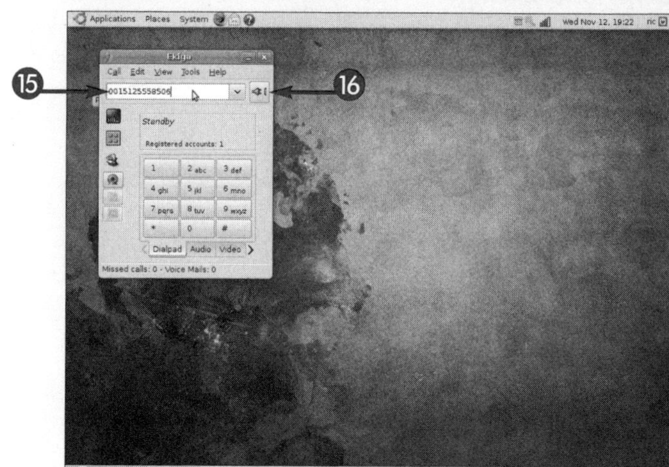

Extra

VoIP is a useful and cost-saving tool, but it can also eat up your bandwidth. If you are on a slower connection or you simply need to limit the amount of bandwidth used by Ekiga, you can adjust the settings to optimize the application.

Click Edit ➔ Preferences to open the Ekiga Preferences dialog box. The Audio Codecs options enable you to select which of the available codecs the system uses. You can select one of the lower bandwidth codecs and disable the higher bandwidth codecs. Note that the lower the bandwidth, typically the worse the quality.

On the Video Codecs tab, you can set a specific limit on the maximum video bandwidth. Note that if you set this too low, and the system is unable to comply with the limit, it will exceed the limit in order to process the video. You can move the Advanced Quality Setting slider control, below the Bandwidth control, to adjust the frame rate and picture quality. Higher frame rates and higher quality will require more processing power and may be limited by the available bandwidth.

Chat with Friends with Pidgin Internet Messenger

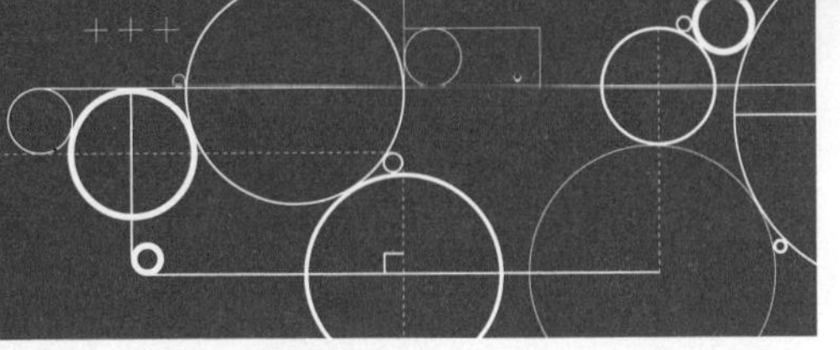

You can use the Pidgin Internet Messenger application to have online chat sessions with your friends. The application enables you to have real-time text message exchanges using accounts from any of the most popular services, including AOL, MSN Messenger, Yahoo! Messenger, and many more.

The first time that you open the application, you will be prompted to set up an account. To do so, you can use the Add Account dialog box. When the system first tries to connect to your new account, you must be connected to the Internet for it to work.

You can add additional accounts at any time by selecting Manage Accounts from under the Edit menu.

Once the system is able to connect to your Internet Messenger (IM) account, a list of your friends who are online will appear in the Pidgin window. Friends that are associated with your account but who are not online at the time are hidden from view.

Note at the bottom of the window the Pidgin status button, which you can use to set a status message for other users to see; for example, if you do not want to be disturbed, you can set your status to Busy or to Away. If you want to remain online but not visible to others, you can select the Invisible option. When you are set as Invisible, you can still send and receive messages, but you will appear to be offline to other users.

Chat with Friends with Pidgin Internet Messenger

SET UP PIDGIN

1. Click Applications ➔ Internet ➔ Pidgin Internet Messenger.

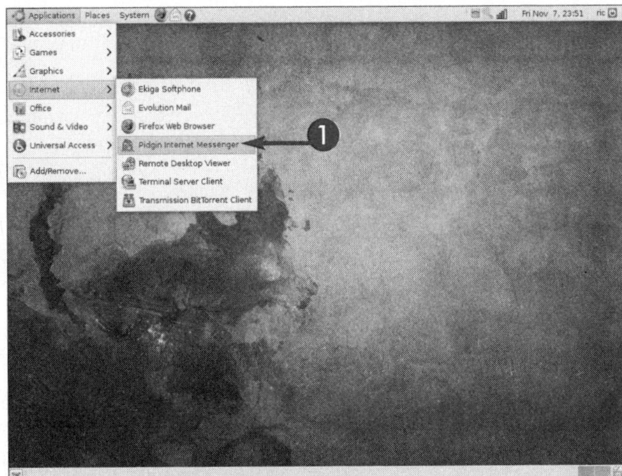

The Accounts setup wizard appears.

2. Click Add.

The Add Account dialog box appears.

3. Click here and select your service.
4. Type your username.
5. Type your password.
6. Click Save.

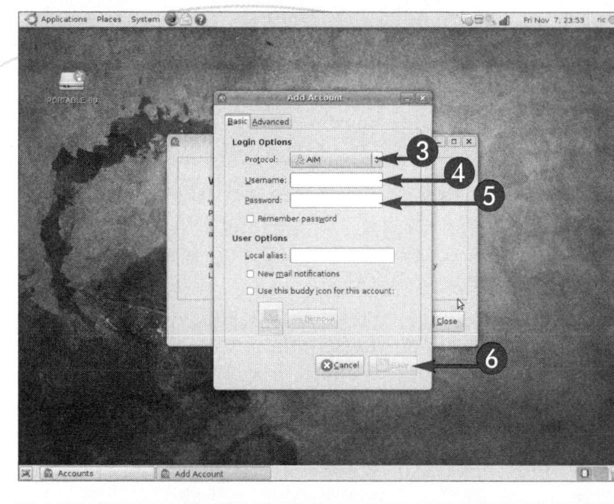

- The Accounts dialog box shows your new account.

7. Click Close.

- Pidgin connects to your account and displays your Buddy List with your contacts.

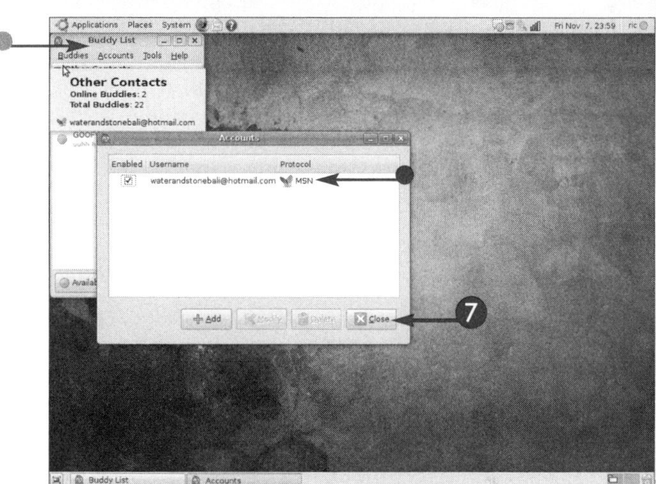

Extra

At the time this book was written, Intrepid Ibex had just been released. Although the vast majority of the applications bundled with Ubuntu 8.10 are quite solid and reliable, there will be applications with a few problems. Pidgin at the time of release was one of those. Now, however, the application is solid.

Whenever the bugs in an application such as Pidgin are numerous, there are a number of individuals working to fix them. Now, the more serious issues have been addressed. This situation is just one example of why it is important for you to keep up with the upgrades and patches that are issued for your Ubuntu system. As bugs are reported, fixed, and patched, the new files will be pushed out to the users. The use of the automatic updates functionality is discussed in Chapter 5.

There are still some small, innocuous bugs in Pidgin. You can check the bugs list located here: http://developer.pidgin.im/wiki/OpenTickets. If you have a problem you are experiencing that does not appear on this list, then you should report the bug so that it can be added to the list and eventually fixed. You can report problems with Pidgin at this address: http://developer.pidgin.im.

continued

Chat with Friends with Pidgin Internet Messenger (continued)

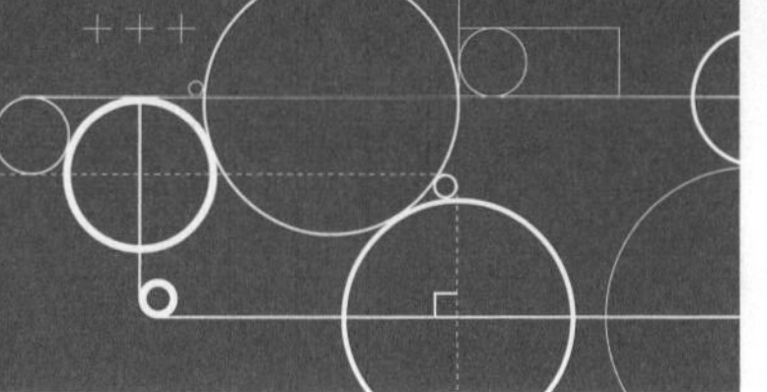

After you have set up Pidgin Internet Messenger, you can chat with your friends online in real time. If your connection is good and stable, the discussion can move very quickly.

You can learn more about the individual contacts in your Buddy List by moving your mouse pointer over their name. When you mouseover a name, a pop-up will appear with details about the person.

When you initiate a chat with a friend, Pidgin opens a chat window and contacts your friend. You both post your messages to the chat window. After you submit a message, it appears in the box at the top of the chat window. As your friend replies, his or her comments are added as well. As the conversation progresses, you wind up with a record of the conversation in your chat window.

If one of your contacts wants to chat with you, you will see a chat window open with his or her name and message. You can reply by typing your response into the chat window. Note that messages cannot be edited after they have been submitted.

You can open as many chat windows as you like; Pidgin makes it possible to have multiple chat windows open at the same time, so you can have multiple conversations going on at once.

You can use the icons at the bottom of the chat window to insert hyperlinks for sharing Web sites and to insert horizontal rules to add visual breaks to the discussion thread. Another option is the Smilies button, which enables you to insert smilies — animated graphical characters — into your discussion.

Chat with Friends with Pidgin Internet Messenger *(continued)*

CHAT WITH A FRIEND

1. Move your mouse pointer over a contact.

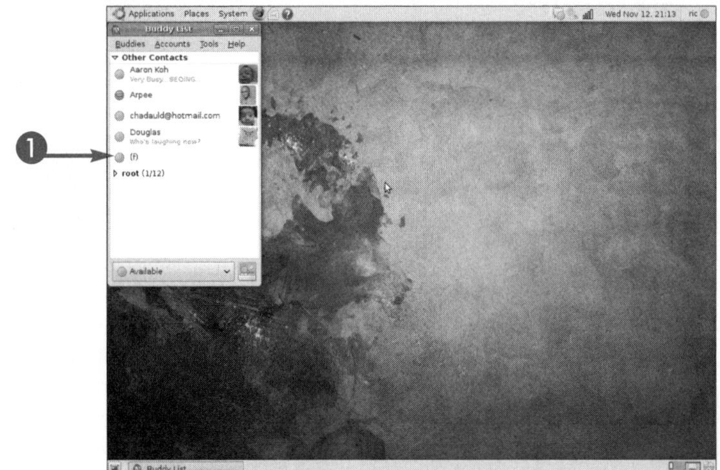

- A pop-up shows the contact's details.

2. Double-click the contact with whom you want to chat.

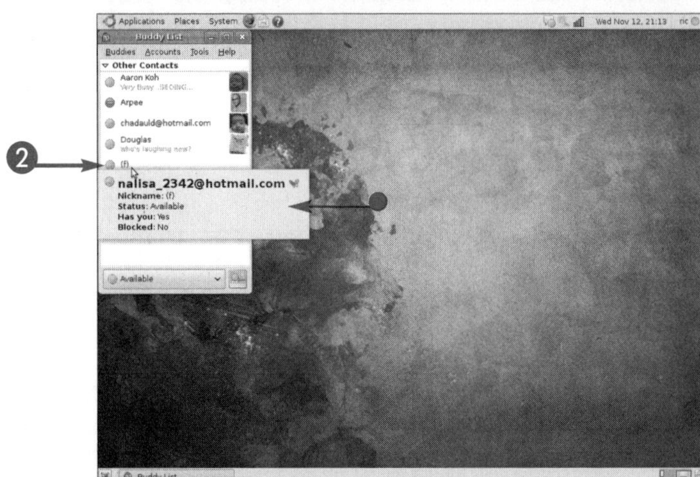

The chat window opens.

3 Type your message and press Enter.

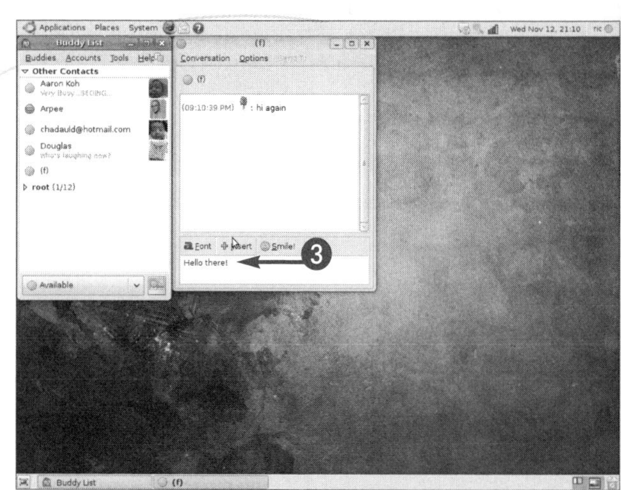

- Your message appears and is sent to the contact.

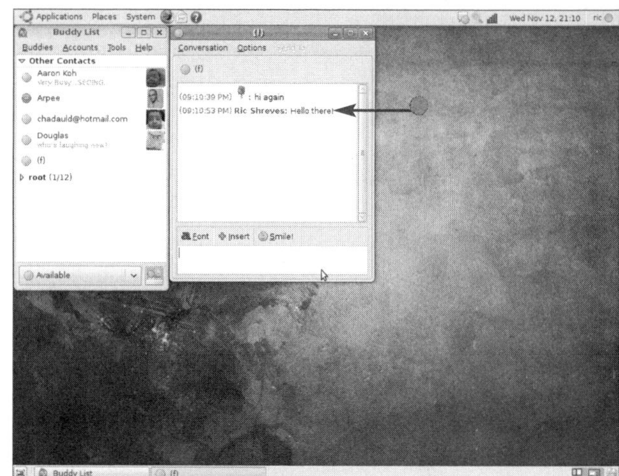

Extra

You can set Pidgin to automatically trigger actions on the occurrence of certain events. This functionality is called *Buddy Pounces,* and it is useful for notifying you when important contacts come online or go away.

Buddy Pounces are accessed under the Tools menu. Click Buddy Pounces and then click Add in the Buddy Pounces dialog box. The New Buddy Pounce dialog box is where you set up the action and specify the trigger. Pounces are associated with users, so start by specifying the Buddy name that you want to be affected. Next, specify the trigger by selecting one or more of the options under Pounce When Buddy. Then specify the action that you want to occur in the Action section. You can open a message window, pop up a notification, send a message, or even execute a command. In the final section are options to make your pounce a recurring event and to indicate whether the pounce is dependent on your status. When you are finished, click Save.

After you have created a pounce, you can edit it by selecting it in the Buddy Pounce dialog box and then clicking the Modify button.

Browse the World Wide Web with Firefox

You can visit and interact with Web sites and other media sources on the World Wide Web by using the Firefox browser. Firefox, one of the world's most popular Web browsers, is included by default in your Ubuntu desktop package. It is easy to use and flexible and gives you immediate access to Web sites.

When you first start Firefox, it will open a predetermined home page. The home page of the Firefox browser in Ubuntu has been set to a Google search page located on the Ubuntu Web site (www.ubuntu.com). If you are connected to the Internet, this default Google search page will be the first thing you see in the browser.

To navigate to a Web site, you type its address in the Address bar at the top of the Firefox window. You can click the green arrow to go to the Web page. Although you can launch Firefox offline and it will allow you to type in addresses, you must be connected to the Internet to view Web sites.

One of the most useful features of the Firefox browser is the ability to open multiple pages and keep them all visible on your screen with tabs. Even though it was possible before tabs to open separate browser windows, a group of tabs is much easier to manage than a group of windows. A shortcut for opening a new tab is pressing the Ctrl key at the same time you press the letter *T*.

Browse the World Wide Web with Firefox

1. Click Applications → Internet → Firefox Web Browser.

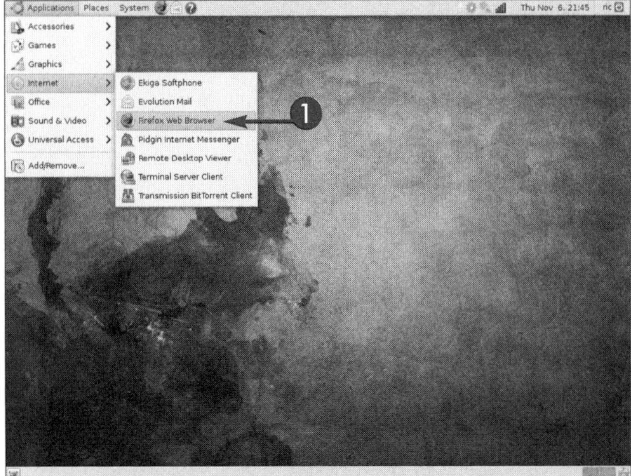

The Firefox browser starts and displays the default home page.

Note: *You need to be connected to the Internet for the page to be displayed properly.*

2 Click File → New Tab.

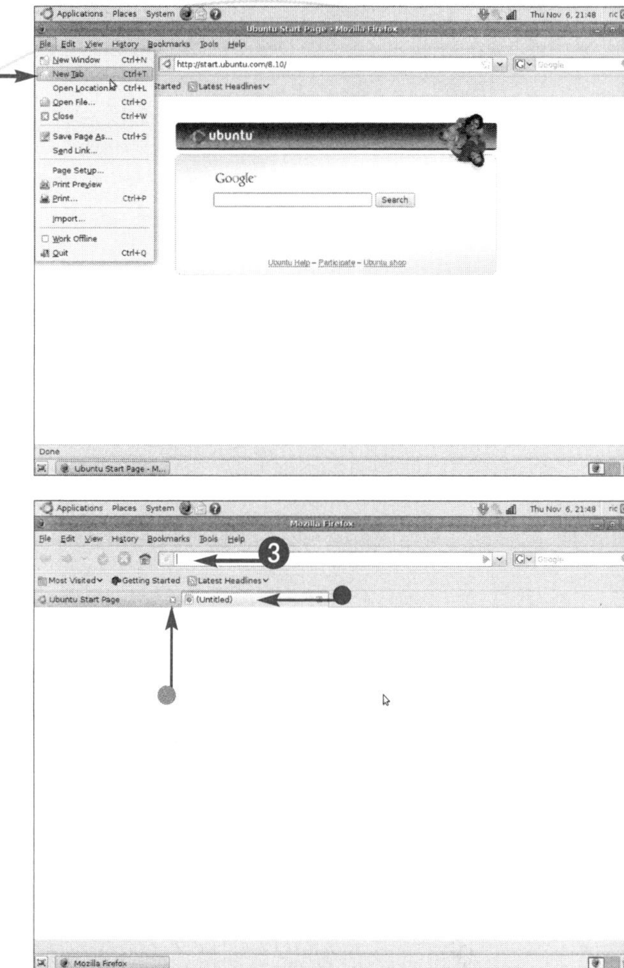

- A new tab with a blank page opens.

3 Type the Web site address that you want to visit and press Enter.

The site opens on the new tab.

- You can close a tab by clicking here.

Extra

The Google search page that Ubuntu sets as the default home page of your Firefox browser is useful, but you may want to change the home page to something else. To change your home page, click Edit → Preferences. When the Firefox Preferences dialog box opens, select the Main tab, if it is not already active. In the Startup section, look for the Home Page text field; this is where you can specify your choice of home page. On the line above the Home Page field, you can specify what happens when the browser starts. After you have made your choices, click the Close button.

To a certain extent, the Google search page is redundant, as your browser has a built-in Web search toolbar at the top right of the application. The search box is always visible. To use it, just enter your search terms in the box and press Enter. The search results will appear in your browser window. Note that the search box has a drop-down list that also enables you to select which search service you want to use.

Remotely Access Windows, Linux, and Macintosh Systems with the Remote Desktop Viewer

You can view the desktops of other computers and control them remotely through the use of Ubuntu's Remote Desktop Viewer. The Remote Desktop Viewer application uses the virtual network computing (VNC) protocol to control another computer that is running a VNC server. This is very useful for troubleshooting a remote machine or for accessing your work computer from your home computer.

Ubuntu's Remote Desktop Viewer is both a VNC server and a VNC client. To access another computer, you will be using the Remote Desktop Viewer as a VNC client. Note that the other computer must be running a VNC server and you must be connected to that computer via a network or the Internet.

When you open the Remote Desktop Viewer, it will automatically detect any VNC servers on the same network as your Ubuntu box. If the computer that you want to access is not on the network or does not appear, you will need to try to connect to it manually. Follow the steps in this section to do so. If there are no difficulties, the desktop of the remote computer will appear in the main pane of the Remote Desktop Viewer application. You can observe what is happening on that computer, and you can move your mouse cursor on the remote computer's screen and control it as if it were your own computer.

Remotely Access Windows, Linux, and Macintosh Systems with the Remote Desktop Viewer

1. Click Applications ➔ Internet ➔ Remote Desktop Viewer.

The Remote Desktop Viewer window opens.

2. Click Connect.

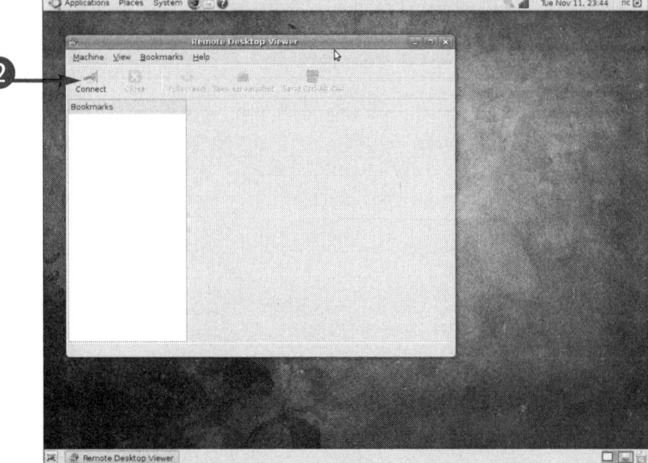

The connection dialog box appears.

3. Type the hostname or IP address.
4. Click Connect.

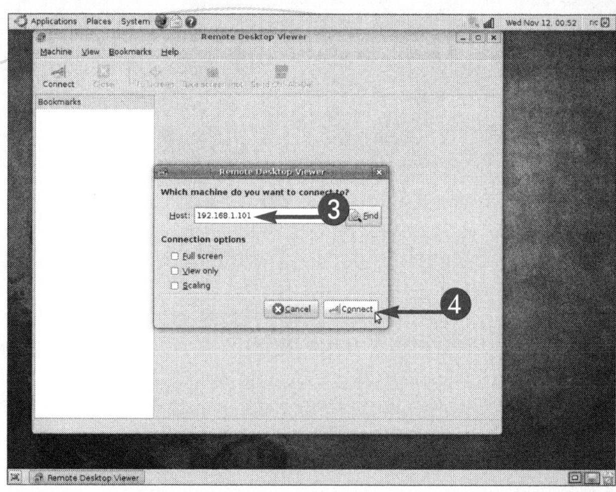

The connection is made, and the remote machine's desktop becomes visible.

- You can now use the remote machine as if you were sitting in front of it.

5. When you are finished, click Close.

The connection is terminated.

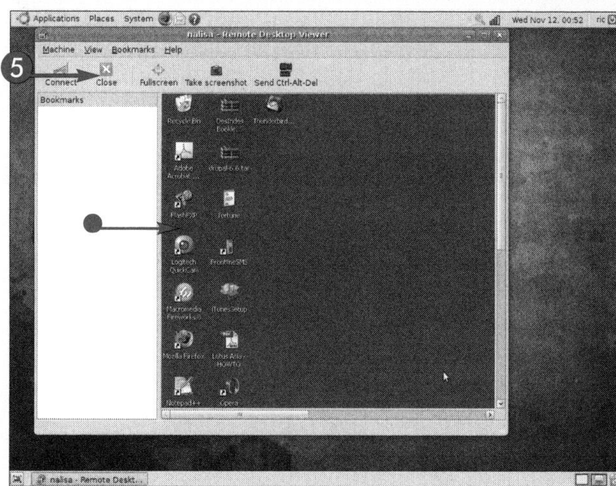

Extra

Making a VNC connection requires the cooperation of a VNC server and a VNC client. Most Linux boxes have some sort of VNC capability, and Macintosh has VNC built into its system. Windows, however, is not bundled with a VNC application.

If you want to connect to a Windows machine, you will need to make sure that a VNC server is installed. One of the easiest to use is TightVNC. There is also a version of TightVNC for Linux and other operating systems. You can download all the different versions from www.tightvnc.com.

After you have installed the VNC server on your Windows machine, you will need to configure it to accept connections. This is usually a simple process, but you will need to follow the instructions of the VNC application that you chose. Make sure that the server is running before you try to connect with the Remote Desktop Viewer.

One important point: Running a VNC server on a Windows machine is potentially risky as it opens up your machine to outsiders. Make sure that you password-protect the machine and, when possible, limit the VNC access to only the IP address of the machine you will use to connect to your Windows box.

Remotely Access Windows Systems with the Terminal Server Client

As discussed earlier, you can use your Ubuntu system to gain access to a Windows machine and control it remotely. Remote access is a powerful tool that lets you operate the Windows machine as though you were sitting in front of it and working with it directly through its keyboard and mouse.

To use remote access, you will need some basic information about the machine that you want to control, including the name or the IP address of the computer, the username, and the password. You enter this information on the Terminal Server Client dialog box's General tab. Note that on this tab, the Protocol drop-down list offers two choices relevant to Windows: RDP, for older Windows 2000 systems, and RDPv5, for Windows XP and newer systems. Select the one that matches your Windows machine's operating system.

After you enter the required information, and if the Windows machine has remote access enabled, you should connect without difficulty. When the connection is made, a new window will open on your Ubuntu desktop showing the Windows desktop. You can navigate and work with the Windows system from within the new window.

You can save connections that you have made by using the Save As button in the Terminal Server Client dialog box. When you save connections, they will be available to you under the Quick Connect drop-down list, making future connections fast and easy.

Remotely Access Windows Systems with the Terminal Server Client

1. Click Applications ➔ Internet ➔ Terminal Server Client.

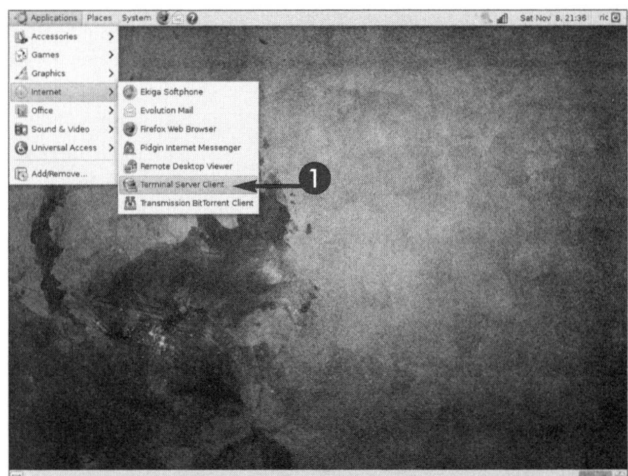

The Terminal Server Client application opens.

2. Type the name of the computer or IP address.
3. Type the username.
4. Type the password.
5. Click the Display tab.

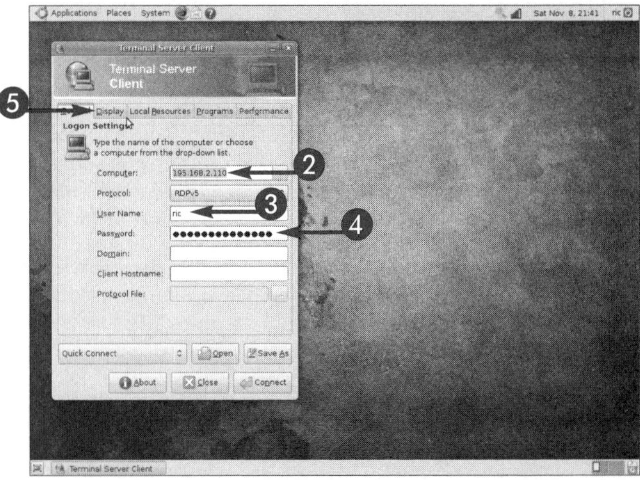

The Display tab comes to the front.

6 Click Use Specified Screen Size.

7 Click here and select the screen size that you want.

8 Click Connect.

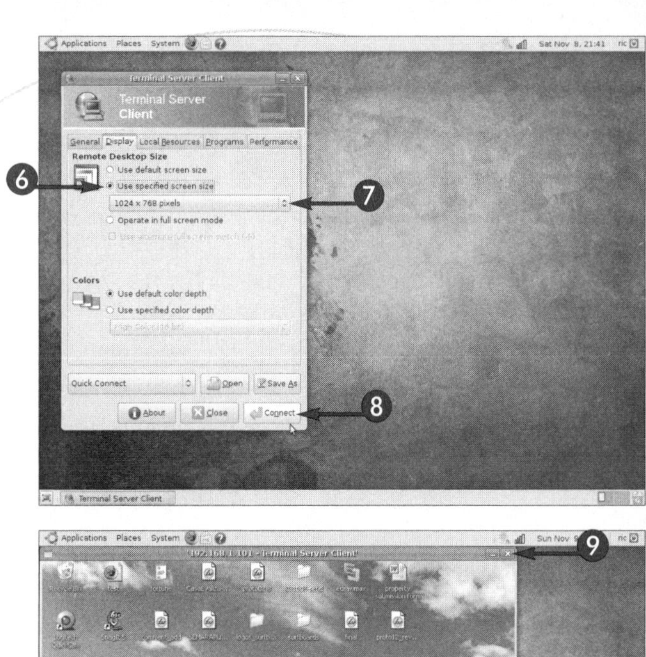

The connection is made, and the other's computer becomes visible on the screen.

- You can now use the remote machine as if you were sitting in front of it.

9 When you are finished, click here.

The connection is terminated.

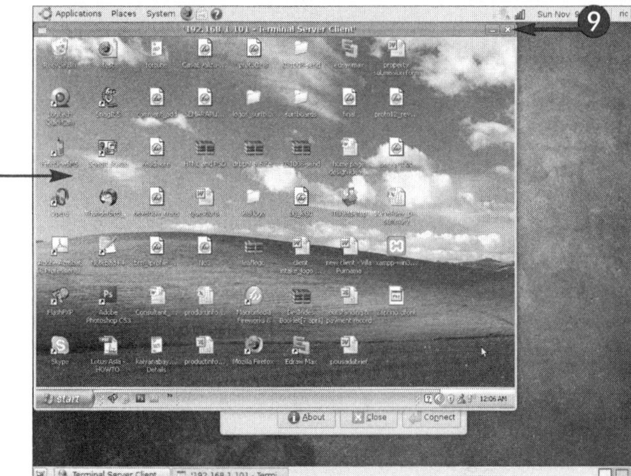

Extra

Using the Terminal Server Client for remote access requires a Windows computer that is configured to accept remote access connections. You must have the Windows machine configured properly, or the Ubuntu application will not be able to make a connection. To set up your Windows machine, first go to the Control Panel and select the System option. In the System dialog box, click the Remote tab and then select Allow Users to Connect Remotely to This Computer. Click Apply. Your Windows machine is now ready to accept remote access requests from your Ubuntu computer.

Note also that you should make sure that your Windows machine requires a username and a password to allow access. Failure to set up a username and password will leave your system dangerously exposed to compromise by remote access.

If your system does not have a username and password set up, then go to the Control Panel and select User Accounts. Click Change an Account and then select the account that you want to modify; generally, this will be the account with Administrator privileges. Set the name and password.

Download Files with the Transmission BitTorrent Client

With the Transmission BitTorrent client, you can download large files quickly and share files on your computer with others. The BitTorrent protocol makes downloading large files easy as it automatically downloads segments of files from multiple servers simultaneously. This approach to file downloads is known as *peer-to-peer.*

The Transmission BitTorrent client is part of the default Ubuntu distribution. You can open Transmission yourself as shown in the steps here or let the system launch Transmission automatically when you click or download a torrent file. Indeed, the vast majority of times that you will use the Transmission BitTorrent client will probably be in the automatic mode as you click torrents that you find online while browsing the Internet.

The main Transmission application window includes a status window, which shows the state of all downloads, as well as a set of controls that let you customize the preferences and configuration. If you have downloaded a torrent file, you can start a download directly from the main Transmission window by clicking the Add button and then navigating to the location of the torrent file on your computer.

Whenever you download a file using the torrent process, a second window will open. The secondary window will be specific to the torrent file that you are working with and will show you the status of the various components of the download. You can stop, start, or pause torrents individually from the secondary window. Transmission enables you to run multiple torrents simultaneously, in which case each download will have its own window, in addition to the main Transmission window.

Download Files with the Transmission BitTorrent Client

1. Click Applications ➔ Internet ➔ Transmission BitTorrent Client.

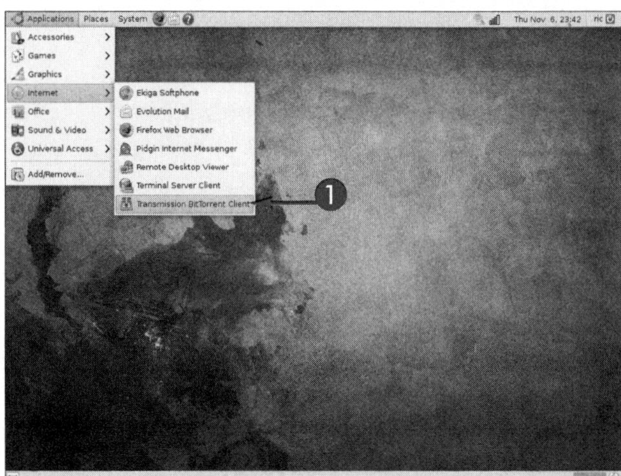

- The Transmission application opens.

2. Click Applications ➔ Internet ➔ Firefox Web Browser.

Firefox opens.

3. Navigate to a site and identify a torrent to download.
4. Click to initiate the download.

   The download dialog box appears.
5. Click OK.

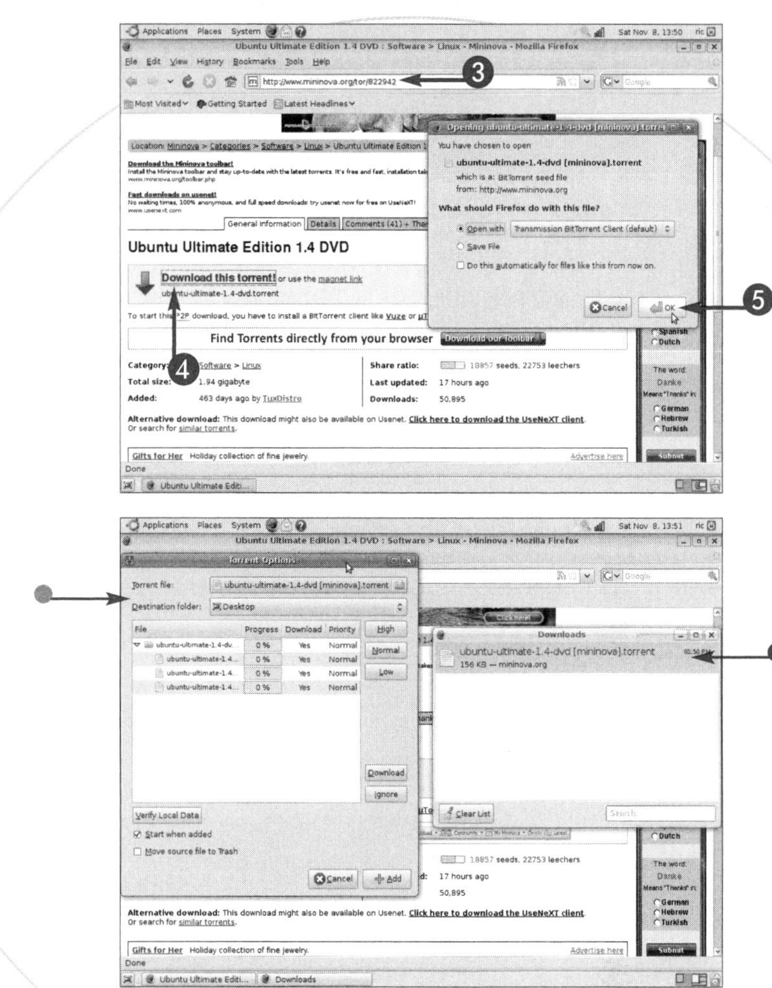

- The torrent file download begins.
- Transmission automatically opens the torrent file and starts to download the related source files.

Apply It

You can create your own torrents for sharing files with others. In fact, the whole credo of the peer-to-peer movement is to enable individuals to share files easily, thereby benefitting the whole. Transmission makes it possible to create and share torrents.

To create your own torrent for sharing, click Torrent ➔ New. The New Torrent dialog box opens. Select the source for your files. You can use either a directory or a specific file. Next, you need to announce that the torrent is available to others. You do this by adding a tracker. Click the Add button and then enter the URL where you announce the torrent's existence. Normally, this will be one of the many torrent directories online. You can add more than one, if you prefer.

Alternatively, you can make your torrent private. Click the Extras button, and the Extras section expands. Click the Private Torrent check box if you want to restrict access to the torrent. Note that in the Extras section, you can also add a comment to your torrent. This is helpful to users and should be done.

Configure an Evolution Email Account

With the Evolution email client, you can send and receive email from your Ubuntu computer.

The first time that you launch Evolution, you will need to go through the steps in the Evolution Setup Assistant to configure the program and add your first account. Before you navigate through the assistant, you will need to know the details for both your incoming and outgoing mail servers. If you lack this information, you can cancel the Setup Assistant and add a new email account later from the Preferences menu under Evolution's Edit menu.

Note that if you have previously used Evolution on another machine or you are upgrading from an older version, you will be offered the opportunity to restore from a backup on the second page of the Setup Assistant. If this is a new setup for you, you can just move on to the next step.

On the third page of the assistant, you add your personal details and email address. The Optional Information section on this page lets you designate the account as your default email account and set up the Reply-To information that will appear on your outgoing email messages.

On the Receiving Email page, you will need to select first your server type and fill in the Configuration fields that are needed for the selected server type. On the next page, Receiving Options, you set the frequency the system will check for new mail and the options for your email storage.

Configure an Evolution Email Account

1. Click Applications ➔ Internet ➔ Evolution Mail.

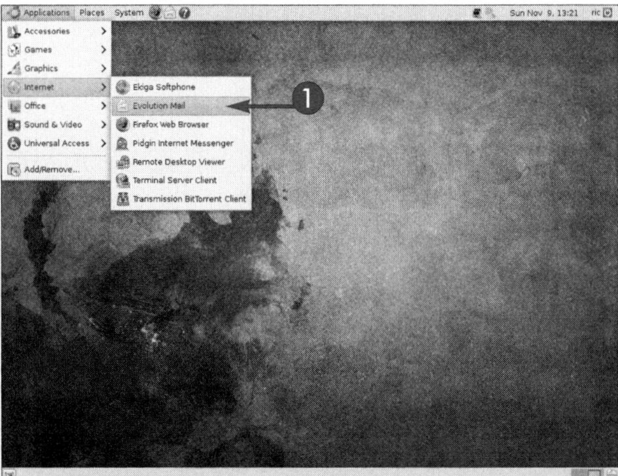

The Evolution Setup Assistant opens.

Note: *This will occur only the first time you start Evolution. You should go through the steps to set up your first account.*

2. Click Forward.

A setup page appears, asking if you want to restore from a backup.

3. If you have no such backup, click Forward.

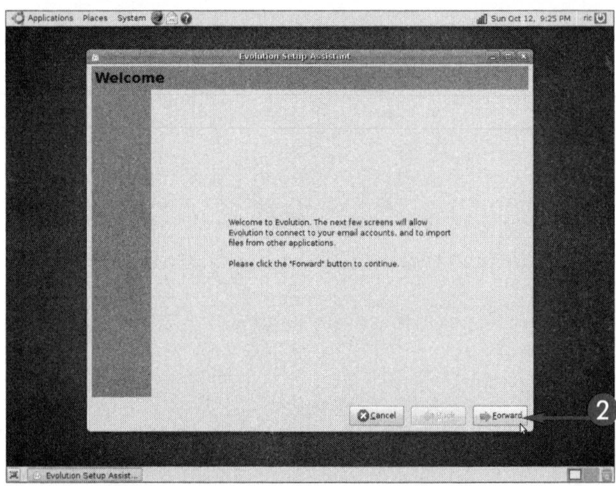

The Identity page appears.

4. Type your name.
5. Type your email address.
6. Click Make This My Default Account.
7. Click Forward.

The Receiving Email page appears.

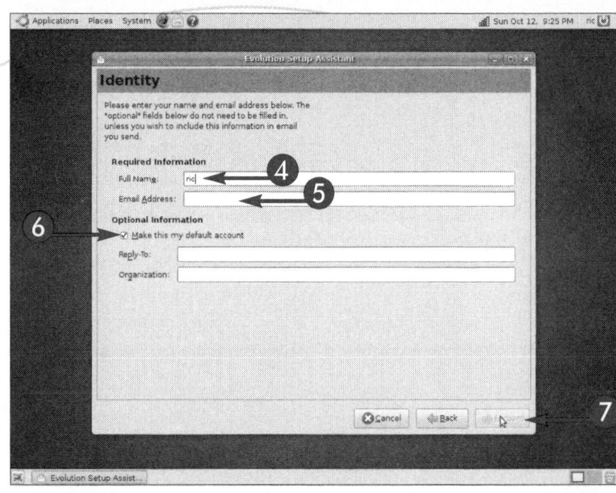

8. Click here and select your incoming mail server type.
9. Type the server's address.
10. Type your email account username.
11. Click Remember Password.
12. Click Forward.

***Note:** Details may vary according to your mail configuration.*

The Receiving Options page appears.

13. Select your options and then click Forward to move on.

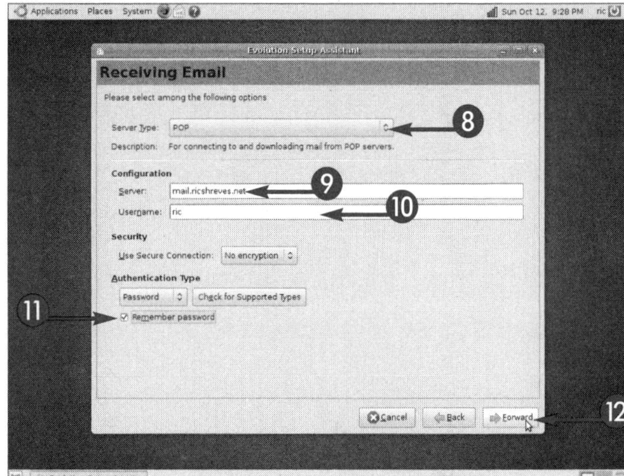

Apply It

Because many people are now using Google's Gmail service for at least one of their email accounts, you may need to know how to set up Evolution to work with a Gmail account. To do so, you must configure both Gmail and Evolution.

First, access your Gmail account. On the top right of the page, click the Settings link. On the Settings page, click the Forwarding and POP tab, locate the Pop Download section, and select either of the options to enable POP. Click Save, and you are done configuring your Gmail account.

Next, you must set up Evolution to access Gmail. Create a new account in Evolution. Click Edit → Preferences. Then select Mail Accounts and click Add. Evolution takes you through a setup wizard. Note the following key settings: Set the receiving mail protocol to POP and the mail server to **pop.gmail.com**. Use the SSL secure connection with the Password Protection option selected. For sending mail, set the server to **smtp.gmail.com**. Select TLS Encryption for the Security option. Click the Apply button on the last screen of the setup wizard, and you are done.

continued →

Configure an Evolution Email Account (continued)

Before you can begin to send and receive email with your Evolution email client, you will need to finish the configuration process.

After configuring your system to receive email, you will need to set up the sending options. On the Sending Email page, you select your outgoing mail server type and add the configuration details to allow Evolution to connect to the server. The Security option on this screen allows you to enable encryption or password-controlled access to your outgoing mail server. Normally, your server determines these options; you cannot control the security options on the server from within Evolution.

The next page, Account Management, asks you to give this account a name. Select something meaningful, as this will appear in Evolution. If you have more than one account enabled in Evolution, these labels will allow you to differentiate between them easily.

The final step in the Evolution Setup Assistant is the Timezone setting. You can use your left mouse button to zoom in on the map and your right mouse button to zoom out. You can also select the appropriate time zone from the drop-down list at the bottom of the screen.

After you finish the setup, the Evolution email client will open. You will again need to enter your email account password. Then the system will attempt to connect to your mail server and download your mail. For this to work, you must be connected to the Internet.

Configure an Evolution Email Account *(continued)*

The Sending Email page appears.

14. Click here and select your outgoing mail server type.
15. Type your outgoing mail server name.
16. Click Forward.

Note: *Details may vary according to your mail configuration.*

The Account Management page appears.

17. Type a descriptive name for this email account.
18. Click Forward.

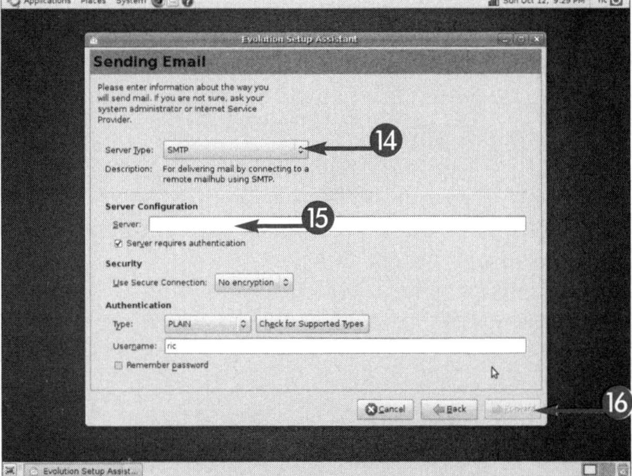

The Timezone page appears.

19. Click here and select your time zone.
20. Click Forward.

The Setup Assistant displays the final confirmation page.

21. Click Apply to finish.

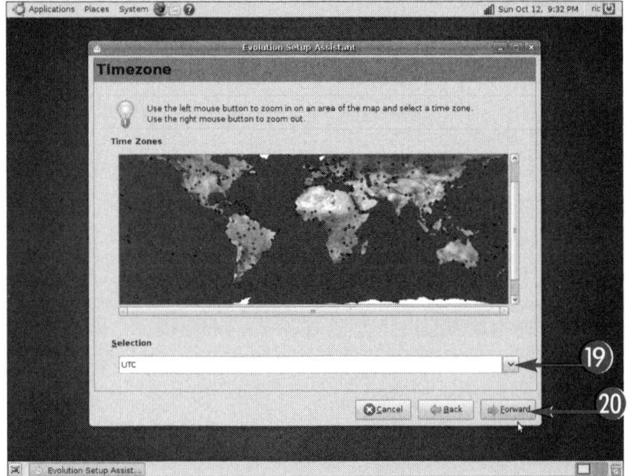

The Evolution email client opens and prompts you for your account password.

22 Type your email password.

23 Click OK.

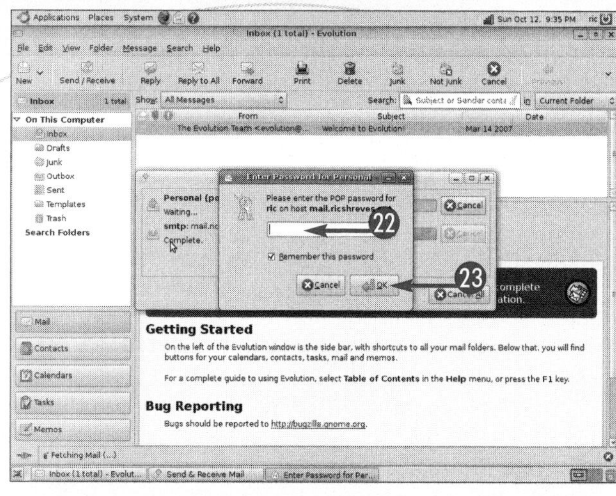

- Evolution attempts to connect to your mail account and downloads any mail.

Note: *For this to work, you must be connected to the Internet, and your account settings must be correct.*

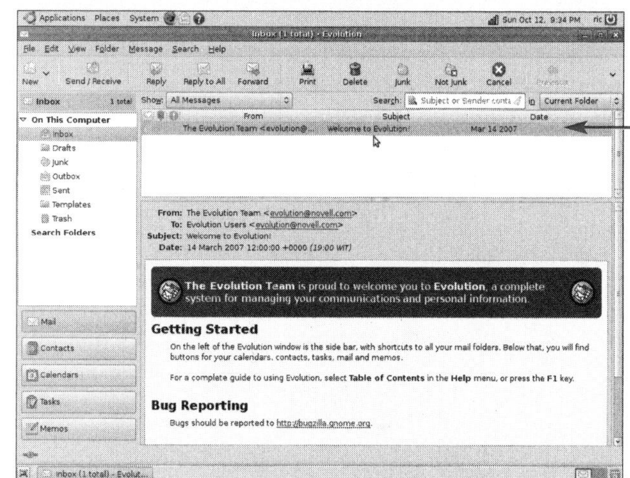

Apply It

You can create automatic signatures to go on your emails in Evolution. The use of standardized automatic signatures — or *sigfiles* as they are sometimes called — adds a professional aspect to your correspondence.

Click Edit → Preferences. In the Evolution Preferences window, select the Composer Preferences option and then click the Signatures tab. On the Signatures tab, click the Add button. The Edit Signature dialog box opens. Give your new signature a name and then enter the text that you want to appear in the large text field. Set the drop-down list on the left to HTML if you want to have more formatting options. Setting the signature to HTML enables you to use styling and to insert active hyperlinks. Note that the formatting, however, will only appear if you send the email in HTML format and the recipient can receive it in HTML format. When you are finished, click Save and Close.

To modify an existing signature, select it in the Signatures window and then click the Edit button.

When you create a new email, your signature will appear as an option under the Signature drop-down list at the top right above the message area.

Compose and Send Email

You can use Evolution to create new email messages and send them to others.

To create a new message, you can follow the steps here or press the Ctrl key at the same time that you press the N key. You type the email address of the recipient on the line labeled To and a subject line for your email in the field next to Subject. The body of the message goes in the large text field at the bottom of the Compose Message window.

When you send your message, you must be connected to the Internet, and your account settings must be correct for the email to go out. If there are problems with your account settings or if you are not connected to the Internet, the system displays an error message, and your email will be saved in the Outbox.

Messages queued in your Outbox can be sent by clicking the Send/Receive button.

There are several other options on the Compose Message window. The Save Draft button on the toolbar saves your message to the Drafts folder, where it can be edited in the future. The Attach button attaches files that you select to your message; those files are sent with the message to the recipient. Undo and Redo are both editing tools that undo the most recent step that you have taken or redo it. The Cut button is for cutting text out of a message. Note the arrow on the right side of the toolbar. Clicking that arrow displays other editing options, including copy, paste, and a search feature.

Compose and Send Email

1. In Evolution, click the New drop-down arrow ➔ Mail Message.

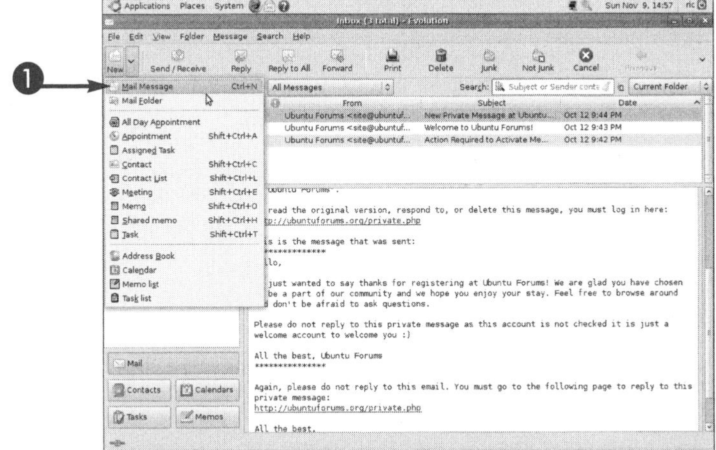

The Compose Message window opens.

2. Type the recipient's address.
3. Type the subject.
4. Type your message.
5. Click Send.

Evolution attempts to send the email.

Note: *For this step to work, you must be connected to the Internet, and your outgoing mail server account settings must be correct.*

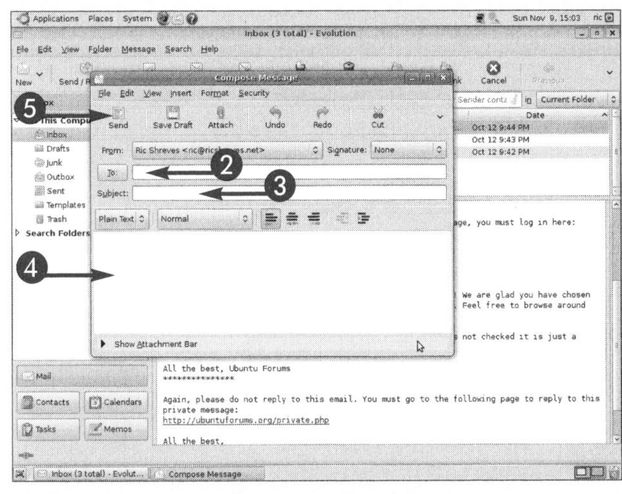

6. Click the Sent folder.

   The sent message appears in the listing on the right.

7. Click the message.

- The contents of the message appear.

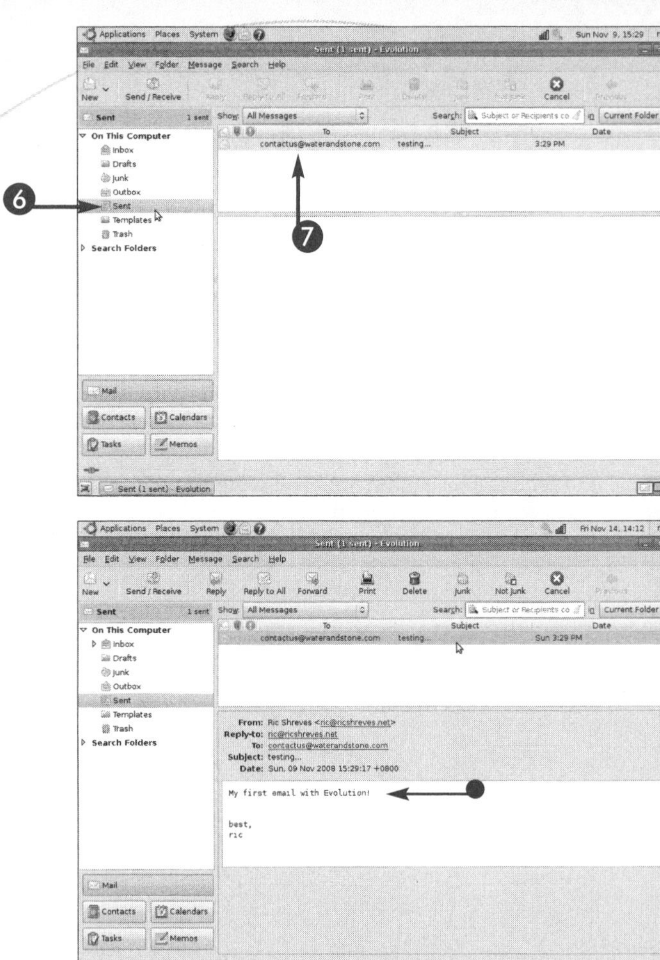

Extra

The menus at the top of the Compose Message window includes a number of important options and features. The File menu repeats several of the options that you see on the main toolbar but also includes the option to create a template out of an email and the Print commands. The Edit menu lists a number of editing options — all common text-editing features that you would see in a text-editing or word-processing program. Note that there is a spell-check option at the bottom of this menu. The View menu controls the display of address fields. By default, only the From, To, and Subject fields are active, but from this menu you can also add a CC or BCC field. Insert includes the attachment controls as well as the ability to request read receipts for your emails and to mark your messages as a priority. Format lets you switch between the Plain Text and HTML formats for your messages. HTML gives you better control over the appearance but may not be supported by all your recipients. The Security menu offers options for encrypting your messages.

Receive and Reply to Email

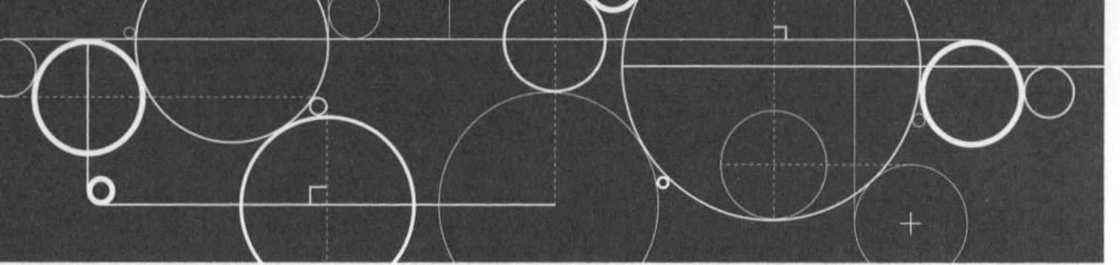

You can receive emails from others and reply to them easily using Evolution. Replies can be sent to the sender of the original email or to everyone on the recipient list.

When you check for new mail, Evolution checks your mail server for new messages and, if any are present, downloads them to your Evolution email client. Note that you must be connected to the Internet for this to work.

New mail appears in your Inbox highlighted in bold on the screen. This highlighting will be removed from the item after you read the new message. If you click a message once to read it, its contents will be displayed in the main window in Evolution. If you double-click it to read it, it will be opened in a new window.

After you read a message, you can click the Reply button to reply to it. This opens a new message window. The new message will be addressed to the sender of the original email and will include the body of the email. If more than one person was sent the original email, for example, if other people were CC'ed, and you want to send your message to all of them, then you select the Reply to All button. Evolution will address the new email to all the people on the original email.

Receive and Reply to Email

1 Click Send/Receive.

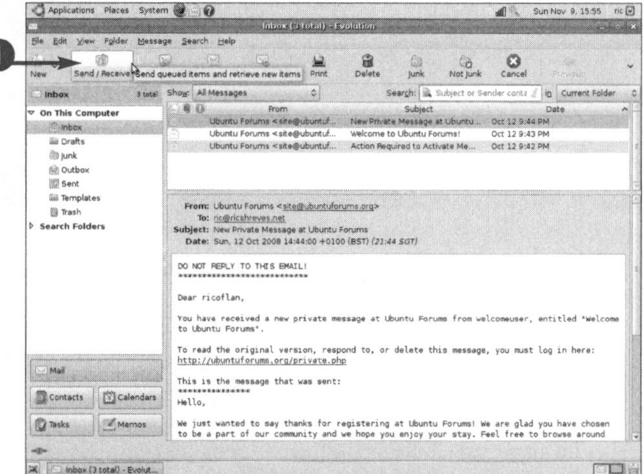

The system attempts to access your mail server and send and receive messages. The status window opens.

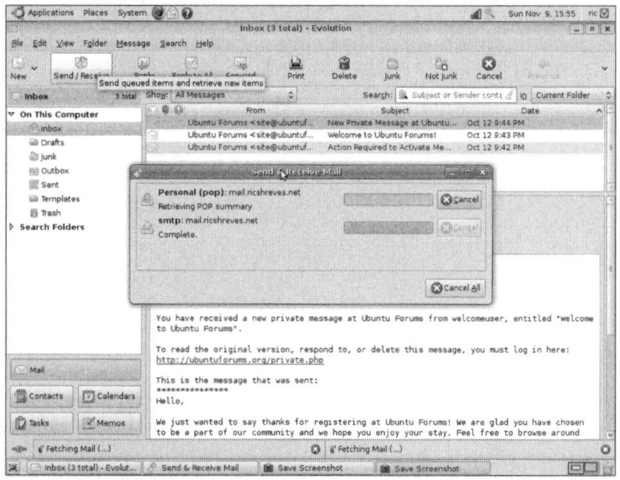

- The new messages appear in your Inbox.

2. Click the message that you want to read.

- The message contents appear here.

3. Read the message.
4. Click Reply.

Note: *You can click Reply to All if the original message was sent to multiple recipients and you want them all to see your reply.*

A new message window opens, containing the previous message and addressed to the sender.

5. Type your reply message.
6. Click Send.

Evolution sends the message to the addressee.

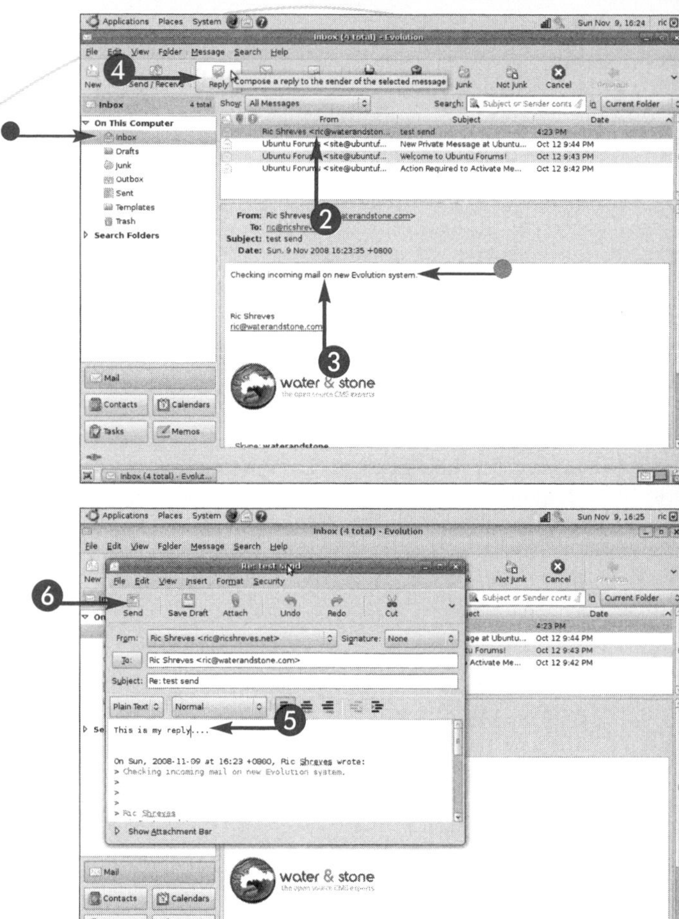

Apply It

With Evolution, you can create templates to use for email messages. *Templates* in Evolution are emails with standardized contents. They are particularly useful as standard responses to common inquiries. You can create a template out of an existing email, or you can create a new message and save it as a template.

To create a template out of an existing message, right-click the message and choose Copy to Folder. In the Select Folder dialog box, click the Templates folder and then click Move.

To make a template from a new message, create a new message, type the contents that you want to appear in the template, and then click File ➔ Save as Template.

In both cases, the message will now be available for use as a template.

To use a template to reply to a message, right-click the message to which you want to reply. From the right-click menu, select Templates and then click the specific template that you want to use. The template contents will be inserted into a new message, along with the text of the original message.

Organize Your Email

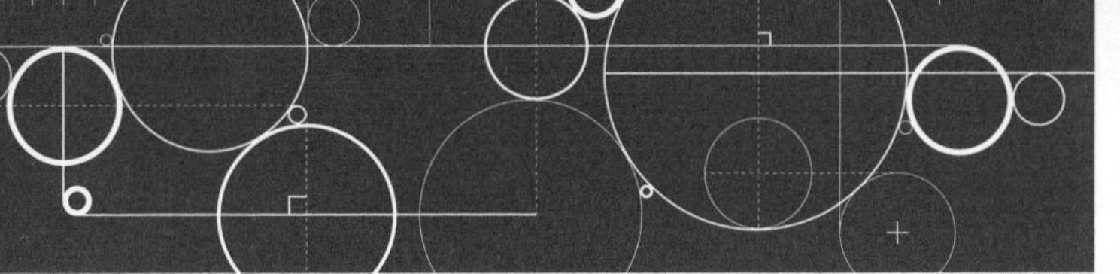

Evolution enables you to create multiple folders to hold your mail and rules that automatically filter the mail upon arrival in your Inbox.

The volume of email that you receive can, at times, be a bit daunting. Evolution makes it easier to manage your mail and keep things organized. By default, your email all goes into one folder, your Inbox. One of the easiest things that you can do to help keep organized is to create multiple folders to hold your mail.

You use the Create Folder dialog box to create a new folder. In the dialog box, you name your new folder. In the window below the name, you can select where you want the folder to appear in your email window. After you create the new folder, it will appear immediately in your Evolution directory tree. To move messages into your new folder, click the messages and drag them to the folder.

Evolution also includes the option to create filters that will route email automatically to the folder of your choice. To create such a filter, you use the Message Filters and Add Rule dialog boxes. You give your rule a name and then create criteria for filtering your mail using the drop-down lists below the rule name. Next, you select the action for the system to take when it detects a message that meets your criteria; in this case, this will be to move a message to a specific folder. Your new filter rule will now automatically route mail that meets your criteria to the target folder.

Organize Your Email

CREATE A FOLDER AND PLACE MESSAGES IN IT

1. Right-click your Inbox and click New Folder.

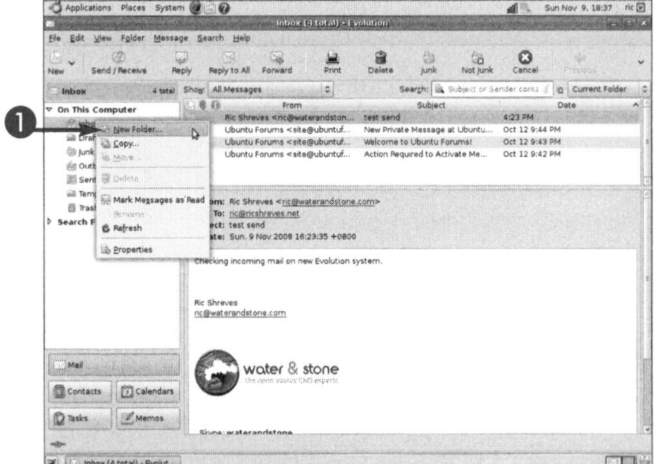

The Create Folder dialog box opens.

2. Type a name for the folder.
3. Select the parent folder.
4. Click Create.

The new folder is created.

You can now place messages in the folder by clicking and dragging them.

In this example, you would drag all emails from Ubuntu forums into the Ubuntu Forums folder.

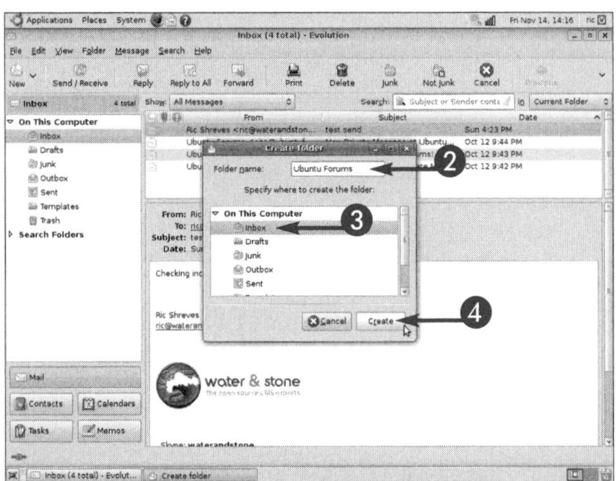

CREATE A FILTER TO HAVE MESSAGES AUTOMATICALLY PLACED IN A FOLDER

1. Click Edit ➔ Message Filters.

   The Message Filters dialog box opens.

2. Click Add.

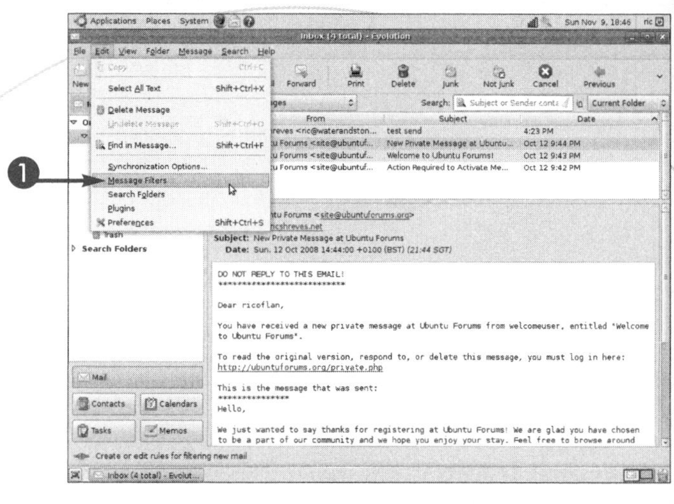

   The Add Rule dialog box opens.

3. Type a name for the rule.
4. Select the criteria.

   In this example, you would choose senders from Ubuntu forums.

5. Click here and select the folder in which the messages will be placed.
6. Click OK.
7. Click OK in the Message Filters dialog box.

   The chosen messages will now be filtered to the folder that you specified.

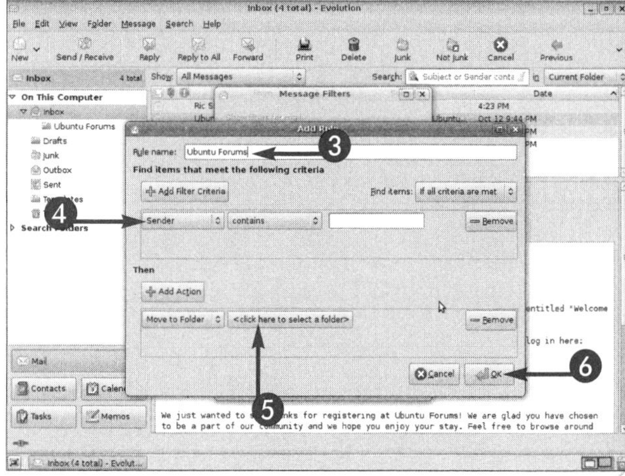

Extra

Another useful organizational tool is the Evolution feature known as *Search folders*. This tool is really a hybrid of a folder and a filter. You should create a Search folder when you find yourself running the same search over and over or when you want to gather emails from numerous folders into a common view.

Search folders do not actually contain any messages, but rather they provide a view of messages that meet a criteria that you determine. That means that the folder contents can change as messages are added or deleted from your system.

Search folders are created and managed from under the Edit menu. Selecting the Search Folders option opens the Search Folders dialog box. Click the Add button to create a new Search folder. The creation process is almost identical to creating a message filter. You need to add criteria and then select the folders that will be searched according to your criteria. All messages located in the folders that match the criteria will be listed in your new Search folder.

Existing folders can be edited from the Search Folders dialog box by selecting the name and then clicking the Edit button.

Using the Junk Mail Filter

Your Evolution email client can help you reduce the amount of SPAM and junk mail that winds up in your Inbox.

By default, the Evolution application comes bundled with two junk mail management programs: Bogofilter and SpamAssassin. These tools allow you to train your system to recognize junk mail and filter your mail more effectively.

When you first begin using Evolution, you should make an effort to train the system by teaching it what is and is not junk mail. Training is simple: select a message and then click either the Junk or the Not Junk button, as is appropriate to the nature of the message. Training begins to be effective with as few as 20 messages, 10 junk and 10 not junk. Over time, as you continue to select messages, the filter becomes increasingly accurate.

Messages marked as *Junk* are immediately moved to your Junk folder. You should review the contents of the folder periodically to make sure that the system is not incorrectly classifying messages as junk. You can set how long these messages are kept in the Preferences dialog box.

Although both Bogofilter and SpamAssassin are installed and available to you in Evolution, Bogofilter is the active plug-in. You can view the junk filter configuration settings in the Evolution Preferences dialog box. Click Mail Preferences and then click the Junk tab. On the Junk tab are the configuration settings for the junk mail filters. The default junk plug-in can be switched from Bogofilter to SpamAssassin if you prefer.

Using the Junk Mail Filter

TRAIN EVOLUTION TO RECOGNIZE SPAM

1. Click a message that you think is SPAM.
2. Click Junk.

   The mail is moved to the Junk folder, and the system's junk filter begins to learn what is considered to be junk.

Note: *You can click a message that is not junk and click Not Junk to further help Evolution learn.*

3. Click the Junk folder.

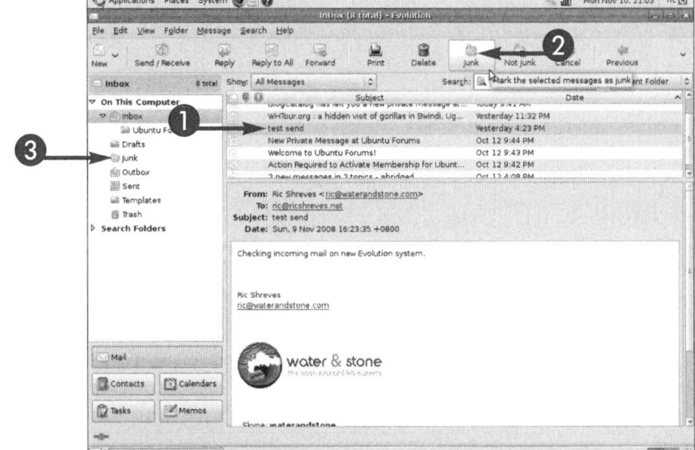

The contents of the Junk folder appear.

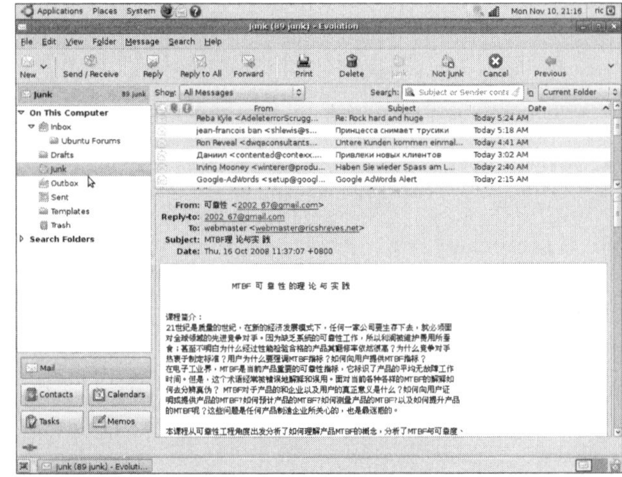

PREVENT YOUR CONTACTS' EMAILS FROM BEING LABELED SPAM

4. Click Edit → Preferences.

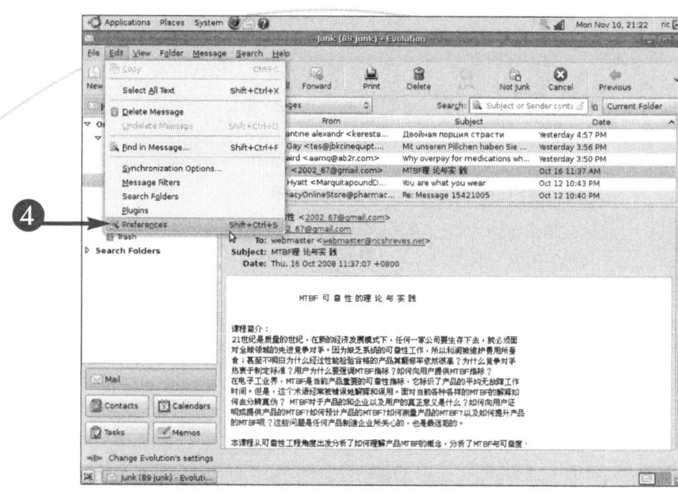

The Evolution Preferences dialog box opens.

5. Click Mail Preferences.
6. Click the Junk tab.
7. Click Do Not Mark Messages As Junk If Sender Is in My Address Book.
8. Click Close.

Now, no emails from contacts in your Address book will be mistaken for SPAM.

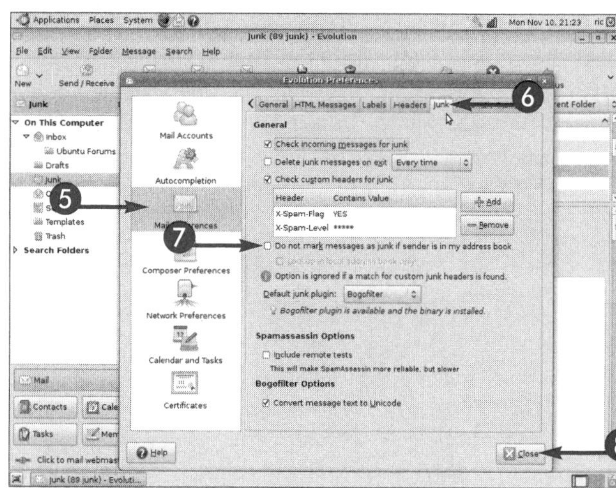

Extra

As experience has made clear, the people who send out SPAM are inventive, resourceful, and dedicated. It is hard for any one application to catch every piece of junk mail that comes in. Although you can train Bogofilter to react appropriately in the majority of situations, it will still miss some junk mail. Just as the SPAMmers react and change tactics, so should you. Do not rely exclusively on one tool to rid your Inbox of unwanted SPAM.

Earlier in this chapter, the section "Organize Your Email" discusses using mail filters to keep your mail boxes in order. You can also use mail filters to help you fight SPAM. If you discover that a particular type of message continues to elude your Bogofilter despite training, consider setting up a mail filter that reacts to the arrival of that type of message and redirects it straight into the Trash. As a mail filter can contain multiple rules and can be edited over time, you can set up a Junk Mail rule that you add to over time and tweak.

A combined approach to combatting SPAM is your most effective strategy to taking back control of your Inbox.

Create a New Contact

You can maintain the addresses of friends, colleagues, and acquaintances by adding new contacts to your Evolution Address book.

The Evolution Address book is quite full-featured, allowing you to create multiple contacts and maintain them either individually or in groups. The close integration of Contacts with the email program makes the two applications naturally complementary.

You can create a new contact from any place within Evolution by opening the Contact Editor. On the Contact tab, you can enter the basic information for the person or company. Note that the File Under drop-down list lets you control how the name will appear in the Contacts window.

Click the Personal Information tab to enter more detailed information about your contact. On the Mailing Address tab, you can enter details for the contact's physical address.

After you have created your new contact, you will see it appear in the top pane of the Contacts window. Click the name to see the details in the main window of the Contact application. You can double-click a name to reopen the Contact Editor and make changes to your entry. Right-clicking a contact opens a menu from which you can perform multiple actions, including sending an email to the contact.

If you have a large number of contacts, you may want to organize them into categories. You can add new categories from the New menu. Management of large contact lists is also eased by the Search box, which appears at the top right of the Contacts window.

Create a New Contact

1 Click Contacts.

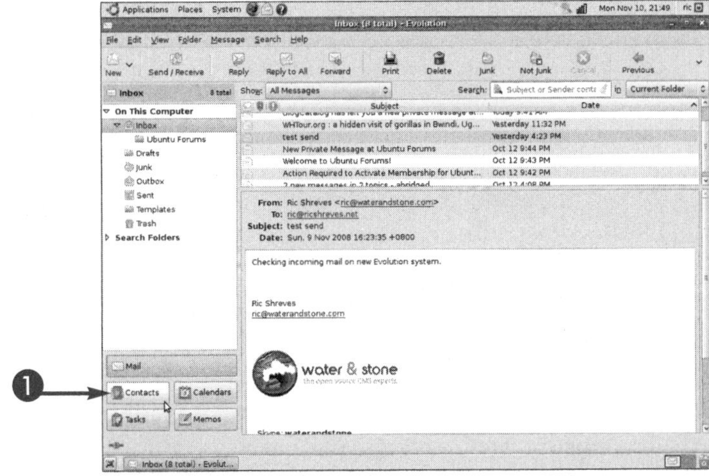

The Contacts pane opens.

2 Click the New drop-down arrow ➔ Contact.

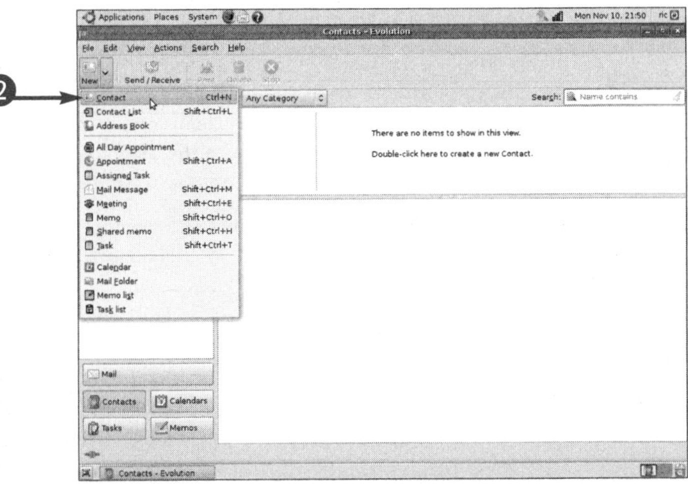

The Contact Editor opens.

3. Type the contact's full name.
4. Type the contact's nickname.
5. Type the contact's email address.
6. Include any other information that you want to about the contact.
7. Click OK.

Evolution creates the new contact.

- The new contact appears in the window.

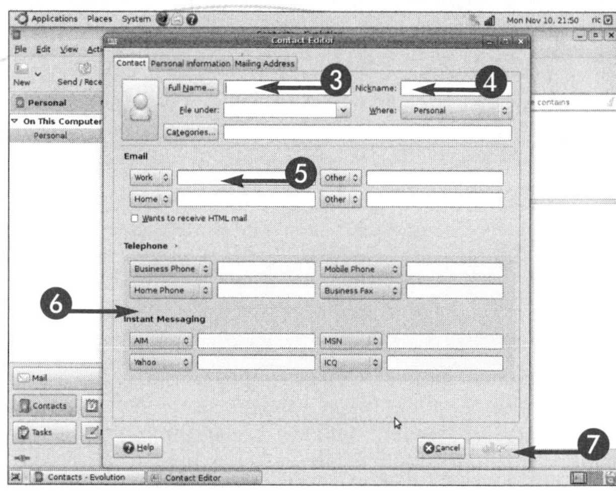

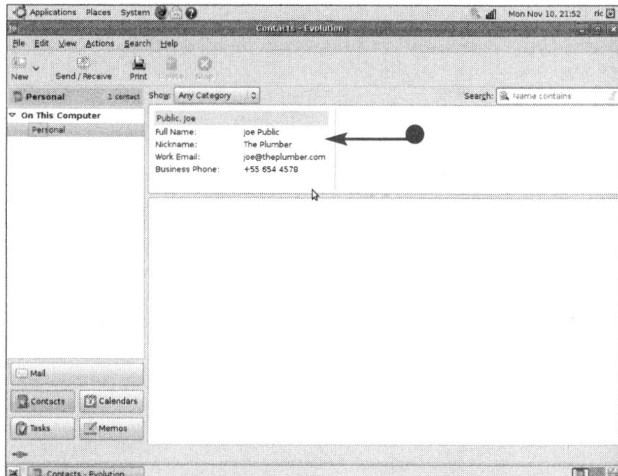

Apply It

Evolution also offers a feature called *Address Book* that makes it easier to manage large contact lists. Although you do not have to use the Address Book feature, if you want to keep your local addresses synchronized with a remote source, for example a Google Gmail address list, or another contact program on your network, then the Address Book function is useful.

You can add a new Address book by clicking New ➔ Address Book. When the New Address Book dialog box opens, select the source and location of the shared Address book, or if you want your local Address book to be the source that is shared, select On the Computer from the Type field, then give the Address book a unique name, and associate a username with it.

If you select Google or WebDAV for the Type field, you must enter the details that will allow your Ubuntu machine to connect with the remote data source.

The Refresh option allows you to set how often the system will check to see if the Address book contents have changed, thereby helping you keep things closely synchronized.

Create Appointments

You can use Evolution's built-in calendar to set events for yourself and others. The system calls events intended for you alone *appointments.* Events that you share with others are called *meetings* and are dealt with in the next section of this chapter, "Send a Meeting Invitation."

To create a new appointment, you first open the Evolution Calendar and then open a new Appointment dialog box. In this dialog box, you provide a summary of the appointment. Note that the summary will appear as the label for the event, so it should be descriptive. You can also enter a location for the appointment and a longer description. The Time, Date, and Duration drop-down lists are necessary to put the appointment on the calendar in the proper place. If your event runs for one or more days, click the All Day Event button on the toolbar. You can set a starting and ending date for all-day events, but not a time. The Recurrence button enables you to set up a recurring event.

Note that under the menus at the top of the Appointment dialog box, there are a number of other choices, including the ability to schedule according to time zones and to classify events as either public, private, or confidential.

After you have added the details of the event and saved it, the new appointment will appear on your calendar.

To see an appointment's details, you can move your mouse cursor over its name on your calendar. If you want to make changes to an existing appointment, double-click it to open an editing dialog box.

Create Appointments

1. Click Calendars.

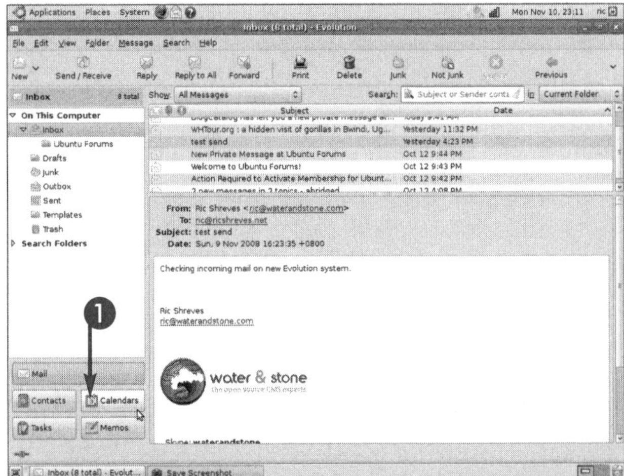

The Calendars pane opens.

2. Click New.

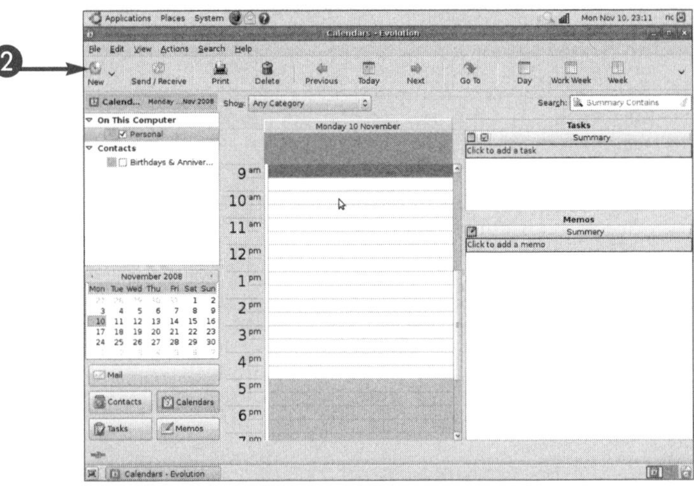

A new Appointment window appears.

3. Type a short description of the appointment.
4. Type where the appointment will occur.
5. Set the time of the appointment.
6. Click Save.

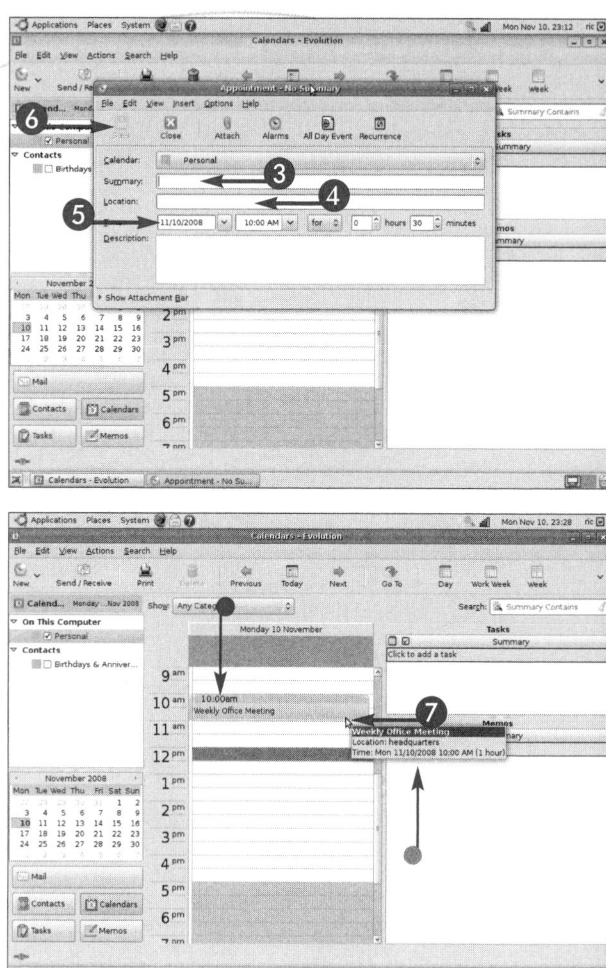

- The new appointment appears on the calendar.

7. Move your mouse cursor over the appointment.

- The appointment details appear in a pop-up.

Extra

Evolution's calendar supports reminders for events. Reminders are a convenient tool for keeping track of upcoming events, and they can help you avoid missing important meetings.

To set a reminder for an event, open the event and click the Alarms button. In the Alarms dialog box, you can select a predetermined time in advance of the event to trigger the alarm. The default alarm notification is a pop-up dialog box.

You can add a custom reminder by selecting Customize from the Alarm drop-down list. When you select Customize, the bottom portion of the window becomes active, allowing you to set the action and the trigger. Click the Add button to open the Add Alarm dialog box. In the dialog box, set the event from the drop-down list and then set the time to trigger the alarm.

Click the Repeat the Alarm option if you want the alarm to be persistent, replaying at a predetermined interval until you dismiss it.

To add a custom message to the alarm pop-up, click the Custom Message box and then type your message in the field at the bottom of the dialog box.

Send a Meeting Invitation

You can use Evolution's Calendar application to set up appointments and invite other people to join them. Evolution calls appointments with multiple participants *meetings* and gives you the ability to notify those people and track their participation.

Creating a new meeting is very similar to creating a new appointment, the key difference being that you must also add participants and notify them. You use the Meeting window to fill in the details about the meeting and invite the participants.

You add a summary to describe the meeting and specify the meeting location. You select the date and time using the drop-down lists, and you can add a longer description if you want to. Then you add the other attendees. You click the Add button to add participants that are not in your contact list. If your want to add persons that are in one of your Address books, the better course is to use the Attendees button, as shown below. In the Attendees dialog box, you can pick persons from your contacts and assign them to roles, if necessary.

You can click the Edit button in the Meeting window to change the role assigned to any attendee. You can also delete attendees by clicking the Remove button.

After you have entered the details of the meeting and selected the attendees, you will be asked whether you want to send notifications to the people on the Attendee list. If you choose to do so, Evolution will send all the attendees a notification email informing them of the meeting and asking them to confirm their attendance.

Send a Meeting Invitation

1. In the Calendars window, click the New drop-down arrow ➔ Meeting.

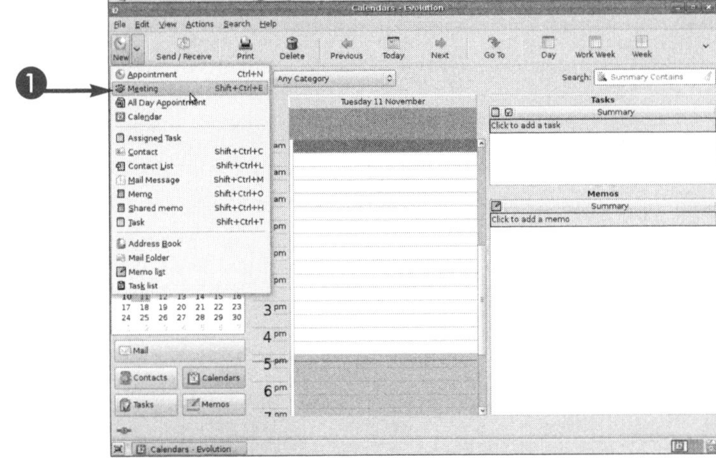

The Meeting window opens.

2. Type a short description of the meeting.
3. Type where the meeting will occur.
4. Set the time of the meeting.
5. Click Attendees.

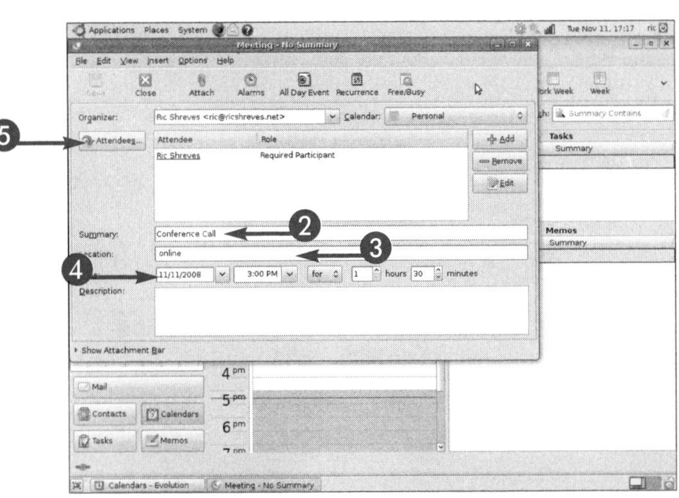

The Attendees window appears.

6 Click the contact(s) to invite to the meeting.

7 Click Add.

8 Click Close.

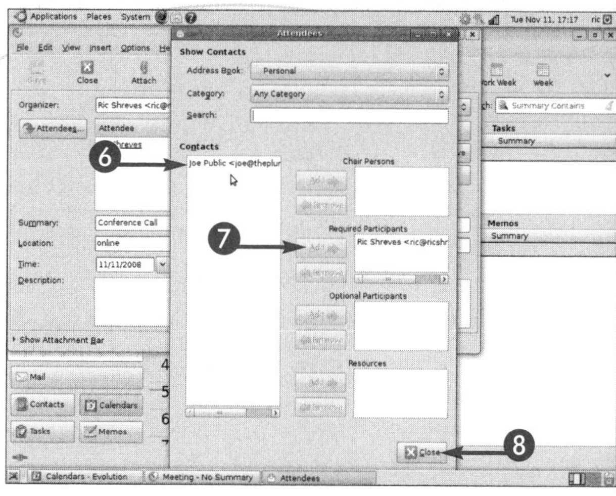

You are returned to the Meeting window.

9 Click Save.

Evolution prompts you to send invitations to the attendees.

10 Click Send.

Evolution sends the attendees an email invitation and adds the meeting to your calendar.

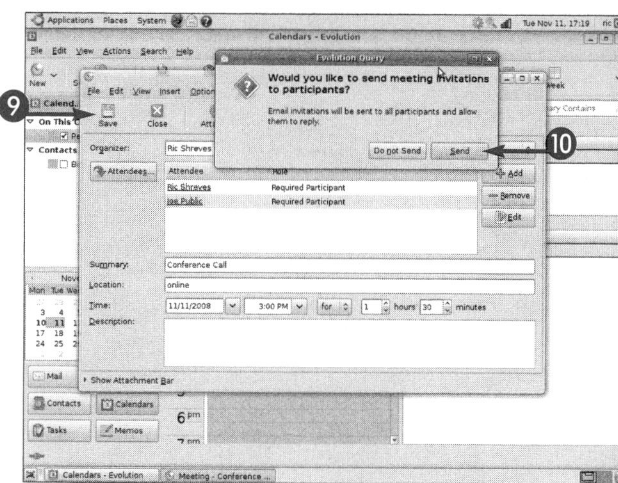

Extra

Calendar invitations are sent from Evolution in the .ics format. This format is known as *iCal* and is readable by the most popular Calendar applications. Attendees will receive an email containing an .ics file that they must add to their Calendar application. Typically, double-clicking the .ics file will trigger the proper process.

After the appointment is in their calendar, they will be able to see the details of the invitation, and, in most applications, they will have the opportunity to accept, decline, or modify the appointment. Whatever they choose will result in an email being returned to you as the meeting organizer indicating the recipient's response.

The iCal format is easy to use and very convenient. The only problems with it are that the email message the attendees receive contains no other information about the appointment and therefore, if the attendees do not expect to receive the notification, they may ignore it or not want to click it for fear that the attachment may harbor a virus or other malicious application. The other problem is, of course, that if the attendees do not have an application with iCal support, then they cannot participate in this shared calendaring process.

Manage Appointments and Meetings

Evolution has a built-in classification schema called *Categories.* You can use Evolution's Categories feature to help keep your meetings and appointments organized. By classifying your events into categories, you can quickly find related items and keep complex calendars with large numbers of events manageable.

The Categories functionality applies across the Calendar, Contacts, and Tasks sections of the application. The Categories tool works by allowing you to associate items with one or more categories. Evolution provides a category filter that you can use to limit the view of items to only those belonging to a particular category, thereby making it easier to find items in large or complex lists. This is particularly useful when you maintain multiple calendars or Address books.

To apply the categories to a meeting or appointment, you must first enable the Categories field. To do so, click View ➔ Categories. The Categories field will now be available on all your calendar events. To assign an event to a category, you use the Categories dialog box, in which you can select one or more categories from the list. After that, the categories will appear in your event's window. After you save the edited event, you will thereafter be able to find this event easily by using the Category filter on the Evolution interface.

To filter items, select the category that you want to see from the Show drop-down list, which is located immediately under the main toolbar in the Calendar, Contacts, Tasks, and Memos consoles. The filter list does not appear in the Mail console.

Manage Appointments and Meetings

1. In the Calendars window, double-click an event.

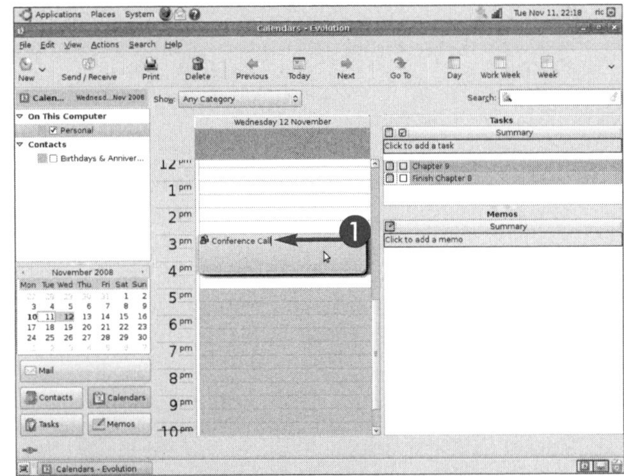

The event's edit window opens.

2. Click Categories.

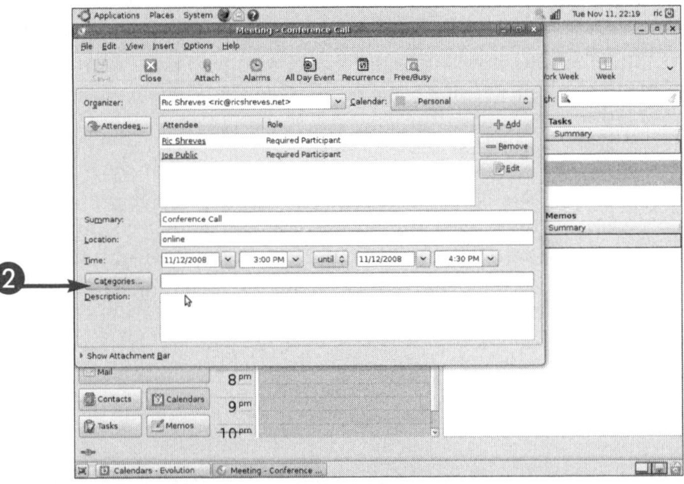

The Categories dialog box appears.

3. Click a category by which you want to classify the event.
4. Repeat step **3** for all the categories for the event.
5. Click OK.

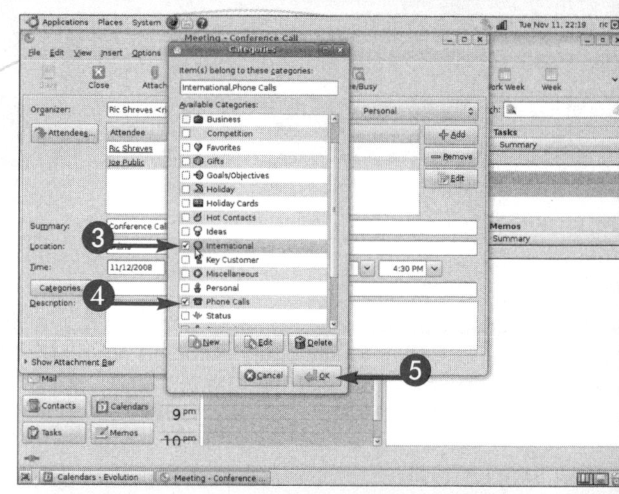

- The categories appear in your event's window.

6. Click Save.

   The event will appear in all the Category lists that you specified.

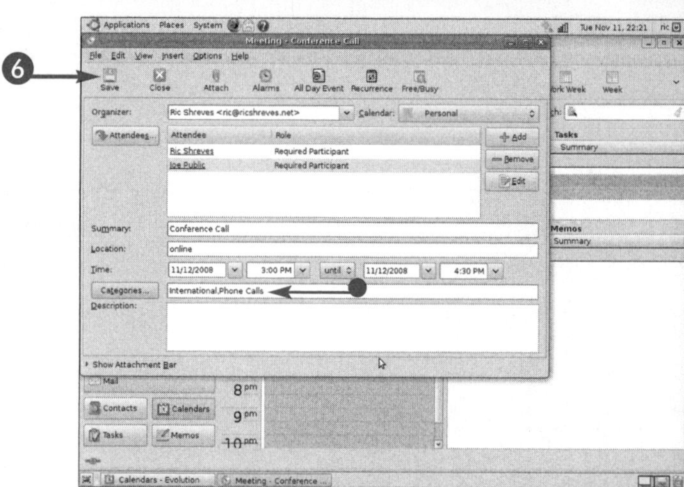

Extra

You can make changes to the default list of categories that comes with Evolution. To edit the Categories list, you need to open an event, contact, task, or memo and click the Categories button. The Categories dialog box includes three buttons: New, Edit, and Delete.

Clicking the New button opens a blank Category Properties dialog box. Use this dialog box to create a new category for your list. Give it a name and then select an icon that will appear beside the category. Note that although the icon is optional, it is very useful because it will appear on any items that are associated with the category. Although the system comes loaded with a number of icons, most of them are in use for other categories. If you want to add additional images to use as icons, you may do so by copying them on to your computer and then selecting them from the Category Properties dialog box.

To edit an existing category, click the name and then click the Edit button. Note that for the system's default categories, you can change only the icon; you cannot change the name of the category itself.

To delete a category, click the name and then click the Delete button.

Create Tasks

You can use Evolution to create tasks and to-do lists. The Tasks functionality enables you to assign tasks and to track the progress as you work on completing them.

The Tasks functionality is built into Evolution and closely integrated with the Calendars functionality and, to a lesser extent, the email system. From the Evolution Tasks view, you can view pending tasks, and you can create and edit tasks.

The Tasks console is the best place for working with your task lists. On the Tasks page, you will see a list of all the tasks in Evolution. Clicking a task displays the details in the lower pane.

You create a new task in the Task window. You provide a short description of the task in the Summary field. You can set a date to begin the task and a date that the task is due, and you can enter a longer description in the Description field, if necessary. Other options in the Task window let you assign the task to a category or set a classification. You can also attach a file to a task using the Attachment option under the Insert menu, or you can drag and drop a file into the Attachment bar.

New tasks appear immediately in the main pane of the Tasks console. Double-click a task to open it for editing. Right-click a task to access a menu of options, including the ability to assign the task to another person or to add it to the calendar.

Create Tasks

❶ Click Tasks.

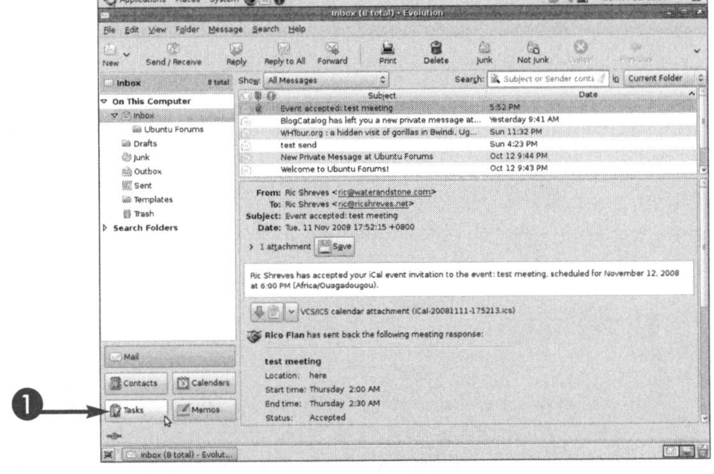

The Tasks pane opens.

❷ Click the New drop-down arrow ➔ Task.

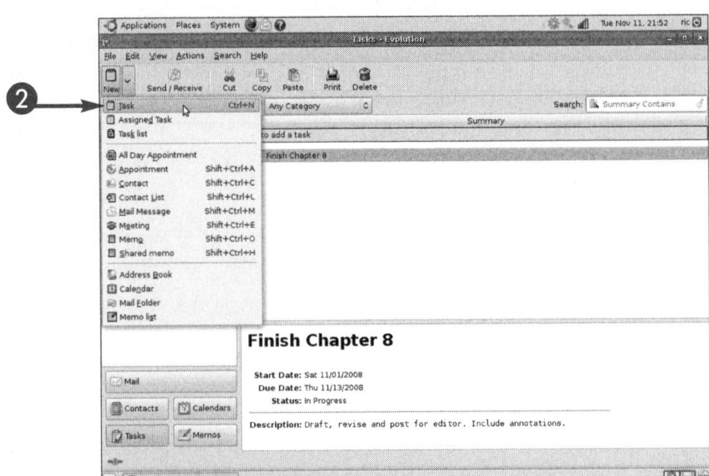

The Task window appears.

3. Type a short description of the task.
4. Type start and due dates.
5. Type a longer description, if needed.
6. Click Save.

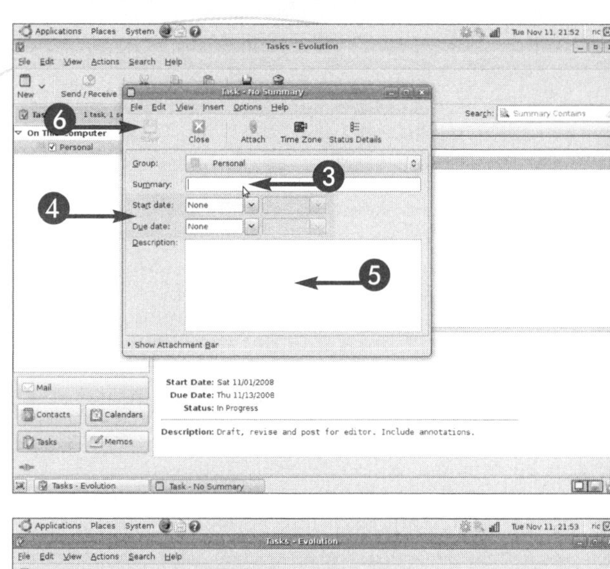

The task is added to your Tasks list.

7. Move your mouse cursor over the task.

- A pop-up displays the task's details.

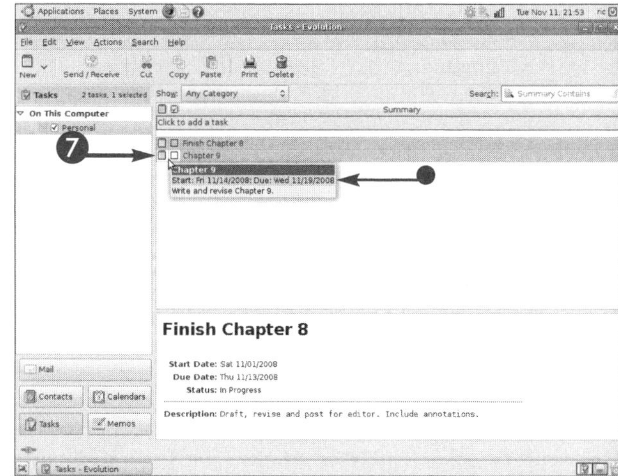

Extra

You can use the Status functionality to track your progress on a task over time. The Status option turns your Tasks console into an organizational tool that helps you stay on top of work in progress and prioritize tasks. Combine it with the ability to assign tasks to others and add them to the calendar, and you have a set of tools that give you basic, but useful, project-management abilities.

To set and manage the status of a task, open it and then click the Status Details button on the main toolbar. The Task Details dialog box that opens enables you to set the status as Not Started, In Progress, Completed, or Canceled. The default setting, regardless of the date you indicate, is Not Started. The Percent Complete field lets you assign a percentage value to the work done to date. The Priority field gives you the choice of Undefined, Low, Normal, or High. Date Completed lets you mark the date and the time that the task was resolved. The last field in this dialog box, Web Page, lets you add a hyperlink to a task. After you have made your changes to the Task Details dialog box, click Close to save your work.

Create a New Document

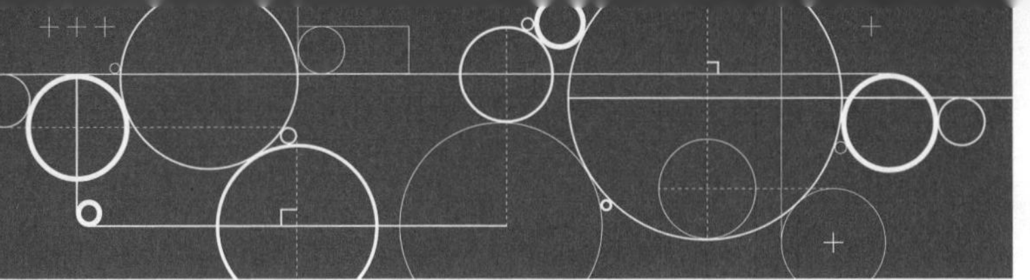

OpenOffice Writer is a powerful and flexible word-processing program that lets you create and edit documents in a number of formats. You can use Writer for simple letters or for complex manuscripts as the application comes complete with all the features and functions that you would expect from a professional word-processing package.

There are several ways to create a new document. When you first launch Writer, the application opens with a new document in the window. Alternatively, if you have closed that document or you want to create another, then you can use the New menu option. Writer also supports a wide array of keyboard shortcuts. There is a keyboard shortcut for most common tasks, including creating a new document. To use the shortcut, you press the Ctrl key at the same time that you press the letter *N*.

The File ➔ New menu has a variety of other options for creating new files. The Spreadsheet, Presentation, and Drawing choices open your other OpenOffice applications. The HTML Document, XML Form Document, and Master Document options are all document formats that you can edit from within Writer. The Labels and Business Cards options are templates that allow you to format a document in a way suitable for those types of items. The last choice, Templates and Documents, enables you to create a new document based on a template.

When your document is open in the window, you can add to or edit the contents freely using the tools in Writer. You can save your work at any time.

Create a New Document

WHEN OPENING WRITER

1. Click Applications ➔ Office ➔ OpenOffice.org Word Processor.

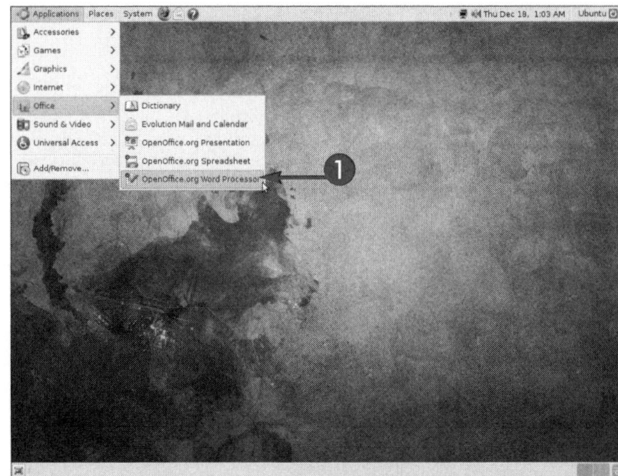

The application opens, with a new document in the window.

- You can type the text that you want in the document.

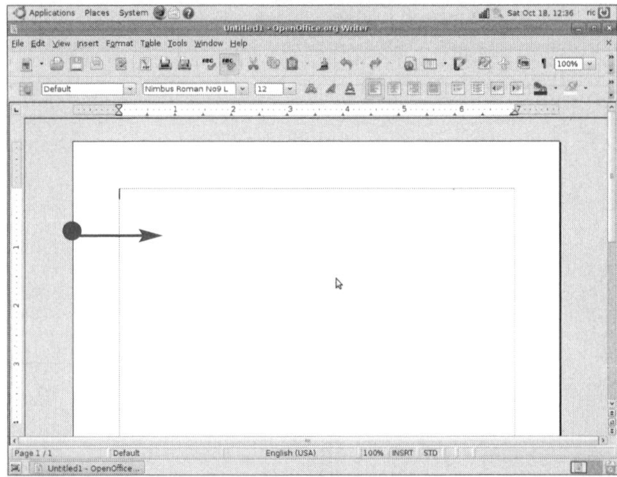

WITH WRITER ALREADY OPEN

1. Click File ➔ New ➔ Text Document.

   A new document appears in the main window.

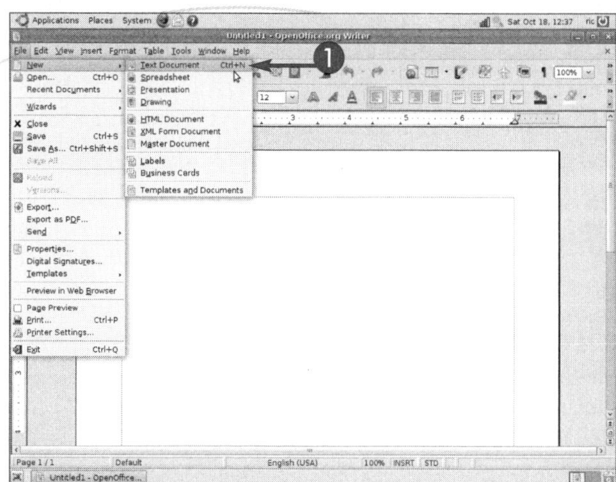

2. Type the text that you want.
3. Click the Save button.

   The changes to the document are saved.

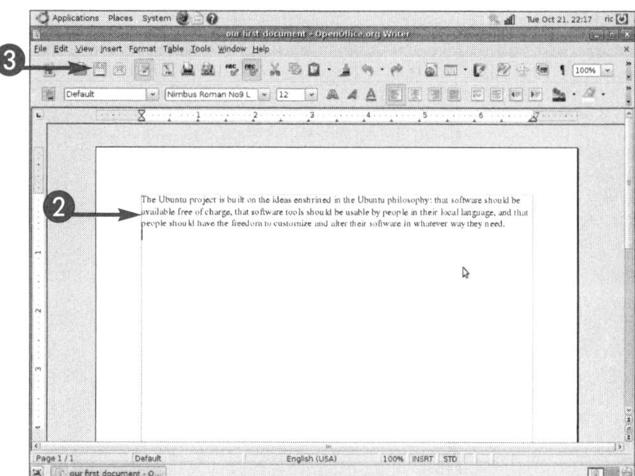

Extra

The Templates and Documents option under File ➔ New allows you to create new documents based on existing templates. Templates provide you with standardized document forms that enable the creation of multiple documents that share common formatting. Templates are most useful for common tasks, such as creating an invoice, a letter, or a form, or for creating long, complex documents that need to have standardized formatting throughout. Using templates, you can set fonts, spacing, common headers, footers, and more, thereby making the creation of new documents easier and assuring visual similarity across multiple documents and multiple users.

The default Ubuntu distribution contains only two templates for use by Writer, Project Proposal and Standard Resume. It is, however, easy to turn a document into a template that you can reuse. You can create a new template out of any document by opening it and then clicking File ➔ Templates ➔ Save. You can edit existing templates by clicking File ➔ Templates ➔ Edit.

Format Characters and Paragraphs

OpenOffice Writer provides numerous options for formatting both the characters in your documents and the paragraphs. By using either the controls on the toolbars or on the menus, you can control colors, sizes, spacing, positioning, and many other attributes of single characters, words, sentences, or paragraphs.

By default, your Writer installation includes a formatting toolbar that contains the most commonly used commands. By clicking the buttons on the toolbar, you can apply font styles and colors, and you can change the font as well as its size. If you click Format ➔ Character, a window opens that offers a number of other choices for controlling the display of the characters.

The formatting toolbar also includes options that relate to the styling of whole paragraphs, including the choice to align paragraphs to the left, right, or center or to fully justify the text. You can also change the line spacing and apply both ordered and unordered list styles. The Formatting ➔ Paragraph menu includes a wide variety of options related to paragraph styles.

Immediately above the editing window, you will notice a ruler control. The ruler allows you to set margins for individual paragraphs or for the page as whole. You can also use this control to set the number of tabs and their spacing.

In addition to manually setting styles item by item, you can apply changes using preset styles, as discussed later in the section "Create a Paragraph Style."

Format Characters and Paragraphs

CHANGE THE FONT

1. Select the text whose font you want to modify.
2. Click here and choose a new font.

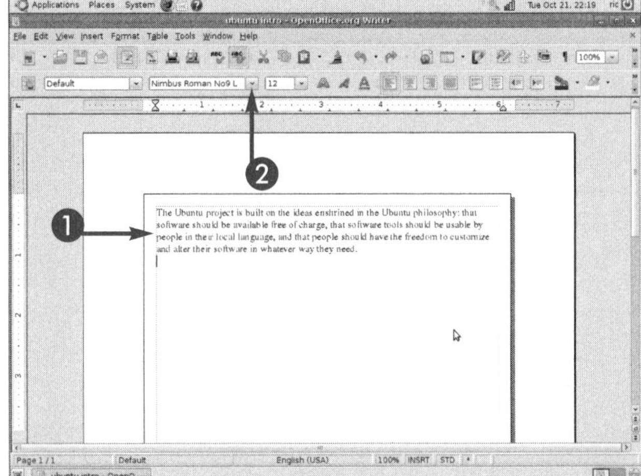

The font changes to your selection.

CHANGE THE FONT STYLE

3. Select the text to which you want to apply a style.
4. Click the style that you want.

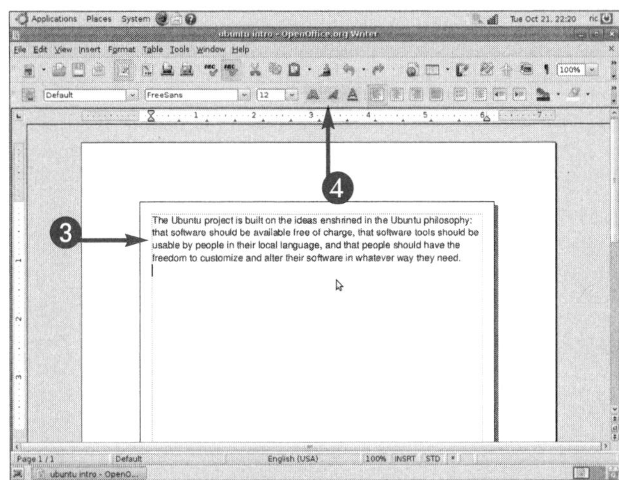

- Your style is applied.

CHANGE THE JUSTIFICATION

5 Select the entire paragraph.

6 Click the justification that you want.

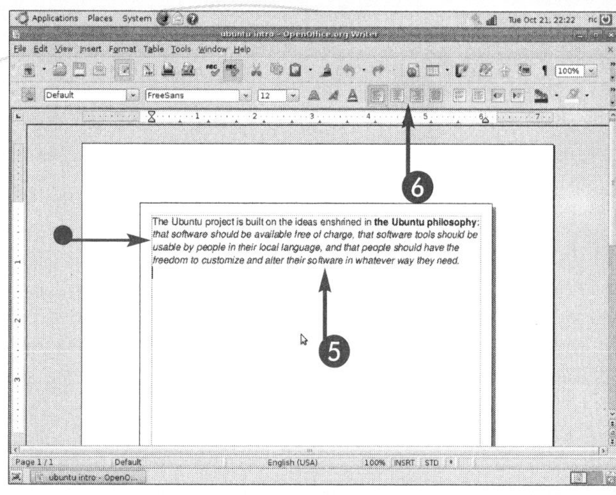

The justification changes.

In this example, the text is now fully justified.

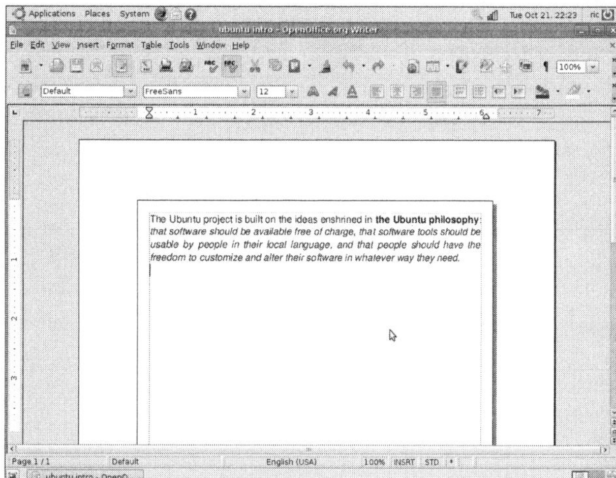

Extra

Under the Tools menu, there are a number of noteworthy specialty formatting options. The Outline Numbering option is useful when you are outlining a topic or creating a table of contents. The Line Numbering option comes in handy at revision time or for creating scripts or timed text. Also on this menu are two options that are essential for the creation of manuscripts for publication: the Footnotes and Bibliography features. Note that if you need to use cross-references or hyperlinks in your document, they can be inserted through the options on the Insert menu.

The Insert, Format, and Table menus all contain additional options that allow you to manipulate your document as needed. Indeed, there are so many choices here that covering all the formatting options available to you is really beyond the scope of this book. Later sections of this chapter cover two of the most common tasks, inserting images and tables, but to really grasp the full range of possibilities, you will want to visit the OpenOffice.org site and download the documentation for Writer. You can find the documentation at http://documentation.openoffice.org/manuals/oooauthors2/0100GS-GettingStarted.pdf.

Work with Styles

OpenOffice.org Writer includes an option to apply styles, which ease the burden of managing document formatting. Using styles, you can control the appearance of items throughout the document and manage them as a group.

When you format documents, you can either do so item by item, or you can apply a style that will handle all the items of the same type. When you define a style, you set the attributes that will be applied to the items.

For example, let's say that you want to indent the first line of the opening paragraph in each section of a document. You have a choice: You can either manually define each individual paragraph according to those rules, or you can apply Writer's default style named First Line Indent and associate that style with the paragraphs that you want to change.

When you use a style to control the formatting of multiple paragraphs, you can affect all the paragraphs by changing the style definition. When you change the style definition, all the paragraphs associated with that style will reflect the change that you made.

By default, Writer includes a set of predefined styles. You can apply those styles by selecting the text that you want to format and then choosing the style from the choices on the Styles and Formatting drop-down list. Clicking More in the Styles and Formatting drop-down list opens a dialog box showing the full list of default styles.

The next section, "Create a Paragraph Style," discusses how to create a new style for use in your documents.

Work with Styles

APPLY A STYLE

1. Select the paragraph to which you want to apply a style.
2. Click here and select More to see all the available styles.

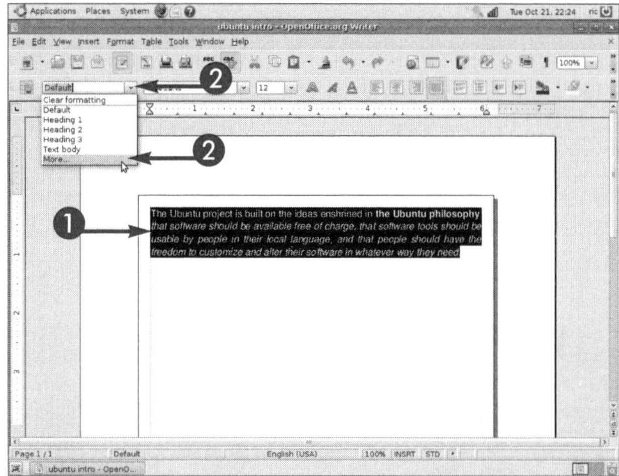

The Styles and Formatting dialog box opens.

3. Double-click the style that you want.

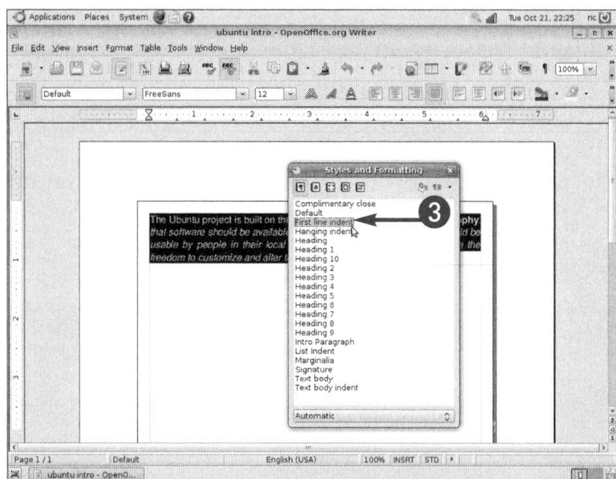

The style is applied to the paragraph.

APPLY THE DEFAULT STYLE

4 Select the paragraph.

5 Click here and select Default.

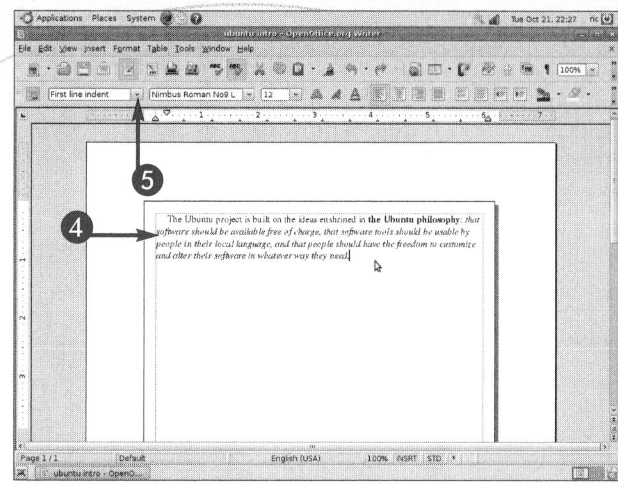

- The Default style is applied to the paragraph.

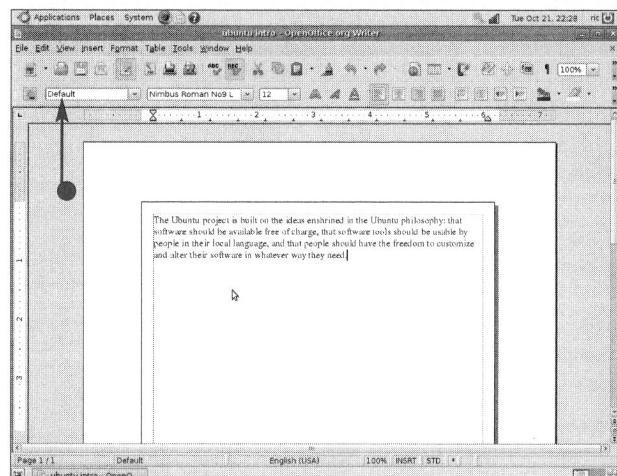

Extra

It is possible to edit an existing style. Click Format ➔ Styles and Formatting or press F11. The Styles and Formatting dialog box opens, displaying a list of the existing styles. Right-click the style that you want to edit and select Modify. The Modification dialog box opens, showing you all the various attributes associated with the style. You can change whatever you want using this dialog box. Navigate through the various choices using the tabs at the top. Note that in this dialog box, you can also rename a style. When you have finished, click the OK button.

If at any time you want to revert to the default style, you can do so by selecting the Reset button on the Modification dialog box. Note also the Standard button in this dialog box; it operates like Reset, but it only affects the tab that is visible at the time you click it. As with most screens in OpenOffice, there is a Help button, which can be of great assistance in demystifying the multiple choices that are associated with this task.

Create a Paragraph Style

If you need something other than the default styles, you can create custom styles. A new style is typically based on an existing style, which you use as a starting point for your own definition.

To make a new style, first create some text to use as a benchmark. If the text is already the subject of a style, you can use that style as your starting point; if not, you can use the Default style. You use the Paragraph Style dialog box to set the characteristics of your new style. You should always start by specifying the first three fields in the dialog box: Name, Next Style, and Linked With. The Name field gives you a label for your style. The Next Style field tells Writer what style to use for the text that immediately follows your new style. The Linked With field is used to create a connection between your new style and another style. The Linked With field should only be used when you want there to be an ongoing association with another style. Be careful with this field, as it means that changes to one style will affect others linked to it.

After you have set the preliminary attributes, you use the tabs at the top of the Paragraph Style dialog box to set the other characteristics that you want your style to exhibit. You can check your work by applying your new style to some text. If you need to make adjustments to your style, right-click its name in the Styles and Formatting list and choose Modify.

Create a Paragraph Style

1. Select the paragraph that you want to use as a starting point for your style.
2. Click the Styles and Formatting button.

   The Styles and Formatting dialog box appears.
3. Right-click the name of the style that is currently applied to the paragraph.
4. Click New.

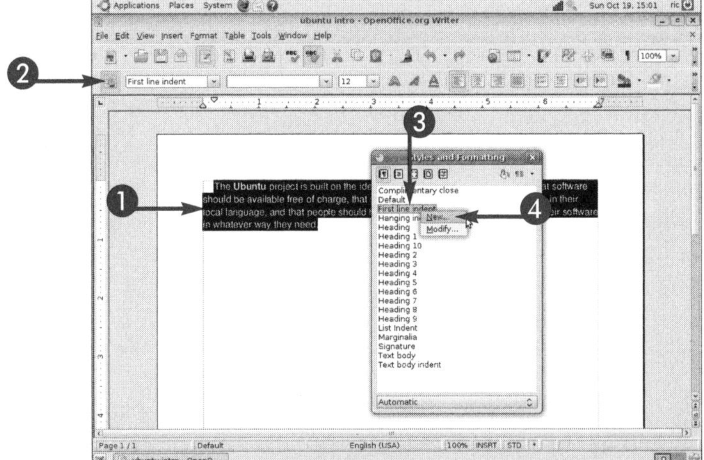

   The Paragraph Style dialog box opens.

5. Type a name for the style that you are creating.
6. Click here and select the style that will automatically be applied to paragraphs just after your new style.
7. Click here and select a style that you want your new style to be linked with, if any.
8. Click one of the other tabs to apply its formatting to your new style.

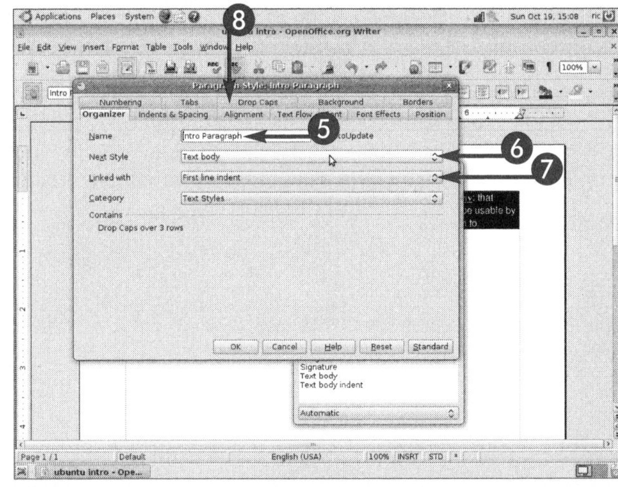

The tab comes to the front.

9 Click the options that you want for your style, such as Display Drop Caps in this example.

- You can click other tabs and apply other formatting to your style as needed.

10 Click OK when finished.

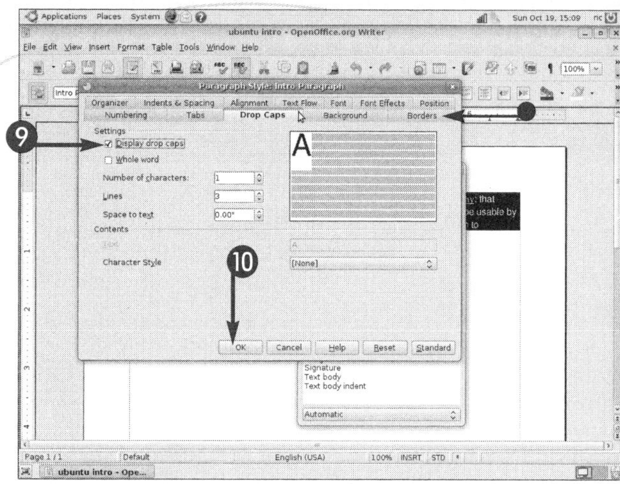

- Your new style is created and applied to the paragraph.

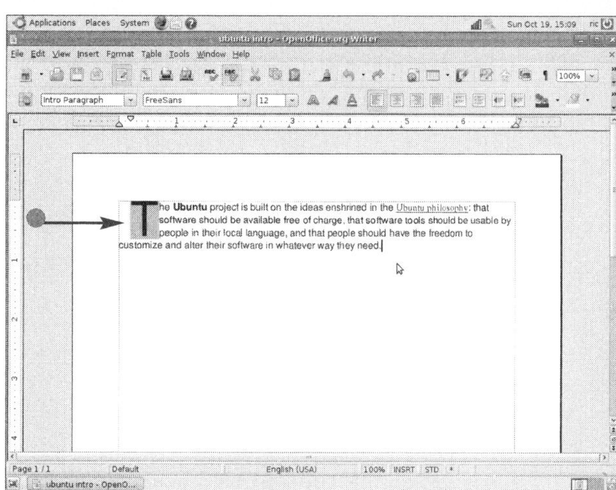

Extra

Writer classifies styles into five categories: Paragraph, Character, Page, Frame, and List. Paragraph styles are used to affect entire paragraphs. Character styles are used to affect a block of text inside a paragraph. Page styles affect your page formatting. Frame styles are used to affect frames and graphics. List styles affect outlines, numbered lists, and bulleted lists.

When you create a new style, you will need to assign it to the appropriate category. Using the categories properly is a useful method for organizing large collections of styles. To view styles by category, use the icons at the top left of the Styles and Formatting dialog box. Note also, at the bottom of the Styles and Formatting dialog box, a drop-down box that contains four filters for your styles: Hierarchical, All, Applied Styles, and Custom Styles. Use the Custom Styles filter to help find the styles that you have defined. Applied Styles shows you the styles used in the document that is open in your window. The Hierarchical filter shows styles that are associated with and dependent upon other styles. All is the default filter and shows all the styles available.

Insert Headers and Footers

You can control the area that appears at the tops and bottoms of your pages through the insertion of headers and footers. *Headers* are areas that always appear at the tops of the pages, and *footers* appear consistently at the bottoms of pages.

When you create a new header or footer, a blank area appears on each page in the corresponding area, in which you can place text or fields common to every page of your document. Pages can support the display of either a header, a footer, or both.

Writer provides quite a range of flexibility for formatting the header and footer regions. Headers and footers can be displayed in either Portrait or Landscape modes. In Landscape mode, the header and the footer appear on the left and right side of the page.

Writer also includes a feature known as *fields,* which allow you to insert into the page information that can be controlled consistently throughout the document. A field, for example, can be used to insert the page numbers automatically or to insert the time, date, or author's name.

After you have created a new header or footer, you can click in the area to enter whatever text you want, or you can go to the Insert menu and choose one of the options from under the Fields submenu. You could, for example, click inside the footer area and then choose the option Page Number from the Fields submenu to insert the page number on every page of your document.

Any text or fields placed inside the header or footer can be controlled by Writer's formatting options.

Insert Headers and Footers

INSERT A HEADER

1. Click Insert ➔ Header ➔ Default.

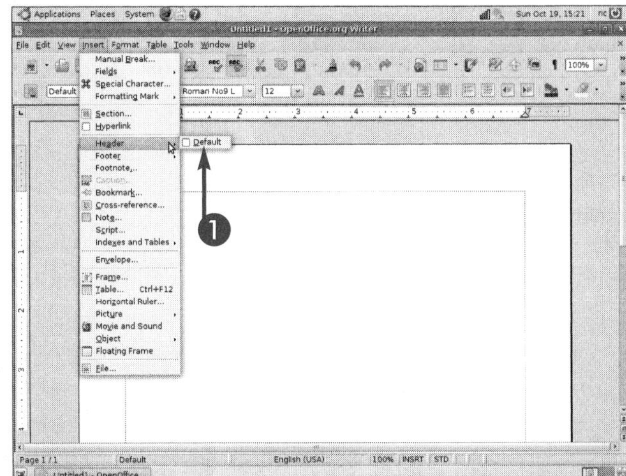

The header area appears in your document.

2. Type the text or insert the fields that you want for your header.

- To insert a field, click Insert ➔ Fields and then the type of field that you want.

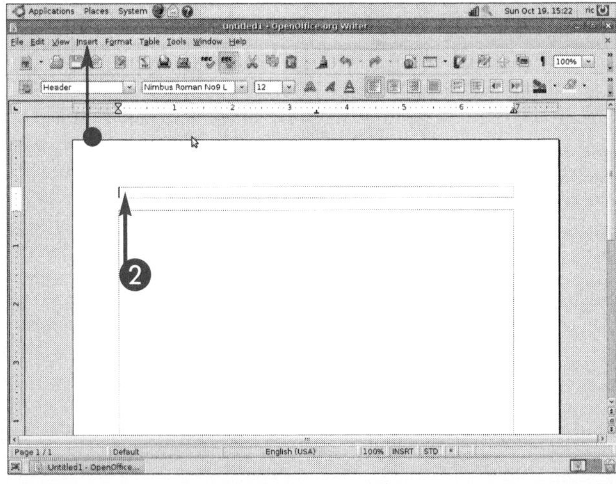

INSERT A FOOTER

1. Click Insert ➔ Footer ➔ Default.

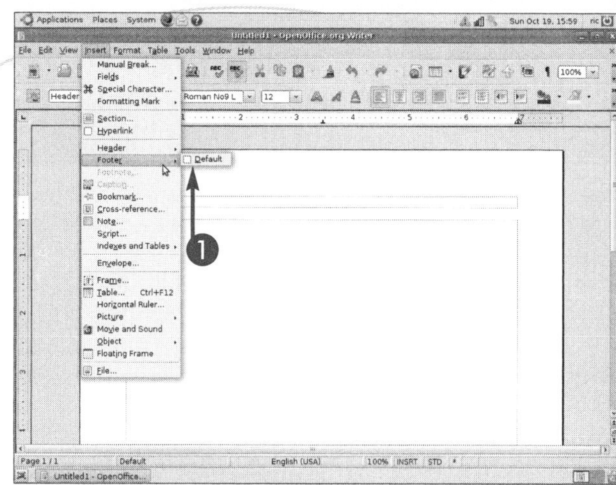

The footer area appears in the document.

2. Type the text or insert the fields that you want for your footer.

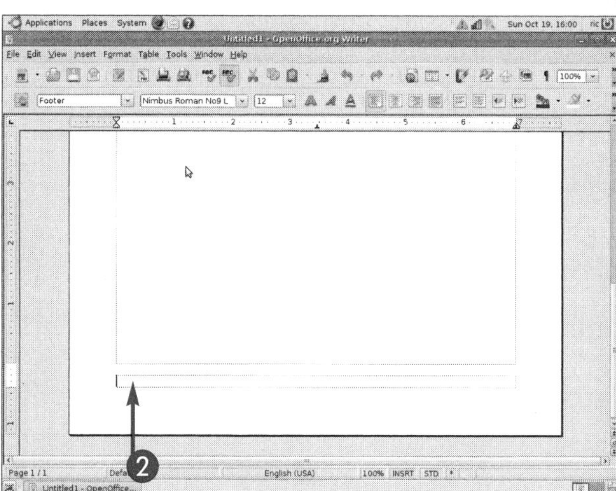

Extra

Page numbers can be formatted in a variety of fashions. The total page count can be paired with the page number to display the total number of pages together with the number of the current page. To create this format, click in the footer area. Type the word **Page**. Next, click Insert ➔ Fields ➔ Page Number. Then type the word **of**. Finally, click Insert ➔ Fields ➔ Page Count. Now, when you view your page, the output in the footer will read, "Page (page number) of (page count)," for example, "Page 1 of 5."

Other page number formats can be achieved by highlighting your page number and then clicking Format ➔ Page. When the Page Style dialog box opens, choose the option Format from under the Page tab. The Format drop-down list contains a list of alternative styles that can be applied to the page numbers. Select the style that you want to use and then click the OK button. Your pages should now reflect the page number format that you selected. Alternating page numbers can be created by choosing from the options under the Page Layout drop-down list on the same tab.

Using Page Formatting Options

You can affect the layout and formatting of your page as a whole using the Page Style options. To view the choices available, open the Page Style dialog box as shown below or by clicking the Styles and Formatting button and selecting the Page Style button at the top of the dialog box that opens.

Using Writer's Page formatting tools, you can set page margins and control headers, footers, and the positioning of text on the page. You can create multicolumn layouts on the Columns tab of the Page Style dialog box. Other options include creating decorative effects, such as adding a background, a border, or a drop shadow to the content area. As mentioned in the previous section, the controls on the Page tab also affect the formatting of the page numbers. The Footnote tab is also useful as it allows you to control the formatting of the footnotes on your pages.

All page formatting can be done through the use of the Page Style dialog box. The default installation comes with a number of page styles. The Default style is applied in all situations in which another style has not been specified. The Default style should be suitable for most uses.

Given the importance of the Default style, you may want to adapt it to suit your typical use. Default page dimensions, for example, are set for the usual North American format — 8.5 by 11 inches. If, however, you use A4 paper, you will want to modify the Default style so that the page contents fit A4 neatly.

If modifying the existing style does not suit your needs, you can create your own styles as you see fit. The creation of new styles is covered in the section "Create a Paragraph Style," earlier.

Using Page Formatting Options

1. Click Format ➔ Page.

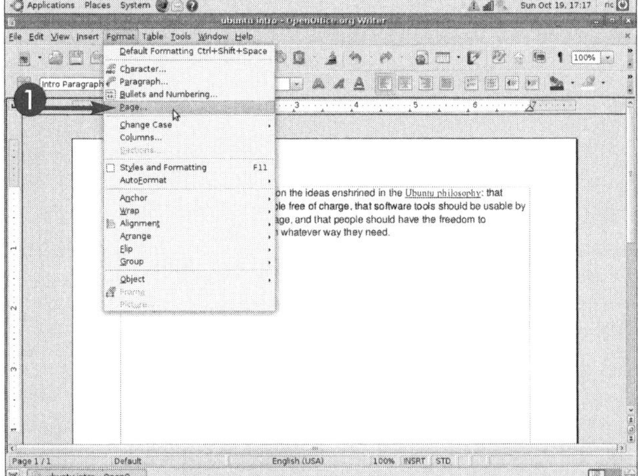

The Page Style dialog box opens.

2. Change the page setup as needed, such as changing the format to A4.
3. Click another tab to change its page settings.

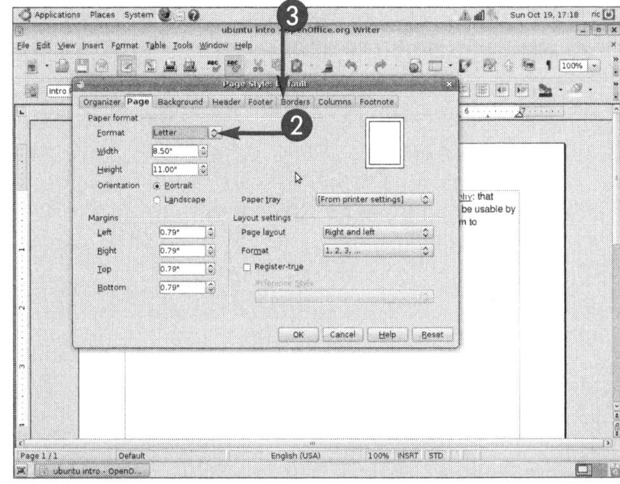

The tab comes to the front.

4. Change its settings as needed.

   In this example, the border line style is set to 0.50 pt, the shadow position to bottom right, and the spacing to .20 inches.

- You can click other tabs and set other page formatting as needed.

5. Click OK.

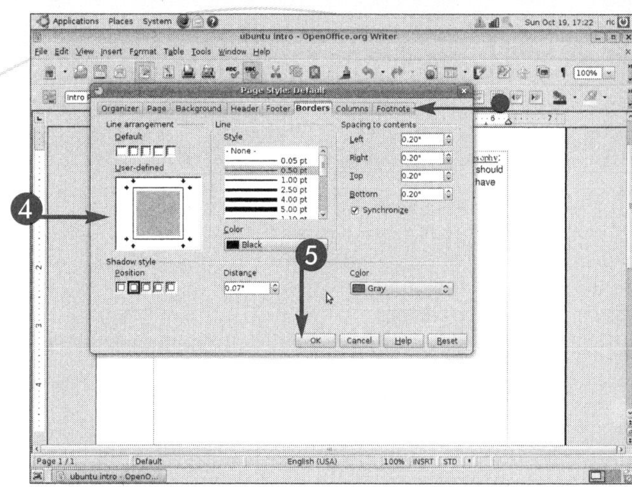

The new page style is applied to the document.

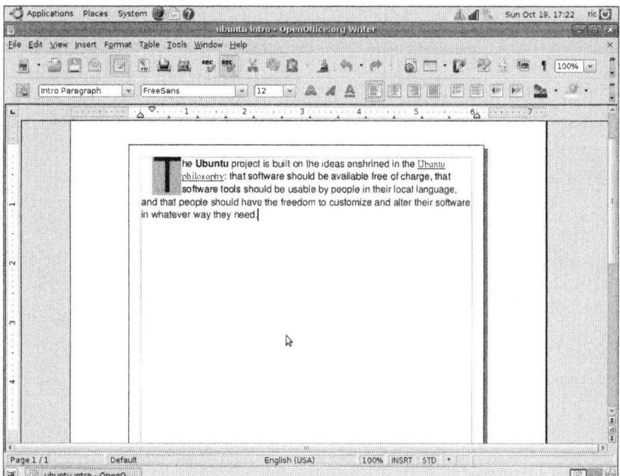

Extra

Writer is distributed with ten different predefined page styles. Although the Default page style is certainly the most important, the other nine varieties deserve mention. You can view the entire list of options by clicking the Styles and Formatting button and then selecting the Page Style button.

There are several styles that are provided to assist with the creation of books and manuscripts. The Left Page and Right Page styles are intended to work together to allow you to create facing pages. The First Page and Index styles create pages suitable for the frontmatter and index of a manuscript. The End Note and Footnote styles supply the most commonly used note formats.

The remaining two styles are of more limited appeal. The HTML style creates a page layout that contains formatting that can be reproduced easily in HTML. If you use this style, remember that you must still save your file as HTML for it to be usable online. The Envelope style is the most specialized style; it is intended to ease the creation and printing of C6 envelopes.

Place Graphics in a Document

You can enhance the visual appearance of your documents by inserting images into them. OpenOffice.org Writer supports the inclusion of most popular image formats, enabling you to use photos or graphics in your documents.

To get started, you need to make sure that the graphics file you want to use is accessible from your local computer. The source of the image does not matter, but the image file itself has to either exist on your computer or be imported from a scanner for Writer to be able to insert the image into your document.

To insert an image, you first place the cursor where you want the image to appear in the text. Then you use the Insert Picture dialog box to navigate to where the image is stored and insert the image in the document.

When the image appears in your document, you will see the Picture toolbar. The toolbar enables you to make minor changes to the image's color or transparency and gives you the ability to rotate the image. If you do not need the Picture tools, you can close the Picture toolbar.

If you want to move the image relative to the text on the screen, you can grab the image with your mouse and drag it to where you want it to appear. Alternatively, if you right-click the image, you will find a number of options that allow you to control its placement and positioning.

Place Graphics in a Document

1. Click Insert ➔ Picture ➔ From File.

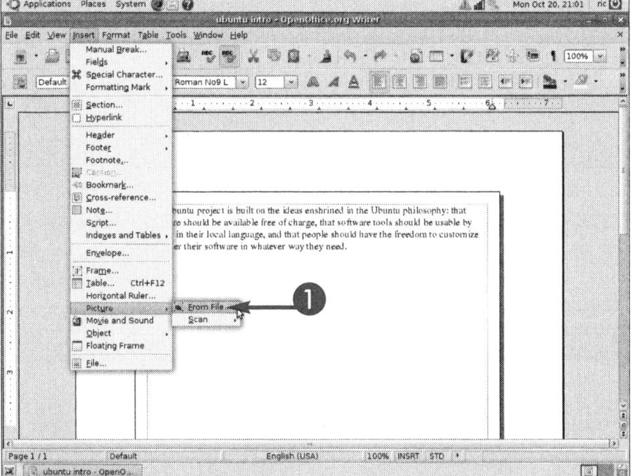

The Insert Picture dialog box opens.

2. Navigate to the folder containing the image file that you want to insert into the document.
3. Click the image filename.
4. Click Open.

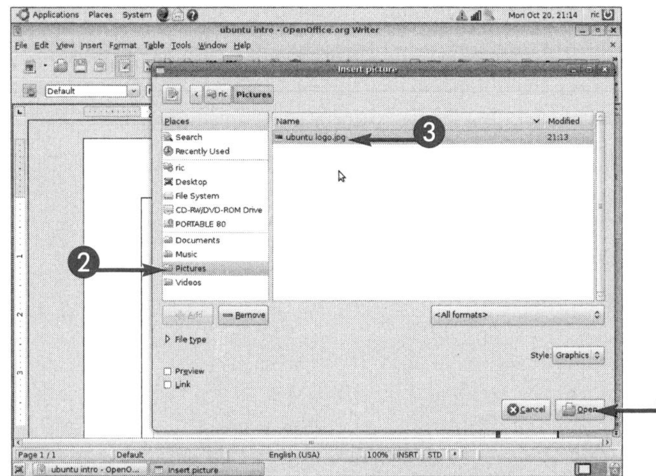

- The image appears in the document.

5. Click the image and drag it to the location in the text that you want it.

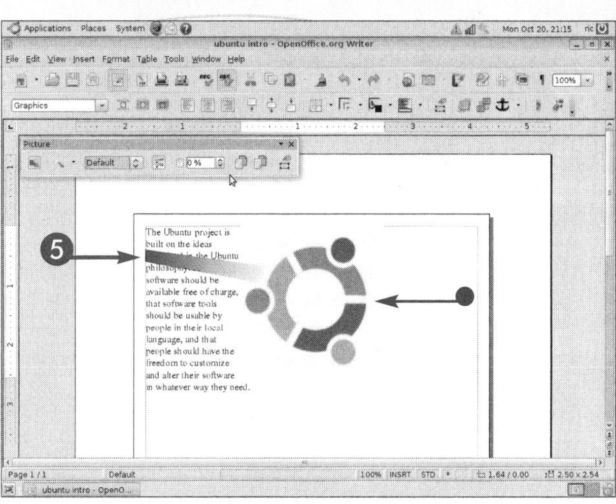

The image is repositioned.

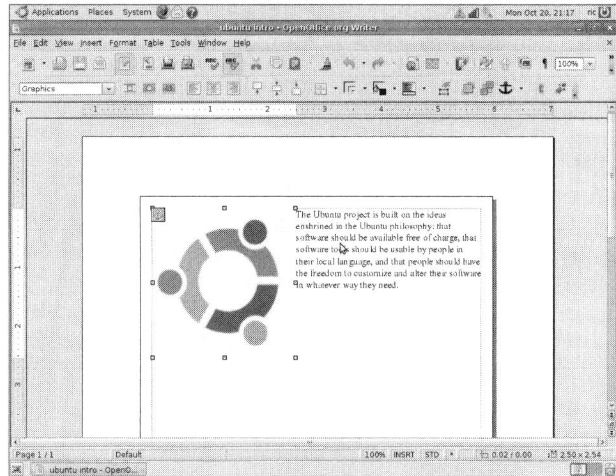

Extra

The Insert Picture dialog box has several useful features. On the right side of the dialog box, below the main navigation panes, are filters that let you change what is displayed in the dialog box's window. The filters enable you to screen out unwanted files and show only the files of a certain type. This feature is very useful when you have large collections of images and you know what file type you are searching for.

On the bottom left are two check boxes labeled Preview and Link. Checking Preview allows you to preview an image directly in the Insert Picture dialog box, prior to inserting it into the document. The Link check box allows you include an image by linking to the image rather than inserting it directly into the document. Linking to an image is particularly useful as it allows you to maintain the image separately from the document. Be aware, however, that if you move the image file, the link will be broken, and the image will no longer appear in your document. Moreover, if you change the image's dimensions, you will want to make sure that it does not break your page layout.

Insert a Table

You can insert tables into your documents through the use of Writer's table-creation tools. Tables are useful for a variety of purposes, including formatting your text and images, controlling complex data, and creating forms.

OpenOffice.org Writer provides a large number of options for handling tables in documents. The application includes both a menu and a toolbar dedicated entirely to tables. To insert a table into a document, you use the Insert Table dialog box, in which you can select the number of columns and rows that you want to include in your table. You can also set several other options for your tables, including table borders.

When your new table appears in the document, the Table formatting toolbar also appears. The toolbar contains a powerful set of tools for manipulating your table formatting. By selecting the icons on the toolbar, you can add or subtract columns or rows from your table. You can also split or merge cells and control the table's visual appearance. The toolbar initially appears floating on the screen, above your document. When you click outside of the table, the toolbar will disappear; it will reappear the next time that you click inside the table. You can also force the Table toolbar to appear by clicking the check box next to the Table option under View ➔ Toolbars.

In addition to using the tools in the toolbar, you can change the height and width of your table by clicking the table border lines and dragging them to the size that you want.

Insert a Table

1. Place your cursor where you want your table to appear.
2. Click Table ➔ Insert ➔ Table.

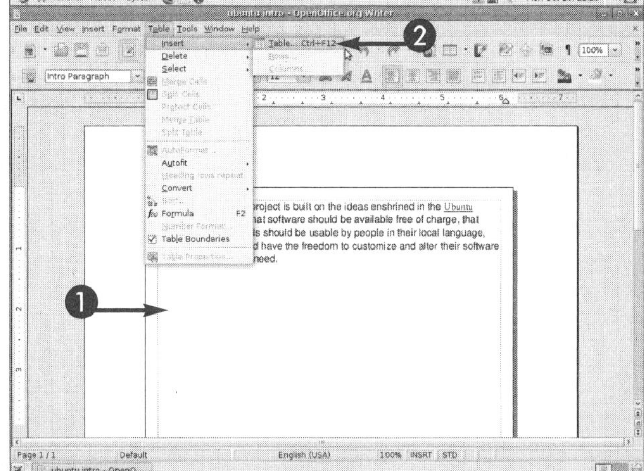

The Insert Table dialog box appears.

3. Click here and select the number of columns that you want.
4. Click here and select the number of rows that you want.
5. Click OK.

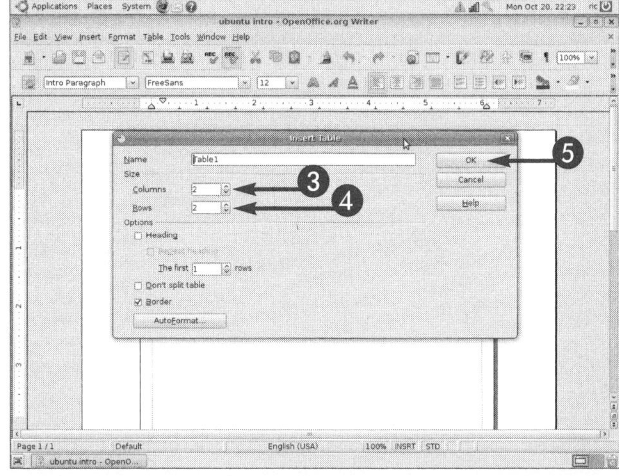

- The table appears in the document.
- If you need to add a row, you can click the Insert Row button.
- If you need to add a column, you can click the Insert Column button.

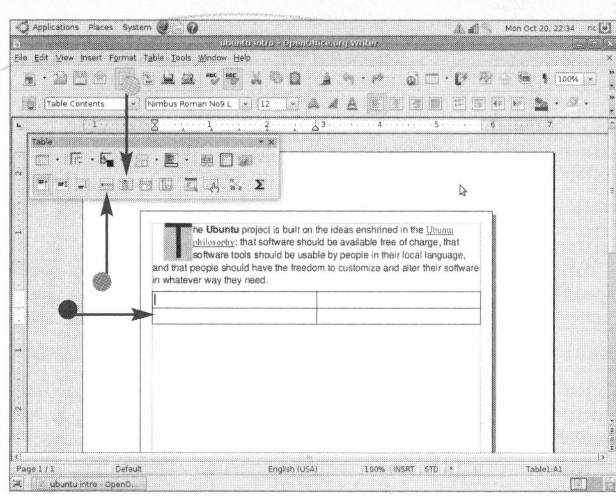

In this example, a new row and column are added to the table.

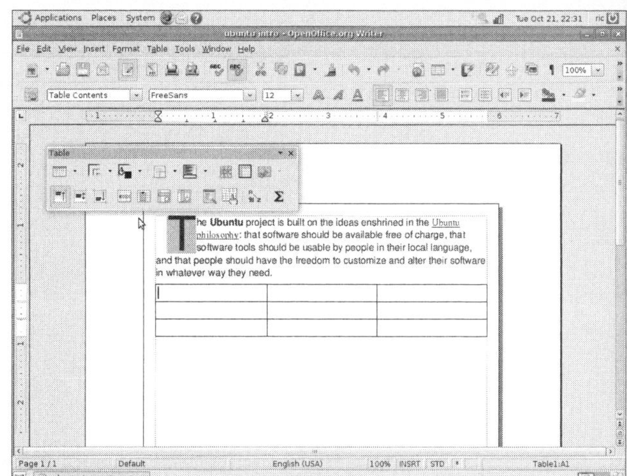

Extra

The Sum function on the Table toolbar enables you to insert mathematical functions into a Writer table, turning your Writer table into a basic spreadsheet. Although the spreadsheet functions in a Writer table are not as advanced as those in OpenOffice.org Calc, there are a number of similarities.

When you click the Sum button on the Table toolbar, a calculations toolbar appears immediately above your document's content area. The calculations bar is extremely useful, as it shows you the name of the active cell and provides you with a number of operators. On the right of the toolbar is a formula field that lets you see your work as you build your formula.

Creating formulas allows you to set up tables that automatically calculate values for table cells based on the contents of other table cells. Operations can be performed on table cells by representing the cells by letter and number, similar to what you would find in other spreadsheet programs. In addition to basic arithmetic operations, you can also employ Boolean operators, statistical operators, and functions such as sine, cosine, and tangent.

Print a Document from OpenOffice.org

You can print documents directly from OpenOffice.org Writer. Printing from Writer gives you a great deal of control over the print output and enables you to print all or only part of a document with ease.

Writer gives you two options for printing: a quick print button and the Print option under the File menu. To perform a quick print, simply click the Print File Directly button on the toolbar. The Print dialog box will open, allowing you to set the configuration of your print job.

The Print dialog box allows you to select a printer and to set the print range. You can print all of a document, just certain pages, or even just part of a page. The Print dialog box also enables you to set the print order and number of copies that will be printed.

You can open the Print Options dialog box from the Print dialog box, which includes a number of additional features, including the ability to print only selected elements — for example, the document's text without the images. The Print Options dialog box also includes the Reversed option, which prints your document from last page to first.

The Properties button at the top right of the Print dialog box opens the Printer Properties dialog box. On the Paper tab, you can set your paper size and page orientation. On the Device tab, you can control a large number of additional printer-specific properties that directly affect the print quality.

Note that after you have sent a job to the printer, you can manage the job using the Manage Print Jobs application discussed in Chapter 6.

Print a Document from OpenOffice.org

1. Click File ➔ Print.

The Print dialog box opens.

2. Click Options.

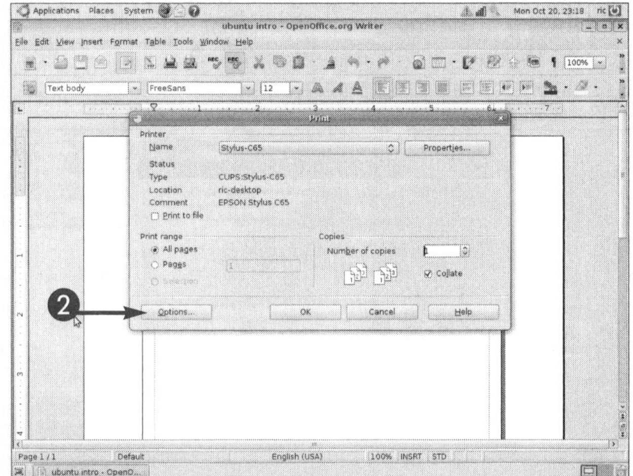

The Printer Options dialog box opens.

3. Click to select the options that you want.

4. Click OK.

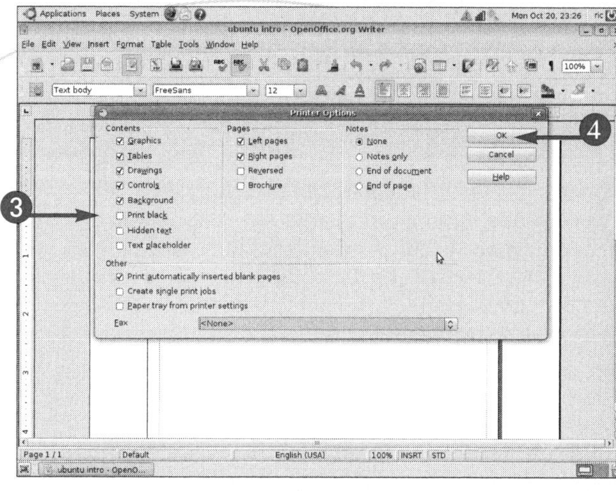

You are returned to the Print dialog box.

- You can click Properties to change the paper and printer settings.

5. Click OK.

The document prints.

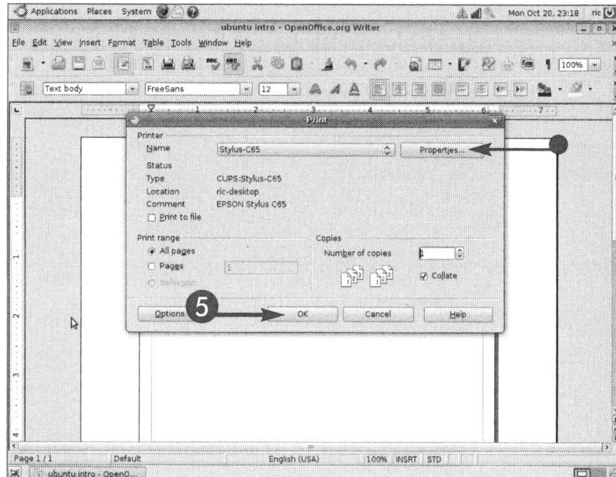

Extra

With the Page Preview command, you can preview documents before you print them, thereby allowing you to check the formatting and page layout as they will appear in the printed document. To use this handy feature, click the Page Preview button or click File ➔ Page Preview.

After you select Page Preview, the main content window will change to show you the pages of your document in full-page view. Use the icons above the Preview pane to navigate through your document. You can view more than one page at a time, or you can zoom in or out to get a better view of your document.

Click the Book Preview icon to view your document as facing pages. The left and right pages will be shown in their proper placement — a very useful feature if you are planning to print and bind your document like a book.

If you are happy with what you see and are ready to print your document, click the Print Page View button to open the Print dialog box.

Create a Basic Spreadsheet

OpenOffice Calc is a powerful and flexible spreadsheet program that lets you create and edit spreadsheets and manage financial data. Although you can use Calc for handling text or as a basic database, the real strength and flexibility of this application lies in the handling of numerical data.

There are several ways to create a new spreadsheet. When you first launch Calc, the application opens with a new spreadsheet in the window. Alternatively, if you have closed that spreadsheet or you want to create another, then you can use the New option. Calc also supports a large number of keyboard shortcuts. There is a keyboard shortcut for most common tasks, including creating a new spreadsheet. To use the shortcut, you press the Ctrl key at the same time that you press the letter *N*.

The File ➔ New menu has a variety of other options for creating new files. The Spreadsheet option is the only new document format that uses Calc. The other choices, including Text Document, Presentation, and Drawing, open other OpenOffice applications. The HTML Document, XML Form Document, and Master Document options are all document formats that you can edit in Writer. The Labels and Business Cards options are Writer templates that enable you to format a text document in a way suitable for those types of items. The last choice, Templates and Documents, allows you to create a new document or spreadsheet based on a template.

When your spreadsheet is open in the window, you can add to or edit the contents freely using the tools in Calc. You can save your work at any time.

Create a Basic Spreadsheet

WHEN OPENING CALC

1. Click Applications ➔ Office ➔ OpenOffice.org Spreadsheet.

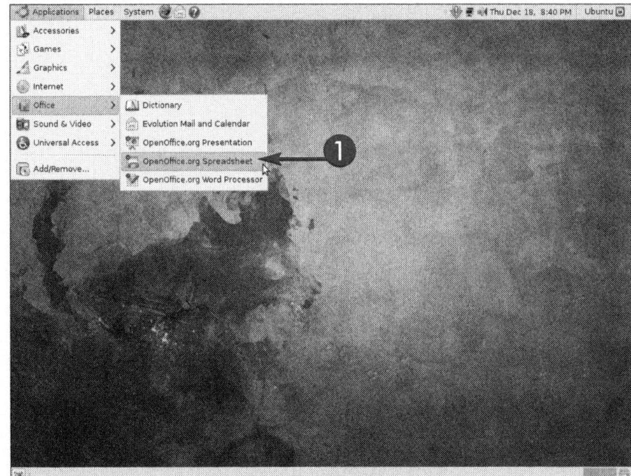

The Calc application opens, with a new spreadsheet in the window.

- You can enter any information or formulas that you want.

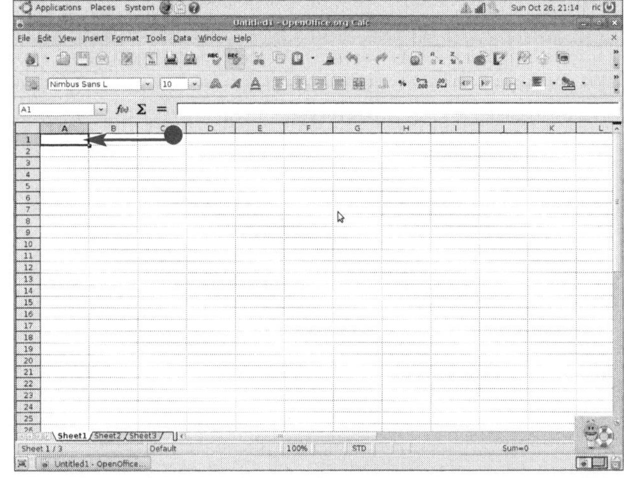

WITH CALC ALREADY OPEN

1. Click File → New → Spreadsheet.

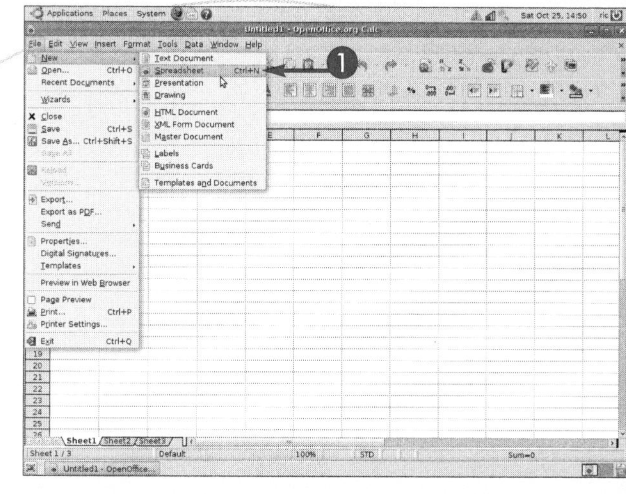

A new spreadsheet appears in the main window.

2. Type any information that you want in the cells.
3. Click the Save button.

   The Save As dialog box appears.

4. Enter a filename.
5. Click Save.

   The changes to the spreadsheet are saved.

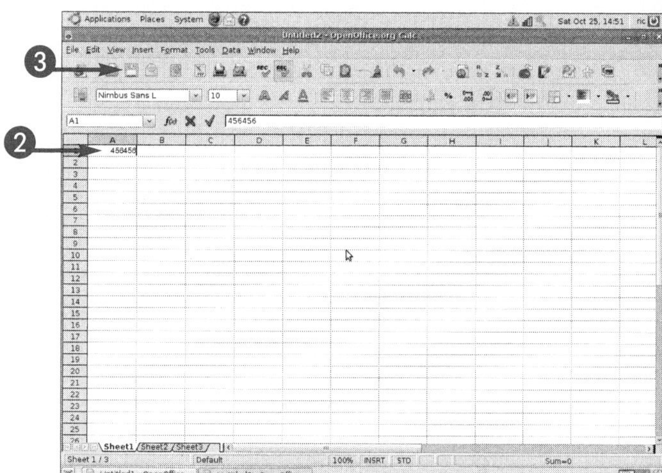

Extra

The Templates and Documents option under File → New allows you to create new spreadsheets based on existing templates. Templates provide you with standardized forms that enable the creation of multiple spreadsheets that share common formatting. Templates are most useful for common repeated tasks, such as creating an invoice, a weekly cash flow report, or a reusable form. Using templates, you can set up formulas, cell formatting, headers, footers, and more, thereby making the creation of new spreadsheets easier and assuring visual similarity across multiple spreadsheets and multiple users.

When you open the Templates and Documents dialog box, you will see a number of directories. Unfortunately, the default Ubuntu distribution does not contain any predefined templates for use by Calc; the directories you see in the dialog box contain templates for other OpenOffice applications. It is, however, easy to turn a spreadsheet into a template that can be reused. You can create a new template out of any spreadsheet by opening the spreadsheet and then clicking File → Templates → Save. You can edit existing templates by clicking File → Templates → Edit.

Create a Formula

You can employ the most powerful feature of Calc — that is, the creation of automatically calculating fields — by inserting formulas into spreadsheet cells. Formulas enable you to specify calculations that will be performed automatically based on the values that you insert into the cells.

Calc includes a number of tools that make working with formulas easy, even for those who are not well versed in working with mathematical formulas. The Formula bar, located immediately above the cells in a spreadsheet, allows you to directly type in a formula, view it, and edit it. To the left of the Formula bar are four additional tools: the Cell Reference list, the Function Wizard, the Sum button, and the Insert Formula button.

To create a new formula, click in the cell where you want the result to appear and then click the Insert Formula button, or type =. You can enter your formula either directly in the cell or in the Formula bar. Working in the Formula bar is generally preferred because the size of the bar makes it easier to see your work. After you have finished entering the formula, press the Enter key or press the Insert Formula button again.

The Formula Wizard enables you to insert complex computations with the aid of a wizard. The wizard includes a large assortment of the most commonly used formulas for financial, statistical, and scientific calculations. Note that you can add the values of cells to formulas by inserting the cell ID numbers into the formulas; the cell IDs are usually visible in the Cell Reference list.

After a formula has been created, you can click the cell to view and edit the formula in the Formula bar.

Create a Formula

1. Type the data on which you want to perform a calculation.
2. Click in the cell where you want the formula results to appear.
3. Click the Function Wizard button.

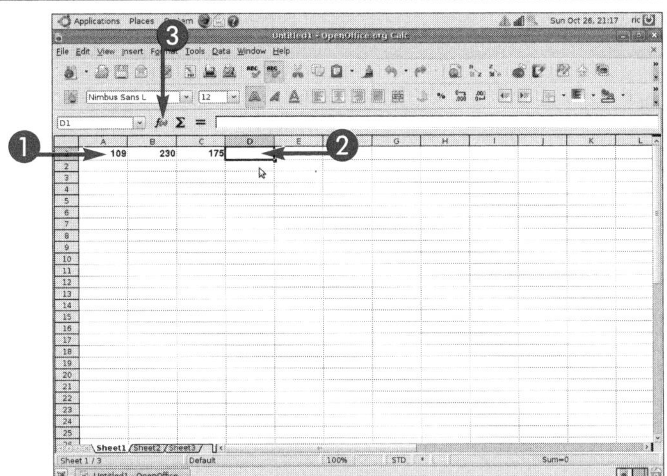

The Function Wizard dialog box appears.

4. Click the function that you want to use.
5. Click Next.

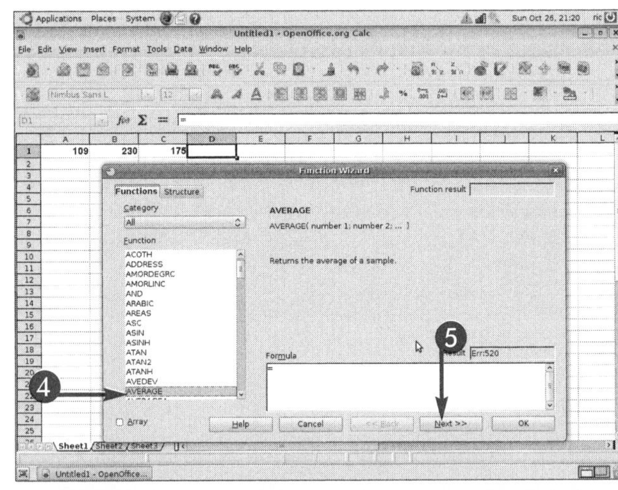

The next step of the Function Wizard appears.

6. Type the ID of the first cell that you want to include in the calculation.
7. Type the ID of the second cell.
8. Type the ID of any other cells that you want to include in the calculation.

- You can use the scrollbar to access as many cells as you need.

9. Click OK.

- The formula appears in the Formula bar.
- The calculated value appears in the cell that you specified for the result.

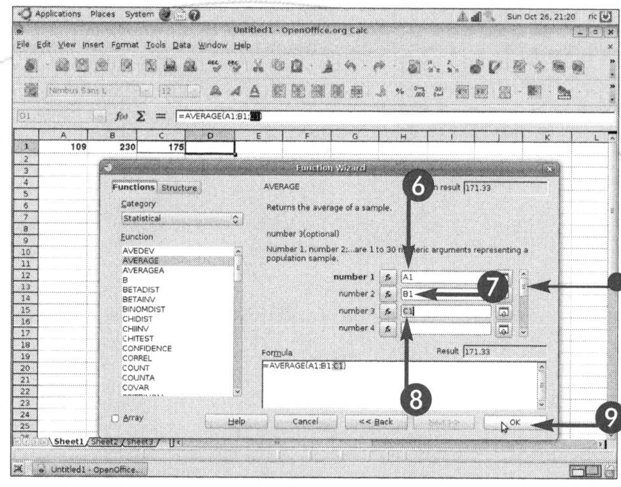

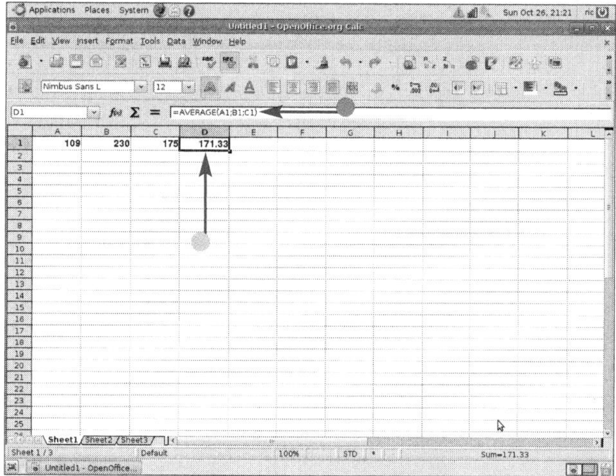

Extra

Under the Insert menu is an option called Function List. Choosing this opens a pane containing a list of all the functions available to the system. The list covers not only basic financial and statistical functions but also a number of useful shortcuts and some powerful features.

The various functions are organized into categories that you can access by using the drop-down list. Last Used keeps a list of the most recently used functions. All, as the name implies, lists all the functions in alphabetical order. The Database option provides a set of formulas that can be used to query database fields. Date & Time is useful for performing date- and time-based calculations. Financial is a list of common financial formulas. Information extracts information relating to the contents of a cell. Logical provides Boolean operators. Mathematical is an extensive list of common mathematical formulas. Array helps extract data into an array. Statistical provides a set of statistics operators. Spreadsheet extracts data about one or more cells relative to their role in the spreadsheet. Text provides operators to combine text and convert numbers to text. Add-in is a list of more exotic operators, many associated with programming functions.

Select and Format Spreadsheet Cells

You can select and format one or more Calc cells simultaneously, allowing you to control the look and feel of your spreadsheet data with ease.

To select a single cell, just click once in the cell. To select multiple cells, click and drag your mouse cursor over as many cells as you need to. You can click a row or column header to select the entire row or column. To select all the cells in a particular spreadsheet, press the Ctrl key at the same time that you press the A key. Selected cells are highlighted, so you can see what is active.

Calc provides a wide variety of formatting options, many of them similar to the formatting functions provided in Writer. The Formatting toolbar, the row of buttons above the Formula Bar, contains shortcuts to most of the basic formatting options. By clicking these buttons, you can control the font type, font size, font styling, cell alignment, number formatting, borders, shading, and more.

For more formatting options, you can use the Format Cells dialog box. This dialog box contains a much wider selection of formatting choices, all divided into tabs across the top. By using the choices in this dialog box, you can control many aspects of cell appearance, and you can also control whether the cell is viewable by others and at print time.

Also, under the Format menu are options dedicated to controlling the formatting of the row, column, sheet, and page. In other words, you can control the appearance of individual cells or any of the other primary elements that make up a Calc spreadsheet.

Select and Format Spreadsheet Cells

USING THE FORMAT CELLS DIALOG BOX

1. Right-click the cells that you want to format.

Note: *In this example, the entire row is selected by right-clicking its ID.*

2. Click Format Cells.

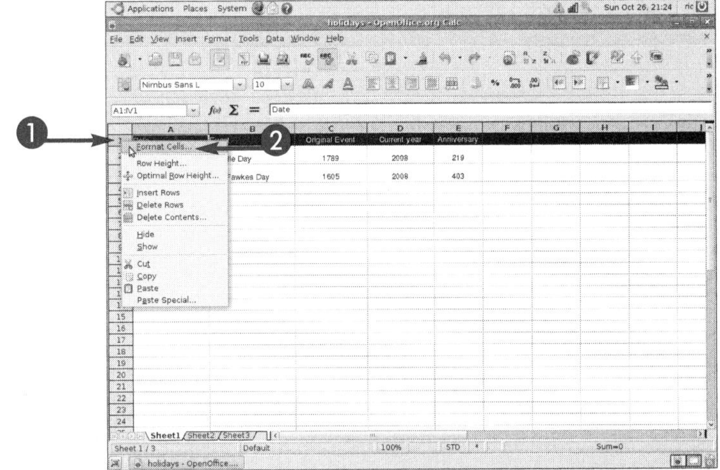

The Format Cells dialog box opens.

3. Click the tab describing what you want to format.

The tab comes to the front.

4. Make the formatting changes that you need.

- In this example, a new background color is selected for the row.

5. Click OK.

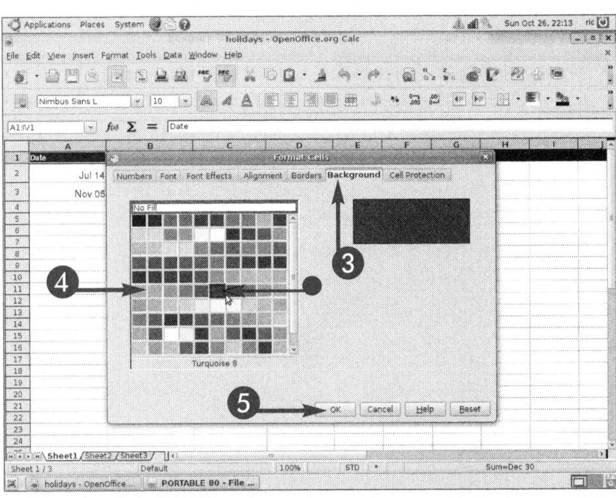

- Your formatting changes are applied.

USING THE FORMATTING TOOLBAR

1. Click and drag to select the cells that you want to format.

- You can click here to change the font color.
- You can use these buttons to apply boldface, italics, or underlining.
- You can use these buttons to change the alignment within the cells.
- You can use these buttons to change number options.

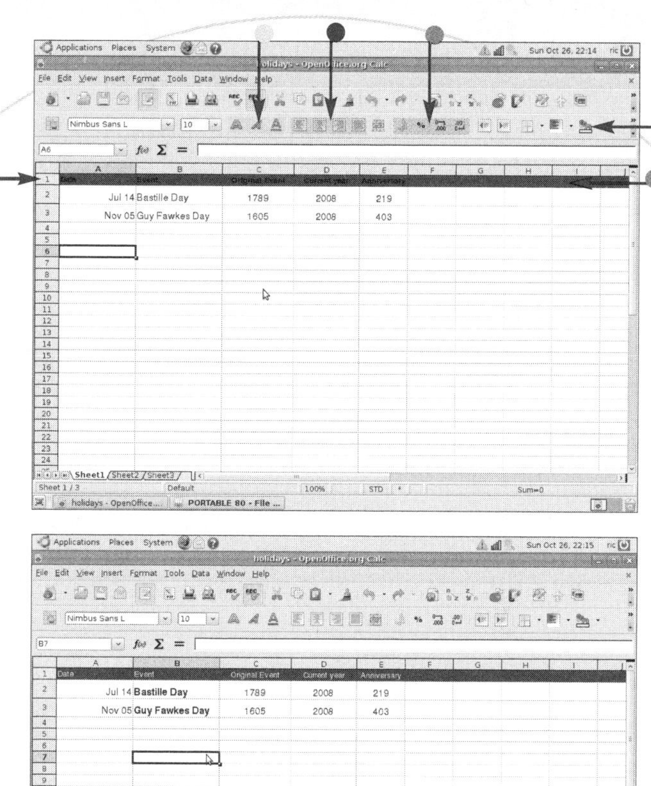

Your formatting changes appear.

Extra

Like Writer, Calc includes a set of predefined styles. You can apply the default styles by selecting the cells that you want to format and then choosing the style from the choices on the Styles and Formatting list, which is accessed by clicking Format ➔ Styles and Formatting. Alternatively, you can click the Styles and Formatting button ( ) and select the style that you want to apply.

Calc comes bundled with five predefined styles. The Default style is used when no other style is specified. Heading and Heading1 are primarily intended for formatting titles. Result and Result2 provide common formatting for total and subtotal fields. The default options are quite basic, and you will most likely want to create your own styles.

To create a new style, right-click an existing style in the Styles and Formatting dialog box and select New. Define the attributes that you want your style to have, name the style, and click OK. Your new style will now be available in the Styles and Formatting list. Right-click the name of your new style and choose Modify if you need to make adjustments.

Insert and Delete Columns and Rows

You can insert or delete columns and rows from your spreadsheets by using the commands on the Insert menu. The ease of modifying spreadsheets is key to making major changes to your layout or data structures.

The Insert menu contains a number of useful commands. Two of the most frequently used are the Rows and Columns options. These commands insert an entire row or an entire column wherever you indicate in your spreadsheet.

To use the commands, you must first select an insertion point for the new row or column. Note that this insertion point should be just *after* where you want to insert a new column or row because Calc inserts a new column into your spreadsheet to the left of the column that you select or above the row that you select.

Rows and columns can also be copied or cut and pasted. To use these options, first right-click the row or column and then choose Cut or Copy from the menu that appears. To insert the cut or copied cells, right-click the row or column in which you want that data to appear and then use the Paste command. The Cut, Copy, and Paste commands can be accessed by right-clicking the row or column, as described here, or from the Edit menu, or you can use the standard keyboard shortcuts Ctrl + C for copying, Ctrl + X for cutting, and Ctrl + V for pasting. You can also click the Cut, Copy, and Paste buttons on the toolbar.

Insert and Delete Columns and Rows

INSERT A COLUMN OR ROW

1. Click the ID to select the column or row that is right after where you want the new one to appear.
2. Click Insert ➔ Columns or Insert ➔ Rows.

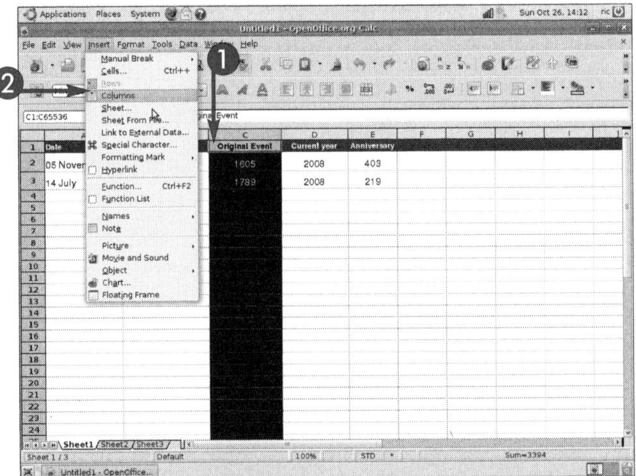

- A new column or row is inserted into the spreadsheet, right before the one that you selected.

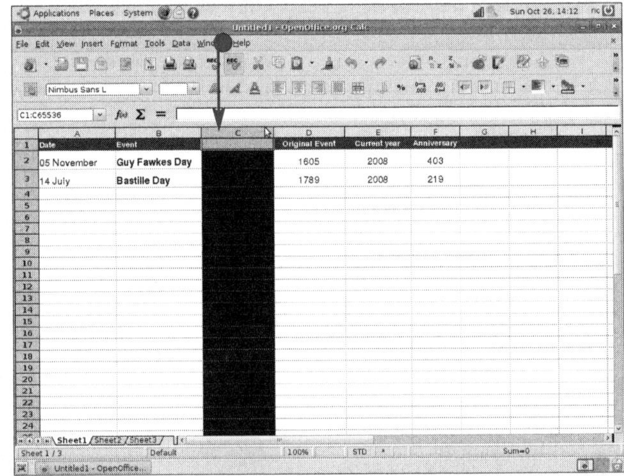

DELETE A COLUMN OR ROW

1. Right-click the ID of the column or row that you want to delete.
2. Click Delete Columns or Delete Rows.

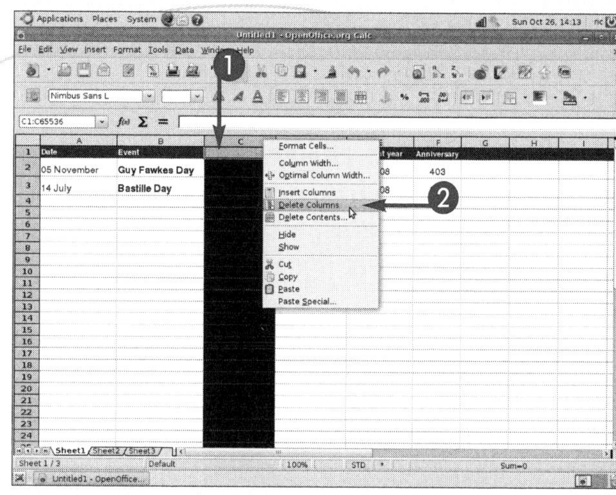

- The column or row is deleted.

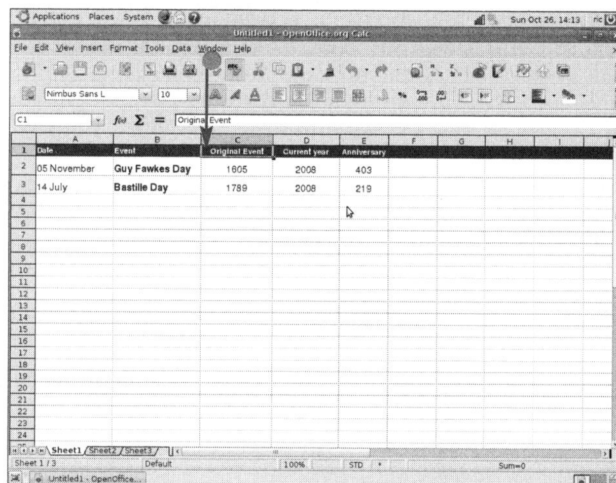

Extra

Right-clicking a row or a column brings up a menu with several choices. Not only are you presented with options to insert items, but you also have the option Delete Contents. Clicking the Delete Contents option opens a dialog box that offers you several choices.

Delete All clears all content of all types from the selected cells, rows, or columns. The Text option deletes text only, but not formats, numbers, formulas, or dates. Numbers removes numbers but leaves text, formats, formulas, and dates. Date & Time removes only date and time values. Formats, text, formulas, and other numbers remain intact. The Formulas option deletes formulas only, but not text, numbers, formats, or dates. Notes removes only the notes attached to the cells. Formats clears the formatting but otherwise leaves the contents unchanged. Objects deletes any objects associated with the selected cells, rows, or columns.

Using these options makes it possible to clear selected portions of your cells without losing work done on other key elements. The smart use of this feature can save you considerable time that you may ordinarily spend reformatting items or re-creating formulas.

Sort and Filter Spreadsheet Data

Once you have data in your spreadsheet, you can filter and sort the data to reorder it and view only what you need. The sorting and filtering tools are not only essential for big spreadsheets containing large amounts of data but are also very useful for smaller spreadsheets.

The Sort and Filter options can be applied to all or only a portion of your data. You use the Sort dialog box to sort your data. This dialog box includes two tabs; the first tab enables you to select the primary and secondary sort criteria, which is labeled by column or row name. If you have used your first row or column as headers, Calc will normally display that as a sort option. You have the choice of specifying up to three layers of sort criteria, and each of them can be either ascending or descending. On the second tab, labeled *Options,* are additional choices to refine the sorting process. If you are sorting the entire data set and have used column headings, check the option Range Contains Column Labels to keep your column headings at the top of the columns.

The Data → Filter option provides a way to select and display data based on criteria that you define. This is most useful if you have a large data set and you want to see only portions of it. The Standard Filter option supplies common filters. More advanced users can create custom filters using the Advanced Filter option.

Sort and Filter Spreadsheet Data

1. Select the cells containing the data that you want to sort.

Note: *If you want to select all the cells, you can press Ctrl + A.*

2. Click Data → Sort.

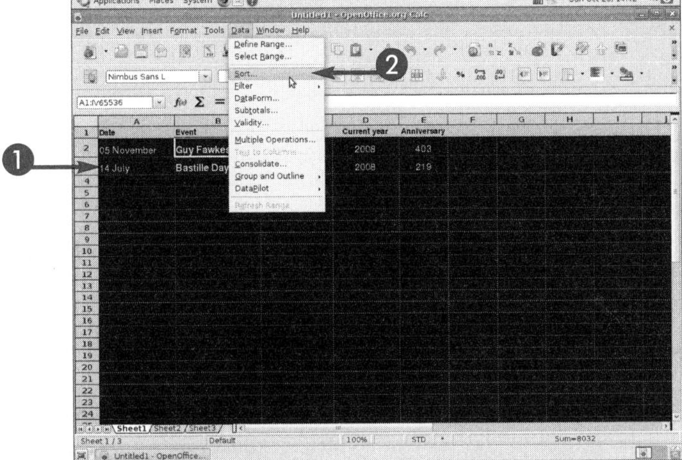

The Sort dialog box opens.

3. Click here and select the column or row that you want to sort by.

- You can select secondary columns or rows to sort by.

4. Click the Options tab.

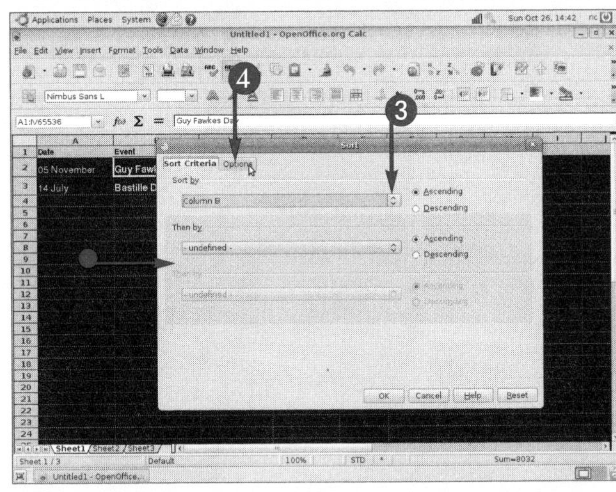

The Options tab comes to the front.

5 If you have column headings that you do not want affected by the sort, click Range Contains Column Labels.

6 Click any other options that you want.

7 Click OK.

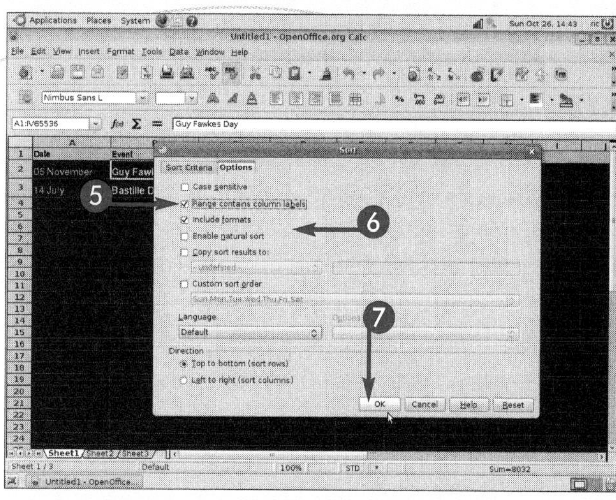

The data in the spreadsheet is sorted.

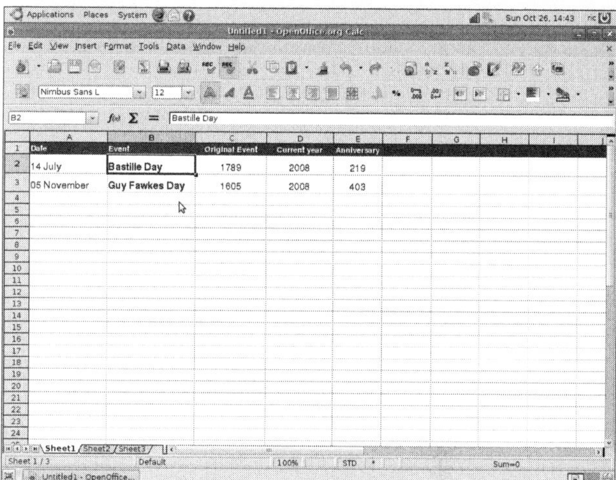

Extra

The Options tab of the Sort dialog box includes several choices that deserve special mention. Case Sensitive, as the name implies, enables you to insist that Calc pay attention to the case of the text in the cells in the course of the sort. In addition, if your spreadsheet includes Asian languages, this option enables sorting by diacritics, character widths, and Kana differences.

The option Copy Sort Results To enables you to specify a target for the output of the sort. You can specify a cell or, more frequently, a range of cells in which you want the results to be copied.

The Custom Sort Order option enables the creation of custom sort criteria. Calc includes several day/date custom sort orders, although these are rather limited in their application. You can create new custom sort orders by clicking Tools ➔ Options. Sort lists can be defined under the section OpenOffice.org Calc.

The Language option lets you set the language to be used for the sort, and for some languages, it also allows the definition of further criteria.

With the Direction option, you can sort either by rows or by columns.

Insert and Format a Chart

Charts provide a way to display data in a visually meaningful fashion. Calc enables the use of a wide variety of chart and graph formats, and each can be customized to suit your needs.

To create a chart or a graph, first enter the data into a spreadsheet. Then use the Chart Wizard to create the chart, which enables you to select from Calc's extensive list of chart and graph formats the type that best suits your data. The Chart Wizard dialog box allows you to specify data ranges and to give names to the various chart elements. You can work through the various steps in the Chart Wizard by either clicking the name in the left panel or by using the Back and Next buttons at the bottom of the wizard.

After the chart is in place in your spreadsheet, you can edit it by clicking anywhere on the chart object. Clicking once selects the chart and causes the Object toolbar to appear above the Formula bar. The Object toolbar enables you to make minor changes to the chart as whole, including setting the order of multiple objects and moving your chart relative to other objects.

Single clicking also causes click-and-drag points to appear on the chart object. You can move your chart by clicking any of the points and dragging the object to the new location. Clicking the corner point allows you to resize the chart.

Insert and Format a Chart

1. Click and drag to select the data that you want to use for your chart.
2. Click Insert ➔ Chart.

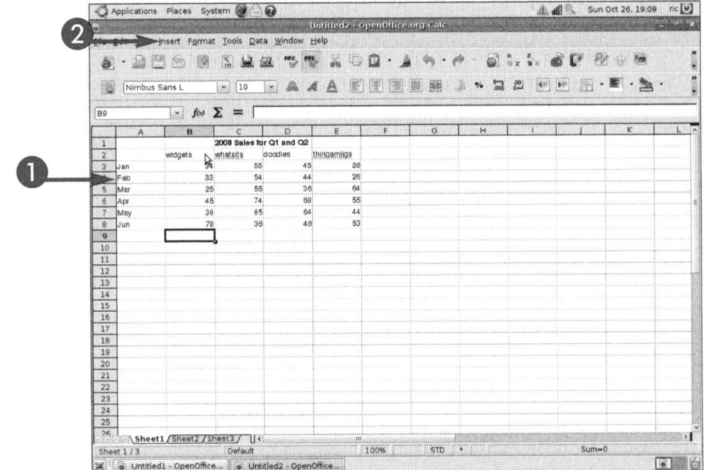

The Chart Wizard appears.

3. Click the chart type that you want.
4. Click Finish.

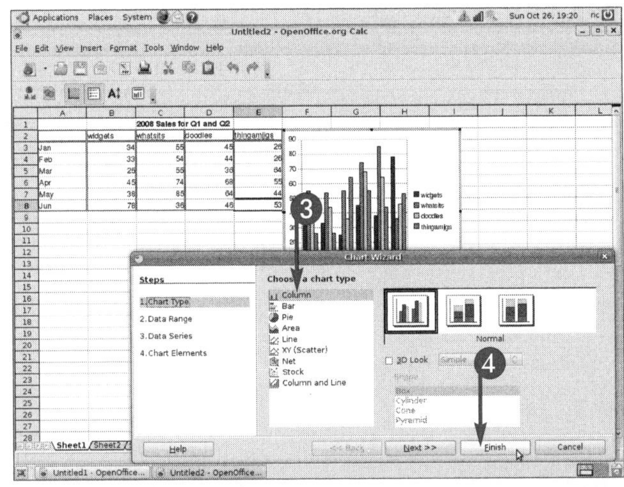

- The chart is generated and displayed in the spreadsheet.

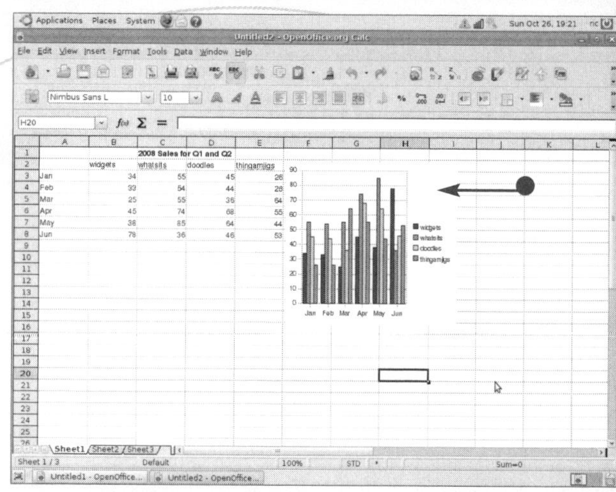

5. Double-click the chart to edit it.
6. Right-click the area around the chart.
7. Click Chart Type.

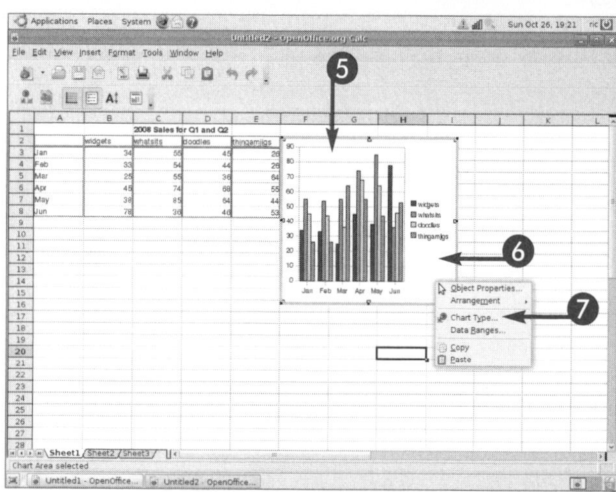

Extra

Calc provides a number of chart and graph formats. The formats are divided into nine categories, each of which includes numerous variations. You can view all the types in the Chart Types dialog box. Column and Bar charts are similar. Both display bars that are proportional to their values. Column charts show vertical bars, whereas Bar charts show the data in a horizontal format.

Pie charts exhibit data in a circular format, in which each data series is a slice of the circle. Calc supports standard pie charts and donut charts. Area charts show values as points on an axis. Variations allow you to show stacked values or percentages. Line charts map data across points on an axis. You can show points only, points with lines, or stacked values. Scatter charts show data as a set of points on the X and Y axis. This chart type relies on a coordinate system for values.

Net charts show values in a web, like a radar grid. Each row of the chart data is a radial arm of the grid. Stock charts indicate trends and ranges. Variants can display subsets or can include the transaction volume. Column and Line charts combine both columns and lines into one display.

continued

Insert and Format a Chart (continued)

Double-clicking on a chart causes the Chart toolbar to appear in place of the Formula bar. The toolbar contains buttons that control certain aspects of the formatting of your chart or graph.

The Chart Type button opens the Chart Type dialog box in which you can change the chart type or add 3D visual effects. The Chart Data Table button displays the data on which your chart is based, if it is not already visible. Other buttons allow you to show or hide the horizontal grid and the chart's legend. You can also scale the text using this toolbar and apply autoformatting, which will override any manual settings that you have applied to the chart.

When you right-click the area around a chart, you access the right-click menu. This menu includes an option labeled Data Ranges. Clicking Data Ranges opens a dialog box that allows you to set the data range that will be displayed in the chart. This dialog box also allows you to control some of the formatting of the data series, including the ability to reorder the data.

You can also control the formatting of the legend attached to your chart or graph. To do so, right-click the chart legend and select Object Properties from the menu. Clicking Object Properties opens the Legend dialog box. In this dialog box, you can set borders, a background, and the transparency for the chart legend. You can also control the font styling and the position of the legend relative to the chart.

Insert and Format a Chart *(continued)*

The Chart Type dialog box opens.

8 Click a Percent Stacked option to compare the percentage the values contribute to a total.

9 Click 3D Look to make your chart values appear 3D.

- You can click here and select a 3D style.

10 Click OK.

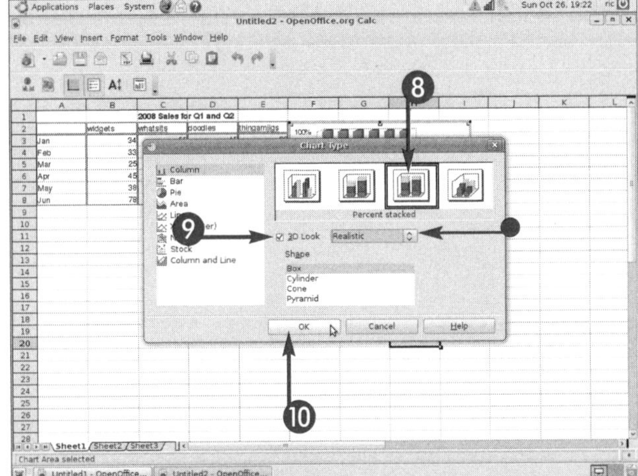

The formatting changes are applied to the chart.

11 Right-click the area around the chart.

12 Click 3D View.

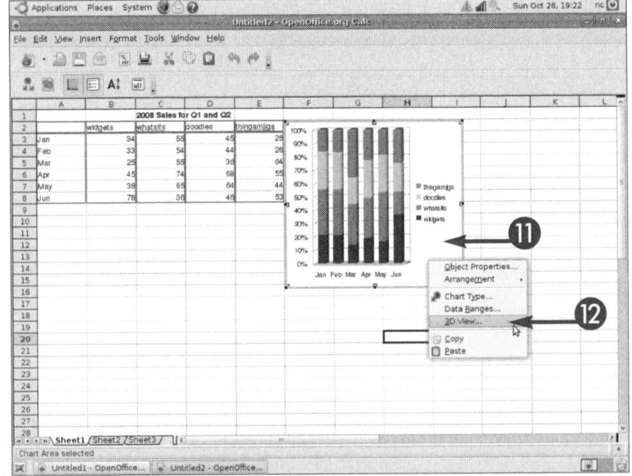

The 3D View dialog box appears.

13. Type the number of degrees for the chart to rotate about the X axis.
14. Type the number of degrees for the chart to rotate about the Y axis.
- You can enter a percentage value to change the perspective.
15. Click OK.

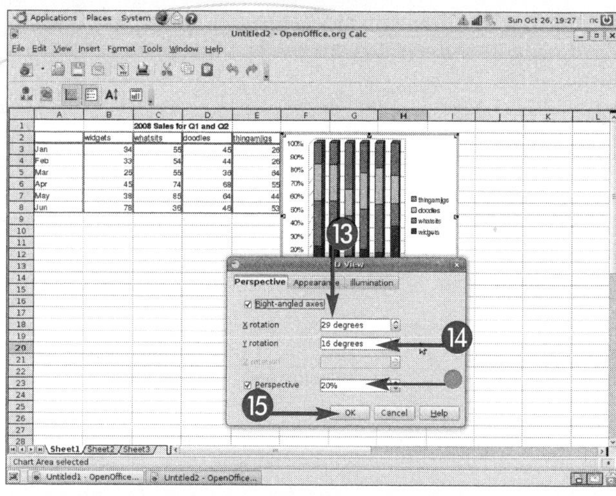

The new formatting is applied to the chart.

16. Click and drag a handle to resize the chart.

The chart is resized.

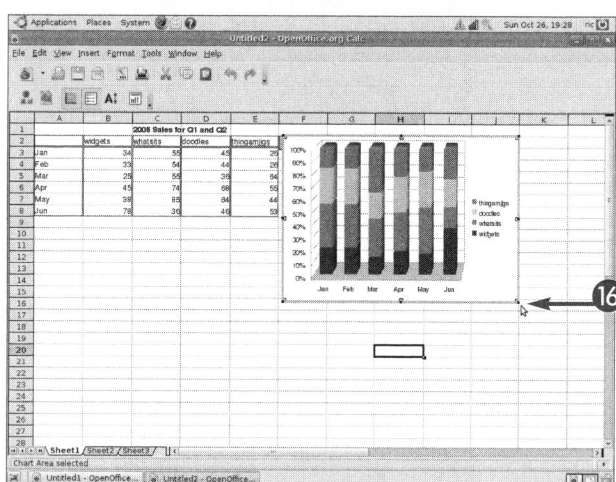

Extra

Often, it is necessary to adjust the formatting of the individual data series in a chart. You can control the appearance of each series and add labels and other useful information for the viewers.

To format a data series on a chart, right-click one member of the series and select Object Properties from the menu that appears. The Data Series dialog box that opens contains eight tabs that give you a great deal of control over the formatting of the series. Select a border for the series on the Borders tab. Click Area to set the color for your series. If you want the values to be displayed along with the series, click the Data Labels tab and select from the options. Choose Show Value As a Number to display the numerical value of each point of the series on your chart. Use the Characters and Font Effects tabs to set the formatting for the data labels. The Statistics tab lets you set error margins for a series. The Options tab lets you set alignment and spacing.

Print a Spreadsheet

You can print spreadsheets directly from OpenOffice.org Calc. Printing from Calc gives you a great deal of control over the print output and enables you to print all or only part of a spreadsheet with ease.

Calc gives you two options for printing: a quick print button and the Print option under the File menu. To perform a quick print, click the Print File Directly button on the toolbar. The Print dialog box will open, allowing you to set the configuration of your print job.

The Print dialog box allows you to select a printer and to set the print range. You can print all of a spreadsheet, just certain sheets, or even just the selected cells of a sheet. The Print dialog box also enables you to set the print order and number of copies that will be printed.

You can open the Printer Options dialog box from the Print dialog box, which includes two additional features: the ability to print only a selected sheet and the ability to print all sheets except blank sheets.

The Properties button at the top right of the Print dialog box opens the Printer Properties dialog box. On the Paper tab, you can set your paper size and page orientation. On the Device tab, you can control a large number of additional printer-specific properties that directly affect the print quality.

Note that after you have sent a job to the printer, you can manage the job using the Manage Print Jobs application discussed in Chapter 6.

Print a Spreadsheet

1. Click File ➔ Print.

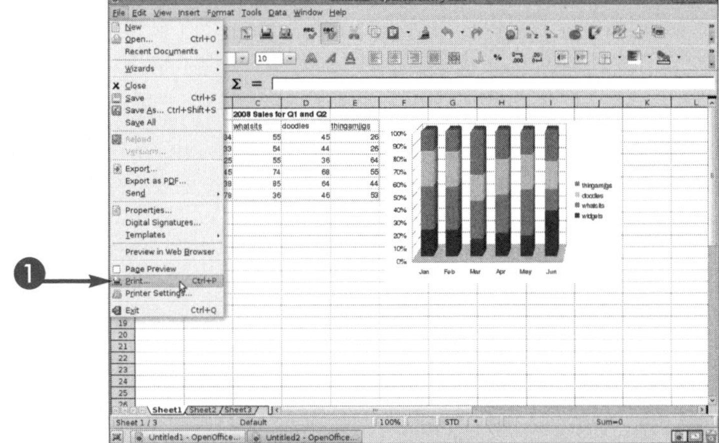

The Print dialog box opens.

2. Click Options.

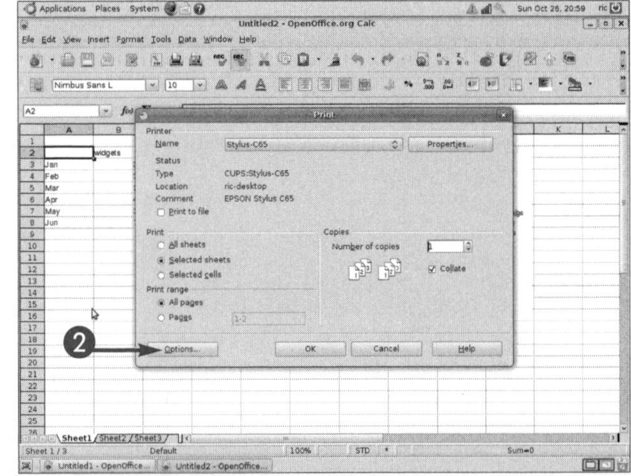

The Printer Options dialog box opens.

3. Click Print Only Selected Sheets, unless you want all the sheets in the spreadsheet to print.
4. Click OK.

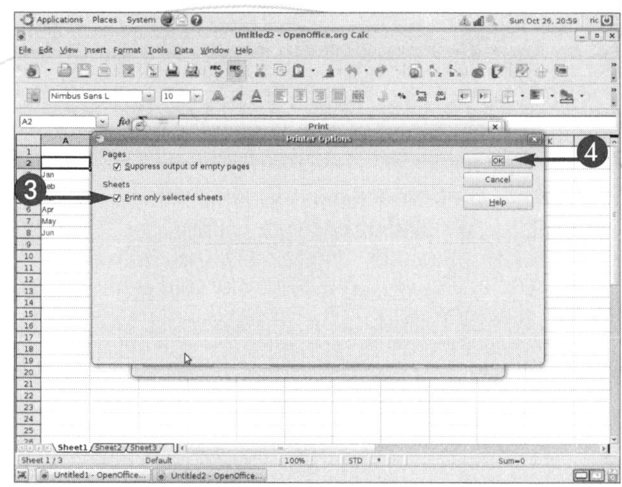

You are returned to the Print dialog box.

- You can click Properties to change the paper and printer settings.

5. Click OK.

The spreadsheet prints.

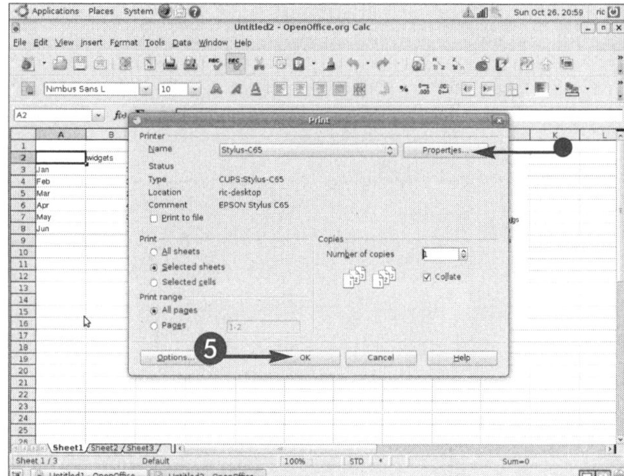

Extra

With the Page Preview command, you can preview spreadsheets before you print them, thereby allowing you to check the formatting and page layout as they will appear in the printed document. To use this handy feature, click the Page Preview button or click File ➔ Page Preview.

After you select Page Preview, the main content window will change to show you the pages of your spreadsheet in full-page view. Use the icons above the Preview pane to navigate through your spreadsheet. You can view more than one sheet at a time, or you can to zoom in or out to get a better view of your spreadsheet.

Click the Format Page button to set additional attributes. The button opens the Page Style dialog box, in which you can set page attributes, including borders, the background, and the header and footer. The Sheet tab of the Page Style dialog box lets you control print order and allows you to exclude elements from the printed document.

If you are happy with what you see and are ready to print the document, click the Print Page View button to open the Print dialog box.

Create a New Presentation

You can use OpenOffice Impress to create slideshow presentations. Slides created with Impress can contain images and text and can be enhanced with a variety of styles and effects. You can create transitions to make your slideshow more visually engaging, and you can add notes and handouts to make the slideshow more useful and informative.

There are several ways to create a new presentation. Impress includes a Presentation Wizard that can be used to quickly set up a new slideshow. The wizard launches automatically the first time that you open the program and thereafter each time you create a new presentation by using the File ➔ New command. You can bypass the wizard by using the keyboard shortcut Ctrl + N to create a new presentation or by selecting Do Not Show This Wizard Again on the wizard interface.

The first step of the Presentation Wizard asks you what you want to do: Create an empty presentation, create a presentation from a template, or open an existing presentation. In the second step, you can select a background for all your slides and customize the appearance of the slides to suit the method that you will use to display the presentation. The third and final step enables you to select slide transitions and timing.

When you create a new presentation, it appears in the central pane of the Impress application containing only one slide, but, as shown in the section "Insert a New Slide and Add Text," you can add additional slides easily.

Create a New Presentation

1. Click Applications ➔ Office ➔ OpenOffice.org Presentation.

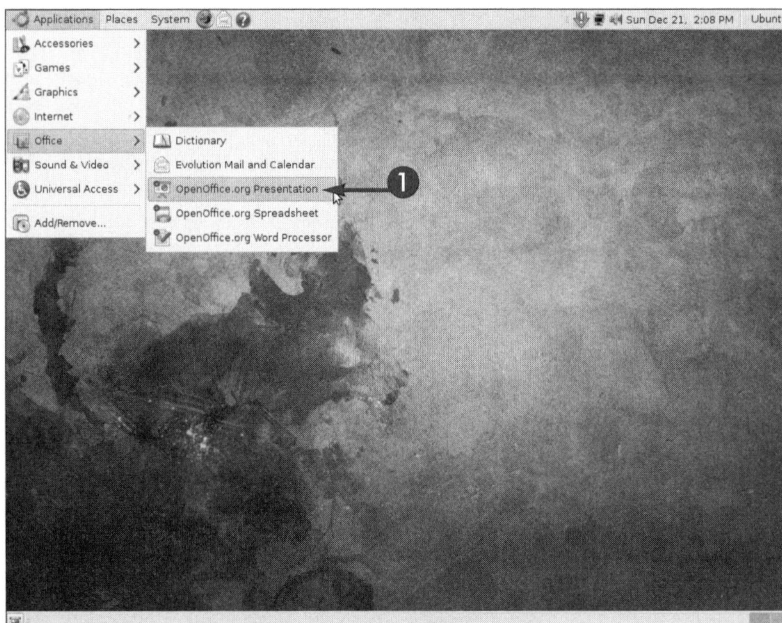

The Presentation Wizard opens.

2. Click Empty Presentation.
3. Click Next.

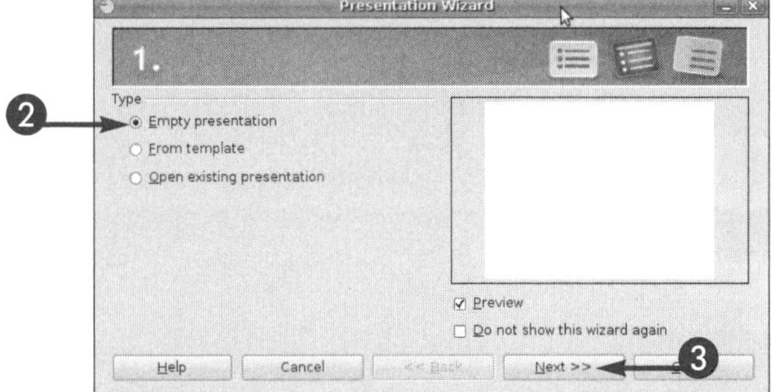

Step 2 of the Presentation Wizard appears.

4. Click here and select Presentations or Presentation Backgrounds.

   The list of presentation templates or backgrounds appears.

5. Click the presentation or background that you want.

6. Click Next.

   Step 3 of the Presentation Wizard appears.

   - You can choose how to transition between slides or the presentation type.

7. Click Create.

   The new presentation is created and displayed for editing.

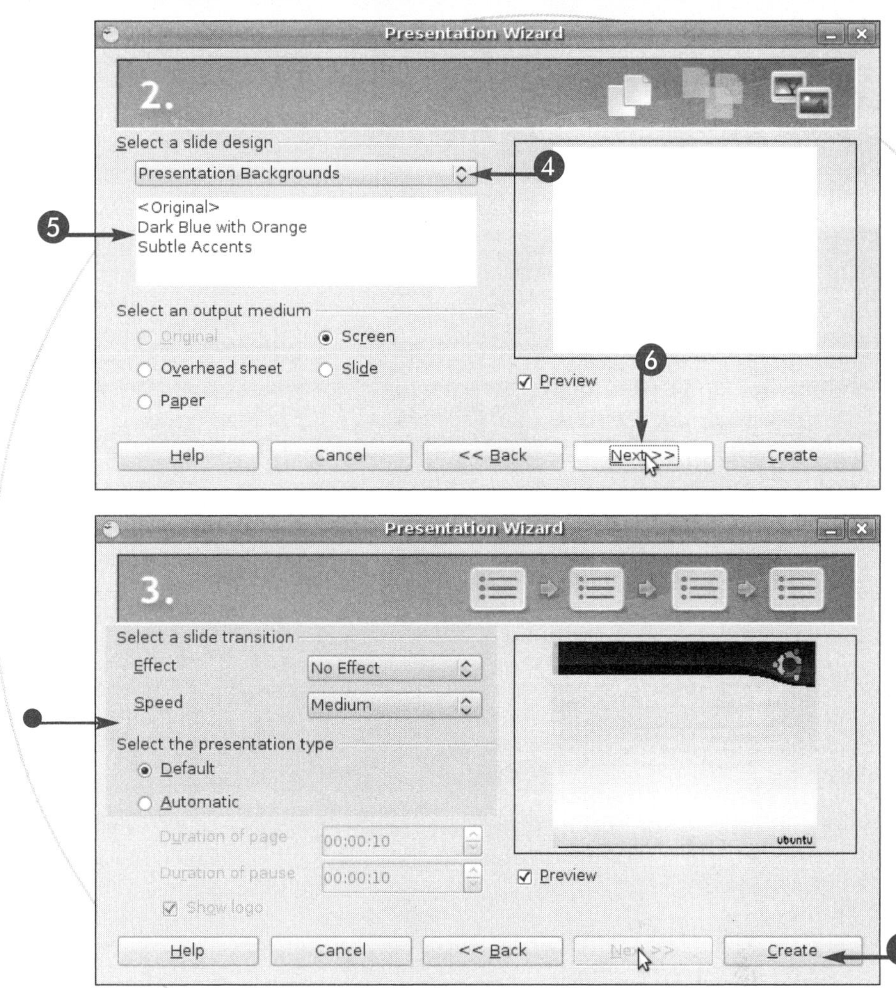

Extra

Both the Presentation Wizard and the File → New → Templates and Documents option enable the creation of new presentations based on existing templates. Templates provide you with standardized forms that enable the rapid creation of a presentation.

When you open the Templates and Documents dialog box, you see a number of directories. Two of the directories, Presentation Backgrounds and Presentations, are relevant to Impress. The Presentations Background directory contains a collection of backgrounds for your slides; using one of these templates does nothing more than create a presentation with a single slide containing the background. Two of the templates inside the Presentation directory, however, are complete multislide presentations. Open the Presentations templates named Introducing a New Product or Recommendation of a Strategy, and you will find a set of seven slides, complete with backgrounds, titles, and formatting — all you need to do is add your own content.

You can also turn an existing presentation into a template that you can reuse. To create a new template out of a presentation, click File → Templates → Save. You can edit existing templates by clicking File → Templates → Edit.

Insert a New Slide and Add Text

You can add new slides to any presentation and create and edit text areas on those slides. Slides can be either based on the other slides in the presentation, or they can be created from scratch. Text can be added either to predetermined areas or to new areas on any slide.

You have several choices for creating a new slide. On the Insert menu are two choices: Slide and Duplicate Slide. The Slide option inserts a new slide with the presentation's default background. If you select an existing slide and then choose Duplicate Slide from the Insert menu, Impress adds a new slide identical to the one that you have selected.

You can also create a new slide by clicking the New Slide button. If no slides are selected in the Slides pane, Impress will create a new blank slide. If a slide is selected, clicking the New Slide button inserts a duplicate of the selected slide.

To add text to any slide, select the Text button on the Drawing toolbar, located at the bottom of the screen. After you have clicked the button, position the mouse cursor on the slide where you want to text to appear and then click and drag to create the text box. When you release the mouse button, the cursor will be inside the new text box; simply type the text that you want.

If your slide is using a preset layout with text areas, you can simply click in the existing text area and begin typing. This method is fast and easy, but you do sacrifice some flexibility.

Insert a New Slide and Add Text

INSERT A SLIDE

1. With your basic one-slide presentation open, click Insert ➔ Slide.

Note: *See the previous section, "Create a New Presentation," to create a basic presentation.*

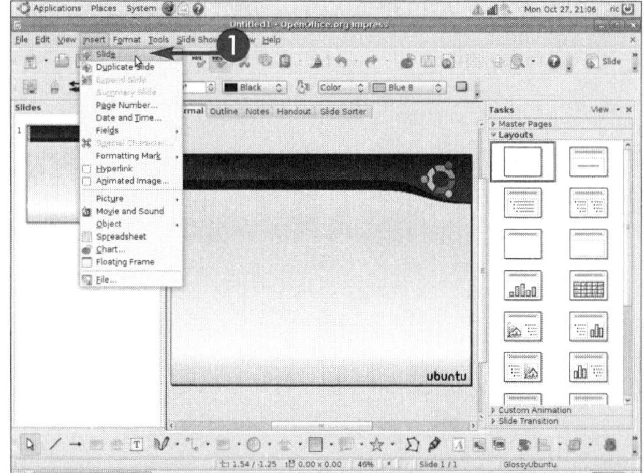

- A new slide appears in the window.

CREATE A TITLE SLIDE

2. Click the first slide.
3. Click the Title Slide layout.

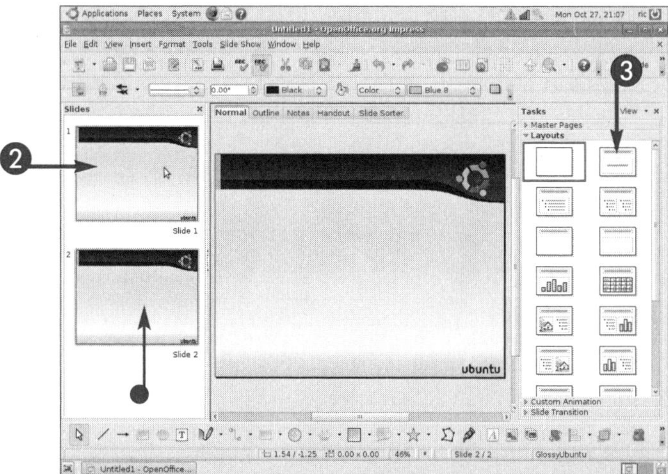

- The Title Slide layout is applied to the slide.

4. Click inside the title box.
5. Type the title of your presentation.
6. Click inside the text box.
7. Type text to introduce your presentation.

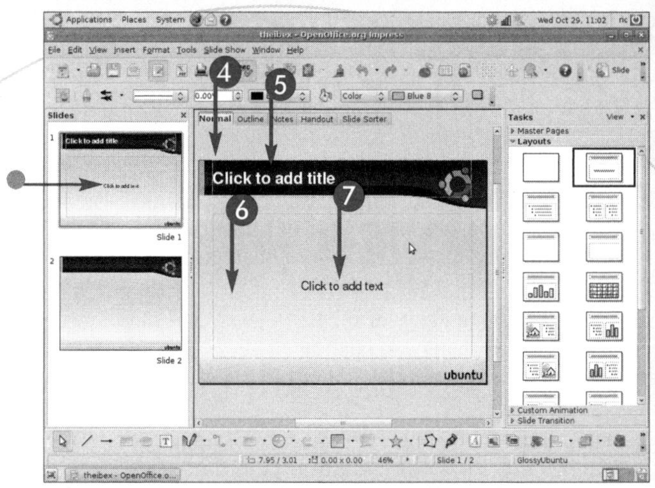

- The title and body text appears in the slide.

ADD TEXT TO A SLIDE

1. Click the slide.
2. Click the Text button.
3. Click and drag where you want your text box.
4. Type your text.

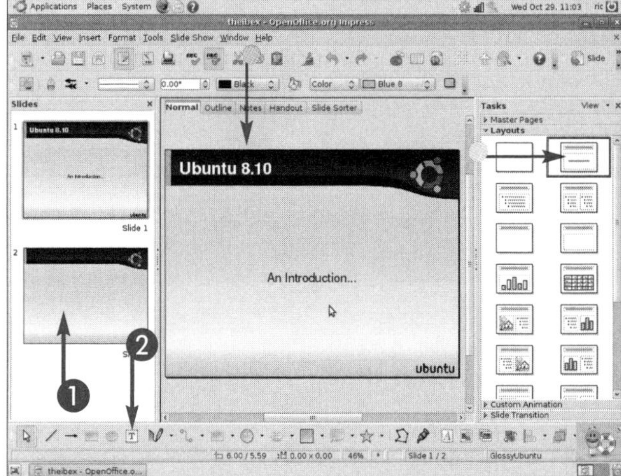

Extra

In the right pane of the Impress window is the Layouts tab. Clicking this tab displays 18 predefined layouts that you can use on any slide. Some of the layouts are simple title slides, and others combine a title area with a text area; still others combine a title with one or more object areas. Object areas can display graphics, charts, or tables.

To apply a layout to a slide, click once on the slide to select it and then click the layout. Impress will automatically associate the layout with the slide. To use the layout, click inside the designated areas on your slide.

To change the layout, click to select the slide and then click the different layout that you want to use; the newly selected layout will appear on the slide, replacing the old layout.

Changing the layout of existing slides can be confusing. If your slide already contains content, changing the layout will not delete the content; Impress will try to rearrange the slide content, and when that is not possible, it will overlay the new layout on your existing content. Although this may create undesired results, you can always rearrange things manually.

Insert Images and Other Slide Objects

You can insert images, graphs and charts, tables, and other media objects into your slides. By adding imagery to your slides, you can create compelling and interesting presentations.

Impress supports a wide array of media objects. Not only can you insert common objects, such as pictures, but you can also add sound clips, movies, and even applets and data objects.

If you are using the Impress layouts to control your slide layouts, images and other objects can be placed by simply clicking inside the appropriate object area on the slide. In this fashion, you can add pictures, charts, and tables. If you want to control the placement exactly, manual insertion of the objects is the best path.

When you insert an image, you have to choose to use either an existing image that is located on your hard drive or a scan of a new image. If you choose to insert an existing image, click the From File option on the Insert ➔ Picture submenu. This opens the Insert Picture dialog box, which you use to insert the image.

Inserting other media types is managed the same way; you merely choose a different media type from the Insert menu. There are dedicated choices for Movie and Sound, Spreadsheet, Chart, and other types of Objects. Pick the one that matches your needs, and Impress will guide you through the process of inserting it into your slide.

Insert Images and Other Slide Objects

1. Click Insert.
2. Click the type of object that you want to insert.

Note: *If you click Picture to insert an image, click From File on its submenu.*

- Alternatively, to insert an image, you can click the From File button.

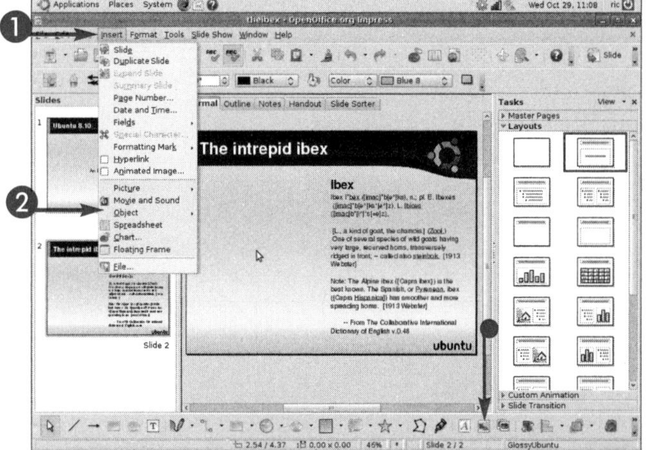

The Insert dialog box for the object opens — in this example, the Insert Picture dialog box.

3. Navigate to the folder containing the object that you want to insert.
4. Click the object filename.
5. Click Open.

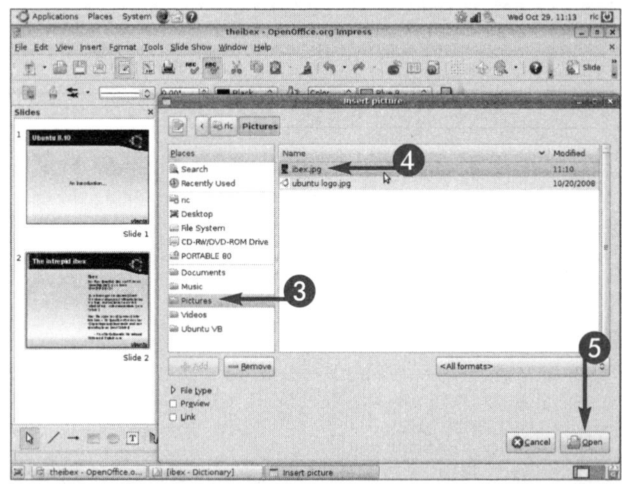

- The object appears in the slide.
- For an image, you can click the handles and drag to resize it to fit the space.

- The image is resized.

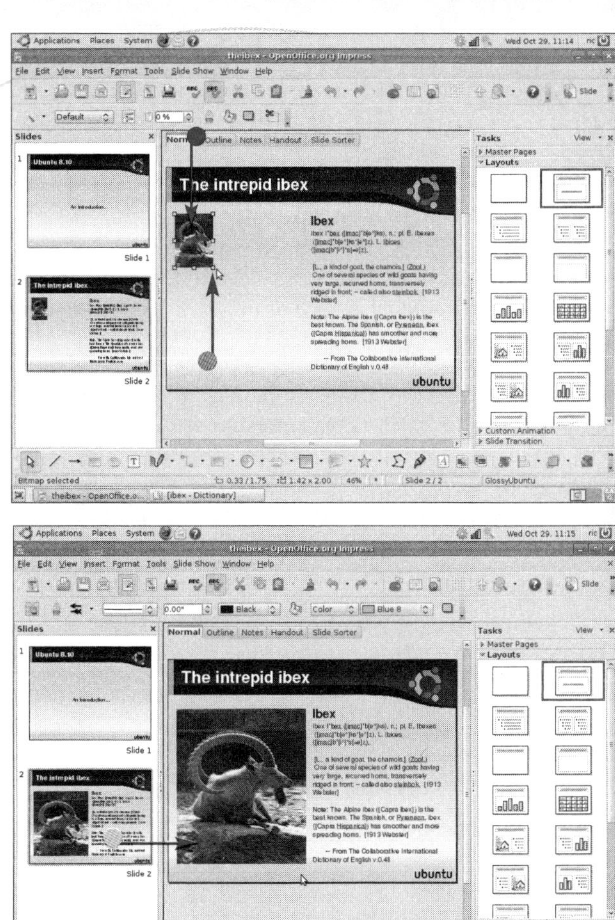

Extra

The Impress application window is divided into three areas. From left to right, they are the Slides pane, the workspace, and the Tasks pane.

In the Slides pane, you can see multiple slides, in order. This is a fast and easy way to navigate through the slides in your presentation. You can rearrange or delete slides from the Slides pane. The Tasks pane, on the right side, has four options: Master Pages, Layouts, Custom Animation, and Slide Transition. Master Pages displays all the masters available. Layouts displays all the layouts in the system. Custom Animation and Slide Transition are discussed later in this chapter in the section "Select a Slide Transition and Add Slide Animation Effects."

The workspace, in the center pane, is where you will do the vast majority of your work creating and editing individual slides. Note the tabs at the top, above the slide: Normal, Outline, Notes, Handout, and Slide Sorter. Normal view is your editing window. Outline shows the presentation as a bulleted point outline. Notes and Handout are where you can create supplemental materials for the presenter or the audience. Slide Sorter is a way to view the entire presentation at a glance and rearrange slides.

Modify the Slide Design and Layout

You can make changes to the design and layout of your slides across the entire presentation or a single slide at a time. Automatic design and layout choices can be easily changed, or if you prefer, you can make changes manually to create a custom tailored appearance for your presentation.

Impress gives you two alternatives for modifying existing slides: either work with the automatic design and style options or modify elements manually. The question of which approach is right for you depends largely on whether you are trying to implement a change across the entire presentation or only to one slide. Changes to the presentation as a whole are best done from the Master Pages tab of the Tasks pane; changes to the master page affect all the slides that are based on that master.

On the Master Pages tab, you can modify your slide backgrounds, fonts, and basic page formatting by selecting from the preexisting master pages. Simply click the master page design that you like, and it will be implemented across the presentation.

Layout options are more useful for individual slides. Click to select a slide and then choose the layout from the Layouts tab in the Tasks pane. Note that if you already have content on your slide, changing the layout may affect it.

If you do not want to apply these automatic options, your best bet is to select the object that you want to modify and make your changes to the text, the item size, and so on yourself. You can edit individual slide contents in the workspace, under the Normal tab. Clicking any object on a slide will make it editable. Changes made to individual slides do not affect other slides.

Modify the Slide Design and Layout

USE A MASTER PAGE TO CHANGE THE DESIGN

1. Click the Master Pages tab.
2. Click the thumbnail of the master page to which you want to change.

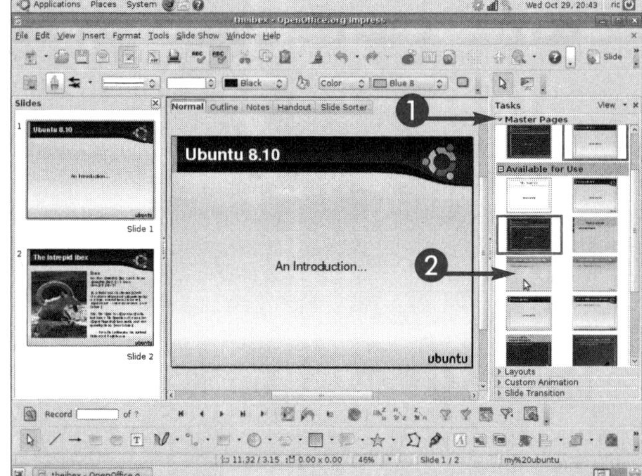

- The new background is applied to the entire presentation.

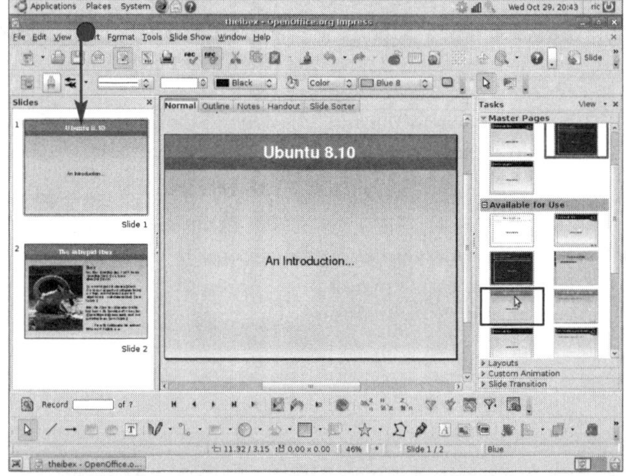

MANUALLY CHANGE THE LAYOUT OF A SLIDE

1. Click the image or other object and drag it to where you want it in the slide.
2. Click the text box and drag it to where you want it.

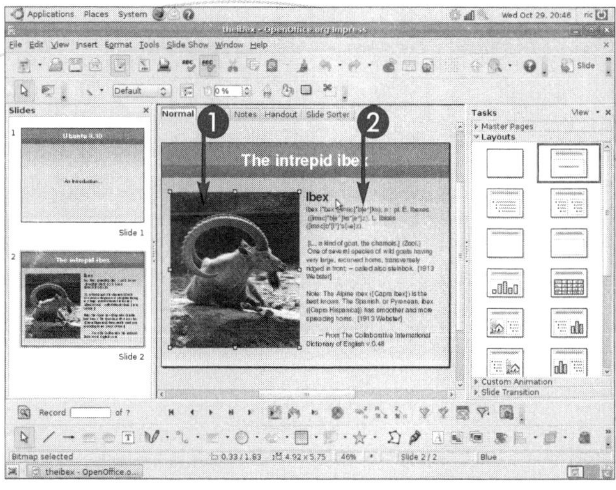

- The layout changes to the slide layout are applied.

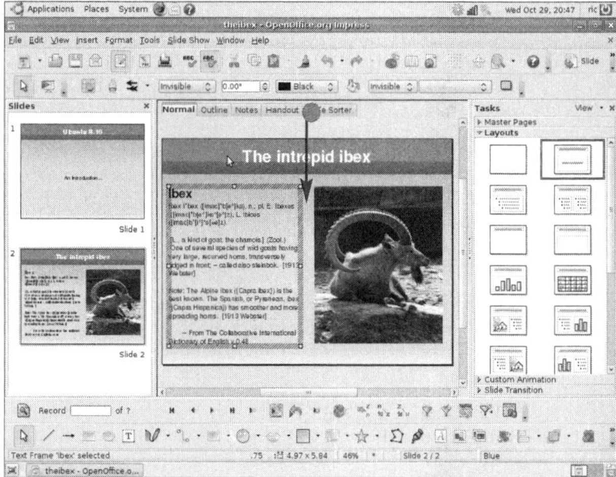

Extra

There are two ways to change the background of an individual slide without affecting the other slides in the presentation. The two methods offer different options, so you need to be aware of both.

The simplest method for changing the page background is to click Format → Page. The Page Setup dialog box opens. On the Background tab, there are multiple options for controlling the slide background. You can choose no background at all, or you can select a bitmap image, a solid color, a gradient pattern, or a hatching pattern. All the options can be edited to a certain degree. Other controls on this tab allow you to set the positioning of the background.

The other option for changing the background, Slide Design, allows you to tap into the templates in the system. Right-click the slide that you want to change in the Slides pane. Click Slide Design. The dialog box that pops up shows you the backgrounds in use in the presentation. You can either select from one of them, or you can click Load to call up a list of all the templates.

Select a Slide Transition and Add Slide Animation Effects

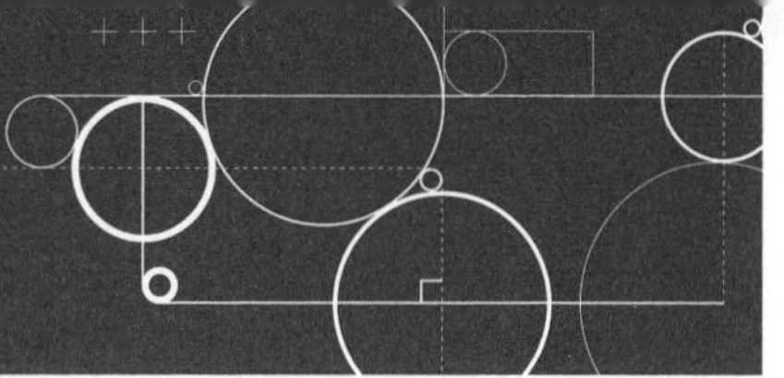

To add motion and interest to your presentation, you can create animated transitions between your slides, and you can also add movement to the objects on the page. Although it is easy to overdue animation effects in a presentation, some animation can help keep the audience's interest and add some polish. Impress supports a set of animation effects that are ready to use.

Applying an animation effect requires you to select the object or pages to be animated and then to select the animation effect. After you have selected the effect, you can fine-tune the settings to make the effect behave as you want it to.

Slide transitions are a type of animation, but they affect the entire slide, rather than just one element on it. To set up a transition, you use the Slide Transition tab in the Tasks pane. You select from the list of the transition effects and check the other options to see if they require adjustment. When you select a transition, it will be previewed in the window. To see the preview again, click the Play button.

To add animation to a slide object, you use the Custom Animation tab in the Tasks pane. You open the Custom Animation dialog box, which displays the options available. Note that there are tabs at the top and a number of options to explore. When you select an animation effect, the animation will be previewed automatically. Note that the Custom Animation tab also has several configuration options that you can use to customize the effect.

Select a Slide Transition and Add Slide Animation Effects

ADD A SLIDE TRANSITION

1. Click the slide that needs a transition.
2. Click the Slide Transition tab.

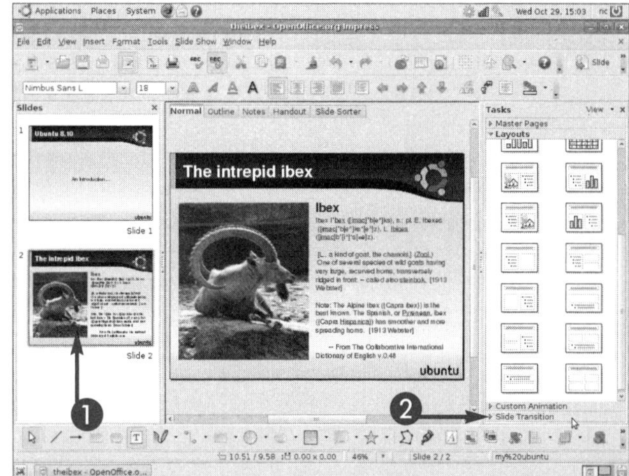

The Slide Transition tab opens.

3. Click the transition that you want.

- The transition is added to the slide.

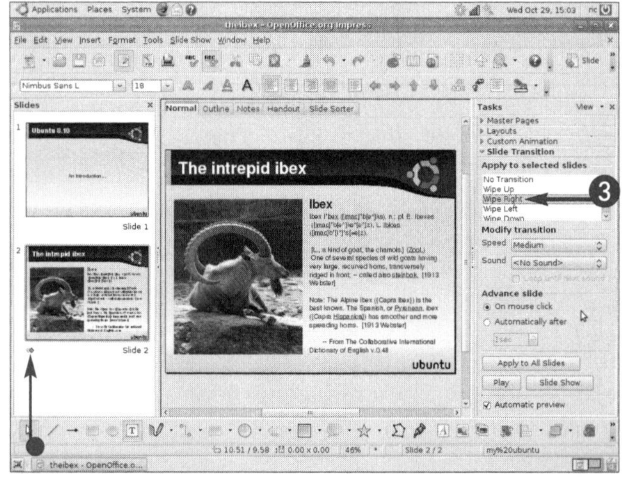

ADD ANIMATION EFFECTS

1. Click the element that will be animated.
2. Click the Custom Animation tab.
3. Click Add.

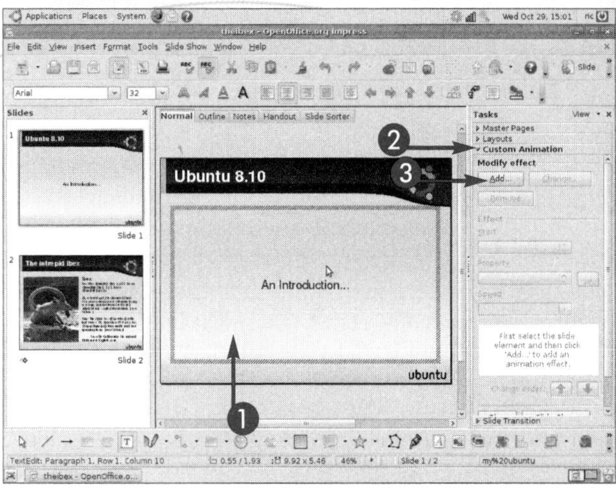

The Custom Animation dialog box opens.

4. Click the animation that you want.
5. Click OK.

The animation effect is now active for the selected element.

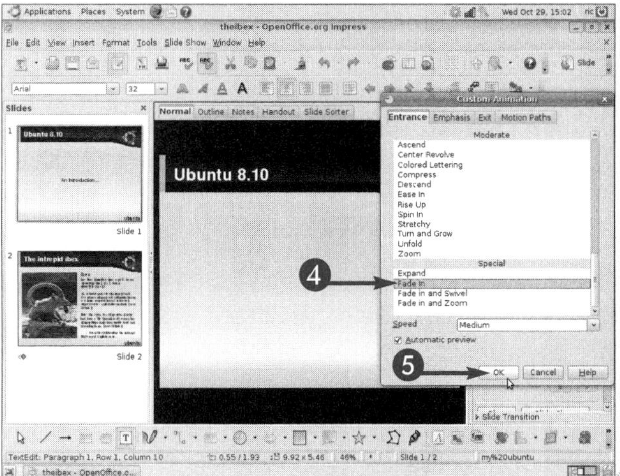

Extra

Managing animation can be time-consuming, and it can also be a real distraction from your message. It is best to try to limit your use of these effects to only those situations where they add to rather than distract from your message.

If you do elect to use animation, check out the options you have for configuring them. After you add animation to an object, you will see that the name of the animation appears in a box near the bottom of the Custom Animation tab. This shows all animations associated with the object. Select an animation and right-click it.

The right-click menu contains several options with which you should be familiar. First, you can determine whether the animation plays immediately when the slide loads or whether it needs to wait for you to click. You can also set the order of the animation, relative to other animations on the same slide. You can set the animation to play at a certain time by using the options under the Timing label. Also worth noting is the ability to tie audio to an animation or to group together multiple objects on a slide to animate them as a set.

Rehearse Slideshow Timings and Change Show Settings

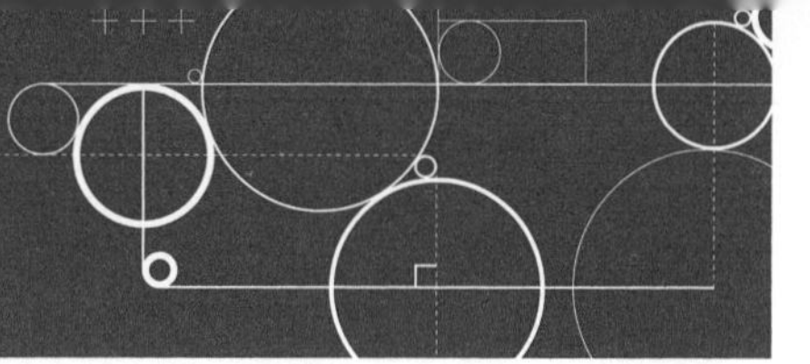

Impress makes it easy to preview and rehearse your slideshow. You can also modify the settings that control the slideshow to make it run as you prefer.

By default, Impress slideshows are set to advance through the slides manually — one slide each time you click the mouse or press the spacebar. You can, however, modify this extensively. You can make shows run automatically, or you can manually advance by element, rather than by full pages. Some people prefer the slideshow to move through the slides at set intervals. The intervals can be the same for all slides, or they can be varied for each slide.

Slide timings can be set manually on the Slide Transition tab of the Tasks pane, or you can preview the slideshow and create the timings automatically by clicking as you watch the slideshow on your screen. The latter method works very well when you are trying to synchronize with a soundtrack or against narration; it is also a very handy way to get a reality check on whether your presentation is moving at an appropriate pace. To access this feature, you use the Rehearse Timings option. As the show plays, click when you want it to advance, and Impress will save your timing automatically.

You can use the Slide Show settings dialog box to choose from a number of configuration options for your presentation. Adjust these settings to control slide and cursor visibility. You can also set the presentation to run automatically and to remain on top of other windows, allowing you to create self-running presentations such as those you would use at a display or a kiosk.

Rehearse Slideshow Timings and Change Show Settings

REHEARSE SLIDESHOW TIMINGS

1. Click Slide Show ➔ Rehearse Timings.

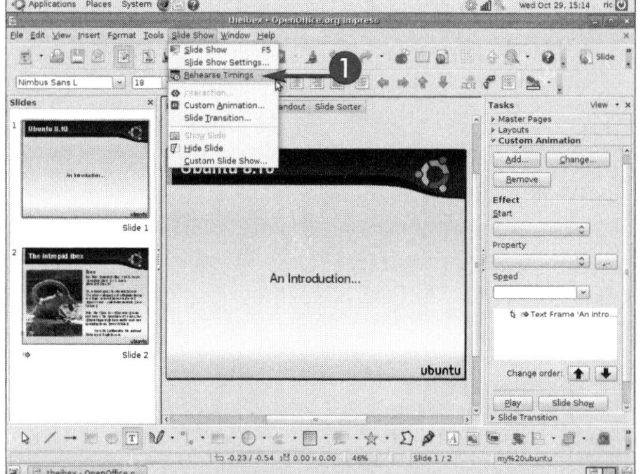

- The first slide appears, and the timer begins to run.

2. Click at the time interval that you want the presentation to advance to the next slide.

3. Keep clicking the timer box at the appropriate times to advance through the slides to the end.

   The timings are now saved by the system and will be used to control the slide sequence in the future.

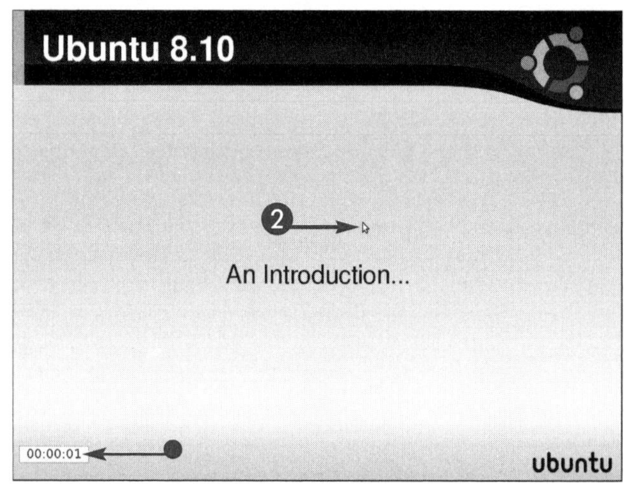

CHANGE THE SLIDESHOW SETTINGS

1. Click Slide Show ➔ Slide Show Settings.

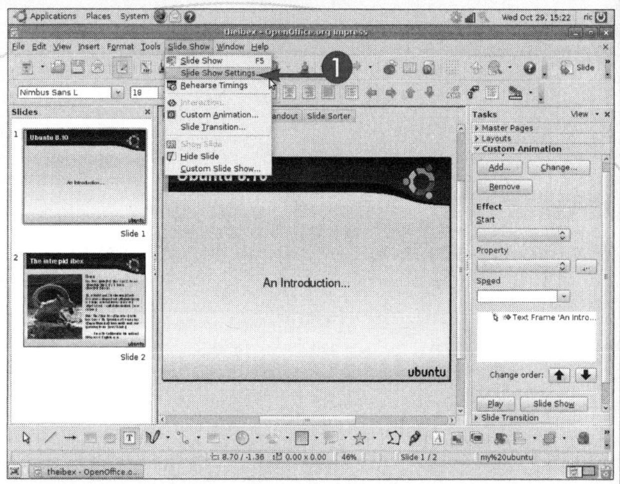

The Slide Show dialog box opens.

2. Click the options that you want, such as Mouse Pointer Visible if you want your cursor to show.
3. Click OK.

The Slide Show settings are saved.

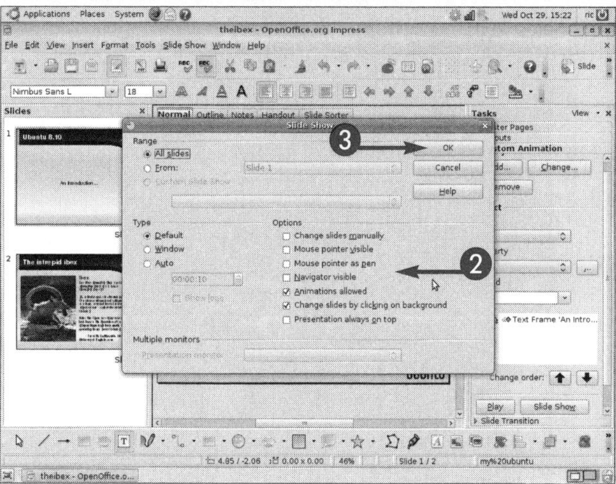

Extra

In some cases, you may want to control the order and timing of the appearance of the objects on individual slides. By default, all objects on a slide will appear at once. This is not always desirable: When all objects appear at once, viewers sometimes have trouble knowing where to focus, or they tune out the speaker while they read the whole slide. If you set up the objects to appear one at a time, you can control their visibility and thereby control to some extent the viewers.

Controlling object visibility is done on the Custom Animation tab of the Tasks pane. Custom animation effects are attached to a currently selected object in the workspace by clicking the Add button. The Effect Start setting allows you to determine the trigger for the appearance of an object. You can control the timing and the rate at which the object appears.

In the box below the Effect controls, you can order the objects to appear in whatever sequence you want. Right-click an object in this box and select Timing from the menu. The Timing tab in the Effect Options dialog box appears. On this tab, you can set an object's visibility on the screen according to timing or in sequence with other objects.

Run Your Slideshow

You can run your slideshow with the touch of a key or the click of a mouse. Once started, the presentation will advance according to your timing marks or your prompts.

At any time during construction or upon completion, you can trigger the display of your slideshow via several methods. The fastest way to start a show is to click the F5 key on your keyboard. Pressing F5 will begin the show immediately.

Another handy tool is the Slide Show button on the Slide Sorter toolbar. Clicking the Slide Show button has the same effect as pressing F5. Unfortunately, this toolbar is not displayed by default. It only shows when you are viewing the Slide Sorter tab in the workspace. Alternatively, you can turn the toolbar on so that it is always visible. To enable the toolbar, click View → Toolbars → Slide Sorter. A third option is to select the Slide Show option on the Slide Show menu. This is a bit slower, but it does the job. Note that in all three cases, the slideshow begins with the slide that is active in the workspace. If you want to start the show from the beginning, you should select the first slide.

Once the show begins, the slides and objects will advance as you have ordered them. If you have set automatic timing, the show will progress on its own. If you have chosen manual advance, you will need to take action to move through the show. To advance the show, either click the mouse, press the spacebar, or use the arrow keys to move forward and backward.

To stop the show at any time, press the Esc key.

Run Your Slideshow

1. Click Slide Show → Slide Show.

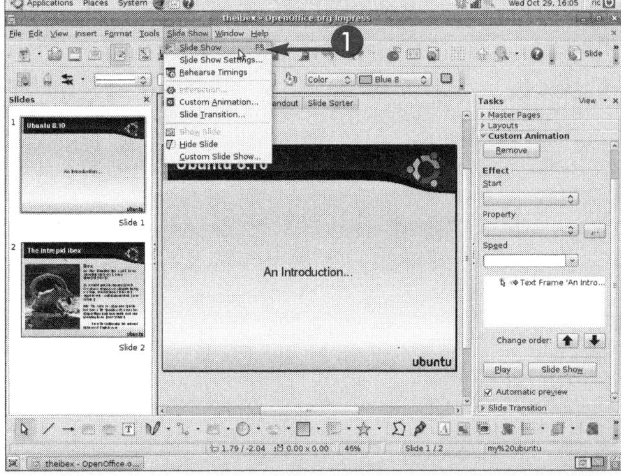

The first slide of the presentation appears.

2. Click the screen.

- If there are any custom animations, they will appear. In this example, the body text from the first slide transitions in via a fade effect.

3 Click the screen.

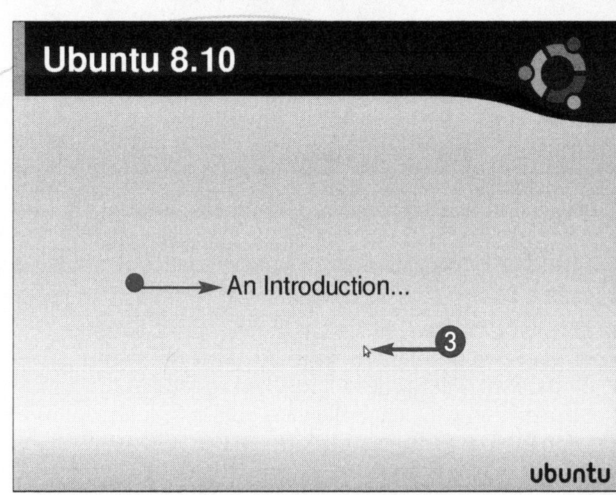

The second slide appears.

4 Click the screen.

5 Keep clicking until you reach the last slide.

Clicking the final slide ends the presentation.

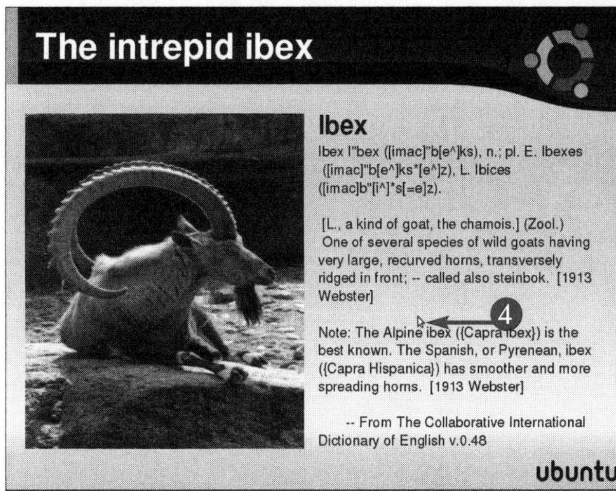

Extra

You can use the Custom Slide Show option to create variations on your slideshow and save them for reuse.

To create a new custom slideshow, click Slide Show ➔ Custom Slide Show. Click the New button. First, give your new custom slideshow a name and then select the slides from the list on the left pane of the dialog box, below the name box. Move the slides to the right pane in whatever order you want them appear in your new show. When you are ready, click OK.

Your new custom slideshow will now be available in the Custom Slide Show window. To play a custom slideshow, you must first click the slide where you want to show to begin. With the starting slide highlighted, click Slide Show ➔ Custom Slide Show. Click once on your custom slideshow, check the box Use Custom Slideshow, and then click the Start button.

Your custom slideshow will now play. It will be controlled by the settings you gave to the original presentation.

Print Slides, Notes, and Handouts

You can print slides, presentations, notes, and handouts with Impress. The application allows you to print all or only part of the presentation and related materials.

Impress gives you two ways to print: a quick print button and the Print option on the File menu. To perform a quick print, click the Print File Directly button on the toolbar. The Print dialog box will open, allowing you to set the configuration of your print job. Clicking File ➔ Print also opens the Print dialog box.

In the Print dialog box, you can select the printer and set the print range. You can print all of a presentation or just certain slides. You can also set the number of copies, which is useful if you plan to pass out your presentation as handouts to your viewers.

You can open the Printer Options dialog box from the Print dialog box, which includes some significant additional features. The Printer Options dialog box allows you to control the printing of the notes for the slides and the handouts. Also on this dialog box are options to help you control the use of ink and paper when you print your presentation. Choosing the Fit to Page option will scale your presentation to make sure that it fits well on the paper size.

Note that after you have sent a job to the printer, you can manage the job using the Manage Print Jobs application discussed in Chapter 6.

Print Slides, Notes, and Handouts

1. Click the Print File Directly button.

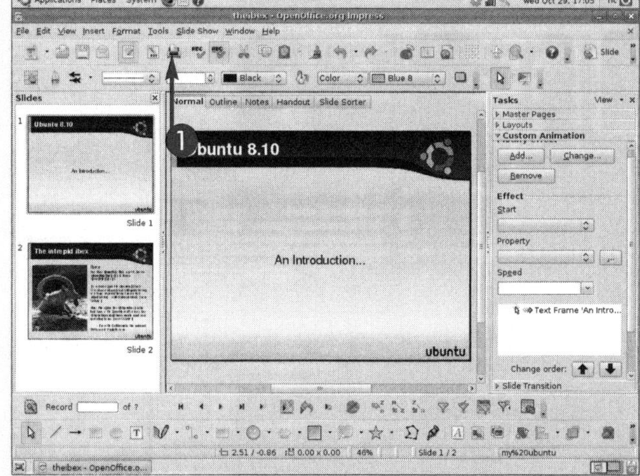

The Print dialog box opens.

2. Click Options.

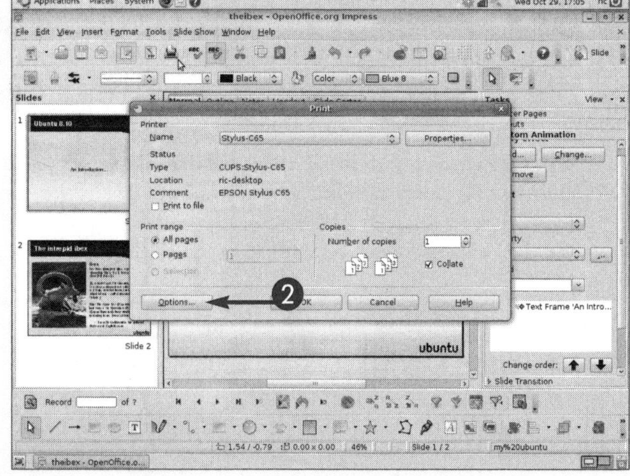

The Printer Options dialog box opens.

3. Click Handouts.
4. Click Notes.
5. Click Fit to Page.
6. Click the ink quality that you want.
7. Click OK.

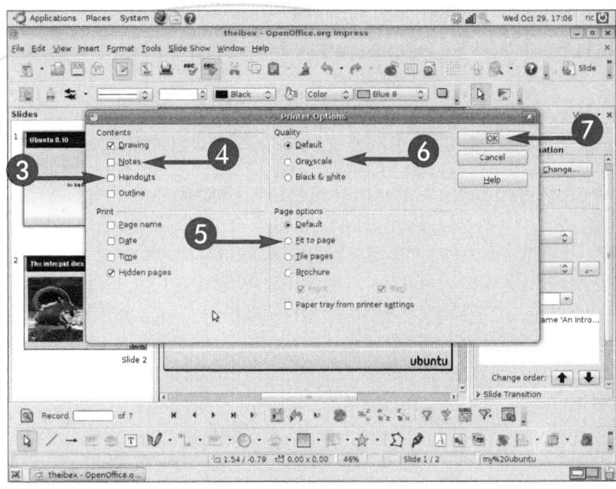

You are returned to the Print dialog box.

- You can click Properties to change the paper and printer settings.

8. Click OK.

The document prints.

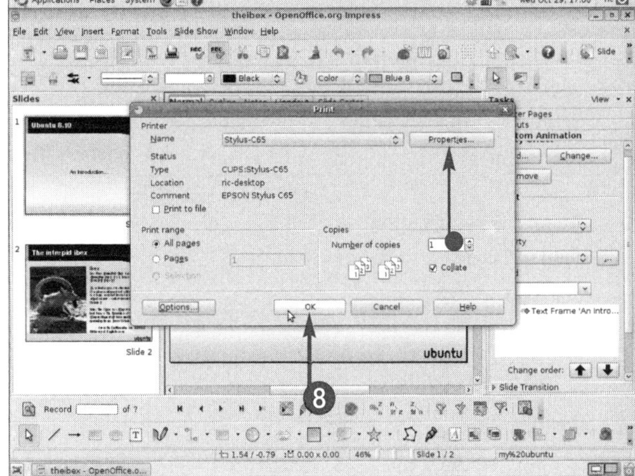

Extra

With Impress, you can publish your presentation as a set of simple Web pages via the HTML Export feature, which you can access by clicking File ➔ Export and choosing the HTML option in the dialog box. This enables you to generate a set of pages, each with its own navigation buttons, to traverse through your slides. Also, the default HTML Export feature includes an overview set of links to jump to any given slide. The output is fairly configurable with options during the Export Wizard that allow you to pick the resolution, image file type, and even any transition sounds that you have selected. You are also presented with several button styles for the navigational links in the Web output.

Although HTML export is probably the most useful, the Export dialog box also enables you to export your presentation in various other formats, including PDF and even Flash. The PDF option is useful when you need to email the presentation to someone who does not have an office suite loaded on his or her machine or to avoid file type incompatibilities. The Flash option gives you the convenience of a single file that you can include in a Web page or other applications.

Create a Flowchart

Draw provides a number of tools that make it easy to create flowcharts and process diagrams. Using the preexisting flowchart elements, you can make simple or advanced charts in no time.

Draw includes a dedicated Flowcharts toolbar. Located off the bottom toolbar, the Flowcharts toolbar includes all the common shapes used to define flowchart elements. You can place flowchart elements anywhere in a document, and you can drag and resize them with your mouse. All flowchart elements are ready for text labels. You do not need to use the separate Text tool to add text to a flowchart element; you can do so right on the element as shown below.

You can change the color of flowchart elements using the color controls on the toolbar immediately above the document window. Click the element and then select the color that you want. Draw will immediately update the element's color to reflect your choice.

Draw includes a Connectors toolbar, which you can use to join together the flowchart elements with linkages that show the sequence clearly. The Connector toolbar is also located off the bottom toolbar and is easily recognized from the shape on the button.

If you want to add additional annotations to your flowchart or label your lines, you can use the Text tool. The Text tool is located on the bottom toolbar and is identifiable by the capital *T* that is on the button. Click the Text tool and then click where you want the text to appear in the document and begin typing. You can set the font, size, and color of your text labels by using the text controls on the Formatting toolbar, located immediately above the document window.

Create a Flowchart

1. Click Applications ➔ Graphics ➔ OpenOffice.org Drawing.
   - The application opens and displays a blank document.
2. Click the Flowcharts button.

   The Flowcharts toolbar opens.
3. Click the shape that you want.
4. Click and drag in the document to create the shape.
5. Repeat steps **2** to **4** to create as many shapes as you need.

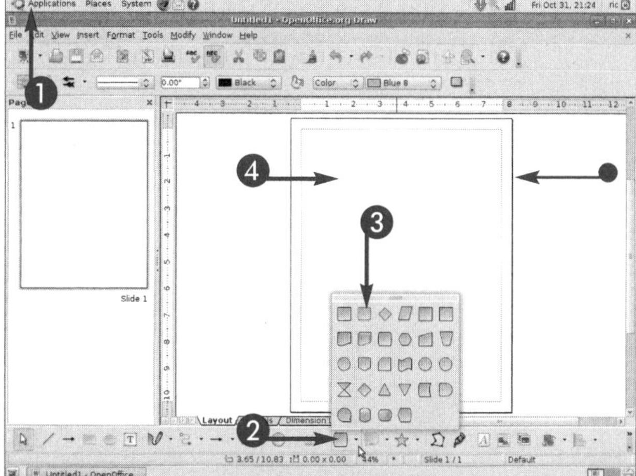

   The shapes appear on the screen.
6. Double-click inside a shape.
7. Type the text that you want for that shape in the course of your flowchart.

   The text appears inside the shape.

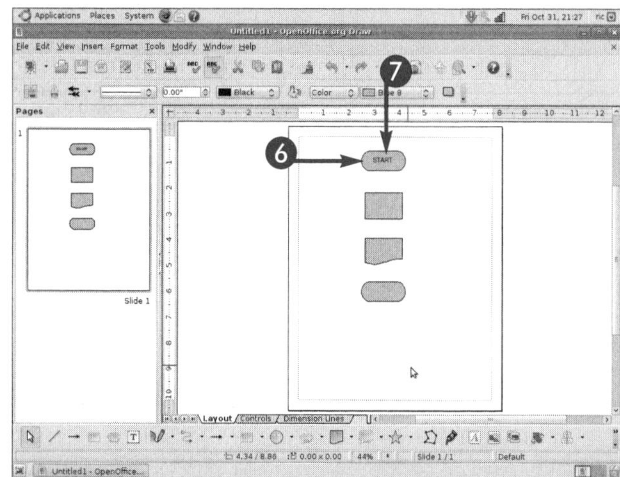

8 Click the Connectors button.

The Connectors toolbar appears.

9 Click the connector that you want.

Note: *For a flowchart, you usually want a connector that ends with an arrow.*

10 Click the shape and drag to connect the arrow to the next shape in your flowchart.

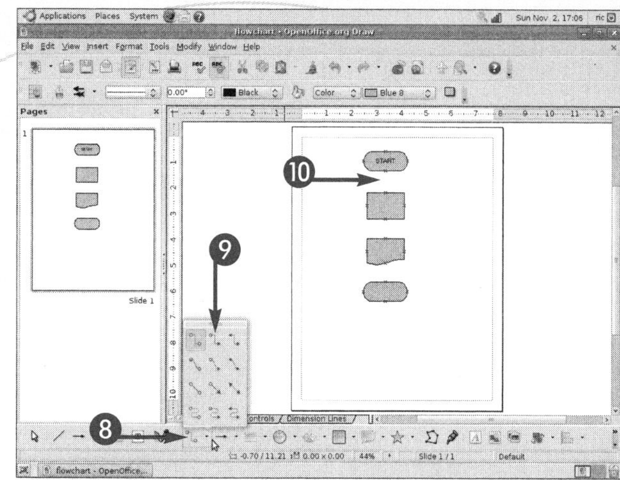

- The connector appears.

11 Repeat steps **6** to **10** for all the shapes in your flowchart.

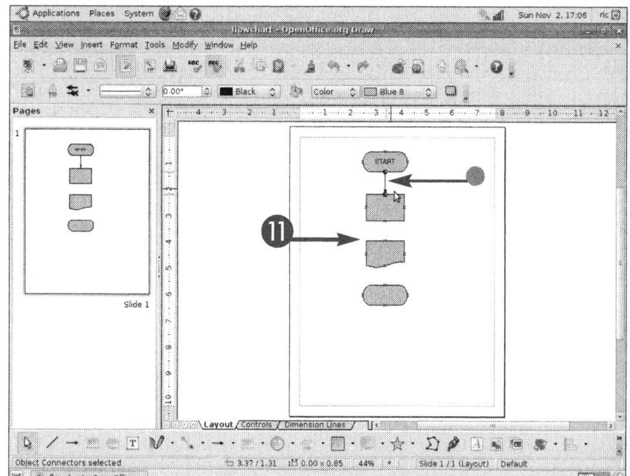

Extra

Draw offers a grid and guides that can help you place and align items. The grid is particularly useful when working with items such as flowcharts. You can enable the grid by clicking View ➔ Grid ➔ Display Grid. The grid appears on the screen as a series of points.

Guides, in contrast, are vertical or horizontal lines that appear in relation to the object. The guides move as you move the object, giving you a point of visual reference relative to the object you are moving. You can enable the guides by clicking View ➔ Guides ➔ Display Guides. Note that guides are also referred to in the OpenOffice system as *snap lines*.

Making the grid and the guides viewable takes some of the uncertainty out of placing items on the screen. If you want to have more help, select the option to "snap" to the grid or the guides. Turning on the snap option will automatically place items exactly on the points or the guides.

You can configure your grid appearance and spacing. To configure your grid, click Tools ➔ Options ➔ OpenOffice.org Appearance.

Create New Shapes

Draw enables you to create new shapes either automatically or manually. The Drawing toolbar, at the bottom of the screen, includes a variety of options for automatically creating shapes, including the Basic Shapes toolbar.

The options you see on the Drawing toolbar are designed to provide you with a number of choices for the easy creation of new shapes. From the left, there are two line-related tools: the Line tool and the Line with Arrow tool. Next on the toolbar are two shape tools: the Rectangle and Ellipse tools. After the Text tool there is the Curves tool, which allows for the creation of curved lines and shapes based on multiple points that you define. After the Connectors tool is the Lines and Arrows tool, which provides greater functionality than the Line with Arrow tool.

Next on the Drawing toolbar comes the most important group of shape tools: the Basic Shapes tool, the Symbol Shapes tool, the Block Arrows tool, the Flowcharts tool, the Callouts tool, and the Stars tool. All of these open toolbars that provide for the automatic creation of basic shapes. You use them all in the same fashion: Click the button to open the toolbar, click the shape, and then click in your document and drag your mouse cursor to create the shape.

If you want to create shapes freehand, the Curves toolbar is your most important tool. Select one of the polygon tools on the Curves toolbar, and you can describe a shape with points, which are then connected with lines and filled.

Once created, shapes can be resized by grabbing the object's handles and dragging them.

Colors for all shapes can be controlled from the color tools on the toolbar above the document window.

Create New Shapes

DRAW A SHAPE

1. Click the button for the type of shape you want to draw.

   In this example, the Block Arrows toolbar is opened.

2. Click the shape that you want, such as the 4-Way Arrow shown here.

3. Click in the document and drag the mouse pointer to form the shape.

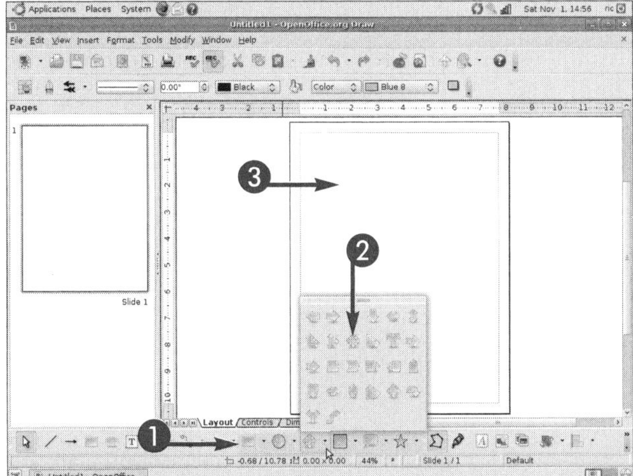

The shape appears in the document.

ADD COLOR TO A SHAPE

4. Click here and select the color option that you want, such as Gradient.

5. Click here and select a color.

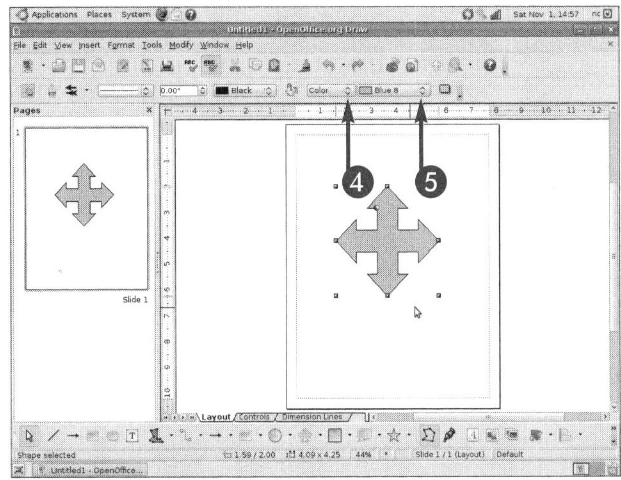

The figure's fill is changed.

DRAW A POLYGON

6 Click the Curves button.

The Curves toolbar opens.

7 Click the polygon button that you want.

Note: *The polygon choices are Polygon, Filled; Polygon 45°, Filled; Polygon; and Polygon 45°.*

8 Click in the document.

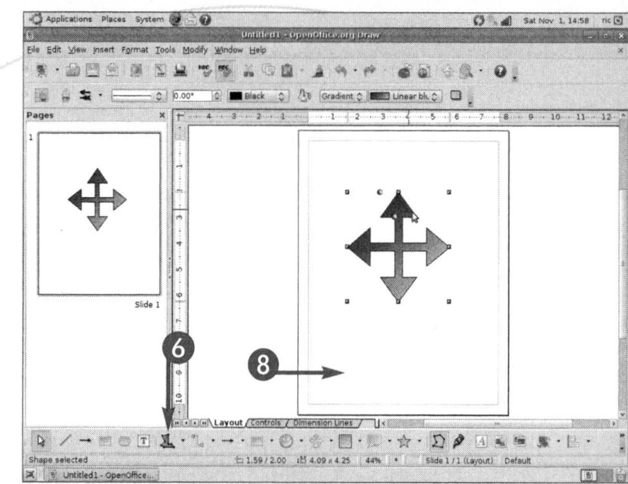

9 Draw the figure.

Note: *This example shows the Polygon 45°, Filled shape.*

- The Edit Points toolbar becomes visible, which you can use to move, insert, or delete points on the edges of the polygon.

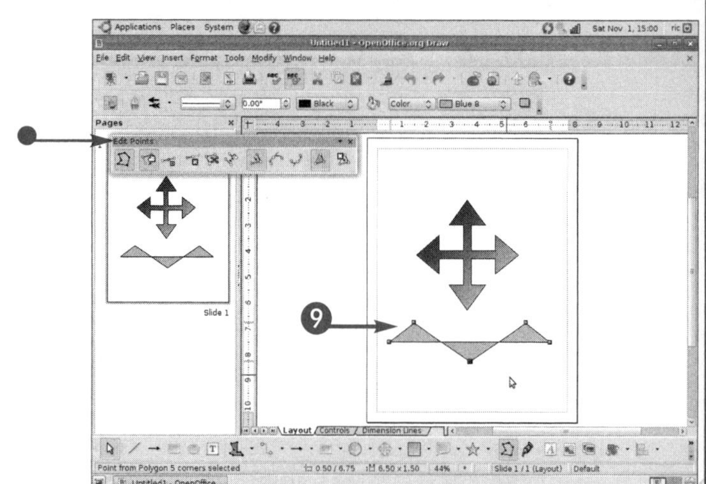

Apply It

You can use the right-click menu to add some visually interesting formatting for your shapes. First, right-click the shape to view this menu. Click Line and the Line dialog box opens. This dialog box not only controls the formatting of lines but also the borders of polygons and circles. Select a style and a color and set the width; then click OK to see the results on your object.

Click the Area option on the right-click menu. In the Area dialog box, you can set the fill for your object, and from the additional tabs, you can configure your fill as you want. Select the Shadow tab and click Use Shadow. Next, click the Transparency tab and click Transparency. Set the Transparency for 80% and then click OK. Your object now has a new fill color, a drop shadow, and is partially transparent.

Finally, click the Position and Size option on the right-click menu. Change the width of the object and then click the Rotation tab. For the Rotation Angle option, set 45 degrees and then click OK. Your object is now wider and has been rotated to the right by 45 degrees.

Change Glue Points on a Shape

You can create or modify connectors on an object by changing the object's glue points. Placing glue points is the way to control where connectors appear on shapes.

Connectors are lines that are used to visually tie one object to another. If you want to join together objects — for example, as part of a flowchart — you will probably use connectors. Connectors join objects at spots on the objects' shape known as *glue points.* The combination of glue points and connectors is very useful as the connections will remain, even if you move or reshape the objects.

By default, Draw objects include four glue points. The default glue points are positioned on the object's top, bottom, left, and right sides.

There is a dedicated Gluepoints toolbar that allows you to add or modify an object's glue points. To use the toolbar, follow the steps below. Alternatively, you can make the toolbar active by clicking View ➔ Toolbars ➔ Gluepoints.

The Gluepoints toolbar contains tools for creating and editing your glue points. You can add a new glue point as shown in the steps below. You can add as many glue points as you want to an object, and although the default glue points are on the object's edge, you can place new glue points wherever you want to, including inside the object.

Change Glue Points on a Shape

1. Click the shape to select it.
2. Click the Connectors button.

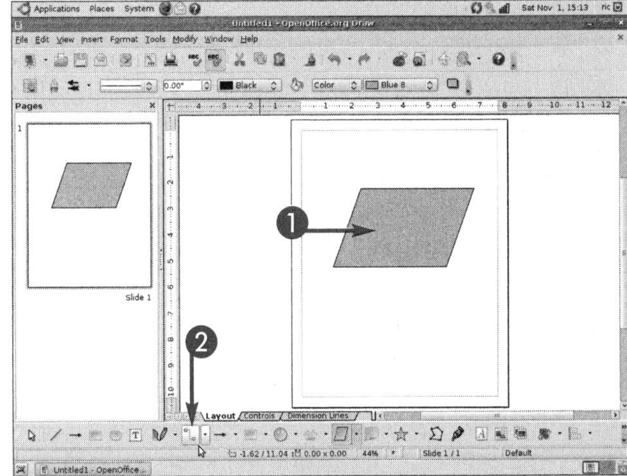

- The object's glue points become visible.

3. Click the Gluepoints button.

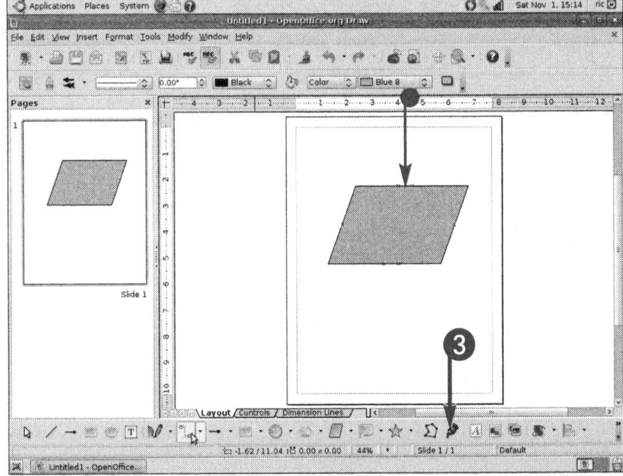

- The Gluepoints toolbar appears.

4. Click the New Gluepoint button.

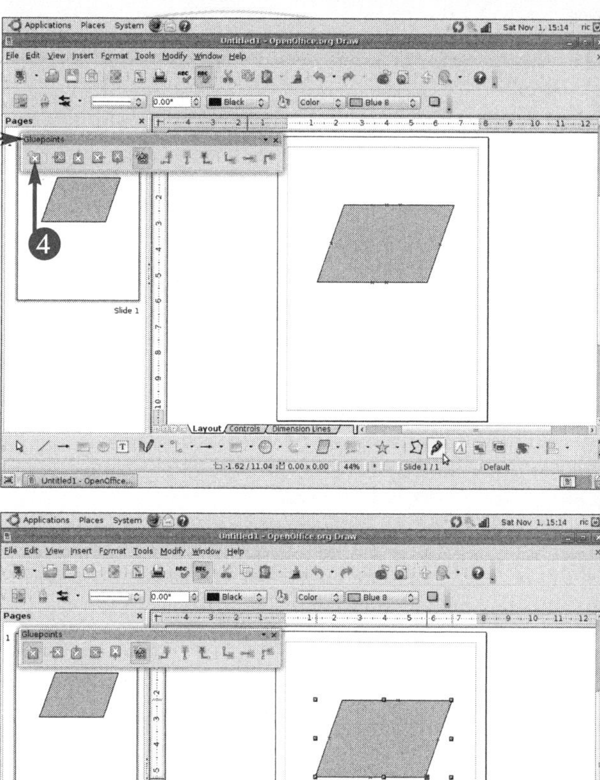

5. Click the shape where you want to place the glue point.

   A new glue point is now available on the shape.

Extra

The Gluepoints toolbar has several additional options with which you should be familiar. Immediately to the right of the New Gluepoint button are four buttons with related functions. Use these buttons to force connections to your object to attach only to the designated points. For example, if you want all connections to your object to be from the bottom of the object, select the Exit Direction Bottom button ( ).

The remaining seven buttons are related to each other. The first of the seven, Gluepoint Relative ( ), makes the placement of your glue points relative to the shape of the object. In other words, if you select this button and resize the object, the position of the glue points will move relative to the shape of the object.

Deactivating the Gluepoint Relative button makes the other six buttons on the Gluepoints toolbar active. The remaining six buttons allow you to fix points inside the shape. By using these options, the glue points do not move, even when the size or shape of the object changes.

For most situations, you will want the Gluepoints Relative button selected, as it reduces complications when you are editing objects.

Align Shapes

The alignment of objects is one of the keys to creating clear and logical charts and illustrations. For flowcharts in particular, the steps in the sequence need to be logically connected to each other, and the visual ordering of those elements is important to maintaining the structure in a meaningful manner. The alignment tools in Draw enable you to modify alignments easily and with certainty.

The alignment tools can be accessed in three different ways. First, on the far-right side of the bottom Drawing toolbar is the Alignment button, which opens the Alignment toolbar. You can control the alignment of items as a group using this tool. The key to using this tool successfully is to select all the items that you want to align and modify them as a group.

Alternatively, you can select a group of objects and then right-click the group. From the right-click menu, choose the Alignment option and select the appropriate action.

You can also use the Alignment option that exists on the Modify menu. Again, you should select the items first and then choose the alignment option that you want to employ.

The alignment options include aligning the objects to the left, right, top, or bottom; for each of these choices, the alignment is based on the edge of the item that is located at the most extreme position in the chosen direction. You can also use alignment to center items. You can align along a center line, either vertically or horizontally.

Note that if you need to modify the spacing and alignment of individual items, you must select and move those items manually. The Alignment tools are for aligning multiple objects relative to each other.

Align Shapes

ALIGN OBJECTS VERTICALLY

1. Click and drag the mouse cursor to select the shapes that you want to align.
2. Click the Alignment button.

   The Alignment toolbar appears.
3. Click one of the top three buttons:

   Click to left-align vertically, to center, or to right-align.

- In this example, the shapes are center-aligned, vertically.

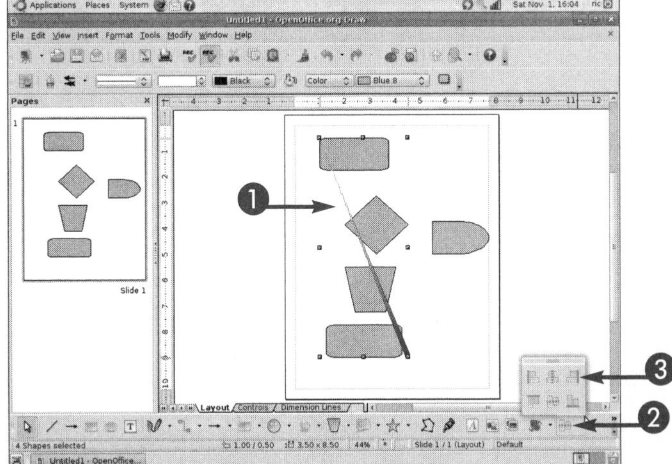

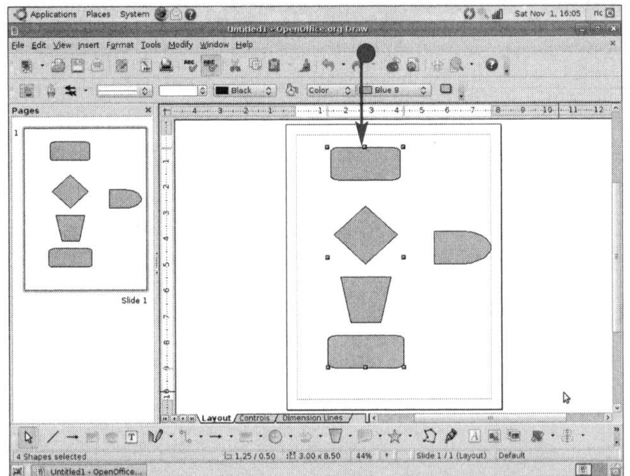

ALIGN OBJECTS HORIZONTALLY

1. Click and drag to select the shapes that you want to align.
2. Click the Alignment button.

   The Alignment toolbar appears.
3. Click one of the bottom three buttons:

   Click [icon] to top-align horizontally, [icon] to center, or [icon] to bottom-align.

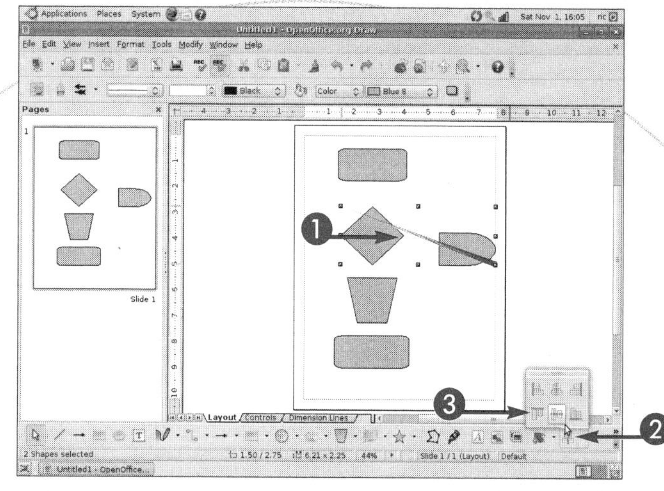

- In this example, the shapes are center-aligned, horizontally.

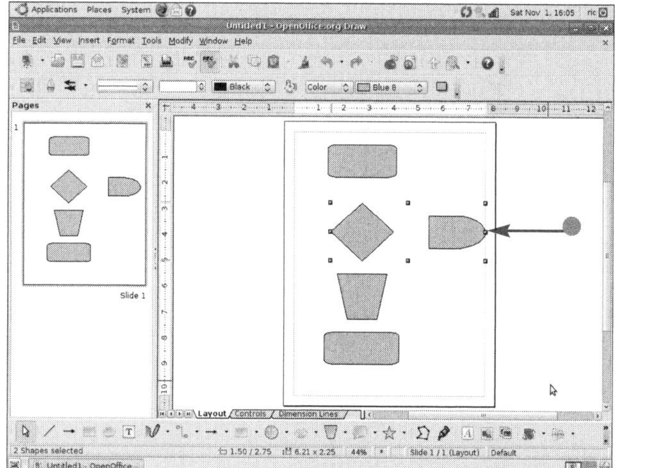

Extra

Just as you can change the alignment of shapes relative to each other, you can change the ordering of the shapes relative to each other. When we speak of ordering in Draw, we are talking about front-to-back ordering, that is, which objects appear in front of, and potentially obscure, other objects.

To set the ordering of an object, right-click the object and select the Arrange option. The Arrange submenu offers a number of choices, all related to moving the object forward or backward in the order of objects on the screen.

Select Bring to Front to move your object in front of all the others on the screen. Select Send to Back to move the object to the back of the order. If you want to move the object one step at a time, select either Bring Forward or Send Backwards. You may need to repeat this step if there are multiple objects on the page. Each time that you select the choice, it moves the object forward or backward one more step.

If you want to move multiple objects simultaneously, select the objects and then choose the Arrange option to move them as a group.

Insert Images

You can add pictures and other graphics files to your Draw documents. The images can be combined with the vector drawings that you create in Draw and can, to a limited extent, be manipulated from within Draw.

To insert an image, you start with the Picture submenu on the Insert menu. The Picture submenu gives you the choice to use either an existing image that is located on your hard drive or to scan in a new image. If you choose to insert an existing image, the Insert Picture dialog box opens, in which you can choose the image on your computer.

Alternatively, you can click the From File button on the bottom toolbar. It works in the same fashion, except that it immediately opens the Insert Picture dialog box.

Note that when the image appears in your document, there will be eight green-colored handles on it. The handles enable you to resize the image by clicking them and dragging the shape. When you move your cursor over a handle, it will change shape to indicate that the handle is active.

To move the image, click it and drag it to the new location on the screen.

Right-clicking an image presents alternative ways to modify the image. The Position and Size option opens a dialog box that enables you to set the image position on the page according to X and Y coordinates. You can also set the image's width and height. A separate tab enables you to rotate the image.

Insert Images

INSERT AN IMAGE

1. Click Insert ➔ Picture ➔ From File.

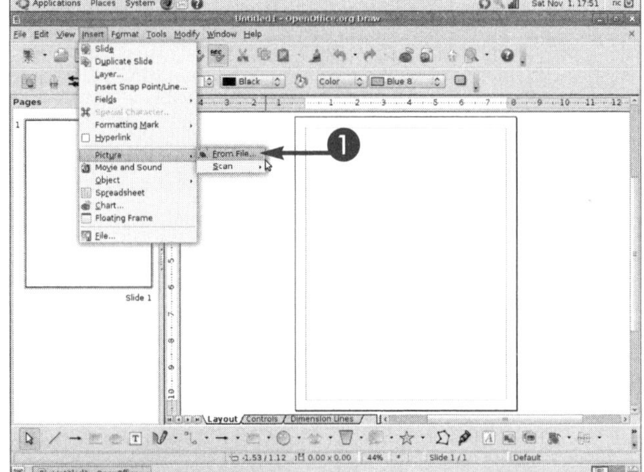

The Insert Picture dialog box opens.

2. Navigate to the folder containing the image that you want to insert.
3. Click the image filename.
4. Click Open.

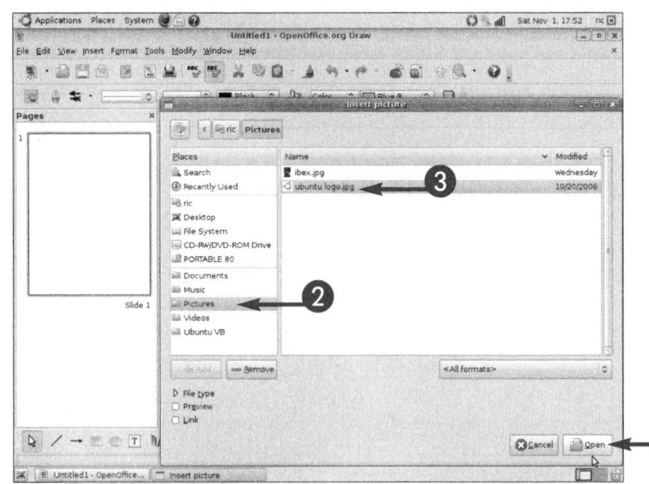

- The image appears in your document.

RESIZE THE IMAGE

5. Click the handles and drag out to increase the image size.

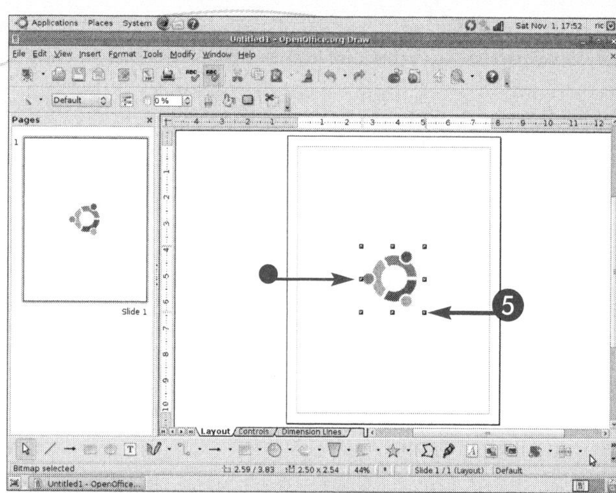

- The image is resized.

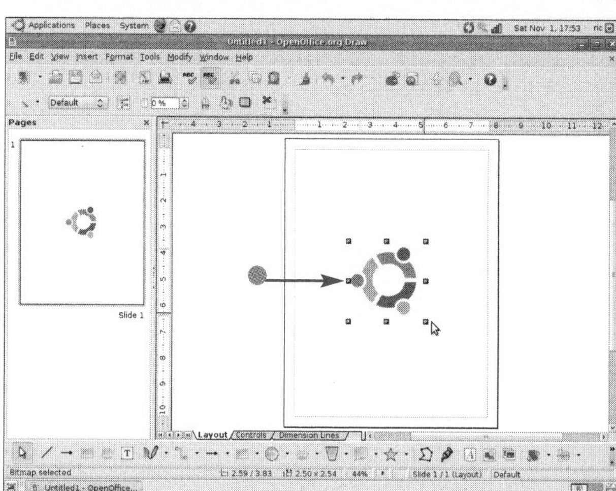

Extra

Not only can you insert images into Draw, but you can also export images created in Draw to a variety of other formats. Documents saved in the native OpenOffice format are usable only by other OpenOffice users. You can, however, export your documents to different formats.

Under the File menu are two options: Export and Export as PDF. The Export option opens a dialog box that offers you 12 different export formats, including the most popular ones: HTML, TIFF, GIF, JPG, PNG, EPS, and BMP.

Although you can also export to PDF from this menu, you will probably want to use the Export as PDF option instead. Selecting Export as PDF opens the PDF Options dialog box, which includes a number of configuration choices for customizing the output. If you are looking to export your document for a printer, you most likely want to export your document in PDF format, using the choices in the PDF Options dialog box to achieve the highest quality output.

Regardless of which format you select, if you need the document to remain editable, it must remain in OpenOffice format. None of the export formats allow you to edit the various individual objects or text fields in your file.

Create 3D Shapes

In addition to creating flat, two-dimensional shapes, Draw makes it possible to create three-dimensional shapes. With Draw, you can control the shape's textures, colors, and illumination to achieve a variety of realistic and striking effects.

3D shapes can be created in three different manners. Draw includes a set of default 3D objects that can be selected from the 3D Objects toolbar and added to a document. There are eight default shapes, including the most commonly used 3D shapes, such as cubes, cones, cylinders, and pyramids. You can see what default 3D objects are available by clicking View ➔ Toolbars ➔ 3D Objects.

There are two options for converting two-dimensional shapes that you have already created into 3D shapes. You can find these on the Convert submenu on the right-click menu. Two of its choices are To 3D and To 3D Rotation Object. The To 3D option to convert a shape to three-dimensional is the simplest; it gives your flat two-dimensional shape depth. The To 3D Rotation Object option takes your shape and renders it in a round format. This is most useful for creating unique 3D shapes, rather than simply adding perspective to a two-dimensional shape.

You can set 3D effects for your 3D shapes by using the 3D Effects dialog box, which has options for controlling the appearance of your object. The 3D Effects dialog box includes multiple tabs for controlling the texture of the shape, the angle of the illumination source, and the depth and shape of the perspective. Using the Effects tool on the Drawing toolbar, you can also select the option Rotation, which allows you to rotate your 3D shape on multiple axes.

Create 3D Shapes

1. Right-click the shape that you want to make 3D.
2. Click Convert ➔ To 3D.

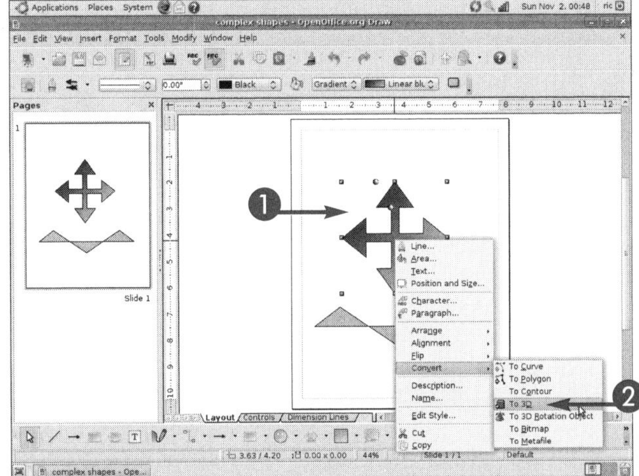

The 3D styling is applied to the object.

3. Right-click the shape again.
4. Click 3D Effects.

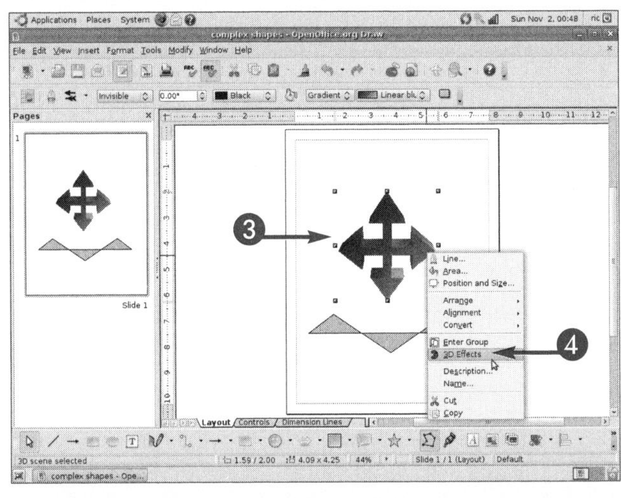

The 3D Effects dialog box appears.

5. Click here and set a percentage for Rounded Edges, such as **20%**.

6. Click here and set a percentage for Scaled Depth, such as **75%**.

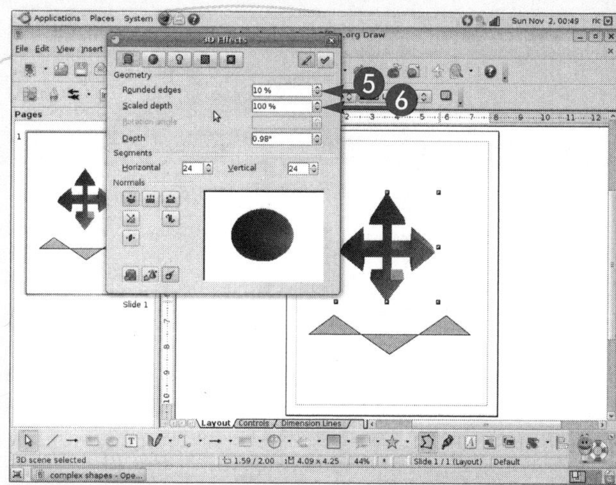

7. Click the Assign button.

- Your 3D effects are applied to the shape.

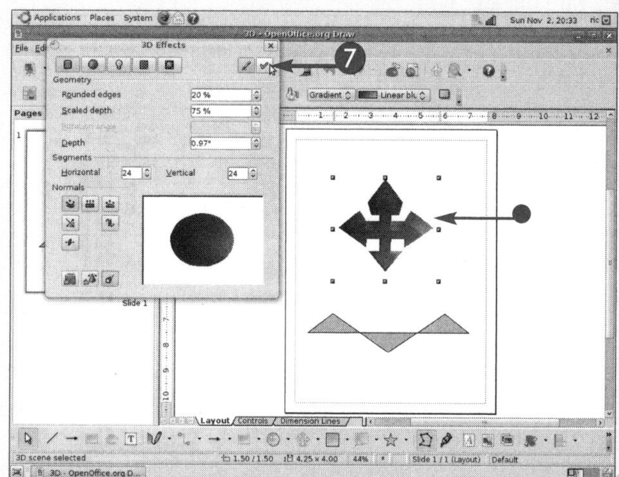

Extra

If you have multiple 3D objects in your document, you can control them all via what Draw refers to as a *3D scene*. A 3D scene is simply a collection of 3D objects that share similar 3D attributes. This is a way for grouping 3D shapes and editing them as a whole. This is particularly useful when you want to work with a common and consistent lighting source to add realism to a set of objects. You can also use this option when you want to combine several objects together to create one new object.

Also, you can convert multiple two-dimensional objects to 3D simultaneously — without grouping them. When you use this approach to create 3D objects, Draw applies differing depths to each object and keeps the objects arranged according to the arrangement order you assigned to the objects. Note that this approach to the conversion of two-dimensional objects gives a different result than you will get by grouping them and then converting the group. When you group objects and then convert, Draw treats the group as a single object.

Play a Music CD

You can use your computer to listen to audio CDs with the Rhythmbox Music Player application. In addition to the Rhythmbox software that is bundled with your Ubuntu desktop, you will need a CD drive, a sound card, and either a pair of speakers or headphones.

When you insert an audio CD into your CD tray, your system will prompt you for an action. The default action for an audio CD is Open Rhythmbox Music Player.

After you open the Rhythmbox Music Player, to see all the files on your CD, click the name of the CD in the column on the left side of the window. The song titles will appear in the main pane of the application. You can choose any song on the list to play, or you can play the whole CD.

As a song plays, you will see the status in a timeline above the main pane. You can drag the slider on the timeline to a specific point in the song if you want to. You can control the volume by clicking the speaker icon at the top right and then moving the slider control up and down to raise or lower the volume level.

Other buttons on the main toolbar let you repeat songs or shuffle the order of the songs on your CD. Clicking the Visualization button will fill the screen with an abstract decorative display that reacts to the audio file being played. The Eject button will cause the song to stop playing and the CD drive to open. The Extract button is for ripping songs, a topic that is discussed later in this chapter in the section "Rip a CD."

Play a Music CD

1. Insert the audio CD that you want to play into your CD drive.

   The Audio Disc dialog box appears.

Note: *By default, this dialog box will have Rhythmbox Music Player selected as the application to open the CD.*

2. Click OK.

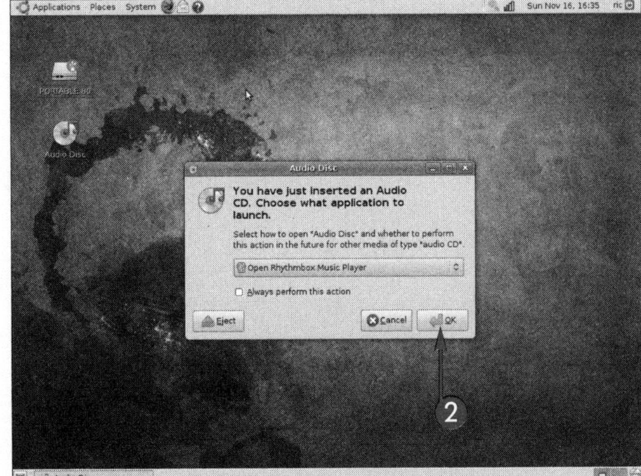

The Rhythmbox Music Player opens.

3. Click the name of the CD.

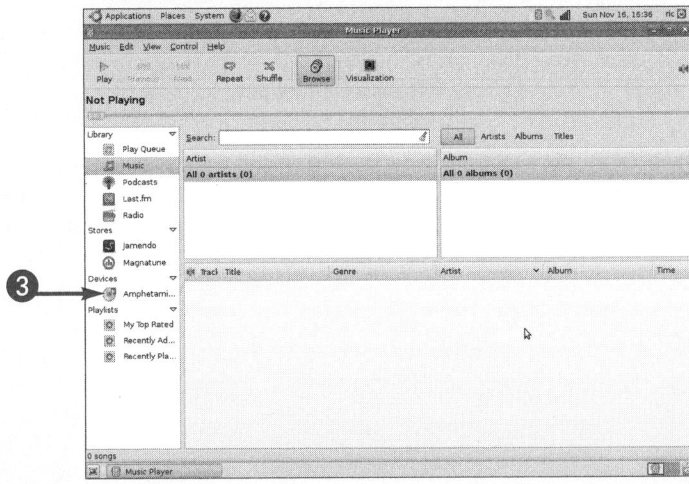

- The songs on the CD appear.

4. Click the first song name if you want to play the whole CD.

Note: *You can click a later song on the CD if you want to start the CD playing from that point.*

5. Click Play.

- The CD begins to play.

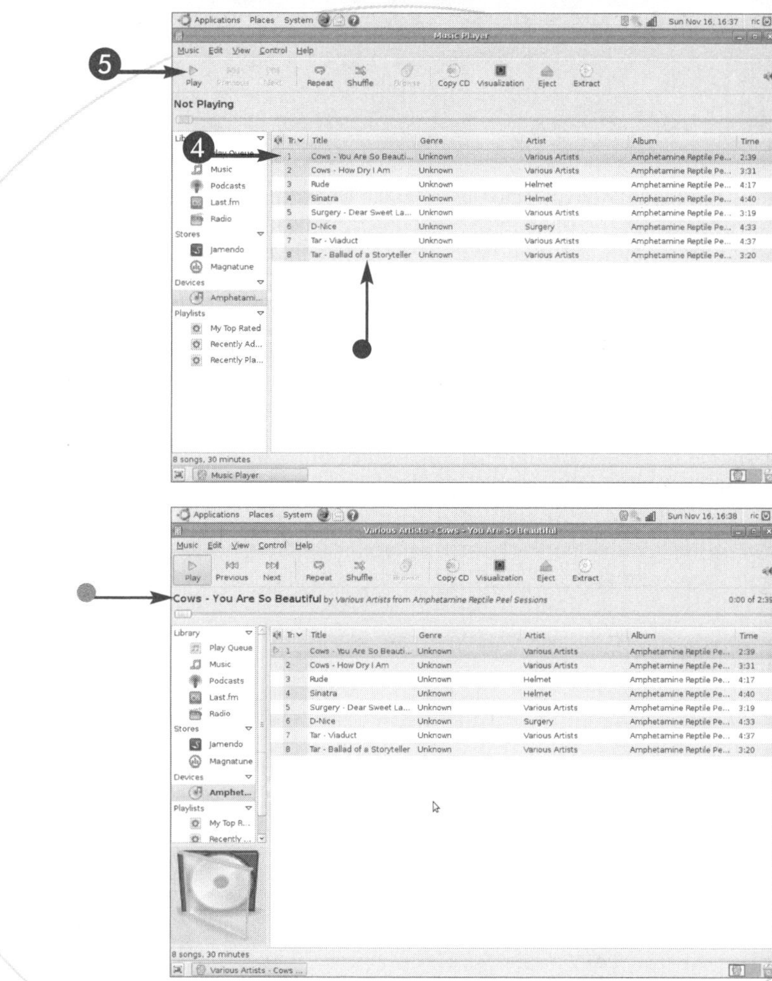

Extra

Rhythmbox is based on Apple's popular iTunes application and works in a similar fashion. Songs on your local hard drive are added to the Library, which you can then manage from within Rhythmbox. You can add songs to the Library by using the Import command on the File menu or by ripping tunes off an audio CD.

Music kept in the Library can be organized into playlists, which appear at the bottom of the left column of the main Rhythmbox Music Player window. You can add new playlists by right-clicking in the Playlists area and selecting New Playlist from the right-click menu. You can name the playlist by typing a name in the window by the icon. After a playlist is created, you can drag songs into it to build your collection.

Information on the songs in your Library can be edited by right-clicking a song title and selecting the Properties option. You can specify a genre or provide ratings for songs to help keep your collection organized. Note also that the songs in your Library or the playlist can be sorted by clicking the column headings in the main pane.

Play a Video

You can play video and movies on your Ubuntu system using the built-in Movie Player application. The player bundled with your Ubuntu installation is the Totem Movie Player that is included as part of the GNOME desktop; it can play music or video and supports both CDs and DVDs.

When you open the Totem Movie Player, if you are connected to the Internet, the application will try to download a list of available content for viewing. The default source of the online information is the BBC. The list of available videos will appear in the sidebar to the right of the main pane.

If you want to play a video file located on your computer, open it in the Totem Movie Player. The movie will play in the main pane of the application. You can pause, go forward, or go backward by clicking the controls under the main pane. The slider control marked Time enables you to move through a video by clicking and dragging the slider. You can adjust the volume by clicking the speaker icon under the main pane. You can hide or display the right sidebar by clicking the Sidebar button next to the speaker icon.

If you would like to view the video in full-screen mode, you can use the Full Screen option on the View menu or press F11 at any time. Note that the View menu also contains controls that enable you to manage other attributes, such as the aspect ratio and subtitles.

Play a Video

1. Click Applications ➔ Sound & Video ➔ Movie Player.

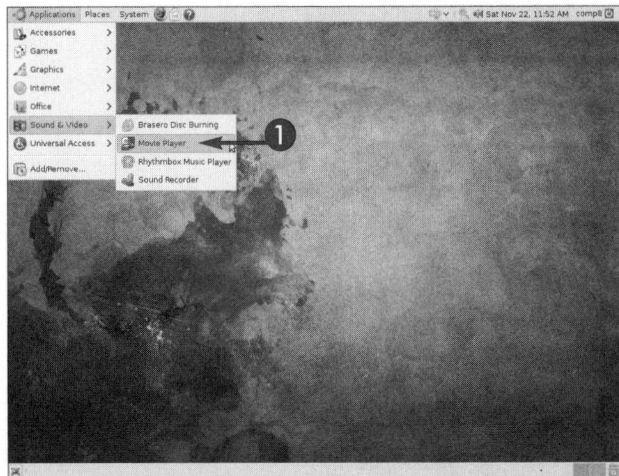

The Totem Movie Player opens.

2. Click Movie ➔ Open.

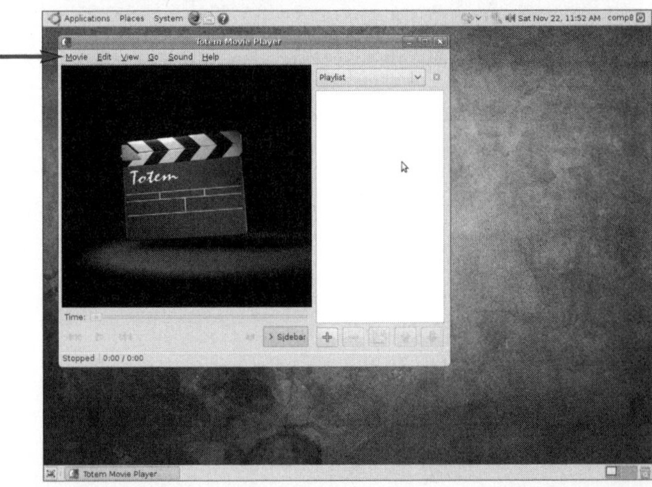

The Select Movies or Playlists dialog box opens.

3. Navigate to the folder containing the video that you want to watch.
4. Click the video filename.
5. Click Add.

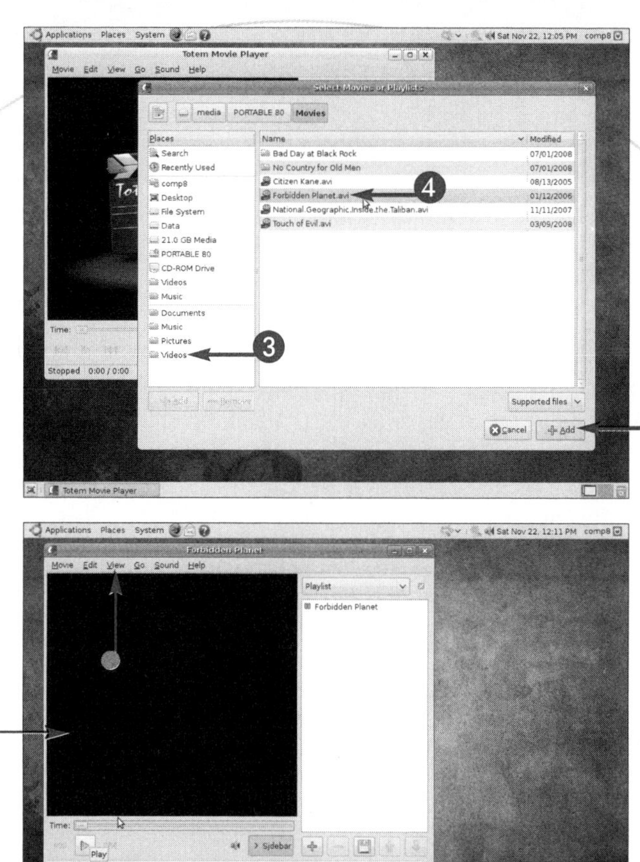

- The movie begins to play in the window.
- You can click View → Full Screen to view the movie full-screen.

Extra

Although the Movie Player can handle most of the common video file formats, you may encounter files that require the installation of additional software. Different digital video file formats require different codecs to decode them. If you try to open a file that is not supported by the default Movie Player, your system will advise you and prompt you to install additional codecs. The system will search locally and can also search the Internet to locate the proper codec.

After the proper codec is identified, the Movie Player will open the Install Media Plugins dialog box. Click to select the plug-ins on the list, and if the system prompts you for permission, click OK. The system may additionally prompt you to supply your administrator's password to install software. Type your password and click Authenticate. The Movie Player will handle the installation automatically from this point, and upon completion, the video file will begin to play.

Note that you will only need to go through this process the first time that you try to open a new format. The next time you open a file of that type, the codec you installed will already be in place.

Burn a CD

You can use the Brasero Disc Burning application to create audio and data CDs. Burning CDs is made easy by Brasero's easy-to-use interface and autodetection capabilities. The Brasero software supports writing CD, SVCD, and DVD format discs.

Note that burning a CD requires the right hardware. The CD drive installed on your computer must be capable of writing CDs. You will need either a CD-R(W) drive or a DVD-R(W) drive.

You can approach the burn process in either of two ways. Either you can start the Brasero application, select the files, and then burn the CD, or you can create a burn folder and make a CD from the contents of the folder. This section demonstrates both methods.

This section first looks at the burn process using the Brasero Disc Burning application. When you first open the Brasero Disc Burning application, the screen that appears prompt you to select the type of project that you want to create. You can select from the following types: Audio Project, Video Project, Data Project, Disc Copy, and Burn Image.

You identify the files that you want to burn in the New Project window and add them to your project. After you insert a disc, you can begin your burn.

The Burn dialog box lets you name the disc and set the disc properties.

Burn a CD

USING THE BRASERO DISC BURNING APPLICATION

1. Click Applications ➔ Sound & Video ➔ Brasero Disc Burning.

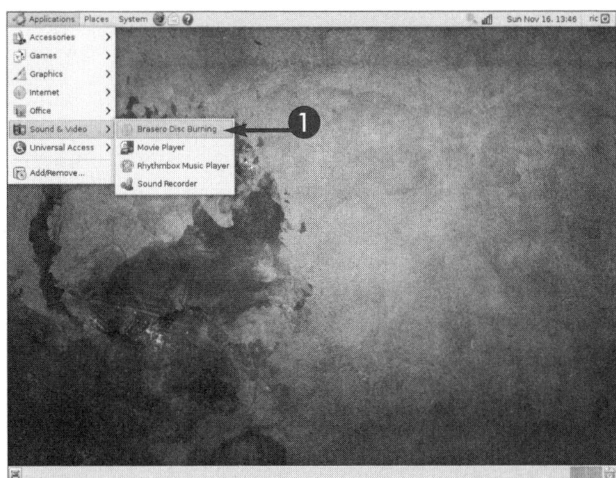

The Brasero start screen opens.

2. Click the type of CD that you want to burn.

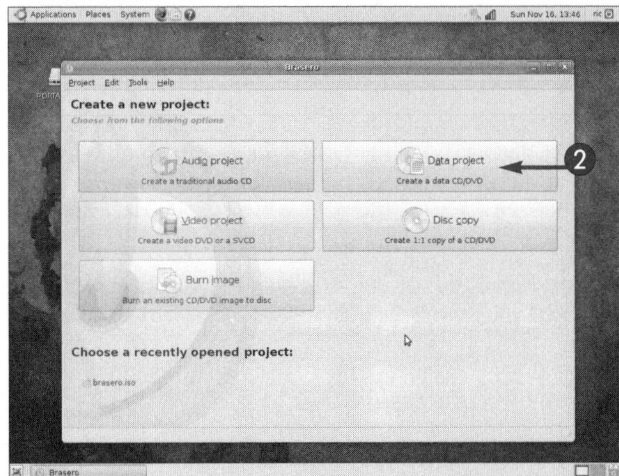

The New Project window opens.

3. Click the Media Size button and click the size of the media to burn.
4. Navigate to the folder containing the files that you want to burn to CD.
5. Click the filenames.
6. Click Add.

   The files will appear in the project window.
7. Insert a blank CD into your CD burner.
8. Click Burn.

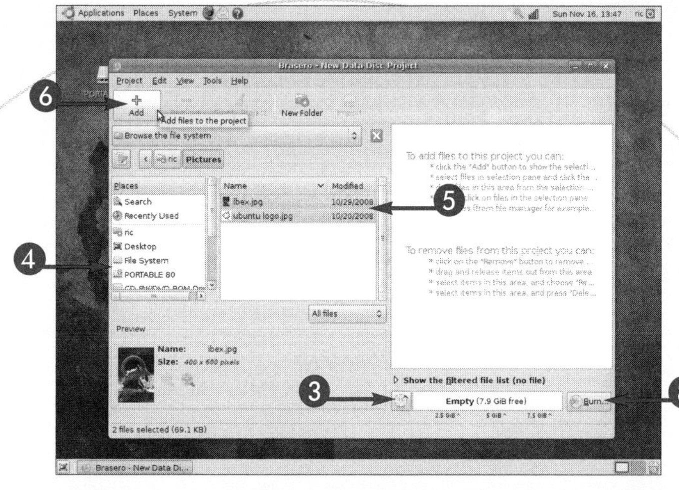

The Disc Burning Setup dialog box appears.

9. Type a name for the CD.
10. Click Burn.

    Brasero burns the files to the CD.

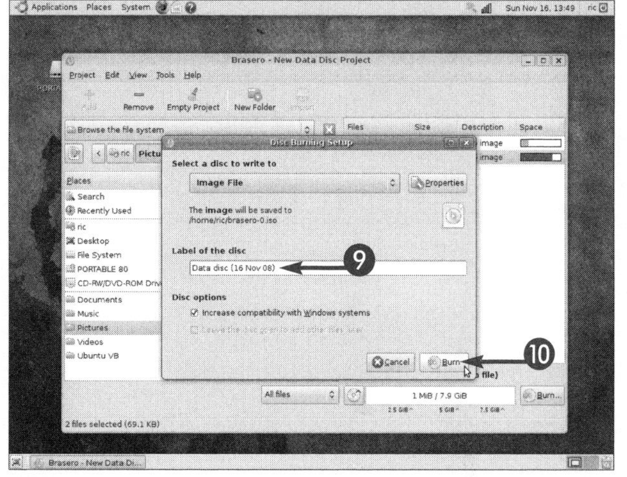

Extra

Brasero supports the CD, SVCD, and DVD formats. Although most people are familiar with CD and DVD, the SVCD format is not particularly well-known. SVCD stands for *Super Video CD,* and it falls somewhere between a normal video CD and a DVD in terms of quality and capacity.

The format is widely used in making karaoke CDs and other types of material in which you need to embed lyrics, interactive menus, text, or hyperlinks, while still maintaining some degree of quality. SVCD supports either two stereo audio channels or four mono channels.

You can fit about 800MB of data in SVCD format. At full quality, you can fit 35 minutes of video on a CD in SVCD format. If you push this format to its limits, you can fit about 100 minutes of video on a disc.

The quality of SVCD playback varies widely, unfortunately. Players that interpret strictly some of the agreed standards in playback will cause aliasing to result, thereby marring the playback quality.

Generally speaking, unless you have a compelling reason to choose this format, you are better off to record in another format, preferably DVD.

continued

Burn a CD (continued)

Burn folders are an alternative way of accumulating a collection of files to burn to a disc. This option is a useful way to create a disc quickly using the File Browser.

To use a burn folder, you open the CD/DVD Creator File Browser. This is essentially a folder into which you can drag files to burn to disc. The easiest way to use it is to maximize this window and then open a second File Browser window. You navigate in the second window, find the files that you want to copy, and then drag the files into the CD/DVD Creator File Browser window.

After you have gathered all the files that you want to burn, you open the Write to Disc dialog box. This dialog box is different than the Disc Burning Setup dialog box you see in Brasero, but it serves the same function. You select the drive in this dialog box and give the disc a name. The final option in the Write to Disc dialog box is Write Speed. Generally, you want to leave the selection to its default choice of Maximum Possible, but if you are having trouble getting your discs to write properly, you may want to choose a slower speed.

When all the settings are adjusted, you can start your CD burn. If all is in order, you will see the Writing Files to Disc dialog box, which shows you the progress as the system writes the data to the disc.

Burn a CD *(continued)*

USING A BURN FOLDER

1. Click Places ➔ CD/DVD Creator.

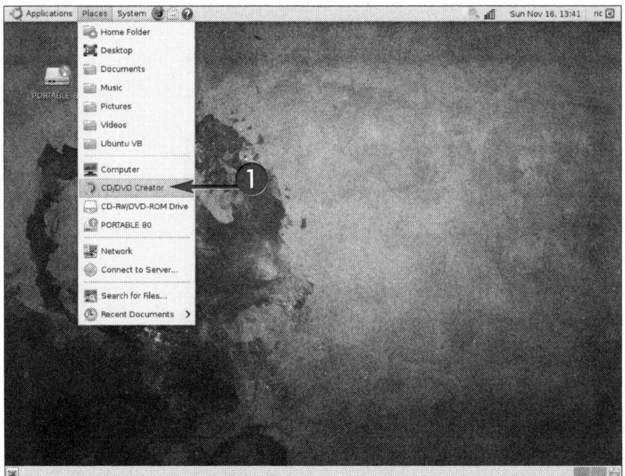

The CD/DVD Creator folder opens.

2. Click Places ➔ Home Folder.

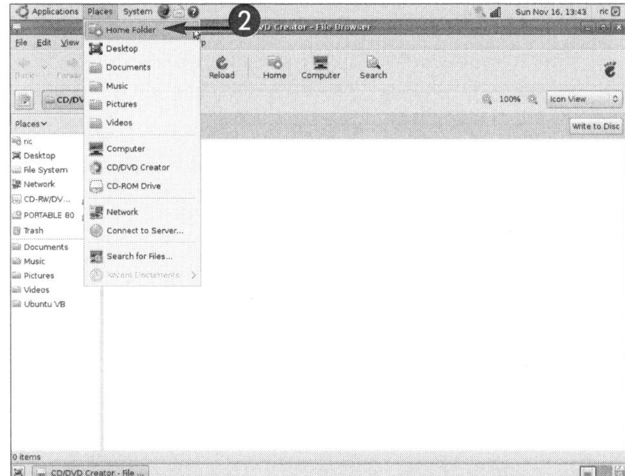

The File Browser window opens.

3. Navigate to the folder containing the files that you want to copy to the CD/DVD Creator folder.
4. Click and drag the files to the CD/DVD Creator folder.

   The files will be added to the project to be burned to disc.
5. Insert a blank CD into your CD burner.

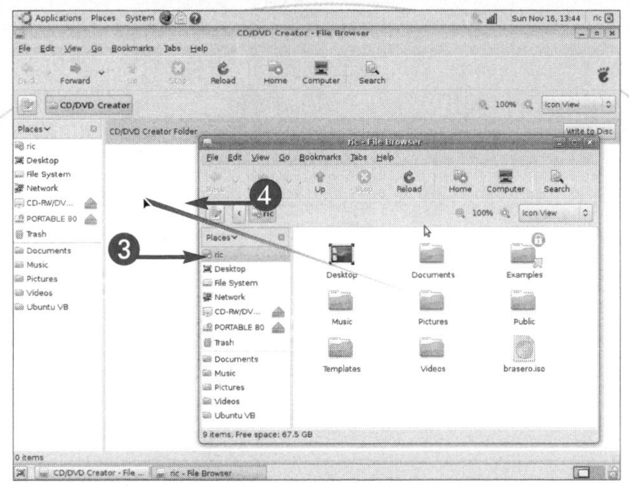

6. Click Write to Disc.

   The Write to Disc dialog box appears.
7. Verify the device to write the image to.
8. Type a name for the disc.
9. Click Write.

   The files are burnt to the CD.

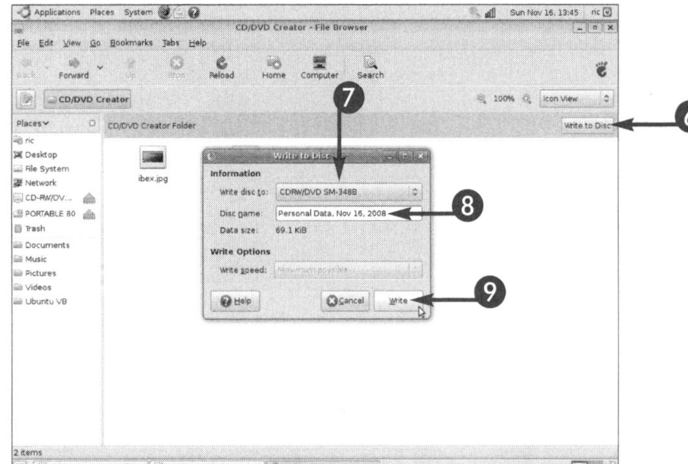

Extra

There are at least three ways to create an audio CD with your default Ubuntu system. First, you can use Brasero, selecting the Audio Project option from the first screen that appears. Second, you can create a burn folder, drag songs into the folder, and then burn the contents of the folder to a CD. The third method is to use the Rhythmbox Music Player. This method has a number of advantages, most particularly the fact that the burn process is based on the Playlists function in Rhythmbox, making it easy to turn your favorite playlist into a CD. Here's how it works:

Open Rhythmbox and create a new playlist. You can use a smart playlist or a static playlist. If you use a static playlist, drag the songs that you want into the playlist. When you are ready, right-click the name of the playlist and select Create Audio CD from the menu, or click the Burn button on the toolbar. Make sure that you have a disc inserted and then click the Create button in the Create Audio CD dialog box.

Rhythmbox will then write the songs on your playlist to the CD.

Rip a CD

You can copy audio files from a CD and keep the files on your hard drive. The process of copying files from a CD to your hard drive is called *ripping a CD,* and this process makes it possible for you to listen to audio files without having to insert the CD into your computer.

In Ubuntu, you rip audio files with the same application that you use to play audio files — the Rhythmbox Music Player.

When you have an audio CD in your CD drive, your CD track listing will show in the main Rhythmbox Music Player pane. Before you begin the ripping process, you can select to copy all or only part of the disc. To begin copying, you use the Extract button, which is only visible when a disc that can be copied is selected. When you click the button, ripping begins immediately. At the bottom right of the Rhythmbox Music Player window, you will see a status bar that displays the progress of the ripping process.

When the rip is completed, your music files will be available in the Music directory on your hard drive. Note that files will be saved in the .oga format.

Files ripped in this manner are automatically added to your music Library. To play files on your hard drive, either double-click the file, which will launch the Rhythmbox Music Player, or open Rhythmbox and play the files from the Library.

Rip a CD

1. Click Applications ➔ Sound & Video ➔ Rhythmbox Music Player.

   The Rhythmbox Music Player opens.

2. Insert a music CD into your CD drive.
3. Click the name of the CD.

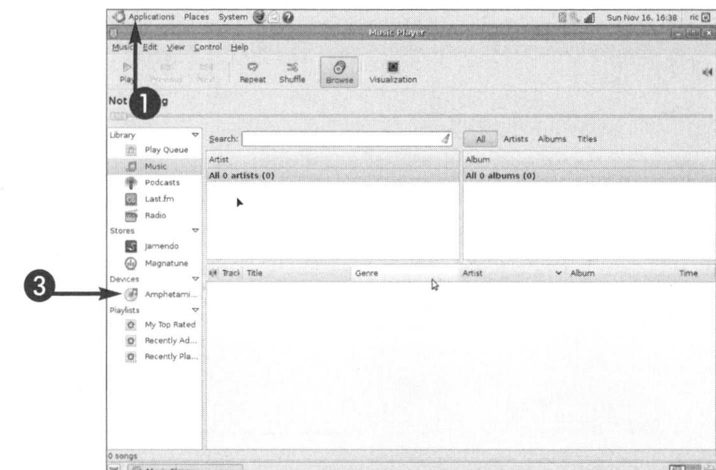

- The tracks on the CD appear.

4. Click Extract.

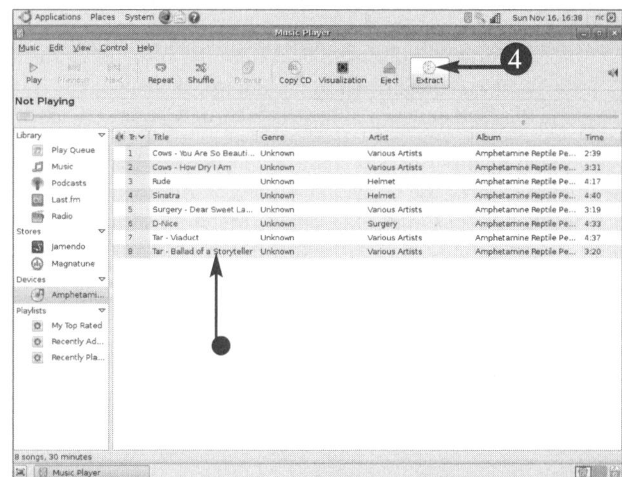

- The application begins to rip the songs and copy them to the Library.

  The status bar will close after it finishes ripping the final track.

5. Click Places ➔ Music.

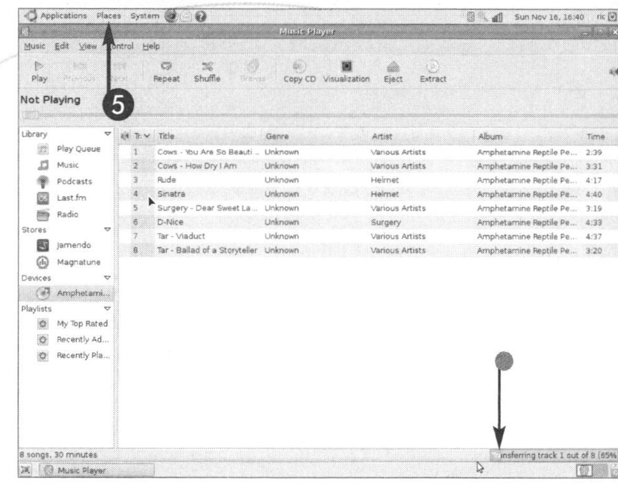

- The song files are automatically organized in your Library and grouped in directories according to the name of the artist.

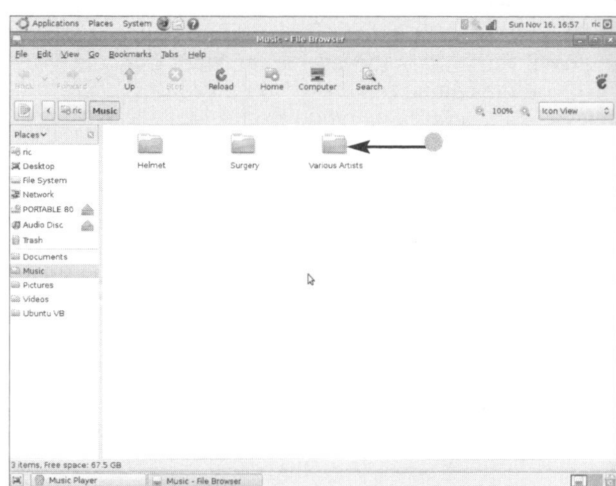

Extra

If you need more flexibility than what is offered by Rhythmbox or you simply want to explore alternatives, there are a number of other applications that can be used to extract audio from different types of media. To review the options, click Applications ➔ Add/Remove. When the Add/Remove Applications dialog box opens, click Sound & Video and then select All Open Source Applications from the Show drop-down list.

If you search for the word **rip** in the Search box, you will see that there are a large number of applications that extract audio from CDs and other media. Two of the most popular are Audio CD Extractor and Serpentine Audio CD Creator. Audio CD Extractor is simple and easy to use, but because it is a specialized tool for extracting audio, it tends to be more flexible than Rhythmbox. Serpentine, on the other hand, has a much more complete feature set and can also be used to extract audio from video files. Another popular application is Grip, which includes integration with the CDDB protocol, which helps you locate track information from an online database.

Record Sounds

With the Sound Recorder application, you can record sounds using a microphone and save them in a variety of formats. You can also use the Sound Recorder to play sound files in several formats.

The Sound Recorder interface is pretty basic, and the application is very easy to use. To record a sound, you click the Record button. To stop recording, you click the Stop button. To play back what you have just recorded, click the Play button. To create a new recording, click the New button, which will launch a second Sound Recorder window identical to the first.

As you record, you can see the level of the input from the microphone on the bottom right. To make a good recording, keep the level high but do not allow the level to reach the maximum. Also, as you record, the display will show you the total recording time.

The Record As drop-down list gives you several choices for recording formats. The default is .oga, which is recorded at CD quality. You can also select CD-quality recordings in either .m4a or .flac format. If you want to create smaller files of lower quality, select the Voice options labeled .wav and .spx.

You can play back a saved file by clicking the Open button and locating the file on your computer. When you open a file for playback, the File Information section of the Sound Recorder application displays basic information about the file, including its name and total time.

Record Sounds

1. Click Applications ➔ Sound & Video ➔ Sound Recorder.

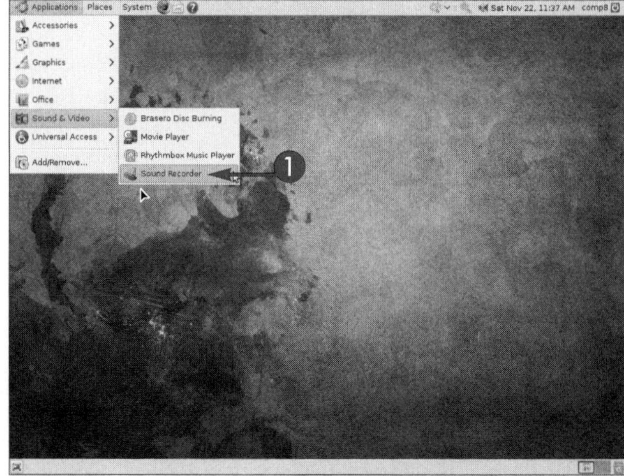

The Sound Recorder window opens.

2. Click here.

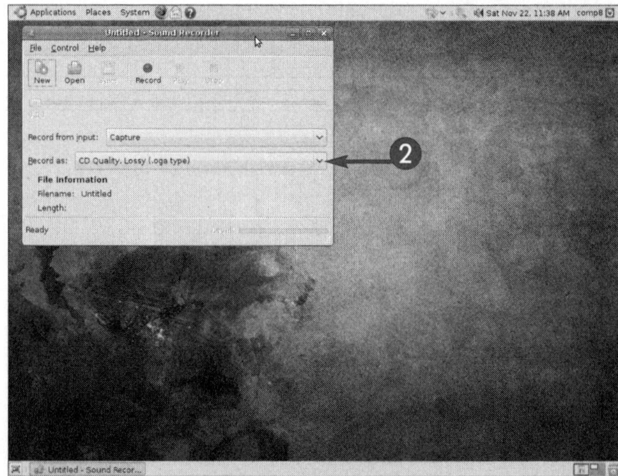

The Record As drop-down list expands to show all the format choices.

3. Click the recording format that you want, such as Voice, Lossless (.wav Type).
4. Click Record.
5. Begin to speak into the microphone or hold your microphone near the sounds that you want to record.

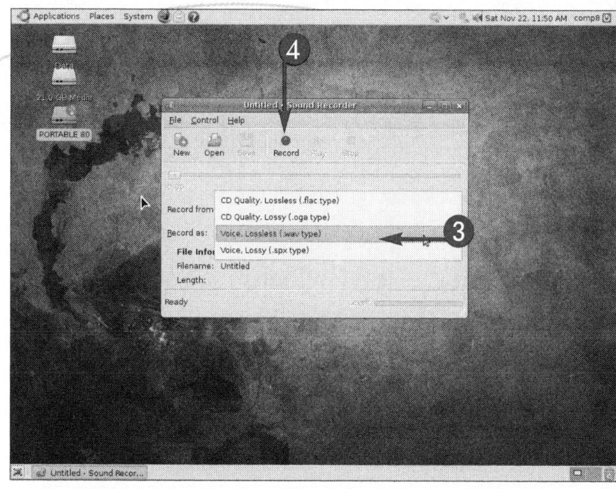

- The sounds are recorded.
- The length of the recording is displayed.

6. Click Stop when you are finished.

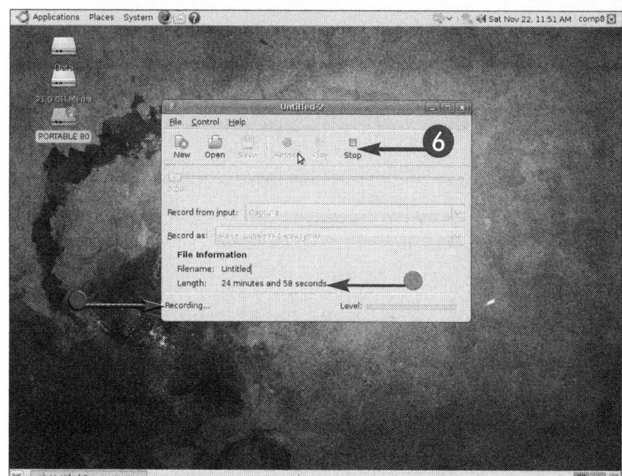

Extra

The GNOME Sound Recorder bundled with your Ubuntu system is a very basic application. Although it is fine for basic voice recordings, if you want to do anything more advanced, you will want to explore other options. Fortunately, you can find other choices using Ubuntu's built-in Synaptic Package Manager.

To view the other options that are available, click Applications ➔ Add/Remove. The Add/Remove Applications dialog box will open, and in this dialog box, you can browse for other programs to install. To see a list of alternative applications, click Sound & Video and select All Open Source Applications from the Show drop-down list.

The Audacity application is worth checking out. This is a very powerful, award-winning open-source application that lets you record and edit audio files. The application has been around for a while and is pretty well-documented. If you are serious about wanting to record sound with your Ubuntu system, you should look at Audacity.

Other applications that merit a look include QARecord, Traverso, Muse, jokosher, Kluppe, and the useful Sound Converter utility.

Understanding the Terminal Command Line

One of the most powerful features in Linux is the ability to access the system directly and run commands from a command line. In Ubuntu, the tool you use to do this is the Terminal application.

Although Terminal is the most powerful way to access the system, it is also the most basic. Unlike your GNOME desktop, with its graphical interface that lets you point and click, in Terminal you work by typing in commands with your keyboard. Instructions are typed at the command prompt, and the system processes them.

Command-line syntax is very particular. You must enter the proper commands in the proper syntax for them to work correctly. The combination of the pure text interface and the sometimes arcane syntax causes many people to feel some trepidation when they first deal with Terminal.

The positive fact to keep in mind is that the system is consistently and mechanically logical. The Terminal application works by a well-defined set of rules, and if you understand those basic rules, you can interact with Terminal safely and efficiently.

To get started, launch the Terminal application by clicking Applications ➔ Accessories ➔ Terminal. Below is what a basic Terminal window looks like:

- Username
- Name of computer
- Home directory
- Cursor

You enter your commands at the command prompt, inside the Terminal window. Many of the commands have multiple and sometimes complex options. When you use one of the commands for the first time, it is strongly advisable to start by using `man` to read the manual for the command in order to fully understand how best to use the command.

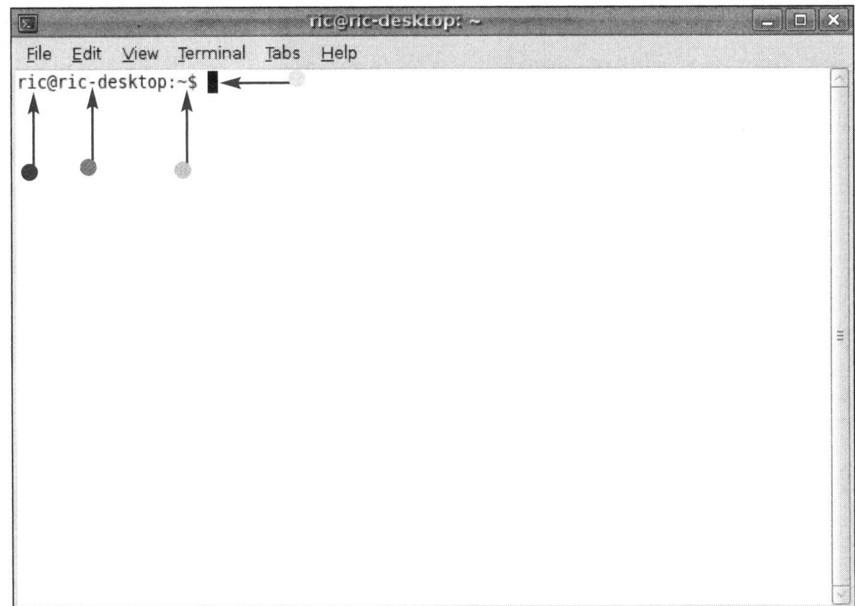

Use the Correct Syntax

The syntax varies with each command. You need to know the exact command to achieve the result. Some commands have only one part; others are more complicated. For example, if you type at the prompt **manual** followed by the name of any command, the system will display a help manual for that command. The two-part `command + target` structure is very common.

As with many commands, there is a long form and a short form for the `manual` command. The short form of the `manual` command is simply `man`. Typing either **manual** or **man** will result in the same output. You must remember that Linux is case sensitive. You must type the commands exactly as indicated. In other words, `Terminal`, `terminal`, and `TERMINAL` are three different words in Linux syntax.

Extend Commands with Options

Many commands have additional options that can be appended to the base command to activate additional features. Options follow the base command and are preceded by a dash character (-). You type a command with an option like this: ***command -option***. For example, the `ls` command lists the contents of the current directory. You can add to the `ls` command various options that provide more information: `ls -s` prints the list of files along with their sizes. `ls -r` prints the listings in reverse order. Options can be grouped together; for example, `ls -rs` prints the list in reverse order together with the file sizes. Sometimes you will see options written out, rather than abbreviated, and preceded by two dash characters (--); this is simply an alternative longhand way of adding an option to a command.

Enter Multiple Commands

You can either enter commands one at a time, or you can group them and submit them at once. The method you pick depends largely on what you are trying to do and how comfortable you are with the system. To group together more than one command, type them as follows: ***command1* ; *command2***. If you do not want `command2` to run until `command1` has been completed successfully, type them like this: ***command1* && *command2***. If, on the other hand, you only want `command2` to run if `command1` fails, type them as follows: ***command1* || *command2***.

Execute Commands with Elevated Privileges

The `sudo` command is a key command you need to know. By default, Linux uses a root account to hold the highest level of privileges and the ownership of many key files. The root password is locked, and you cannot login as root directly. If you want to work with directories or files that are not owned by your account, you will need to preface your commands with the command `sudo`. This special command gives you temporary access to the file and allows you to run your commands. Note that this command is normally only usable by someone with administrator-level access. To use the command, type it as follows: **sudo *command***. If the system prompts you for a password when you use the `sudo` command, type your user password, not the root password.

Get Help

There are three commands that can be used to get help while inside the Terminal window. The commands are `manual`, `info`, and `help`. The `manual` command is very helpful if you are just starting out; there are manuals for all the commands. To call up the manual for a command, simply type **man *command***. For example, to get the manual for the `manual` command, type **man man**. Also useful as a starting point is the manual for the introduction to the command line: `man intro`. The `info` command is very similar to the `man` command; it displays documentation. Although there are man pages for most every situation, there are fewer info pages available. The `help` command is always available. Simply type ***command* -h** or ***command* --help**, and you will see a summary of the command's usage.

Reset the Terminal

If you find yourself trapped inside some screen that you cannot seem to escape or the screen has become so cluttered you simply need to clear the mess and start afresh, you can do so. Under the Terminal menu are two useful commands: Reset and Reset and Clear. Choose Reset if you have lost the cursor and need to recover the command prompt. Choose Reset and Clear to reset Terminal and clear the Terminal screen. Alternatively, you can always open a new tab in your Terminal window. Each time a new tab opens, it starts with a clear screen and a command prompt. As a third alternative, if you only want to clear the screen, just type the command **clear** at the command prompt. If you find yourself trapped inside a command or a screen you do not seem to be able to exit, you can also type **C** as you hold down the Ctrl key. The combination Ctrl + C gets you out of almost any situation.

Understanding Essential File Commands

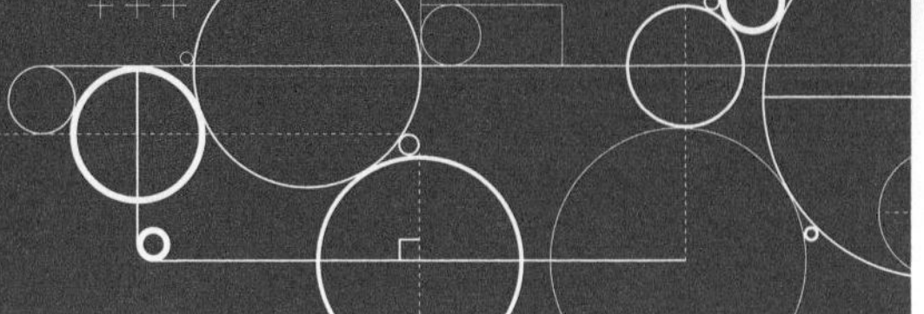

Being able to quickly and easily find your way around the files and directories in your system is one of the essential skills you need to work comfortably from the command line. This section discusses getting around the directory tree and working with the files you find there.

Creating Files and Directories

To create a new empty file, use the command `touch`, specifying after the command the name to be given to the new file. For instance, to create a new text file named "example," you would type **touch example.txt**. This creates a new empty file in the active directory. To create the new file in a subdirectory, simply enter the name of the subdirectory before the filename. In this example, the new file will be created inside the subdirectory named "examples": **touch examples/example.txt**.

If you want to create a new directory, you can do so from the command prompt by using the command `mkdir`. Type the command, followed by the name that you want the new directory to bear. For example: `mkdir mydirectory` creates a new directory named "mydirectory."

Naming Files and Directories

Naming files in Linux is easy and flexible, but there are a few key rules that must be respected. First, filenames are case sensitive. Second, you must escape characters that are not upper- or lowercase letters, numbers, periods, hyphens, and underscores. The escape character is the backslash (\). Additionally, you can enclose a name that uses whitespace with quotations to have the multiple words treated as a single filename.

One of the advantages of the Linux naming convention is that file extensions are optional. However, even though you do not have to add a particular extension to the end of a file to get it to work, it is very useful to have the information for reference. Among the most common extensions are the following:

EXTENSION	USED FOR
.txt or .text	Text files
.jpg or .jpeg	A common image format, widely used for photographs
.html	HTML files
.gz	Compressed file archive
.rar	Compressed file archive
.png	Portable network graphics, a commonly used format for graphics
.tif or .tiff	A high-quality image format often used for photographs
.gif	A lower-quality graphic image format

Moving between Directories

If you need to move from one directory to another, you will need to know the name of the directory and in some cases, the path. Moving down the directory tree, from broader to more specific directories, requires you to know the name of the directory. Moving up the tree can be done without knowing the name of the parent directories.

TO DO THIS	TYPE THIS
Move up one directory	**cd ..**
Go to the root directory	**cd /**
Go to your home directory	**cd** or **cd ~**
Move between multiple levels	**cd *the/full/directory/path***

If you are unsure where you are, type the command **pwd**, which will print on the screen the name of the working directory.

Listing the Directory Contents

The `ls` command is used to list the contents of a directory. Simply type **ls**, and the system will display a list of all the contents of the active directory. There are a number of options that can be employed. Among the more useful options are these:

OPTION	DESCRIPTION
`-a` or `--all`	Shows all the files, including those normally hidden
`-d` or `--directory`	Reports on the directory itself, not the contents
`-k`	Shows the file sizes
`-r` or `--reverse`	Prints the list in reverse order
`-R` or `--recursive`	Shows the contents of all the subdirectories inside your directory
`-t` or `--sort=time`	Orders the results by the last changed date
`-x` or `--sort=extension`	Shows the results sorted by file extension and then by filename
`-l` or `--format=long`	Displays the long form of the output, which shows you much more information about each file, including the owner, the last modified date, the size, and the read/write status

Learning More about a File

If you need more information about a file than you can get from the list command, there are two commands that can help you. First, the `file` command tells you the nature of the contents of the file. To use this command, type **file *filename***. The output in the Terminal window will be a description of the file contents — for example, `ASCII text`. This may not tell you the contents, but it can at least tell you what you need to view the file.

If you want to take a quick peek at the contents, use the `head` command. `head` displays the first few lines of data from the file. To use it, type **head *filename***. You can use the option `-n` to specify how many lines will print. Note also there is a parallel to the `head` command — the `tail` command. `tail` works in exactly the same fashion, but instead of producing the first few lines, it produces the last few lines of the file.

continued

Understanding Essential File Commands (continued)

The file-related commands outlined in this section enable you to find and manage files and directories. Using only basic commands, you can create, copy, move, and delete files. Combine those skills with the ability to locate files and examine their contents, and you have the tools you need to handle the vast majority of basic file-related tasks. Instructions for managing files, particularly large numbers of files, are not only faster when executed from the command line, but also have the added advantage of providing a knowledgeable user with more information.

Note that virtually every command has at least a few options available to it. Understanding the options is one of the keys to getting the most out of the Terminal application. Although the information in this section provides a useful starting point, use the system documentation and help files to learn the full extent of each command.

Finding Files

The command prompt provides powerful commands that let you search for, and within, directories and files. The two most useful commands are `find` and `grep`.

find

`find` allows you to search across multiple directories to identify files that meet the criteria you define. By default, `find` searches through the directory tree beginning with directory you are in. Alternatively, you can specify a directory to be searched by adding the path to the command. There are many options available for this command, and as they are a bit complicated in their syntax, you should explore this further via the `man` command. Among the most useful options are these:

OPTION	DESCRIPTION
`-name` *`filename`*	Searches for a specific file by name
`-user` *`username`*	Finds files owned by a particular user

grep

`grep` is a powerful command that enables you to search within files. Using `grep`, you can search through multiple files to find a particular word, phrase, or string of numbers. Note that in many Linux help files, you will see the term "pattern" used to mean a word, phrase, or a string. `grep` goes line by line through the files, searching for the string you specify, and then prints on the screen only those lines that contain the pattern. A number of options exist for this command. Among the most useful are these:

OPTION	DESCRIPTION
`-i` or `--ignore-case`	Returns the results regardless of the capitalization pattern
`-n` or `--line-number`	Prints out the lines and the line numbers where the system finds the pattern
`-w` or `--word-regexp`	Restricts the results to whole-word matches only
`-v` or `--invert-match`	Returns all files that do not match the pattern — the inverse of the normal command

Copying Files and Directories

Use the `cp` command to copy a file or a directory. You need to specify the name of the file that you want to copy and give the copy a name as well. A command to copy a file named "example" would look like this: `cp example copy.of.example`. As written, that command makes a copy of the file named "example" and leaves it in the same directory as the original; the name of the new file will be copy.of.example. Copying the file will not alter the contents, but if you want to preserve the attributes of the original file — for example, the creator, group, and permissions — you need to add to this command the option `-p` or `--preserve`. Note that if you specify a name for the file that already exists in the directory, the new file will overwrite the old file of the same name. Copying directories works in the same fashion: `cp original.directory duplicate.directory`. This command copies the directory named original.directory and creates a copy of it named duplicate.directory. Note that if you want to copy all subdirectories and their contents, you must add the option `-R` or `--recursive`.

Moving Files and Directories

Moving a file or a directory requires the use of the command `mv`. You must include with this command both the name of what you want to move and the target, that is, where you want to move it. For example, if a user wanted to move the file mydoc from the Desktop directory into the Documents directory, he or she would type **mv mydoc ~/Documents**.

Similarly, if the user wanted to move the subdirectory today, which is located in the active directory, into the subdirectory tomorrow, the user would type **mv today tomorrow**. The result would be that the directory today is now a subdirectory of the directory tomorrow. To move directories that are not inside the user's active directory requires the user to specify the path to the directory.

Note that you can also use the `mv` command as an easy way to rename files. To rename the file yesterday to today, you would type **mv yesterday today**.

Deleting Files and Directories

To delete a file or a directory, use either the command `rm` or `del`. The only thing you must specify here is the name of the file or directory that you want to remove. To delete the file mydoc, you type **rm mydoc**. To delete a directory along with its contents, use `rm` plus the option `-R` or `--recursive`. You can also use the command `rmdir` to delete directories. Type **rmdir** along with the name of the directory. Note that if the directory contains files, you must delete them first; attempting to delete non-empty directories with the `rmdir` command results in an error message.

If you use the command `rm`, the file is removed; it is permanently deleted, and there is no command to restore it. A safer way to handle this task is to use the command `del`, which will delete the file but will ask you to confirm the action before permanent deletion. This provides at least a level of confirmation that can help you avoid a costly mistake.

Understanding Useful System Commands

Using the Terminal application, you can get a very complete picture of what is happening with your system. You can also manage the system's users and applications using just the command prompt.

As seen earlier in the book, you can gain insight into system processes, create users, and install and manage applications using a variety of applications bundled with Ubuntu. However, if you would like to learn how to do all that using just one application, Terminal is the answer for you. With powerful direct access to the system via the command prompt, you can perform any of the tasks necessary for site maintenance and management.

Gaining Insight into System Status

There are a significant number of commands designed to give you insight into the functioning of your system. Basically, you can expose every process from the command prompt. You have direct access into the system and are in the best position to obtain accurate information on all aspects of the system's operation. Here is a listing of some of the most commonly used commands:

COMMAND	FUNCTION
`df`	Displays the total file system disk usage. Try using it with the option `-h` to render the output into a more easily readable form.
`du`	Displays the disk usage of the active directory.
`free`	Displays the amount of free and used memory.
`ifconfig`	Reports on the network usage.
`ps`	Lists the processes you are running as a user.
`top`	Displays a more detailed picture of system usage, including processes and resources.
`uname`	With the option `-a`, prints out complete system data, including your kernel information.
`lsb_release`	With the `-a` option, displays the version information for the Linux release you are running.

Working with Users

Managing users and permissions is an area in which Terminal excels. Although the tools discussed earlier in this book may look friendlier and easier to use, it is often faster to obtain information on users and permissions by using the command prompt, particularly when you have a large number of users on the system.

Obtaining User Information

If you need to obtain information about the users on your system — who they are and what they are doing — you can do so using the following commands:

COMMAND	FUNCTION
`whoami`	Displays your identity.
`who`	Displays a list of all users currently logged in to the system.
`w`	Lists which users are currently logged on to the system and what they are doing.
`ps -u` *`username`*	Lists all the processes used by that particular user.
`last`	Lists recent activity. Follow this command with a username to find out the last time the user logged in to the system.

Creating and Deleting Users

The traditional manner for adding a new user to a Linux system is to use the command `useradd`. However, your Ubuntu system should have an additional package installed named adduser. The adduser package enables the use of two very handy commands: `adduser` and `deluser`.

Note that you have to invoke `sudo` to use these commands, as this is a system administrator–level task. To create a new user with `adduser`, type **sudo adduser *username*** at the prompt. The system automatically assigns an appropriate user ID and group ID, creates the default home directory, and sets the initial configuration options and permissions.

Use the command `sudo deluser` *`username`* to delete a user from the system. The command can also assist you with backing up or removing the user's account and files.

If `adduser` and `deluser` fail to function properly in your Terminal application, use the Synaptic Package Manager to verify the installation of the adduser package.

Managing Permissions

Every file has permissions attached to it. Permissions tell the system who is entitled to do what with the file: Can the user read the file? Write to the file? Execute the file? The permissions system is largely responsible for Linux's reputation as a secure computing system. It also means that there will be times when you will want to adjust the permissions of a file.

To view a file's permissions, use the `ls` command with the `-l` option, as discussed in the previous section, "Understanding Essential File Commands."

Adjusting file permissions from the command prompt means using the command `chmod`. The syntax for this command is a bit complicated, but perfectly logical. To structure this command properly, you must follow this formulation, expressed here in English: `chmod` [*`user`* or *`group`*] [*`enable`* or *`disable`*] [*`permission`*] [*`filename`*] — and expressed here in terms of the actual syntax you must use: `chmod` [a/o/g/u] [+/–] [r/w/x] [*`filename`*].

OPTION	FUNCTION
a	Changes the privilege for all users
o	Changes the privilege for other users
g	Changes the privilege for the members of your group
u	Changes the privilege for yourself
+	Adds permission
–	Deletes permission
r	Permission to read
w	Permission to write
x	Permission to execute

Here are two examples: To add permission for yourself to write to a file named example.txt, you would type **chmod u+w example.txt**. If you wanted instead to prohibit others from reading the file example.txt, you would type this: **chmod o-r example.txt**.

To change permissions on files that are owned by root, preface the command with `sudo`.

Installing Packages

`apt-get` is a powerful suite of commands that support the installation of additional software packages to your Ubuntu system. Although an increasing number of users now rely on the Synaptic Package Manager to handle software searches, installations, and maintenance, the purists will still no doubt prefer `apt-get`.

The `apt-get` commands are numerous, but taken together, they allow you to search for new packages, install them, install any dependencies, and thereafter maintain the packages. When the time comes to remove the package and all its supporting files, you can once again turn to `apt-get` to perform that task.

The syntax is typically expressed as `apt-get` *`task package.name`*.

TASK SYNTAX	FUNCTION
`install`	Installs the package
`build-dep`	Searches the repositories and builds a list of dependencies that need to be installed
`remove`	Removes the package from the system
`purge`	Removes from the system the package together with all of its configuration files
`upgrade`	Installs an upgrade of a package

Note that you will need to preface this command with sudo. You should also be aware that there are a large number of other options for use with this command; therefore you should examine the manual for this command before you begin.

INDEX

NUMBERS

SYMBOLS

A

B

C

D

INDEX

G

H

INDEX

I

J

K

L

M

N

INDEX

S

INDEX

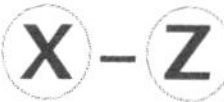

...all designed for visual learners—just like you!

Master VISUALLY®

Your complete visual reference. Two-color interior.

- 3ds Max
- Creating Web Pages
- Dreamweaver and Flash
- Excel
- Excel VBA Programming
- iPod and iTunes
- Mac OS
- Office
- Optimizing PC Performance
- Photoshop Elements
- QuickBooks
- Quicken
- Windows
- Windows Mobile
- Windows Server

Visual Blueprint™

Where to go for professional-level programming instruction. Two-color interior.

- Ajax
- ASP.NET 2.0
- Excel Data Analysis
- Excel Pivot Tables
- Excel Programming
- HTML
- JavaScript
- Mambo
- PHP & MySQL
- SEO
- Vista Sidebar
- Visual Basic
- XML

Visual Encyclopedia™

Your A to Z reference of tools and techniques. Full color.

- Dreamweaver
- Excel
- Mac OS
- Photoshop
- Windows

Visual Quick Tips

Shortcuts, tricks, and techniques for getting more done in less time. Full color.

- Crochet
- Digital Photography
- Excel
- iPod & iTunes
- Knitting
- MySpace
- Office
- PowerPoint
- Windows
- Wireless Networking

For a complete listing of Visual books, go to wiley.com/go/visual